Routledge Revivals

Regional Problems and Policies in Italy and France

First published in 1970, *Regional Problems and Policies in Italy and France* examines the problem of regional imbalance in two important countries of Western Europe and emphasizes that policies aimed at promoting regional development must form an integral part of national economic policies.

The book is divided into three parts—part I: Regional Problems and Policies in Italy; part II: Regional Problems and Policies in France; and part III: Regional Policy: Three Issues. Part I and II analyze how regional policy in France and Italy has moved away from the public assistance type of intervention into new, broader approaches which require reorganization of traditional procedures, change in economic structures, introduction of new products and methods of production, movement of workers between areas and occupations, and shifts in geographical distribution of population and employment. Part III explores regional planning and growth centres or growth areas in the light of Fench and Italian experiences. It further analyses the regional effects of the EEC and gives a brief account of how British regional problems and policies would be affected by the membership of Community. This volume is an essential reading for students of Western European governmental policy and the European Economic Community.

I0083935

Regional Problems and Policies in Italy and France

Kevin Allen and M. C. MacLennan

Routledge
Taylor & Francis Group

First published in 1970
by George Allen & Unwin Ltd

This edition first published in 2024 by Routledge
4 Park Square, Milton Park, Abingdon, Oxon, OX14 4RN

and by Routledge
605 Third Avenue, New York, NY 10017

Routledge is an imprint of the Taylor & Francis Group, an informa business

© George Allen & Unwin Ltd 1970

Publisher's Note
The publisher has gone to great lengths to ensure the quality of this reprint but points out that some imperfections in the original copies may be apparent.

Disclaimer
The publisher has made every effort to trace copyright holders and welcomes correspondence from those they have been unable to contact.

A Library of Congress record exists under LCCN: 78586314

ISBN: 978-1-032-88847-7 (hbk)
ISBN: 978-1-003-53995-7 (ebk)
ISBN: 978-1-032-88849-1 (pbk)

Book DOI 10.4324/9781003539957

REGIONAL PROBLEMS AND POLICIES IN ITALY AND FRANCE

KEVIN ALLEN

AND

M. C. MACLENNAN

University of Glasgow

London

GEORGE ALLEN AND UNWIN LTD

RUSKIN HOUSE MUSEUM STREET

FIRST PUBLISHED IN 1970

© *George Allen & Unwin Ltd* 1970

ISBN 0 04 330165 7

PRINTED IN GREAT BRITAIN
in 10 *on* 11 *pt. Times type*
BY T. AND A. CONSTABLE LTD.
HOPETOUN STREET, EDINBURGH

TO
KIRSTEN AND ELISABETH

PREFACE

This volume is the result of a research project, extending over a period of three years, in the Department of Social and Economic Research in the University of Glasgow. The project was generously assisted by a grant from the Nuffield Foundation and it is right that our first acknowledgment should be to them. The aim of the project was to examine regional problems and policies in Western Europe. At an early stage we had to decide on the number of countries to be covered in the study. The alternatives were to cover a large number of Western European countries, with the consequent danger of superficiality, or to undertake a more intensive investigation of a smaller number of countries. In the end we concentrated our attention on the two particularly important and interesting cases of Italy and France. The first two sections of the book analyse regional problems and policies in these two countries. Both sections are written very much with the British reader in mind. We next had to decide whether it was necessary to have a section on Britain. We decided against this for a number of reasons. First, it seemed reasonable to assume that many British readers are familiar with the situation in Britain which has already received considerable attention. Secondly, we were fully aware that Dr Gavin McCrone of Brasenose College, Oxford, and formerly of this University, was writing a volume on British regional policy, now published in this series under the title *Regional Policy in Britain*. Indeed, Dr McCrone was initially involved in this project prior to his going to Oxford and has continued to be in close touch subsequently. Thirdly, it proved possible to incorporate our views on Britain in appropriate places throughout the book and particularly in Part III. While, therefore, there is no specific section on Britain, in a sense the whole book is concerned with the lessons to be drawn for British regional policy from the Italian and French experiences.

One of the pleasantest parts of writing a book of this type is the number of contacts that develop in the course of the work. From such contacts must arise many acknowledgments of indebtedness. For our work on France we wish to acknowledge the useful discussions which M. C. MacLennan had with Professor M. Penouil of the Faculté de Droit et des Sciences Economiques de Bordeaux and Professor Louis Davin of the University of Liège. For our work on Italy we wish to acknowledge in particular the valuable help given by Drs V. A. Marsan, A. Benzoni and F. Brunelli of the IRI and

Professor Del 'Angelo and his colleagues of SVIMEZ in Rome who were particularly helpful during the preparation of the Italian part of the study when K. J. Allen was generously provided with working facilities within the SVIMEZ offices. Throughout the whole study we have derived considerable benefit from our association with Dr McCrone. In the first year of the project, he spent time in Belgium studying both Belgian regional problems and the regional problems of the European Community, and his work there has been of great value to us. Of course, the writing of this work has involved us in many debts to our colleagues in this University. We would mention particularly Professors D. J. Robertson and T. Wilson.

We would also like to express our thanks to Mrs E Patterson, Miss M. Nelson and Mrs M. Christie for their patience and efficiency in typing the various drafts.

Since some of the above acknowledgments are to public officials, we should emphasize that any errors or omissions of fact or mistakes in judgment which remain are the sole responsibility of the authors.

K. J. ALLEN
M. C. MACLENNAN

CONTENTS

xi

INTRODUCTION

In the past few years most Western European governments have become increasingly concerned with the problem of regional imbalance within their economies and have responded by developing an increasingly wide range of policy measures and spending increasing amounts of funds to deal with it. Perhaps the most important development has been the gradual emergence of the view that policies aimed at promoting regional development must be considered as an integral part of national economic policies or plans for increasing national output, and not as *ad hoc* welfare schemes for alleviating the higher than average levels of unemployment which arise from time to time in different localities. This wider view of 'the regional problem' has had at least two important consequences.

It has, firstly, compelled governments to examine the nature of regional development and regional policy more rigorously. This has become necessary since regional development policy is now part and parcel of the range of measures employed by governments to manipulate the level and rate of growth of demand and to influence the organization and exploitation of resources so as to attain a rapid growth of national output. It is no longer enough to think in terms of relieving local unemployment; the problem has become the much wider one of organizing and activating regional economies so that both regional and national economic growth may be stimulated. This broader approach immediately poses extremely important and difficult questions. It is possible to reduce local unemployment by relatively isolated increases in demand and inter- and intra-regional transfers of resources on a fairly small scale. The promotion of growth in a regional economy requires a much greater degree of change in economic structures, involving the introduction of new products and methods of production, the movement of workers between areas and between occupations, and the acceptance of sometimes quite significant shifts in the geographical distribution of population and employment. All this means much more scientific study and research. It is simply not socially acceptable that such important alterations in the conditions of life should be made on the basis of individual and at times unrelated decisions.

The second consequence follows directly from the first. The new, wider definition of regional development means that it must be organized more firmly on a national basis, so that the compatibility of a certain rate or form of development in one region with that in

xiii

the others and in the economy as a whole may be known and assessed. This in turn requires the reorganization of traditional procedures and sometimes the creation of new ones in order that the regional dimension of the economy may be more clearly exposed and policies to influence it efficiently implemented. At the same time, the forms of local government have to be recast to allow a wider regional approach to be adopted.

Parts I and II of this book have attempted to analyze how regional policy in France and Italy has moved away from the public assistance type of intervention into these new, broader approaches. There are several reasons why a comparative study of these two countries is of interest in Britain. In both countries the disparities in the living standards and economic performance of different regions are very much larger than in the United Kingdom. The policies studied are therefore serious responses to what is, in both countries, a major national issue. Since the Second World War, thinking and action on the problem of regional development have progressed from a position which was much less organized and sophisticated than in the UK to a point where interested British observers concede that they may have lessons to learn. This is not simply an interest in something different although that, quite validly, exists. The adaptations imposed by a wide-ranging regional development policy have in some respects been more boldly accepted and worked through than in the United Kingdom. Finally, both France and Italy have economies of a type basically similar to the mixed economy of the United Kingdom. There are, of course, interesting points of dissimilarity but they are by no means so great, or so much based on ideological or philosophical differences, as to render academic a study of their regional policies.

In our study of French and Italian regional policies we have tried to avoid the mere cataloguing of actions and legislation, and have sought rather to analyze the changing view of regional development which produced them and to examine them critically in this perspective.

In Part III of the book we have singled out three of the many issues involved in regional policy and attempted to analyze them in rather greater detail and in the light of the French and Italian experiences. We discuss first regional planning. This is a topic in which all countries concerned with regional development are currently much interested. It is, however, a field in which the creation of new administrative procedures seems to have gone rather faster than the analysis of what these bodies could most profitably do. Chapter 12 has some suggestions to make on this point. Of special interest here is the French experience. France possesses perhaps the most organized system of regional planning in Western Europe, combined with twenty-five years' experience of the day-to-day job of making economic planning models work. This mixture of theoretical techniques, administrative ingenuity and innovation and a sense of the practical limitations of both of these is worth study by anyone involved in regional development policy.

The second issue discussed is the idea of growth centres or growth areas. This concept has now gained favour as the most efficient principle on which to base the development of a regional economy and it has had a definite influence on both French and Italian regional policy. It is, however, a concept of deceptive simplicity— a simplicity which tends to disappear when the first practical questions are asked. The French and Italian experiences are an expecially intriguing context in which to examine the idea of growth areas. In France the notion of selectivity has been interpreted and applied for the most part in a geographical sense. In Italy, on the other hand, attention has in addition been directed to the possibility of *industrial* selectivity in the form of the proposed interrelated industry complex for the Bari-Taranto growth area. The many different interpretations of the term 'growth area' in the United Kingdom suggests that this comparison might be of some use at the present time.

The analysis of the regional effects of the EEC in Chapter 14 hardly needs justification. Membership of the EEC has affected both the nature of the regional problem and the direction of regional policy in France and Italy. Although concrete evidence is hard to come by, that which exists is well worth study in any country applying for membership of the Community. The diversion of resources to certain regions, at least initially, in defiance of the signals of the market in the context of a complete customs union throws into sharp relief the fundamental question of whether regional development hinders or facilitates the rate of growth of national output in open economies heavily dependent on international trade. In view of the importance of these issues to the UK, an attempt has been made to indicate how British regional problems and policies would be affected by membership of the Community.

Regional intervention in the United Kingdom, in quantitative terms, has seen a considerable expansion between 1966 and 1969. The expenditures on the programmes have risen considerably. By 1969, the Board of Trade alone was spending £300 million per annum on regional development effort. There is reason to believe that this period will be seen later as being one of unprecedented generosity, when the benefits of such intervention were but little evaluated and the contribution of regional development to national growth was more of a hope than a firm fact. It seems likely that the future will see a more critical approach, a greater concern that regional development should make the fullest possible contribution to national development, or at least an attempt to limit its costs. In these respects, the Italian and French regional experiences and policies are illuminating, no less so in that they are members of the highly competitive EEC towards which the United Kingdom aspires.

PART I

REGIONAL PROBLEMS
AND POLICIES IN ITALY

'Quando il solo nome di regionalista pare a voi come una bestemmia, una minaccia, un tradimento: oh, allora, per Dio, le nostre debolezze e le nostre miserie sono le debolezze e le miserie di tutta l'Italia! . . . E non crediate io esageri o mi faccia, dinanzi a voi vincere da me stesso: tutt'altro! Siete mai stati laggiù, nel mezzogiorno?'[1]

Il Mezzogiorno e lo Stato Italiano
G. Fortunato

[1] 'When even the name of regionalist seems to you a blasphemy, a threat, a betrayal: oh, for God's sake, our weaknesses and our miseries are the weaknesses and miseries of all Italy! . . . And don't think that I exaggerate to win you to my side: far from it! Have you ever been down there, in the South?'

INTRODUCTION

These chapters are aimed at providing a survey of the southern Italian problem and the policies pursued in an attempt to resolve it. Regional problems exist, of course, in northern Italy. Shortage of space, however, precludes a detailed examination of northern problems and the policies involved, except in as far as they impinge or affect southern problems and policies. In any event, nowhere in the North do regional problems reach the level or intensity of those in the South, while the policies developed are much weaker than their southern counterparts.

There are four chapters. Chapter 1 is devoted to a discussion of the southern problem—the form it takes, its size and intensity, and the way it has evolved and changed over time. An attempt is made to go beyond a superficial description of the problem and to examine in some detail the economic structure of the South in an attempt to isolate the main explanatory factors behind its backwardness. Chapter 2 is concerned with the policies pursued up to 1965 in an attempt to resolve the southern problem. The stress is laid on industrial policy. Chapter 3 continues this discussion of policy, analysing the situation after 1965 and presenting a picture of current policy. Finally, Chapter 4 examines the results of policy and draws conclusions from the previous chapters.

CHAPTER 1

THE PROBLEM OF SOUTHERN ITALY AND ITS ORIGINS

The South is composed of the eight regions of Abruzzi, Molise, Campania, Puglia, Basilicata, Calabria, Sicily and Sardinia plus the two provinces of Latina and Frosinone in the region of Lazio. Very roughly, it is the area south of Rome and is the operational area of the Cassa per il Mezzogiorno (Fund for the South)—the main body responsible for southern development. The area of the South amounts to 40 per cent of Italy and holds a population of 20 million, 38 per cent of the Italian population. The South has an area almost equal to that of Greece but with more than double the population; it has an area equal to that of Czechoslovakia yet with a population 5 million in excess. The three states of Benelux have a population merely 2 million in excess of southern Italy, while the three Scandinavian countries have a total population which is 3 million less than that of the South. The size of the area and its population, relative to Italy as a whole, inevitably makes the problem of development all the greater.

In terms of virtually all the conventional indicators of regional disequilibrium—migration, income per head, activity rates, unemployment, growth—the South represents a severe problem. It is worth while discussing some of these indicators briefly in order to give a quick picture of the problem before moving on to a more detailed discussion of the southern economic structure.

Emigration has been a common means whereby the southerners have tried to better themselves. Between 1885 and 1915 about 5 million people left the South—the greater proportion going to the Americas. The inter-war period saw a considerable slowing down in the rate of emigration—a result of immigration controls in the receiving countries and efforts by the Italian government to curb the outflow. In the post-war period, however, emigration was again running at a very high level. Between the two Census years, 1951 and 1961, net emigration from the South amounted to more than 2 million people, of which slightly over half went to the North of

19

Italy.[1] The population of the South in 1951 was 18½ million. The rate of emigration was accelerating in the late 1950s and early 1960s with increasing proportions of the emigrants going to the rapidly expanding North of Italy. The Italian recession of 1964 and 1965 reduced the level of emigration considerably. The improved economic situation after 1965 saw a further upsurge.[2]

An indication of the severity of the post-war migration is the fact that, between 1951 and 1961, fourteen out of the thirty-two southern provinces suffered an actual fall in population. Of the remaining eighteen provinces one saw no change and the rest had population increases. Only one province, Naples, had an increase in population in excess of the north-west Italian average of 12·3 per cent and this was as a result of very high natural increases, and not immigration as in the north-west. In fact, all the southern provinces were characterized by net emigration varying, as a percentage of the 1951 population figures, from 1 per cent in Naples to almost 25 per cent in the province of Enna. The social and economic consequences of the heavy migration which took place in many of the provinces was very serious.[3]

High levels of regional emigration, for the most part, reflect lack of opportunities within a region and/or the presence of better opportunities elsewhere.[4] As indicators of opportunities, or rather lack of them, it is usual to refer to data for income per head, unemployment, underemployment, activity rates and growth. These are discussed in this order below.

[1] For an interesting and comprehensive treatment of southern migration both within and outwith the South, see S. Cafiero, *Le Migrazioni Meridionali*, Giuffrè, 1964. Also by the same author 'Le Migrazioni dal Mezzogiorno', in the symposium *Mezzogiorno e Politica di Piano*, Laterza, 1964.

[2] Net emigration from the South to the North and abroad in the 1960s was as follows:

1960—155,000	1962—193,000	1964— 96,000
1961—265,000	1963—138,000	1965— 64,000
		1966—141,000

The figures are taken from Comitato dei Minstri per il Mezzogiorno, *Studi Monografici sul Mezzogiorno*, 1967, p. 75.

[3] S. Cafiero, *Le Migrazioni Meridionali*, op cit.

[4] Migration is, however, not dependent purely on economic factors. Cafiero in the references above stresses that much of the movement, particularly within the South, was towards the large centres and away from the more isolated smaller communities in spite of the scarce number of new jobs available in the former. Migration is often more a movement away from the agricultural communities rather than to better opportunities elsewhere. A. Predetti in his book *Le Componenti Economiche, Sociali e Demografiche della Mobilità Interna della Popolazione Italiana*, Milan, 1965, argues that only 58 per cent of Italian migratory movements are explicable in terms of economic variables.

THE PROBLEM OF SOUTHERN ITALY AND ITS ORIGINS

By British standards, the disparity in income per head between North and South is enormous. In 1966, southern income per head at current prices was only about 53 per cent of the comparable northern figure. As with migration, there were considerable differences between individual regions both within the North and the South. Lombardy and Liguria, for example, heading the income per head tables in the North, had an income per head which was almost three times that of Calabria—the poorest of the southern regions. All the northern regions have an income per head higher than even the most prosperous southern regions of Puglia and Sardinia.[1] In 1966, income per head at current prices in the South was at the level enjoyed in the North about ten years earlier. Measured at constant prices, the South was, in 1966, hardly at the 1951 northern level.

Unemployment and underemployment in the South, according to the official figures, is not very serious, though there is reason to believe that the figures are inaccurate and do not fully reflect the phenomena that they purport to measure. In 1966, unemployment in the South was about 4·5 per cent as against 3·7 per cent in the North.[2] The official underemployment figures also generally show the difference between North and South as being relatively insignificant and indeed, reflecting the caution with which these figures must be treated, for 1966 show the South with 11 people defined as underemployed for every thousand people employed compared with 12 in the North.[3]

If activity rates are measured in terms of numbers in the labour force as a percentage of the total number of inhabitants, the rate in the South in 1966 was 51·6 per cent for males and 15·3 per cent for females. Comparable figures for the North were 59·8 per cent and 22·4 per cent respectively. Much of the regional disparity in male activity rates is, however, explained by age structure differences between the two regions—the South having a high proportion of children in its population. Activity rates using the male population aged fourteen years and above gives virtually identical rates between the two regions—81 per cent in the South and 80 per cent in the North. Age structure differences, however, go little way in explaining

[1] G. Tagliacarne, 'Misura della Disuguaglianze Interprovinciali dei Redditi e dei Consumi', *Studi di Mercato*, 1968, no. 4; reprinted in *Informazioni Svimez*, June, 1969, no. 11. The figures are for 1967.

[2] The figures in the text measure unemployed as a percentage of employed plus unemployed.

[3] ISTAT, *Annuario Statistico Italiano*, 1967. The underemployed are defined as those people who in the sample had worked for less than 33 hours a week 'for reasons of an economic character attributable to the shortage of a greater supply of work'.

21

the considerable regional disparities in activity rates for females. The point is often made that the differences are not solely a reflection of the differing economic conditions between North and South, but also the different mentalities of the two regions.[1] Our own view is that this explains but a small part of the regional disparities in female activity rates.

There are many ways in which south Italian growth can be measured, though as a quick indication of changing economic conditions, real income per head is probably best. Table 1.1 shows income per head at 1964 prices between 1951 and 1964 in the North and South of Italy.

TABLE 1.1

GROWTH OF INCOME PER HEAD AT 1964 PRICES

	1951 income per head ('000 lire)	1957 income per head ('000 lire)	1957 index 1951= 100	1962 income per head ('000 lire)	1962 index 1951= 100	1964 income per head ('000 lire)	1964 index 1951= 100
South	126·3	155·5	123·1	197·3	156·2	211·3	167·3
North	243·8	323·8	132·8	442·9	181·7	464·8	190·6
Italy	200·1	261·2	130·5	353·1	176·5	373·0	186·4

Source: Comitato dei Ministri per il Mezzogiorno, *Relazione sulla Attività di Coordinamento*, 1965, Vol. II, p. 47.

It is not difficult to see that on the basis of these figures, the disequilibrium between North and South, far from decreasing, is actually increasing. However, on the basis of income per head at current prices, the picture is more optimistic, as shown in Table 1.2 below.

In terms of current prices the South manages to gain slightly on the North. It is a debatable point as to which is the better indicator of southern development. Many writers take their choice between the two depending on the theme or picture they wish to depict. The pessimists and the critics use constant prices, the optimists current prices. It is not in fact possible, without more details of price changes in the two areas, to know which of the two measures is the more representative of the phenomena it is intended to reflect. The important point, however, is that even if we use the measure more favourable to the South, the disequilibrium in income per head is

[1] Comitato dei Ministri per il Mezzogiorno, *Studi Monografici sul Mezzogiorno*, 1967, p. 83.

diminishing only very slightly, and indeed, if the present trend were to continue, it would be well past the end of the century before the disparities disappeared.[1]

Although the growth of income per head in the South has been disappointing relative to the North, it is important to remember that the North has enjoyed one of the fastest rates of growth in Europe. Relative to most other European countries, and certainly relative to the more backward areas of Europe, the South has done exceptionally well. We return later to the question of what yardstick should be used to assess the South's progress.

The brief outline of the southern problem given above has been

TABLE 1.2

GROWTH OF INCOME PER HEAD AT CURRENT PRICES

	1951 income per head ('000 lire)	1957 income per head ('000 lire)	1957 index 1951= 100	1962 income per head ('000 lire)	1962 index 1951= 100	1964 income per head ('000 lire)	1964 index 1951= 100
South	110·9	168·3	151·8	247·9	223·5	308·8	278·4
North	231·1	344·8	149·2	521·0	225·4	629·7	272·5
Italy	186·4	279·1	149·7	421·1	225·9	513·5	275·5

Source: Comitato dei Ministri per il Mezzogiorno, *Relazione sulla Attività di Coordinamento*, 1965, Vol. II, p. 47.

intended merely to provide a quick sketch before moving on and studying the position in greater detail. There are, of course, innumerable other statistics which could illustrate further the poverty of southern Italy and the extent to which it represents a very serious

[1] The reader will have noticed that the figures in the tables only go up to 1964. The reason for this is that more recent figures are calculated in a different manner and it is not possible to make them strictly comparable with the earlier figures. The trend between 1964 and 1966 shows the South gaining slightly on the North in terms of income per head at current and constant prices. Taking 1964 as 100, southern income per head at current prices was 118 in 1966 and the comparable figure for the North was 113. On the basis of 1963 prices and still taking 1964 as 100, the South reaches a level of 108·6 in 1966 as against 106·1 in the North. The arguments in the text above are hardly changed by these trends. A series from 1951 to 1966 would still show the disparity between North and South increasing on the basis of real income per head and falling slightly when measured in current prices. For further details of the later figures, see Comitato dei Ministri per il Mezzogiorno, *Relazione sull'Attuazione del piano di coordinamento degli Interventi Pubblici nel Mezzogiorno*, Vol. I, 1967.

regional problem. For example, 16 per cent of the southern population of six years and above are illiterate as opposed to 4·1 per cent in the North. Infant mortality—reckoned as the number of children who died in the first year of life per thousand live births—is 43·8 in the South and 28·9 in the North. The number of still-births per thousand births is 28·0 in the South and 14·6 in the North. The number of persons per room in the South, at 1·4, is 40 per cent higher than the comparable figure for the North.[1] There is no great shortage of statistics illustrating the poverty of the South.[2] It should, of course, be kept in mind that we are discussing the South relative to northern Italy which is itself still poor compared with Western Europe generally.

Most of the statistics used so far, to varying degrees, do no more than merely describe the problem. They show, as it were, the tip of the iceberg. In order to understand rather than describe the southern problem, it is necessary to go deeper and examine the southern economic structure vis-à-vis the North. This is the next task—to examine the quantitative and qualitative structure of the two regions with a view to explaining the problem and laying the foundation for our later discussion and evaluation of policy.

THE ECONOMIC STRUCTURE OF SOUTHERN ITALY

The southern Italian economic structure is characterized by a heavy weighting of agriculture and a low weighting of industry. It is from this structure that many of the region's problems arise.

---

[1] These figures are taken from *Relazione sulla Attività di Coordinamento*, 1965, op. cit., except for the housing figures which are taken from ISTAT, *Annuario Statistico Italiano*, 1965. The housing and illiteracy figures are for 1961. All the others refer to 1964.

[2] The four most convenient sources of general data on Italy and its regions are: (1) *Compendio Statistico Italiano*, (2) *Annuario Statistico Italiano*. Both are prepared annually by the Istituto Centrale di Statistica. (3) *Un Secolo di Statistiche Italiane: Nord e Sud* 1861-1961, published by Svimez. This massive volume of over a thousand pages is a mine of information, with the data often broken down even to provincial level. Its contents vary from the income, investment and production type of figures to the more prosaic figures of crime, people living in caves, illiteracy, etc. It is a pity that this volume was published before the 1961 Census figures became available. Much of its data for this reason only covers the period up to 1951. (4) *Informazioni Svimez* (published twice monthly). This bulletin is an invaluable source of information on southern Italy, bringing statistics up to date, informing of legislative, administrative and juridical changes together with reprints and/or summaries of some of the more important articles on Italian regional problems.

Table 1.3 below shows the gross product by sector in the North and South for 1966.

TABLE 1.3

GROSS PRODUCT BY SECTOR IN 1966 AT FACTOR PRICES

	Gross product (milliard lire) South	Percentage distribution South	Gross product (milliard lire) North	Percentage distribution North
Agriculture, forestry and fishing	1,690	24·8	2,535	11·2
Industry	2,330	34·3	11,206	49·5
Tertiary activities	2,786	40·9	8,884	39·3
Total	6,806	100	22,625	100

Note: The figures are for the private sector only.
Source: Comitato dei Ministri per il Mezzogiorno, *Studi Monografici sul Mezzogiorno*, 1967, p. 29.

The figures in Table 1.3 give a broad indication of one of the South's main problems: a heavy weighting of agriculture which in Italy as a whole has a lower productivity than industry. But the problem is worsened by the fact that both agriculture and industry in the South have a lower level of productivity than in the North. Both these points are illustrated in Table 1.4 below which shows an estimate of value added per employee by sector for 1964.

TABLE 1.4

VALUE ADDED ('000 LIRE) PER EMPLOYEE BY SECTOR

	Agriculture	Industry	Other
South	654·4	988·7	990·0
North	917·6	1675·0	1302·0
Italy	798·1	1515·0	1212·0

Source: Compiled from data in Comitato dei Ministri per il Mezzogiorno, *Relazione sulla Attività di Coordinamento*, 1965, Vol. II, pp. 102-5.

The table shows the considerable differences in productivity between North and South in the three sectors. Value added per employee in southern agriculture is about 70 per cent of that in the North, while the difference in industry is even greater with value added per employee in the South being around 60 per cent of the northern level. Calculations based simply on the three sectors show these differences in productivity as being the main explanatory factor behind the low overall level of value added in the South relative to the North. About 35 per cent of the difference between North and South in overall value is explained by the different structures and the rest by differences in productivity.[1] The next two sections take a look at the two sectors of agriculture and industry in the South and try to explain the reasons for the low levels of productivity.

I. AGRICULTURE

There is, of course, no single explanation of the poor productivity of southern agriculture: the reasons are many—poor quality of land, small unit size, fragmentation of units, lack of capital, lack of modern techniques and equipment, the system of tenure, *inter alia*. Many of these are interconnected, but taken together they present conditions which are not conducive to high productivity.

Much of the cultivated land in the South is hilly or mountainous. Of the 11·7 million hectares under cultivation, 28 per cent is mountainous, 54 per cent hilly and only 18 per cent plain. A large proportion of cultivated land in the South is on slopes of more than 15 degrees—about 55 per cent as against 46 per cent in the North. The difference may not seem great, though a more careful examination (see Table 1.5) shows that a much higher proportion of steep sloping land in the South is without drainage systems. This gives rise to serious soil erosion.

Southern holdings are frequently too small to allow economic use of modern equipment and techniques. 'Pulverization is an evil common to all Italian agriculture, in the North as well as in the South, however, in the South it assumes much greater importance.'[2] Table 1.6 below shows the percentage of farms falling into various

---

[1] The calculation was made by giving the northern structure to the South and applying southern value added per employee to the various sectors and calculating the difference between overall value added on this basis and actual overall value added in the South.

[2] *Relazione sulla Attività di Coordinamento*, 1965, op. cit., p. 128.

TABLE 1.5
CULTIVATED LAND ACCORDING TO ITS ANGLE OF SLOPE AND
THE PROPORTION WITHOUT DRAINAGE SYSTEM

Slope up to 15°	Proportion with no drainage systems	Slope 15°-30°	Proportion with no drainage systems	Slope 30°+	Proportion with no drainage system
South 43·8	34·4	35·4	30·5	20·8	18·7
North 53·4	10·7	26·2	12·1	20·4	12·4

Source: Comitato dei Ministri per il Mezzogiorno, *Relazione sulla Attività di Coordinamento*, 1965, Vol. II, pp. 160-1.

size brackets in 1961 in the two regions. A quick glance at the table shows that nearly 40 per cent of southern farms are of a size less than 1 hectare and 80 per cent are less than 5 hectares.

TABLE 1.6
SIZE DISTRIBUTION OF FARMS IN HECTARES

	-0·5	0·51-1·0	1·01-5·0	5·01-20	20·01-100	100+	Total
South	19·9	17·7	44·0	15·0	2·9	0·5	100
North	15·4	12·5	43·1	24·6	3·9	0·5	100

Note: One hectare=2·471 acres.
Source: Comitato dei Ministri per il Mezzogiorno, *Relazione sulla Attività di Coordinamento*, 1965, Vol. II, pp. 126-7. The figures are for 1961.

The picture given by examining the percentage of cultivated area in various farm sizes is slightly brighter than that given in Table 1.6, although almost a fifth of land is being cultivated on farms of less than 5 hectares. This is shown in Table 1.7.

It should, of course, be remembered that some of these farms will be part-time ventures although there is no reason to think that this should not be just as true in the North as in the South. In fact, probably a greater proportion of northern holdings are part-time.

Some of the smaller farms are, in fact, very profitable. Small holdings of 4-5 hectares in irrigated or highly fertile zones, and cultivating specialized crops, can be economic, though larger holdings, even in these conditions, give more than proportionately higher returns. Many of the smaller southern holdings are, however, neither in irrigated nor highly fertile zones and in consequence are well below the size which is commonly accepted as being economic.[1]

Another evil common to both North and South, though slightly more common in the South than the North, is that of fragmentation. Only 29·9 per cent of cultivated land is cultivated as a single piece against 34·6 per cent in the North. As much as 20 per cent of southern land is cultivated in holdings which are made up of between five and

TABLE 1.7

PERCENTAGE OF CULTIVATED AREA IN FARMS OF VARIOUS SIZES (IN HECTARES)

	-0·5	0·51-1·0	1·01-5	5·01-20	20·01-100	100+	Total
South	1·0	2·5	19·4	24·5	21·0	31·6	100
North	0·6	1·4	16·3	34·4	20·1	27·2	100

Source: Comitato dei Ministri per il Mezzogiorno, *Relazione sulla Attività di Coordinamento*, 1965, Vol. II, pp. 126-7. The figures are for 1961.

ten non-contiguous pieces as against 18 per cent in the North. Fragmentation, damaging even to traditional agricultural systems, is even more at odds with the needs of modern agriculture where the extension of mechanization, irrigation and specialization of crops make even greater the importance of homogeneity and contiguity of land within a holding.

The small holdings and high levels of fragmentation inevitably make southern agriculture undercapitalized and the methods of cultivation are often archaic. Modern mechanized methods are not generally suited to the agricultural system described above. The low income secured from this system anyway severely restricts the pos-

[1] It has been estimated that, in general, a holding would be reasonably economic if it was of 10 hectares in good plain and 15 hectares in good hill country. In the poorer hill country and in the mountain zones a holding would need to be above 20 to 25 hectares if it was to be economic. See Mario Bandini, 'Considerazione sulla Struttura delle Aziende Agricole nell' Europa dei Sei' in *Scritti di Economia e Statistica in Memoria de Alessandro Molinari*, Giuffrè, 1963.

sibility of using modern and often expensive methods. The level of mechanization in southern agriculture is very low.[1]

Although, on the whole, southern agriculture is in a poor condition, it is capable of considerable development through rationalization, irrigation and the application of modern techniques and ideas. Some areas in the South have seen great improvement through land reform schemes where a Gross Marketable Product of almost a million lire per hectare is quite possible.[2] These schemes, however, cover only a small proportion of the total southern cultivated area and large proportions of the non-irrigated and non-reformed areas remain predominantly engaged in cereal cultivation and pastoral activity—neither of which give high yields. Some of these areas are not capable of being developed except at enormous expense, and more extensive holdings with consequential depopulation seems the only answer.

There is a considerable need for great changes in southern agriculture, not only because of the direct impact that higher productivity in agriculture would have on the southern economy as a whole, but also because of the potential indirect impact of the sector. A richer agriculture would expand demand for non-agricultural goods and services thus giving greater possibilities for industrial development. Without a more prosperous agriculture, the problem of developing industry is all that much greater.

The problem of securing agricultural development in a sector riddled with tradition and bolstered by illiteracy is very great. It is indeed a revolution which is needed—a vast rationalization and reorganization of the sector with a considerable movement of the labour force into alternative employment and locations.[3]

[1] It is not easy to find a good measure of mechanization. The number of tractors, however, gives a reasonably good indication of the levels of mechanization so far attained in southern Italian agriculture. In 1964 the South had a mere 15 per cent of the total Italian tractors. In *Relazione sulla Attività di Coordinamento*, op. cit., 1961, it was estimated that the value of agrarian capital in the South was 35 per cent of that available in the North. A further indication of the backwardness of the South in terms of modern technique and equipment is that southern expenditure on agricultural production goods and services was a mere 9·1 per cent of gross saleable product in 1962 as against 19·6 per cent in the North. See G. de Rossi, 'L'Agricoltura Meridionale' in *Mezzogiorno e Politica di Piano*, Laterza, 1964.

[2] *Land Reform in Apulia, Lucania and Molise.* Bari, 1964.

[3] There has of course already been considerable movement out of agriculture. Between 1951 and 1961, about 900,000 people left agriculture. The annual movement tended to accelerate in the late 1950s and early 1960s, slowed down during the Italian recession of 1964-5, but gained momentum again as the economy recovered after 1965.

II. INDUSTRY

The development of industry in southern Italy is essential, not only because of its immediate repercussions in terms of income and employment but also because, by providing employment opportunities outside agriculture, it will take pressure off that sector and allow for its further development. Because of the importance of industry in this respect and because much of southern policy is currently aimed at industrial development, it is worth while making a fairly detailed examination of this sector.[1]

We have already seen in Table 1.3 above, that industry in the South carries little weight relative to the North. Southern industrial gross product is only 34·3 per cent of total gross product arising from the private sector as against 49·5 per cent in the North. Measured in terms of value added, industry accounted, in 1964, for 29 per cent of total (private plus public) southern value added as against 49 per cent in the North. With only 29 per cent of total southern value added originating in industry, the South has a structure more similar to an underdeveloped country than one of Western Europe. Belgium, for example, has a proportion of 41·3 per cent; France 47 per cent; Germany 53 per cent; Britain 46·4 per cent. The southern proportion is similar to Cyprus with 25 per cent; Chile with 28 per cent and Malta with 31 per cent. It is hardly consoling to see the South in a more favourable position than Burma with 20·1 per cent.[2]

By far the greatest proportion of Italian industry is concentrated in the North. Though holding 38 per cent of the Italian population and responsible for around 22 per cent of Gross National Product, the South in 1964 contributed only 15 per cent of Italian industrial value added.

The industries which do exist in the South are frequently inefficient and often operating in traditional sectors—a point which is discussed in more detail later. The position can however be briefly illustrated. In 1961, of the South's 864,000 industrial employees (out of a national total of 5·6 million), 384,000 were working in production units of not more than ten employees, i.e. 44 per cent were employed in firms which were broadly of an artisan or pre-industrial character.

---

[1] For an extremely comprehensive and interesting study of the southern industrial structure see C. Turco, *La Struttura dell' Industria Meridionale e la Politica di Sviluppo Industriale del Mezzogiorno*, Svimez, 1966 (mimeographed). Many of the figures in this section are taken from this book.

[2] The international comparisons in the text are from ISTAT, *Annuario Statistico Italiano* 1965, and are for the year 1963.

Giving strength to this point, over 20 per cent of industrial employees in the South were in units of not more than two employees. Against these figures, the north-west of Italy[1] had 82 per cent of its industrial employees in units of more than ten employees while only 2 per cent were in units of not more than two employees.

Although industry in general is poorly represented in the South, there are some sectors which are as well represented in the South as the North and of a similar organizational form. In point of fact, it is principally one sector, manufacturing, which is well out of line with the rest of the country in terms of its development, productivity and structure. The other sectors, construction, electricity, water, gas and the extraction industries, have an economic weight which corresponds with the South's economic importance measured in terms of southern gross product as a proportion of that for Italy as a whole.

The construction industry is a case in point. Furthermore, with 80 per cent of its employees in local units of more than ten employees it is not organizationally different from the rest of the country. Its growth, in terms of value added, has been less than that of the North though with a six-fold expansion between 1951 and 1964, as opposed to the eight-fold expansion in the North, there is little room for complaint. There has been a steady expansion in Italy generally of the medium-sized firms in this sector, a tendency which has been only slightly stronger in the North and reflecting the trend of increased mechanization in the industry. Electricity, gas and water share similar comments concerning structure, growth and territorial distribution. All these sectors are now under public ownership and their geographical distribution is largely determined by population and regional levels of prosperity. Inevitably, therefore, the South has a share of these sectors which is commensurate with its economic importance. Only the electricity industry is out of line, being slightly over-represented in the North, though this is largely explained by the hydroelectric plants in that region. Lastly, the extraction industries. In terms of value added, the South is in a fairly favourable position with 30 per cent of Italian value added and almost 40 per cent of the nation's employees. The industry in the South, with a doubling of value added between 1951 and 1964, has however not done as well as that in the North, which has seen a three-fold expansion over the period. There has been a decline of employment in the small and very large (500-plus employees) firms in the sector. The medium-sized firms, however, have seen a quite rapid expansion

[1] Piemonte, Val d'Aosta, Liguria, Lombardy. The north-west is the most industrialized area of Italy.

in employment. The extraction industry in the South is not strictly comparable with the North. While in the North natural gas represents the main part of the sector, the South is still predominantly working lignite, zinc and sulphur—all of which declined rapidly in the 1960s as a result of increasingly heavy international competition. These sectors can be expected to decline further in the future. The South is, however, moving rapidly into the extraction of crude oil, gas and potassium salts which offer good opportunities of high productivity development. Although the extraction industry has done much worse in terms of growth than the other sectors considered above, this cannot to any great extent explain the poor performance and position of industry generally in the South. Responsible for only 4 per cent of the South's industrial production, it is far too small to make any appreciable impression on the southern industrial position as a whole.

It is to the manufacturing industry that one must turn in order to understand the industrial backwardness of the South. The manufacturing industry is a vital sector for a region like the South without many basic materials and particularly one with excessive numbers employed in agriculture. Greater development of manufacturing would not only bring the direct benefit of additional employment in the region but also, by reducing the pressures of agriculture, contribute to the growth of that sector also. The southern manufacturing sector at present, however, has considerable shortcomings.

Although manufacturing industry is the principal southern industrial sector, it carries far less weight than in the North. In 1965, 62 per cent of the South's total industrial value added arose from manufacturing industry, while in the north-west of Italy, in line with other advanced countries, it was 80 per cent. The great majority of Italian manufacturing output is in the North. Only 13 per cent of national manufacturing value added in 1964 was in the South. A large proportion of the southern manufacturing employees work in extremely small firms and it is obvious that much of the sector is of an artisan character. According to Census data for 1961, only 46 per cent of the sector's employees were in local units of ten or more employees and 29 per cent were in units of two or less. The corresponding figures for the north-west were 82 per cent and 6 per cent.

In order to understand the poor placing of the South in manufacturing relative to the North, it is worth while briefly examining the structure of the sector in a little more detail in order to discover the types of manufacturing industry in the South and how these compare with the North. To do this it will be necessary to divide the industry into two sectors: traditional industry and modern industry.[1]

Traditional industries are those mainly concerned with the exploitation of local agricultural resources and directed principally at supplying provincial and, at most, regional markets. The production forms are mainly family or artisan, using antiquated techniques. They frequently enjoy relatively protected markets for geographical reasons and the products often have a fairly low income elasticity. The market conditions and the production forms do not make the sector a dynamic one.

Modern industries are those industries involved in the working of materials from a variety of sources and aimed at markets for the most part outside their immediate area of operation. They are not geographically protected and need to be organized at high levels of efficiency if they are to remain competitive and survive. Their output has a fairly high level of income elasticity while their organizational structure makes them capable of responding to market opportunities. An important point is that they rely to a considerable extent on a multiplicity of technical and economic interrelationships with other firms and sectors.

It is not easy in practice to divide manufacturing industry into these two groups of traditional and modern. Turco[2] makes a meaningful division, however, by considering the traditional industries to be made up of food and tobacco, clothing, furs, wood and non-metallic manufacturing. The modern industries include textiles, engineering, chemicals, petro-chemicals, paper, rubber, printing and publishing, cinematograph and 'various'. On this breakdown, the South's manufacturing output is fairly evenly divided between traditional and modern industry. In 1964, southern value added by traditional industry was 504 milliard lire against 568 milliard lire for modern industry. The picture in the North was quite different, with 82 per cent of total value added in manufacturing arising from the modern sector. The South had about 25 per cent of national value added in the traditional industries but a mere 8·7 per cent in the modern. Even the figure of 8·7 per cent overstates the presence of the modern manufacturing sector in as far as the engineering group—forming a very important part of the modern manufacturing sector—is made up for the most part of units with two or less employees. Thus, though included in the modern sector for the purposes of the calculations above, it would be more meaningful to classify them in the traditional manufacturing sector.

[1] The division and the calculations below are taken from C. Turco, op. cit.
[2] ibid.

Not only does the South have a heavier weighting of traditional industry, which in Italy as a whole has a value added per employee of 30 per cent below that of modern industry, but southern traditional industry has a value added per employee which is only about 90 per cent of the comparable northern figure.[1] It is interesting to note that the disparity of value added per employee in modern industry between North and South is slightly less than it is with traditional industry.

Let us summarize our discussion of the southern economic structure. First, it is heavily weighted with the conventionally low productivity sector of agriculture. Secondly, southern agriculture has even lower levels of productivity than the North. Thirdly, manufacturing industry is poorly represented in the South and much of that which exists is in the traditional sector where productivity is usually low. Fourthly, productivity in both modern and traditional manufacturing sectors is lower than in the North though the slightly lower level of productivity in the modern manufacturing sector is partly explained by the inclusion, in our calculations, of artisan and family type engineering workshops in the modern sector.

III. THE ORIGINS OF THE SOUTHERN PROBLEM[2]

The disparity in economic well-being between North and South is no new phenomenon. The South is a problem of long standing and one to which many writers have given attention.[3] Some historians trace its origins to the Roman wars with Carthage; others go back merely to the feudalism imposed by the Normans and yet others lay stress on the maladministration and inefficiency of the Spanish occupation. For the economist, however, it is the period since Unification (1861) which is of special interest; not only because some, albeit small, amounts of statistical data are available from that date, but also because it was after Unification that the position in the South clearly deteriorated. What happened in the South after Unification is a good illustration of the damage which can be done by the forced union of an economically advanced and a backward region if adequate provisions are not made for the transition.

[1] This is calculated using value added at current prices for the Census year of 1961.

[2] The author is grateful to Alberto Benzoni for comments on an earlier draft of this historical section and admits to having made extensive use of his article, 'Il Mezzogiorno nello Stato Italiano', Il Veltro, No. 6, 1962.

[3] A very good anthology on the Southern Question is A. Carrà, Orientamenti e Testimonianze sulla Questione Meridionale, Célèbes, 1965.

THE PROBLEM OF SOUTHERN ITALY AND ITS ORIGINS

There is little doubt that the South was poorer than the North at the time of Unification and had a much lower potential for development. The industrial structure was weaker than in the North. A higher proportion of its industry was artisan in character and the North, even at Unification, had most of Italy's limited liability companies. Southern industry was much more protected than its counterpart in the North. External tariffs were about four times higher than those in the rest of the country. Much of the larger-scale industry in the South was foreign-owned or state enterprise. There was a serious lack of an entrepreneur class.

Southern agriculture was also inferior to that of the North. The climate was harsh and the land was poorer due to the lower proportion of plain and to serious erosion in the past. Capital was scarce and the distribution of land, on the basis of a feudal or semi-feudal relationship between landowners and cultivators, was inefficient. These were the two extremes: the big landlord and the small peasant. The former was often absent. Between the two were the parasitic intermediaries. The small peasants lacked the means to improve their situation, while the big landowners often lacked the inclination. The natural conditions in which agriculture operated were made worse by malaria on the coast and plains. This forced the population into the poor hilly land. The increasing pressure of population in the hill towns led to the greater cultivation of woodland and pastureland which aggravated the erosion problem, damaged the lower basins and, incidentally, also aided the spread of malaria. There were some irrigated zones of intense cultivation in the South though these covered less than 10 per cent of the South's cultivated agricultural area.[1] For the rest, the main crop was grain cultivated inefficiently on poor land. At Unification, output per person employed in agriculture is estimated to have been about 20 per cent below that of the North.[2]

The South was at a further disadvantage relative to the North at the time of Unification in terms of communications. The Bourbon fear of antagonizing the old ruling classes and encouraging the new bourgeoisie led them to keep taxes, and therefore public expenditure, low. Tax rates were well below those in the North and, after meeting the costs of the army and servicing debts already contracted, there was little remaining for other public works. Communications were in an almost medieval condition. Railways were virtually non-existent

[1] A. Benzoni, op. cit.
[2] *Un Secolo di Statistiche: Nord e Sud* 1861-1961, Svimez, and also R. S. Eckaus, 'The North-South Differential in Italian Economic Development', *The Journal of Economic History*, September 1961.

with only 99 km. of track as against 1,798 km. in the country as a whole.[1] The roads network was extremely poor at both provincial and communal level. The mileage of roads was small and the system poor in quality and scarcely integrated.[2] So poor were transport facilities that the region cannot really be considered as a single geographical unit but must be seen rather as a series of local and isolated markets: so isolated that local harvest failures could cause large price changes which had serious effects on local communities.[3] Large parts of the North had navigable rivers and canals, good roads and the start of a railway network. In terms of literacy also, the South was backward relative to the North. Eighty-nine per cent of the population aged six years and above were illiterate as against 67 per cent in the North. Finally, in this list of deficiencies, the South even lacked a system of standard weights and measures.

The high tariffs, poor communications, poor agriculture and inefficient industry inevitably meant a society with low levels of material well-being and low levels of international trade relative to the North. The former is difficult to quantify. One assessment, calculated on the basis of the number of days that a workman had to work in order to buy a quintal of grain, put the difference between North and South at about 12 per cent.[4] Such an estimate can only be tentative and subject to many reservations though it may not be too far out if, as mentioned above, productivity in the vital sector of agriculture was about 20 per cent lower than in the North. Overseas trade is much better documented.[5] The available data show the importance of foreign trade per inhabitant in the North as being similar to that of Western Europe as a whole while the South is much lower. At the same time the South was largely importing consumer goods while the North was importing a far greater proportion of raw materials, fuels and semi-finished industrial goods. The North, during the decade or so before Unification, had seen a considerable increase in such imports while the South saw no similar change.

Up to the end of the nineteenth century there was, as we shall

[1] Interestingly, however, the South had the first stretch of railway constructed in Italy; built in 1839 in the Naples area.

[2] P. Saraceno, *La Mancata Unificazione Economica Italiana a cento Anni dall' Unificazione Politica*, Giuffrè, 1961.

[3] C. Rodano, *Mezzogiorno e Sviluppo Economico*, Laterza, 1954.

[4] P. S. Labini, 'Osservazioni sull' Evoluzione Economica del Mezzogiorno' in *Scritti di Economia e Statistica in Memoria di Alessandro Molinari*, Giuffrè, 1963.

[5] A. Graziani, 'Il Commercio Estero del Regno delle Due Sicilie dal 1832 al 1858' in Vol. 10 of the *Archivio Economico dell' Unificazione Italiana*, Torino, 1960. Also see P. Saraceno, op. cit.

see, very little widening of the gap between North and South largely because the forty years after Unification was a period in which the Italian economy in general grew very slowly. Although the gap did not appear to widen, these were years in which changes were taking place which were eventually to allow the North to move rapidly ahead of the South. In addition to these changes, a number of general policy measures were taken by the new State which adversely affected the development of the South.

One measure which, perhaps surprisingly, did little initial damage to the South was the substitution of Piemontese external tariffs for the much higher external tariffs of the Kingdom of the Two Sicilies and the immediate dismantling of tariffs between the various Italian States. One might have expected that southern industry would have been hard hit by such changes. This, in fact, proved not to be the case and indeed industrial employment in the South up to 1881 rose faster than in the North, though much of the expansion was in female employment and thus probably of an artisan character.[1] The explanation of the rapid industrial expansion may lie in the continued relative isolation of the southern economy up to about the mid-1880s combined with the stimulus given by the rapid expansion of southern agriculture in the quarter-century after Unification.

Soon after Unification, the new State began an impressive programme in the South aimed at bringing the southern communications network, and infrastructure generally, up to northern standards. The majority of the State's expenditure on roads went to the South while, for the next fifty years or so, 50 per cent of the funds for aqueducts and water improvements likewise went to the South. A large railway-building programme was started soon after Unification which gave the South a third of the nation's track by the mid-1880s and brought the South up to the northern level of track kilometres per square kilometre of territory by the turn of the century.

The improved communications which were becoming significant by the mid-1880s were not wholly to the South's advantage since they laid it open to the more competitive northern industries. Between 1881 and 1901 there was a massive fall in industrial employment in the South and a rise in the North.[2]

As mentioned above, before the 1880s southern industry undoubtedly benefited from the very rapid expansion of southern

---

[1] For data on employment trends after Unification, see *Un Secolo di Statistiche Italiane: Nord e Sud* 1861-1961, op. cit.

[2] Taking 1871 as 100, industrial employment in the South was 147·3 in 1881 and 103·6 in 1901. The same index for the North gives 122·1 and 130·8 respectively.

agricultural output and income following Unification. In the first fifteen years, agricultural output expanded at a rate which was not exceeded until after the end of the Second World War. The expansion arose largely from foreign demand for fruit and wine.

The rapid agricultural expansion in the South was halted after 1887, when pressures from northern industry resulted in a protective duty being imposed on many foreign industrial goods but particularly textiles and metals. At the same time, largely a result of pressures from the big southern landlords, a protective duty was placed on grain which was suffering heavy competition from North America. These protective measures, which with modifications were to last until the 1940s, were to have grave consequences for the South and indeed Italy generally.[1] One of the most serious consequences for the South was that France took retaliatory tariff measures against Italian wine and this at a time when the French vineyards were being hit by Phylloxera and when prospects for southern wine in the French market were therefore extremely good. Another damaging effect for the South arose out of the policy of protecting Italian grain. This did not help the small farmer who was often producing only for his own consumption. What it did do was to preserve the extensive cultivation system in the South and indeed extend the area devoted to grain, with further encroachment on pasture and forests and consequential aggravation of the problems of erosion.

In spite of the general policy measures above, and in some cases perhaps even because of them, the disequilibrium between North and South does not appear to have increased much up to the end of the century. Italy as a whole in this period was developing only slowly, and indeed in the last decade of the nineteenth century income per head was only just about equal to that of 1861-1870.[2] Net investment over the period was only about 3-5 per cent of national income. Agriculture in the South expanded at a rate similar to the North though industry lost some weight.

Evidence to support the contention that the South, on the surface at least, was keeping fairly well in line with the North up to the turn of the century can be found in a fascinating article by Tagliacarne[3]

[1] One disadvantage for Italian industrial development arising out of the protective measures was that they impeded the development of the engineering industry which was not protected and which was burdened with the higher prices of the protected and inefficient basic metal industries.

[2] A. Benzoni, op. cit.

[3] G. Tagliacarne, 'Lo Sviluppo Economico delle Regioni Italiane in Tre Quarti de Secolo (1885-1961)' in *Scritti di Economia e Statistica in Memoria di Alessandro Molinari*, Giuffrè, 1963.

in which he calculates an economic index for the two regions. The relationship between the North and South over time on the basis of this index is shown in Table 1.8.[1]

TABLE 1.8

Year	1885	1895	1905	1915	1925	1938	1951	1961
Index	67·8	66·4	64·6	60·1	55·4	57·6	50·4	46·7

More important perhaps than such global figures, though less quantifiable, is the fact that most evidence seems to indicate that, although the South on the surface was keeping fairly well in line with the North (though there was a continued strong disequilibrium between them), conditions had been created, or were present, in the North which were to enable it, after the turn of the century, to move rapidly ahead of the South. Conditions in the North were becoming much more conducive to a rapid growth of both industry and agriculture. The agricultural structure of the South was little changed from the time of Unification. The big landlords without initiative remained as did the small peasants lacking means. Although there had been some redistribution of land, this was almost wholly confined to ecclesiastical and public land. The almost feudal agricultural conditions were little changed by 1900 from what they had been in 1860 or even 1800. The North, in the meantime, never so troubled by the big landowners, had developed an agricultural structure and system which was not much out of line with Europe in general. On the industrial side, the North had a higher proportion of fairly large firms and a smaller proportion of industrial employment in the artisan sector. The industrial protection of the mid-1880s had encouraged further industrial development of the North, inefficient though it may have been. Northern industrial development was further aided towards the end of the century by the development

---

[1] The basic Tagliacarne index is the sum of nine indices of economic conditions for which data was available over the period. The indices are (1) telegrams sent, (2) taxes on agricultural and property incomes, (3) taxes on buildings, (4) income tax, (5) succession taxes, (6) registration taxes, (7) stamp taxes, (8) tobacco purchases and (9) money deposits in credit and postal institutes. The index is calculated as the average percentage that the nine indices make of the two regions. Thus, for example, in 1885 the South had an average percentage of the nine indices equal to 30·7 per cent of Italy and the North naturally had a percentage of 69·3. The population at that time in the South was 39·5 per cent of Italy. The index for the South and North is now expressed as the index calculated over the percentage population. This gives an index of 1·15 for the North and 0·78 for the South. In Table 1·8, the index for the South is calculated as a percentage of that for the North.

of hydroelectricity, all but about 10 per cent being generated in the North. Fuel costs remained between 30 and 50 per cent lower in the North than the South until after the end of the Second World War.[1] Finally, in spite of the significant improvements in the southern communications network, the North at the turn of the century was still better endowed than the South.

It was at the end of the nineteenth century, when Italy entered its phase of take-off into self-sustaining growth, that the changes which had taken place in the North since Unification, and the lack of similar changes in the South, began to show results. Over the next forty years, income per head in Italy rose by 70 per cent while industrial output increased by 300 per cent. The growth of agricultural output, however, slowed down and between 1900 and 1940 increased by only 26 per cent as against 36 per cent in the previous forty years.[2] The greater weighting of agriculture in the South would therefore in itself have accentuated the disequilibrium. The situation has however worsened by the fact that the South, with its archaic structure, was not even able to equal the national growth of agricultural output. Agricultural output hardly increased at all in the South and virtually the whole of the national increase occurred in the North. In industry, the South saw a decline in employment of about 10 per cent between 1901 and 1936 as against an increase of around 50 per cent in the North.

It is thus hardly surprising that the gap between North and South widened rapidly between 1900 and the outbreak of the Second World War. The calculations based on the Tagliacarne index in Table 1.8 above, show this trend. The gap was yet wider by the late 1940s.

The poor economic structure of the South and the backward character of the individual sectors which made up this structure prevented the South from exploiting the rapid Italian economic growth in the twentieth century and represent the main explanation of the widening disequilibrium between 1900 and 1950. There were, however, a number of other factors operating during this period which intensified the disequilibrium.

Firstly the two great Italian war/post-war inflations, in a way, benefited northern industrial development in that capital was quickly written off. The greater investment in fixed capital in the North placed it at an advantage during the inflations relative to the South where investments were to a greater extent in paper titles. Secondly, the attempts to extricate the Italian banks from their difficulties in the early 1920s and the setting up of IRI further consolidated the

---

[1] P. Saraceno, op. cit.   [2] A. Benzoni, op. cit.

North's industrial advantage in as far as the rescue operation was inevitably directed towards shoring up the existing industrial structure and therefore mainly concerned with the North. Thirdly, two particular policies of the Fascist administration widened the gap. First, the attempt to secure self-sufficiency in grain, coinciding with the virtually complete isolation of the Italian economy after 1929, damaged the South since it resulted in yet more land, about 12 per cent more, being turned over to grain with consequential inroads into pasture and woodland and further aggravation of the problem of erosion.[1] The second policy measure taken by the Fascist administration and which had deleterious effects on the South, was the control of migration both within and outside Italy. This put additional pressures on the already overworked land in the South, leading to further encroachment on forests and pastures. Fourthly, the First World War saw a considerable improvement of communications in the North in order to expedite the movement of troops and goods to the Northern front while the Second World War brought far greater destruction to the South than the North.[2]

The disequilibrium which would anyway have widened as a result of the structural deficiencies of the South was accentuated by the factors and policies above. The disequilibrium in 1950 was far more serious than it had ever been.

[1] The more flexible agricultural structure of the North is indicated by the fact that the 'battle for grain' saw higher output per hectare in that region. A. Benzoni, op. cit.

[2] For details of the extent of the damage, see the article by G. Pastore in Vol. 1 of *Cassa per il Mezzogiorno: Dodici Anni* 1950-62, Laterza, 1962.

CHAPTER 2

SOUTHERN REGIONAL POLICY UP TO 1965

The number of time periods into which one can divide policies for the South is inevitably arbitrary. Most observers agree, however, on three major points: 1950 with the creation of the Cassa per il Mezzogiorno; 1957 with the start of a serious southern industrialization policy; and 1965 with the introduction of new legislation for southern development, considerable expansion of the funds involved and the efforts to integrate national and regional planning. This chapter is concerned with the first two periods though with much greater attention being paid to the years after 1950.

I. POLICIES FOR SOUTH BEFORE 1950

Southern policy prior to 1950 can be divided into two phases, the first lasting until about the turn of the century and the second operating between then and around 1950.

Immediately following Unification, the new State, recognizing the relative backwardness of the South, implemented policies which it was hoped would give *de facto* as well as *de jure* Unification. Policy was aimed primarily at levelling the infrastructure endowment between the North and South, particularly with respect to communications and water supplies. The new State, up to about the turn of the century, was spending more than half of its expenditure on communications and water in the South. As mentioned in the previous chapter, considerable improvements were effected. Policy was however almost wholly directed at infrastructure during this first phase though there were some feeble attempts at redistributing land, but this mainly involved ecclesiastical and public land—the latter often a very marginal quality.

The second phase of southern policy started around the turn of the century and involved more positive measures 'not only having the aim of levelling conditions but also of creating conditions in favour of the South relative to the other regions of Italy'.[1] This new

---

[1] P. Saraceno, op. cit., p. 13.

phase of policy was centred around a number of special laws for the southern regions: Sardinia in 1897, Naples in 1904, Basilicata in the same year, Calabria in 1905 as well as a special law for the southern provinces, Sicily and Sardinia in 1906 which aimed in the first instance at 'carrying out public works considered necessary for economic and social development and for which the general legislation was not adequate to ensure execution'.[1] The special laws aimed mainly at providing adequate domestic and agricultural water supplies though they also included other important aspects such as the power of the State to give support to communes which were not financially capable of executing the tasks laid out in the general laws. They also included measures to improve southern agriculture by easing the burden of taxation on the small farmers and creating agricultural credit institutes. The unfortunate point was, however, that the funds allocated were small in comparison with the size of the problem and, more important, the agricultural policies in particular were more appropriate for a northern type of agricultural structure where credit facilities and water supplies were the most serious obstruction to growth. In the South there was a need, before the benefits of the former could be fully enjoyed, for structural reorganization and for comprehensive and integrated land improvement programmes stretching from the hills to the sea. The agricultural provisions were therefore largely wasted since they were being applied to a structure which was not, on the whole, capable of exploiting them.

Common to most intervention until the late 1950s, industry was largely—but not wholly—neglected in the measures for southern development. In 1904 the special law for Naples provided for industrial zones and fiscal as well as customs concessions for industry locating there. The fiscal and customs concessions were extended to the rest of the South in 1906. Naples, however, remained the 'showcase of the South' as far as industrial development was concerned.

Between the wars, the measures of the pre-1914 period were consolidated and to some extent extended. There was an attempt to undertake more integrated and comprehensive public works policies while some, though too few, integrated land-reform and land-improvement schemes were begun. The general reluctance to interfere much with the agricultural holding structure unfortunately remained. Industry continued to be largely neglected though some of the state-controlled IRI firms in engineering and metals industries were located in the South—again mainly in Naples.

[1] ibid., p. 13.

It is, of course, always necessary to see any policy measures in the context of their period. Viewed in this light, the efforts to secure southern development in the period following Unification and up to the Second World War were not inconsiderable and it is certainly quite wrong to argue that the southern problem was completely neglected. For such an early period in fact, the measures were quite impressive and in advance of similar policies in other European countries. Though well intentioned, the policies were not, however, adequate to overcome the disequilibrium between North and South and indeed, as we have seen, the gap widened—particularly after 1900. The failure of policy to narrow the gap or even to hold it arose out of a number of factors. Firstly, the means available to execute the legislation were limited and much of the policy remained as aspirations. Secondly, the conceptual economic framework on which policy could be based was hardly developed. Policies were pursued in almost complete ignorance of what should be done or what would result from particular measures. Thirdly, measures were too often *ad hoc* and unrelated to each other. In agriculture in particular there was a need for comprehensive schemes—schemes which would change the farm holding structure and range over large areas. Without this, the efforts were largely wasted. Fourthly, policy concentrated too much on agriculture and infrastructure and too little on industry. Lastly, and perhaps most important, the measures to aid the South were more than offset by a number of general economic policy measures and trends which worked against the South and which have already been mentioned earlier: the protectionist policies after the mid-1880s, the wars and inflations of the first half of the twentieth century, and the control of migration during the Fascist period. All these, and others too, helped to widen the disparities—disparities which would have anyway been difficult to resolve given the more flexible northern economic structure, its closer proximity to the North European markets, its higher quality of labour, its lower fuel costs, its better agricultural conditions and its larger entrepreneural class.

II. THE CREATION OF THE CASSA PER IL MEZZOGIORNO

The period following the Second World War was one of great difficulty for the whole of Italy.[1] The most pressing priority was the

---

[1] For a very good description of Italian economic difficulties in the period immediately following the Second World War and indeed Italian economic development to the mid-1960s, see G. H. Hildebrand, *Growth and Structure in the Economy of Modern Italy*, Harvard University Press, 1965.

reconstruction of the economy after the war and occupation. To a very large extent, and this is true of any period of crisis, sectional interests like the South were temporarily forgotten, other matters taking higher priority. The South was largely neglected in the attempt at national recovery and any measures taken were largely of an emergency character in order to deal with the South's most elementary and serious deficiencies with respect to sewerage and water.

The political manœuvrings leading to the creation of the Cassa per il Mezzogiorno, and the start of serious intervention in the South are not unimportant in explaining the form which the Cassa eventually took and its early policies.[1] The victory of democracy in the 1948 elections was followed, in 1949, by a wave of strikes and invasions of the land. The latter phenomenon had its centre in the southern regions and mainly in Sicily, Puglia and Calabria. The extreme left, rejected at the elections, tried to provoke more militant action. The South offered very good material for such action with its vast number of peasants, labourers, unemployed intellectuals and underemployed city proletariat. The national economic difficulties lying behind the troubles of 1949 were very great. Public debt was high and the government was having difficulty in acquiring funds. Unemployment was also very high. Economic reconstruction was still far from complete and the economy had been hard hit by cuts in exports which were particularly severe in textiles and, with the rapid recovery of Germany, engineering. Agricultural prices were falling as a consequence of depression at home and difficulties in recovering past overseas markets.

Although it was obvious that, for political reasons, there was a need for a dramatic new approach to the southern problem, the national economic conditions of the time recommended prudence rather than audacity—a policy at most of first-aid rather than one of structural modifications which would necessarily be slow to yield results. The first few years of intervention by the Cassa, as we shall see, smacked strongly of first-aid.

It is wrong, however, to see the creation of the Cassa solely in political terms: there were other factors involved. First, there was developing a better understanding of the southern problem as a result of improved statistics and, more important, the rapid emergence of the relatively new subject of development economics. Particularly important in this context of understanding the problems and evolving

[1] For an interesting discussion of the factors surrounding the creation of the Cassa, see the article by P. Campilli in *Cassa per il Mezzogiorno: Dodici Anni, 1950-62*, op. cit., Vol. I.

policy was the creation of SVIMEZ at the end of 1946.[1] This group, through to the present day, has had an influence on policy beyond its size. Second, there was a recognition that the effects of earlier efforts had not been satisfactory. They had been generally unco-ordinated, badly planned and poorly administered and for more successful policies there was a need for a supra-ministerial body. Third, it was becoming recognized that there were possible national economic benefits to be derived from southern aid. In particular, the South if developed was seen as a possible major market to replace, if only temporarily, those lost overseas.[2] In the early efforts of the Cassa there was in fact probably too much stress on the South as a market than as a producing region. A final factor behind the creation of the Cassa was that interest in a comprehensive set of measures for the South was stimulated by an early offer by the World Bank of considerable funds if comprehensive development plans were evolved— an offer, incidentally, which in its original form was never taken up. Nevertheless, the eventual creation of the Cassa owes much to the original discussions and interest aroused.

In 1950, largely in response to these factors, the Cassa per il Mezzogiorno was created.[3] It marks the beginning of a more serious, cohesive and, on the whole, beneficial policy for the South.

The policies pursued following the creation of the Cassa can be divided broadly into three periods of time. First, the pre-industrialization period of 1950 to 1957. Second, the industrialization period 1957 to 1965 and finally the period after 1965 with the prorogation and financial strengthening of the Cassa and the evolution, if not implementation of stronger national and regional planning. Any division of this nature is never completely satisfactory. The pre-industrialization period was not entirely lacking in industrial policy

[1] SVIMEZ, Association for the Industrial Development of southern Italy, was founded on December 2, 1946. It has the aim 'to promote, in a spirit of effective national solidarity and with an overall approach, the detailed study of economic conditions in the South of Italy, in order to propose concrete programmes of action and work intended to create and develop in southern Italy and the Islands the industrial activities which best meet such needs as have been ascertained' (Article 2 of the Statute of the Association). For a discussion of the history of SVIMEZ and its role in southern development and an invaluable collection of SVIMEZ studies, see *Il Mezzogiorno nelle Ricerche della Svimez*, 1947-1967, Giuffrè, 1968.

[2] The most important and influential contribution, arguing that development of the South would stimulate employment and income in the whole of Italy, was *Economic Effects of an Investment Programme in Southern Italy*, edited by SVIMEZ, Rome 1951.

[3] Law 646, 1950. Legislation in Italy is frequently referred to by number and year. This practice is followed in these chapters.

and the pre-planning period was not entirely lacking in plans; yet the division we have chosen is meaningful and makes for ease of exposition. The next two sections cover the first two phases of policy. The third phase—current policy—is treated in Chapter 3.

III. THE PRE-INDUSTRIALIZATION PERIOD: 1950-1957

The creation of the Cassa in 1950 represented a major watershed for southern policy. The main criticisms of earlier policies had been that they were too fragmented, unco-ordinated and lacking a proper sense of direction. Furthermore, the funds involved were nowhere near sufficient for the problem in hand. With the creation of the Cassa it was hoped that these faults would be largely remedied.

The Cassa is an executive body under the control of a Committee of Ministers for the South with parliamentary responsibility for the Cassa's activities. The Committee of Ministers was composed of those ministries which would have an important role to play in southern development.[1] The Committee of Ministers had the responsibility of drawing up a long-term plan (initially ten years) of what were called extraordinary works, aimed at the development of the South. The works were to be organic, i.e. the work of the Cassa was to cover intervention in fields which would usually have involved a number of ministries with the attendant problems of co-ordination. The so-called ordinary policies of the government extend over the entire national territory. Each ministry intervenes in the sector which lies within its own sphere of authority, very often without prior consultation with other ministries dealing with related sectors. Because the policies are not co-ordinated, their potential economic efforts become dispersed. It was hoped that the Cassa, because of its supra-ministerial character, would escape such difficulties.[2]

Although the efforts of the Cassa were intended to be organic, it was of course necessary that its interventions be co-ordinated with the ordinary administration. Although intended, this co-ordination proved difficult to implement in practice, even though the Committee of Ministers should have provided a useful forum for such co-ordination. The individual ministries were operating on different

[1] The Ministries initially involved were those of Agriculture, Forestry, the Treasury, Industry and Commerce, Public Works, Labour and Social Welfare and Transport. It was later enlarged to include the Ministry of State Holdings, Tourism and Education.

[2] For a discussion of the early organization, expectations and role of the Cassa, see E. Massaccesi, 'Regional Economic Development Policies in Italy' in *Area Redevelopment Policies in Britain and the Countries of the Common Market*, us Department of Commerce, 1965.

time-scales in their planning—many of them in fact planning on an annual basis. Worse still, there was little co-ordination even in the drawing up of their annual plans which were presented as *fait accompli* rather than being discussed in the first instance with other ministries.[1] The creation of the Cassa did not ease these problems of co-ordination. The extent to which the Cassa could take a lead in co-ordination was slight. There could be no bullying of ministries on particular policies. The ministers within the Committee of Ministers had responsibility to Parliament for their own ministry and could not be swayed either by fellow-ministers or the Cassa itself. The Cassa thus played a rather strange role. With its own interventions, say an irrigation scheme, it could never be sure that the ordinary administration would co-ordinate its activities to coincide with its own actions, while the relatively unco-ordinated actions of the individual ministries often left the Cassa to clear up the mess —but often many years after the event. In the capacity of clearing-up and filling the gaps left by the ordinary administration the Cassa played an important and useful role. It was a role which the Cassa increasingly had to play though completely contrary to the original idea that it should be additive to the activities of the ordinary administration and not substitutive.

The Cassa was endowed with a considerable amount of money. For its first ten-year plan it was allotted 1,000 milliard lire (about £600 million). Although in principle it was to be spent evenly over the ten-year period, the Cassa in fact often spent future income. What did the Cassa do with the money?

A first general point is that the Cassa never had a particular quantified global objective for its spending. It never declared itself to be aiming for, say, so much growth in the South. Its aim was broadly that of aiding the social and economic progress of the South.

The direction of the Cassa's spending before 1957 was basically non-industrial and most of its effort went into agriculture and infrastructure. Of the original allocation of 1,000 milliard lire, it was intended that 77 per cent was to go to agriculture, 11·5 per cent to water supplies and drainage, 9 per cent to road building and 2·5 per cent to the tourist sector.

Even as early as 1952 there was a reorganization of the proposed expenditures. In that year, its funds were increased to 1,280 milliard

---

[1] A procedure was established in 1959 whereby discussions took place prior to decisions in order to get increased co-ordination between the various ministries. This, though preferable to the earlier chaos, was a long time in implementing and indeed little response was observed prior to the drawing up of the Italian National Plan and Law 717 in the mid-1960s.

lire and its plan extended to 1962. The priorities or direction of spending were slightly modified. The so-called Twelve Year Plan of 1952 allocated 69 per cent to agriculture, 29 per cent to transport, communications, aqueducts and drainage, and 2 per cent to tourism. Industry still does not appear on the lists.

The concentration on agriculture and infrastructure in the pre-industrialization period was a consequence of a number of factors, pressures and ideas.

First, the concentration on agriculture. Agriculture represented of course the main economic sector of the South and there is always a temptation to concentrate effort on developing or supporting major economic sectors. There was, however, also a feeling that the poverty of the South was a result largely of its poor agriculture.[1]

To a large extent, however, the Cassa's early agricultural policy had the character of 'assistance' rather than the objective of promoting increased productivity.[2] Its interventions through land reform and land improvements (drainage and irrigation) were carried out over wide areas even though costs were frequently high and the economic benefits of action in some of the areas were very low. There was little concentration of effort in areas or sectors where the return would be highest. Land coming available through land reform was frequently distributed in holdings well below their most economic size.[3] The spreading of effort, common also outside the sphere of agriculture, was not corrected until the mid-1960s.

In the context of the pre-industrialization period, a policy of 'assistance' rather than 'efficiency' is perhaps understandable. It was clear that something needed to be done in order to improve the conditions in the South and in particular increase employment and income, no matter how slightly. To a large extent it was considered that aid should be given *in situ*. It was never expected that there would be any large-scale and immediate industrial development in either the North or the South so that the prospect of heavy emigration out of the agricultural areas was not envisaged—at least not on the scale on which it finally took place. The economic miracle in the North, and the fairly rapid though geographically concentrated southern industrial development, took the authorities by surprise.

[1] A. Molinari was one of the major opponents of this idea and argued that industry represented the major hope for southern development. See A. Molinari, 'Necessità ed Urgenza di Industrializzare il Mezzogiorno' in the volume *Contributi allo Studio del Problema Industriale del Mezzogiorno*, SVIMEZ, 1949.

[2] We shall see later that this character of assistance was also present in other fields where the Cassa operated.

[3] M. Bandini, 'Six years of Italian land reform', *Banca Nazionale del Lavoro*, Vol. X, 1957, pp. 169-213.

After agriculture, infrastructure took the next largest portion of the Cassa's funds. The big allocation for infrastructure expenditure was for three main reasons. First, there was an obvious need to endow the South with basic infrastructure—water, drainage, communications, etc.—at least approaching that of the North. Secondly, there was a hope that this endowment of infrastructure would be followed spontaneously by industrial development. Thirdly, it was thought that the expenditure involved in providing infrastructure would give a considerable fillip to southern income, not only by the direct impact of the expenditure but also through the regional multiplier effect. In this respect and also in respect of the hope for spontaneous industrial developments there was to be considerable disappointment.

The regional multiplier effect of infrastructure expenditure in the South was very low. It varied, according to the type of infrastructure, from $1 \cdot 07$ (railway works) to $1 \cdot 35$ (road works). The low multiplier was largely the result of very high leaks through imports from the North and abroad. In road works, for example, the marginal propensity to import from the North was $0 \cdot 22$. The marginal propensity to import from abroad was $0 \cdot 23$. With railway works, the marginal propensities to import from the North and abroad were $0 \cdot 34$ and $0 \cdot 29$ respectively.[1]

As with agricultural intervention, infrastructure provision was largely spread and with very little evaluation of its likely contribution to southern development. It was again largely relief work rather than part of a distinct policy for growth.

The attitudes and actions of the Cassa towards industry during the period 1950 to 1957 were both interesting and disappointing. There was little attempt to gain industrial development through the use of incentives. The prime industrial incentive at this time was through the credit system. Law 298 of 1953 had created three medium-term credit institutes having the role of providing loans for southern Italian industry.[2] But although this move overcame the earlier quantitative lack of credit in the South, the rate of interest charged on loans was not very favourable, being set initially at $5\frac{1}{2}$ per cent. The amount of credit conceded by the three institutes up to 1957 was relatively

[1] F. Pilloton, *Effetti Moltiplicativi degli Investimenti della Cassa per il Mezzogiorno*, Guiffrè, 1960. This work was based on the earlier *Effects of an Investment Programme in Southern Italy*, edited by Svimez, Rome, 1951.

[2] The three institutes were ISVEIMER which operated on the southern mainland, IRFIS for Sicily and CIS for Sardinia. For an account of the development of credit policies in the South, see G. Dominici, 'Credit Policy for the Development of Southern Italy' in the Banco di Roma's *Review of the Economic Conditions in Italy*, November 1964.

insignificant. Between 1954 and 1957 inclusive, they financed a total of 806 projects to a value of almost 100 milliard lire—a value less than that conceded in 1963 alone (137 milliard).[1]

The lack of attention to industry in this period is explicable in terms of a number of factors. First, the belief mentioned above that agriculture was the main key to southern development and the sector where most resources needed to be placed. Secondly, and very important, there was a belief that industry would move of its own accord once the right environment had been created. Infrastructure was considered to be the major ingredient for such an environment. It was hoped furthermore that the development of agriculture and the incomes arising out of infrastructure works (increased through the regional multiplier effect) by expanding the southern markets would provide an attraction for industry to move and develop in the South. Lastly, there was a reluctance to interfere overmuch in Italian industrial development. The need for high levels of competitiveness in Italian industry was very great if the Balance of Payments situation was to be improved. It must be remembered that the period up to the mid-1950s was still largely a period of reconstruction in Italy.

Any hope that large-scale industrial development would take place spontaneously in the South was grossly optimistic. There were few reasons why northern industry should consider a southern location and indeed very important reasons as to why they would be reluctant to move to the South. There was a plentiful supply of labour in the North while the major markets were also there or in Europe, to which of course the North was in greater proximity. In spite of the efforts of both the Cassa and the ordinary administration, the level of infrastructure provision was still below the northern level. The communications network in particular was deficient relative to the North. The distance from major markets and the poor communications system were important deterrents to industrial location, but the main impediment was undoubtedly the lack of industry. The grave shortage of any industrial development in the South inevitably made it proportionally more difficult for industrial development to take place. Industry A was reluctant to go South because Industry B, its main supplier, did not exist, while Industry B, needing A as a market, could not develop without A. Industrial development of a region is largely self-sustaining after a particular point. The South was nowhere near this take-off stage. It was optimistic to hope for any large-scale industrial development.

It is sometimes possible to compensate for the lack of external

[1] *Cassa per il Mezzogiorno, Dodici Anni* 1950-1962, op. cit., Vol. V, p. 84.

economies through incentive schemes. The almost total lack of such schemes up to 1957 made the prospect for industrial development of the South doubly difficult. The industrial investments of the period 1951 to 1957 are in fact, as one would expect, rather disappointing relative to the period after 1957 when a more positive industrialization policy was being pursued. Gross industrial investments at 1954 prices between 1951 and 1957 showed an annual percentage increase of 9·6 per cent as compared to 18·3 per cent between 1957 and 1962 and 26·6 per cent between 1959 and 1964.

IV. THE INDUSTRIALIZATION PERIOD

This section deals with the attempts at industrialization in the period 1957 to 1965.[1] Many of the measures discussed below remain in some form after 1965, though that year is best treated as a watershed as far as there was then a reorientation of policy towards more planning and a not inconsiderable reorganization of the incentive schemes.

The belief that the South could be developed mainly through agriculture and the provision of infrastructure was crumbling in the mid-1950s. It became increasingly recognized that if there was to be adequate industrial development more positive measures would need to be evolved.

The slowness with which more positive measures were taken to encourage the southern industrialization is a major point of criticism of southern policy. It was only with Law 634 of 1957 that industry forms an important part of southern development policy. Indeed, because of internal political problems and government instability, it was not until the end of 1958 that the regulations to implement Law 634 appeared and not until 1959 that the Law actually entered into operation.

It can be argued that if industrialization had been more strongly pursued earlier, the problems of southern development would have been less difficult. By 1957, the North had completely recovered from the war and had developed an environment which was highly suitable and encouraging to further industrial development. The problems of persuading industry to give up the external economies found in the northern location or even the problems of making existing southern industry capable of competing with their northern counterparts were all the greater as a result of the Cassa's tardy action in the field of industrial development.

The reasons for the late intervention are many, though there are probably three major explanatory factors. First, although the belief

[1] For an excellent survey of this period see C. Turco op. cit.

in development through agriculture and infrastructure was crumbling in the 1950s it was long in dying. Secondly, the political conditions of the early and mid-1950s did not favour a more positive policy, the government being weak. Thirdly, Italy was still, at least in the early 1950s undergoing a period of reconstruction with a considerable need for exports. There was no desire to risk sacrificing efficiency and national welfare for the South. The association of weak regional policies with weak economies is common to many countries. In Britain, for example, the main peg of British regional policy, the Industrial Development Certificate, was applied in a diffident fashion until the late 1950s, and particularly to exporting firms. To a large extent, regional policy is, in the short term at least, a luxury. It could be argued that it was only by the late 1950s that Italy could think of a more even distribution of the cake rather than increasing it. By the late 1950s the Italian period of reconstruction was virtually completed and the balance of payments in a healthy condition and it was then possible to give more serious consideration to southern industrial development.

Tardy though the efforts to industrialize the South may have been, the move once made, was at a serious and sophisticated level. A wide range of measures to promote industrial development were introduced. The actions taken in the period under review can be broadly classified into three types: compensation, stimulation, simulation. Under the first head, of compensation, are the vast range of financial and fiscal incentives which were introduced in an attempt to compensate industry for the difficulties it was likely to meet by moving to, or expanding in, a southern location. Under the second head, stimulation, are the direct measures to gain industrial development through the movement of state-controlled firms to the South in order to play the role of propulsive industries plus the attempt to locate more demand in the South through the government contract award system. Thirdly, simulation refers to the growth centre policy which was evolved in this period. Through the geographic concentration of development—an essential aspect of growth centre policy—it was hoped to simulate the conditions of the North and in particular to create industrial external economies.

The three aspects of compensation, stimulation and simulation are discussed in turn in the next three sections.

1. COMPENSATION

By 1965 the authorities had built up a considerable array of incentives to encourage southern industrial development. Their value as a proportion of total revenue varied considerably depending on investment size, sector and location though on average they had a value higher than those available in any other European country.[1] Most of these incentives originated with Law 634 of 1957 though some were slightly modified by Law 623 of 1959 and other minor incentives were added between 1957 and mid-1965 when a revised scheme was introduced. The incentives available by early 1965 can be grouped into five main types—fiscal, grants, financial, share holding, and 'various'. The intention now is to look at these in turn.[2]

Fiscal incentives

The fiscal incentives involved the partial or complete exemption from six forms of tax or duty and were available for firms setting up, expanding or modernizing in the South. The first, and most important, was the ten-year exemption from tax on industrial incomes (*Imposta di Richezza Mobile*). The normal rate for this tax lies between about 28 and 36 per cent depending on income. Secondly, firms could gain exemption from customs duties on materials and machinery required for constructing and equipping the plant. On average these duties would amount to about 15 per cent of the value of imported materials and machinery at the time when the incentive was first introduced, though the liberalization of trade in Europe after 1957 saw a continued diminution in their value. These same items, incidentally, were also exempted from the less important equalisation tax (*Imposta di Conguaglio*) which had an average value of around 4 per cent. The third fiscal incentive was partial exemption from turnover tax (*Imposta Generale sull'Entrata*) on equipment and machinery which was not imported but produced in Italy. The tax was reduced to half the ruling rate which up to 1965 was about 3·3 per cent of purchase price. These three fiscal incentives were the most important in terms of value. The remaining three were first, exemption from taxes on registration and mortgage fees with a value equal to about

[1] Ackley and Dini, in 1959, estimated that the value of the incentives averaged about 9 per cent of revenue. See G. Ackley and L. Dini, 'Tax and Credit Aids to Industrial Development in South Italy', *Banca Nazionale del Lavoro*, December 1959. A more comprehensive survey which shows the differences in value according to investment size, sector and location can be found in ILSES, *Ricerca sul Grado di Convenienza dell'Insediamento delle Industrie in Relazione ai Vigenti Incentivi Diretti*, Milan, 1965 (Mimeographed).

[2] All the incentives discussed below are in the context of the southern mainland. There are sometimes slight variations in application and value for Sicily and Sardinia. Only when the differences are important are they mentioned.

1 per cent of the assets involved,[1] second a reduction by 50 per cent of the excise duty on electric power and third, local authorities could concede partial or total exemption from local taxes on industry. These taxes amounted to between 7 and 8 per cent of industrial income.

Grants

As a result of Law 634 in 1957, the Cassa gained the right to make grants to small and medium sized enterprises (fixed assets not in excess of 6 milliard lire) locating or expanding in the South. The criteria for determining the size of these grants were both subtle and complex.

In simple terms, grants of up to 25 per cent of building costs, including supply roads, sewers and water systems,[2] were available to firms. For machinery and equipment the grant could be up to 10 per cent of costs on condition that the goods had not already been exempted from customs duties. For machinery and equipment purchased from southern suppliers, the grant could rise to a maximum of 20 per cent.

The figures given above are maximums. In the case of machinery and equipment the actual value of the grant was decided by the Cassa and the Special Credit Institutes. No specific information is available concerning the criteria for award though one would suspect that they reflect those used in awarding building grants discussed below.

The criteria for the percentage grants given for buildings are clearly laid down so that a firm considering a southern location could easily calculate the probable award. The criteria are interesting in as far as they reflect the attitudes of the authorities concerning the desirable direction and form of industrial development.

The size of building grant was determined by three factors. On each factor a firm could be awarded up to 25 percentage points. The final grant is the arithmetic average of the percentage award for each factor.

The three factors were:

(a) *The industrial sector and size of enterprise.* Industry was divided into three groups. The percentage points awarded varied according

---

[1] The estimate of 1 per cent is very rough. There is a great complexity of these taxes. For a brief exposition see Cassa per il Mezzogiorno, *Summary of Measures to Promote Industrialisation in Southern Italy*, 1963, p. 9.

[2] The maximum was in fact 40 per cent for water-reserve and water-supply systems.

to the industrial group of the applying firm. The points awarded were highest for modern industry (22-25 per cent) and lowest for traditional industries like foodstuffs (9-16 per cent). The middle group was a mixture of both types of industry and had percentage points of between 17 and 21. The actual points awarded within these ranges (e.g. the range of 22-25 per cent) were determined by the size of the investment, with more points for the higher investment levels. The size of investment required to qualify for a particular percentage was clearly laid down. A firm, for example, in the first category above (22-25 per cent) would receive 22 percentage points if its investment was below 50 million lire, 23 points for 50-200 million lire, 24 for 200-500 million lire and the maximum of 25 above 500 million lire.

(b) *Investment per employee.* The percentage points awarded under this criterion varied inversely with the value of investments per employee. There was greater variation in possible points under this criterion than with the first criterion above, varying from 5 per cent for an investment per employee beyond 12 million lire to 25 per cent for less than 4 million lire. Obviously the aim was to favour the smaller firms—firms which have a relatively greater need for non-repayable grants. But, perhaps most important, there was also the aim of encouraging the development of the more labour intensive firms and industries.

(c) *Location.* The third criterion, location, is interesting in as far as it reflects the extent to which the authorities were trying to pursue a growth centre policy. In an attempt to develop the growth centres rapidly, they received preferential treatment. The percentage points were higher for firms locating or expanding in the growth Areas or Nuclei and even within the Areas and Nuclei[1] there was a differential. Industry within the *agglomerati* (industrial zones) of the Areas and Nuclei secured higher grants than those outside.[2] There is one further qualification; Areas and Nuclei were classified into three groups according to the levels of industrialization already achieved with higher grants for firms in the less developed Areas and Nuclei. Points under the criterion of location were awarded as follows:

---

[1] There were, and still are, two types of growth centre—the small 'Nuclei' and the very large 'Areas'. Growth centre policy is discussed in more detail under the heading of 'simulation' below.

[2] The preferential treatment for the *agglomerati* was in order to concentrate development within the geographically large Areas and Nuclei and thus reducing the cost of infrastructure per firm.

	Area of Nuclei	*Agglomerati*
Area of Nuclei with a 'ratio'* up to 1·5 per cent	20	25
Area or Nuclei with a 'ratio'* of 1·5 to 2·8 per cent	16	20
Area or Nuclei with a 'ratio'* above 2·8 per cent	12	15
Outside an Area or Nuclei	10	

* The percentage of employees in firms of more than ten employees as a proportion of the resident population. This was the measure of industrialization mentioned in the text above.

The inclusion of location as a criterion and the openly[1] preferential treatment for growth centres in the grant system is particularly interesting for, although the differentials are small, they are virtually unique to Italian regional policy. In point of fact, growth centres were furthermore favoured in as far as grants could be awarded even to 'large' firms—investments in excess of 6 milliard lire—if they were in an Area or Nuclei though the award was made solely for the first 6 milliard lire.

To conclude this section on grants, the final grant awarded was determined by the three criteria above and was the arithmetical average of points awarded under each head. As the maximum award under any head was 25 per cent, it is obvious that the maximum possible grant was 25 per cent. This maximum would go to a firm in the modern industrial sector (say, chemicals) with a high level of investment (above 1,500 million lire) but with a low investment per employee (less than 4 million lire) located in a relatively undeveloped Area or Nuclei (say, Avellino) and operating within the *agglomerato*. The lowest grant, 8 per cent, would be for a traditional industry (say, foodstuffs) with a low level of investment (below 50 million lire) but with a high level of investment per employee (over 12 million lire) located outside an Area or Nuclei.

[1] In a covert fashion, preferential treatment for growth centres has existed in other countries. In Britain, for example, the fact that industry in growth centres had guaranteed assistance between 1963 and 1966 irrespective of the level of unemployment in the area, represented preferential treatment for these areas. See pages 308-309 below.

Financial incentives

These are the oldest type of incentive and based on the supply of medium term loans at favourable rates of interest by the three special credit institutes of ISVEIMER, IRFIS and CIS mentioned above. The loan could cover specified proportions of a firm's investment and at specified, lower than market, rates with the difference in interest rates being met by the Cassa. The credit institutes had existed since the early 1950s when they played an important role in ensuring adequate supplies of industrial credit for the South, but it was only in 1957 that the rate of interest was to any great extent subsidized and thus only then that favourable finance represents an important incentive for southern industrial development.[1]

By 1965 the following conditions held:

(*a*) Loans were available for small and medium sized enterprises (fixed investments not in excess of 6 milliard lire) setting up, expanding or being converted in the South. The loans were for a maximum duration of fifteen years with a maximum two-year loan utilization period in which interest was not paid and a further three-year period of grace when interest, but not principal, was paid. The rate of interest was fixed at 4 per cent. A firm could receive a loan as well as a grant but the total capital 'financed' by these two could not exceed 85 per cent of total investment. Plants with fixed investments above 6 milliard lire could secure loans at 5 per cent interest rates.

(*b*) *Special loans*: From 1959 loans were available for small and medium sized firms at 3 per cent interest rates though with a top limit of 1·5 milliard lire for new plant and 500 million lire for expansion or conversion of old plant. In neither case was the loan to exceed 70 per cent of the cost of the project. The repayment terms were a little more stringent than on the 4 per cent loans—there being no period of grace although there still was the important two year loan utilization period. Again the maximum duration was fifteen years.[2]

[1] This is not to belittle their pre-1957 role when they ensured a supply of credit for the South when credit generally was scarce in Italy.

[2] The power of these special loans was incidentally diluted in as far as, at the same time that this special concession was made for the South, a similar concession was agreed for small and medium sized firms in the North (Law 623). These firms, whose invested capital was required to be below 1·5 milliard lire, were eligible for special loans of up to 500 million lire for the construction of new plant, and 250 million for expansion or conversion, at 5 per cent interest. Their duration (ten years) was less than in the South and they could not exceed in value more than 70 per cent of the total project cost.

The criteria for deciding whether a firm secured a 'special loan' as opposed to an ordinary loan were not made public.

Provision of risk capital

An interesting and quite unique aspect of Italian incentives was the creation of bodies to subscribe risk capital to firms. The aim is, however, not simply to subscribe capital but also to encourage and develop entrepreneurship—very important in the context of the South. The assistance, both financial and technical, is expected to be temporary in as far as the promoted firms are expected eventually to buy back the capital subscribed and to be able to continue without further assistance.

There were, and still are, two main bodies engaged in this type of intervention, ISAP[1] and IN-SUD.[2] The former is largely a private body in the sense that it was created outside special southern legislation. It has the objective of promoting and helping in the creation of new industrial activity through the subscription for a minority of share capital. Its shareholding by 1964 amounted to about 7 milliard lire in firms with a total capital of 51 milliard lire.

IN-SUD is of more recent origin, being constituted by special legislation in 1963 by an amalgam of sections of the Cassa, Breda Finanziaria and various banks and credit institutes. The main difference between IN-SUD and ISAP lies not only in the fact that IN-SUD is more of a public body but also that it is normally expected to assume majority shareholding. By 1964 it was already holding 3·6 milliard lire in firms with a total capital of 36 milliard lire.

Both the bodies described above operate on the mainland. Similar organizations are to be found on the islands. In Sicily there is SOFIS[3] which has been operating since 1957 and up to 1964 had taken shares to the value of 9·3 milliard. It has had the right to take majority shareholding since 1961. In Sardinia two existing institutes were amalgamated in 1964 to form FINSARDA[4] though up to that date their investments had been very small.

Various

There are two remaining incentives which could be classified under the head of compensation: transport concessions and technical assistance.

[1] *Istituto per lo Sviluppo Delle Attività Produttive.*
[2] *Nuove Iniziative per il Sud.*
[3] *Società finanziaria siciliana di investimenti industriali.*
[4] *Società finanziaria sarda.*

The first, transport concessions, can be dealt with quickly as it was, quantitatively, one of the least important incentives. The concession allowed a reduction of up to 50 per cent in the cost of rail transport (within Italy) of goods, materials and machinery needed for the creation, expansion or modification of industrial plant with a further reduction of up to 20 per cent for sea transport between the mainland and Sardinia.

Technical assistance for southern industrial development is in the hands of IASM.[1] This body has the general role of promoting and advising small and medium-sized industrial firms, though to some extent it is also operating in non-industrial fields. It was constituted in 1961, promoted and financed by the Cassa in collaboration with the three special credit institutes, but it was not until 1964 that it had organized itself internally and was ready to meet its commitments.

Its main efforts so far have been five-fold. Firstly, promotion—an attempt to interest foreign and Italian industry in a southern location by advertising and personal contact. Secondly, it has aided firms in market analysis, taxation, fiscal and administrative aspects. Advice has also been given on technical aspects of location and expansion. Outside consultants have been employed where necessary. Thirdly, the institute has helped the bodies controlling the newly formed Areas and Nuclei with the unprecedented judicial, fiscal and administrative questions with which they have been faced. Fourthly, the institute has also helped in the field of tourism, giving advice to local authorities or individual enterprises concerning location, preparation of sites, organization, advertising, etc. The fifth role which the institute has played is that of study and research. The research has been of an applied character and concerned mainly with the preparation, often with the aid of outside consultants, of data and material for specific and general studies of southern development problems and prospects.

Of all the measures aimed at industrializing the South, the creation of IASM has perhaps been one of the more important. The returns, in terms of development, from information, advice and cajoling are very high. Without such an organization the incentives themselves would have a lesser impact. Incentives, no matter how high, are

---

[1] *Istituto per l'Assistenza allo Sviluppo del Mezzogiorno.* For further details on this organisation, see A. Molinari, 'Institute for Assistance in the Development of Southern Italy' in *Review of Economic Conditions in Italy,* Banco di Roma, May 1962. For a more up-to-date summary of its role and activities, see Comitato dei Ministri per il Mezzogiorno, *Relazione sull'Attuazione del Piano di Coordinamento Degli Interventi Pubblici nel Mezzogiorno,* 1967, Vol. I.

largely wasted if firms lack the knowledge and ability to make use of them. Although other existing Italian bodies could in theory play the role of IASM, in practice they would be likely to act more slowly and in a more bureaucratic manner.

The aspect of compensation in brief

By early 1965, and largely as a result of the legislation introduced in 1957, the authorities had created a strong and interesting system of incentives, ranging from fiscal and financial concessions to those of transport. The incentives were geared towards the modern sectors of industry and geared also towards the pursuit of a growth centre policy. The general aim was to secure as much efficient industrial growth as the funds allowed. This was necessary for the funds available for industrial development, even after 1957, were small. The Cassa allocated only 12 per cent of its total 1950-1965 funds, about 250 milliard lire (£150 million), for industrial incentives. This was intended to cover the eight-year period 1957 to 1965. It is obvious that a great amount of selection needed to be exercised. The fact that regional funds in Italy are not open-ended as in the United Kingdom is an important point. The allocations for the Cassa's industrial interventions were in fact too small to aid all feasible applicants. The incentives available in Italy after 1957, because of the shortage of funds to fulfil the policy, had less power than they would appear to have on paper. Applications were considered in a very stringent manner.

As with most regional incentive schemes, the Italian incentives favoured the more capital intensive enterprises in as far as they were, to a large extent, based on concessions which gravitated on capital. It is, of course, true that the more capital intensive industries are in general also modern and fast growing, so those enterprises receiving the larger incentives would be the ones with the greatest growth potential. The incentives, furthermore, favoured the fast-growing industries in that the tax concession favoured firms with high profit margins.

Other than the shortage of funds to support the incentive schemes, the most important failings of the 1957 legislation were two-fold. First, and a shortcoming which was overcome in 1961, the scheme proposed in 1957 lacked any strong, positive industrialization machinery. Incentives are largely passive in character. They encourage those firms who know of their existence and value and those firms so organized as to be able to exploit them. Until the creation of IASM in 1961, there was no body capable of playing the positive role of promoting the idea of southern industrial development and

61

aiding firms to organize themselves so as to be eligible for assistance and capable of fully exploiting the incentives available. The second major shortcoming was that the incentives proposed in 1957 did not favour the location of the big enterprises with investments in excess of 6 milliard lire. In consequence, there was little development of large-scale private industry and the South had to rely for its pro-pulsive firms on the state-controlled firms who, a point discussed below, were obliged to locate specified proportions of their new industrial development in the South.

2. STIMULATION

Although the incentives in Law 634 of 1957 represented an important step forward in the South's industrialization policy, perhaps the most important aspect of the Law lay not in the incentives but in confirming the policy of using the state-controlled firms[1] as an important part of the policy for southern industrialization. Law 646 of 1950 (Article 4) had demanded that the investments of the state-controlled firms be so distributed as to encourage greater equilibrium between North and South and that at least 60 per cent of their new industrial investments be located in the South. Forty per cent of their total investments were required to be in the South by 1964-5. Although introduced in 1950, these provisions were of relatively little importance up to the mid-1950s when the majority of the investment by the state-controlled industries was of a replacement and modernization character. This was particularly true of IRI.[2] Although the state-controlled firms adhered to the rules concerning new industrial investment, the absolute amount involved was slight. By 1957, the state-controlled firms had only 19·5 per cent of their total investments located in the South. The 1957 confirmation of the 1950 Law came at a time when the firms were about to start a considerable investment programme. They adhered to the Law in

[1] There are seven groups of these firms though by far the most important are IRI (Istituto per la Ricostruzione Industriale) and ENI (Ente Nazionale Idrocarburi). These two account for over 90 per cent of the annual investments of the state-controlled firms as a whole. The main activities of the state-controlled firms are heavy capital intensive industries: iron and steel, cement, engineering, ship-building, petroleum, petro-chemicals; and a number of services like telephones, radio and TV. For a discussion of the state-controlled firms, their history and roles, see M. V. Posner and S. J. Woolf, *Italian Public Enterprise*, Duckworth, 1967.
[2] For a discussion of the role and policy of IRI in the South up to 1955 see Ministero dell'Industria e del Commercio, *L'Istituto per la Ricostruzione Industriale*, Vol. III, report by P. Saraceno, Turin, 1956.

respect of the geographic division of this investment and indeed virtually all their new industrial investment was in the South. By 1964, 45·4 per cent of their total investments were in the South.

The southern investments by the state-controlled firms after 1957 were very large, both in absolute terms and relative to total southern industrial investments. Between 1957 and 1964, their southern industrial investments amounted to 1,161 milliard lire,[1] with a further 800 milliard between 1965 and 1968. These investments represented a considerable proportion of total southern industrial investments. Almost 45 per cent of southern gross industrial investment (at current prices) between 1957 and 1964 was accounted for by the state-controlled firms. The weight of their investments increased over the period. In 1964 they represented 54 per cent of southern gross industrial investments against 26 per cent in 1957 and 34 per cent in 1960. In the first half of the 1960s, increased industrial investments by the state-controlled firms represented about two-thirds of the increase in total southern industrial investment.

There are two further points of interest about the southern investments of the state-controlled firms and both concern direction—firstly sectorially and second geographically.

Table 2.1 below shows the sectorial distribution of southern investments by the state-controlled firms between 1957 and 1964.

The table shows the large proportion of investments in basic heavy industries. The concentration on this sector can be explained in two ways. First there was a belief that without these basic industries the prospects of gaining non-basic industry was slight—a belief that basic industry represents a form of infrastructure. The second point, however, and perhaps an ungenerous one, is that the choice of sector was anyway limited to a large extent by the type of activities of the two major bodies, IRI and ENI. These, the former for historical reasons and the latter for strategic reasons, were mainly engaged in basic industry.

The geographic direction of the investments by the state-controlled firms has been mainly towards the newly declared growth centres. 'Experience has shown the need not to disperse the effects but to concentrate and thus multiply the attractive power of the new initiative.'[2]

---

[1] Industrial investments represented a high proportion of total investments—about 80 per cent.

[2] Comitato dei Ministri per il Mezzogiorno, *Relazione sulla Attività di Coordinamento*, 1965, Vol. I, p. 140.

The sheer amount of investment and its immediate multiplier effects has undoubtedly been a considerable stimulus to southern income. Further industrial development around the basic industries has however been disappointing. They have not so far played the role of propulsive industries. It must be remembered, however, that many of the plants have not yet, or only recently, attained full

TABLE 2.1

SOUTHERN INVESTMENTS BY STATE-CONTROLLED FIRMS
1957–1964 BY SECTOR

Sector	Investment (milliard lire)	Composition
Mining and Petroleum	245·2	17·3
Manufacturing	667·4	47·0
Iron and Steel	416·8	29·4
Engineering and Shipbuilding	70·5	5·0
Petro-chemicals	85·3	6·0
Cement	17·6	1·2
Others*	77·2	5·4
Electricity†	249·1	17·6
Communications (telephones, TV, radio)	170·6	12·0
Transport	83·6	5·9
Various	3·3	0·2
Total	1,419·2	100·0

* Textiles, paper, glass, rubber, foodstuffs and a list of 'difficult to classify'.
† 1957-1962. The sector was nationalized in 1962.

Source: C. Turco, *La Struttura dell' Industria Meridionale e la Politica di Sviluppo Industriale del Mezzogiorno*, p. 203, SVIMEZ (mimeographed).

production, and surrounding development could not anyway be expected to take place quickly. On the other hand, the haphazard manner in which the plants were located, with little or no evaluation of whether or not it would be feasible for supporting and product-using firms to locate around them, makes one doubt whether much further development could have been expected.

The most recent major industrial investment decision by the state-controlled firms has been the announcement of plans to establish the Alfa-Sud (part of the IRI group) car plant outside Naples. The plant, which is to cost about 260 milliard lire, is planned to be in production by 1971. Output is expected to run at 25,000 vehicles per annum and employ around 15,000 people. The plant should, in itself, make a large contribution to southern industrial development, but the hope in the South must be that it will encourage ancillary industrial development. British observers, with their own experience in mind, may be inclined to scepticism over the prospect of ancillary development around a motor plant. The movement of the motor-car industry into Britain's depressed areas had a disappointingly small effect in terms of ancillary development. There appears to be more ground for optimism in the Alfa-Sud case. First, planned output of the plant is about two and a half times as great as the Scottish motor plant. This difference in size is likely to give greater prospects of supplying firms locating in the South in as far as there is a greater likelihood of these firms being able to operate at a size which is sufficient to give rise to the economies of scale required for efficient production. Secondly, there exists within Italy, and within IRI, institutes and facilities which could be used to encourage ancillary development—more so than in Britain. IASM will undoubtedly attempt to promote ancillary activity, while within IRI there exists the means of gaining ancillary development, not only through its own engineering sector, but also through its finance company, SME.[1] Whether IRI will be inclined to take a positive part in encouraging ancillary development is, however, a moot point. It needs always to be remembered that the state-controlled firms need to raise money on the open market and have a responsibility to their shareholders.[2] They have only limited prospects for engaging in non-commercial operations and some of the Alfa-Sud ancillary development may not be wholly profitable—at least in the short run. But the basic point made above remains—that the size of the main plant gives greater prospects for spontaneous ancillary development than was the case in Scotland.

[1] *Società Meridionale Finanziaria per Azioni*. The company was founded in 1899. Its main activity was the production and distribution of electricity in the South. Following the nationalization of the electricity industry in 1962, it received considerable compensation and broadened its field of operations taking part shares in desirable companies. It operates mainly in the South, with about 80 per cent of its intervention being in that region. Currently, it has share capital of 122 milliard lire and is controlling and influencing sectors which range from cement to supermarkets. For further details see IRI and SME Annual Reports.

[2] For a further discussion of the role and limitations of IRI in the promotion of southern development see G. Petrilli, *Lo Stato Imprenditore*, Cappelli, 1967, pp. 169-205.

One potentially important aspect of southern industrial policy as operated in 1965, and indeed since 1950,[1] and which should come under the head of stimulation, is that of the 'reserve' of contracts and works by the public administrations. This law of *'quinto'* demanded that the public administration 'must reserve one-fifth of the global amounts of their contracts for supplies and processing for industrial establishments, including small and artisan concerns, in the South'. In principle the aim of the law was good—giving a stimulus to southern industry in the form of assured markets which under more competitive conditions it might not have secured. It represented a form of infant industry protection. In practice, there is evidence that the reserve was not adhered to or enforced, and in 1965 new arrangements were introduced in order to ensure greater compliance.[2]

3. SIMULATION

This final section covers the last of the trinity of measures to promote southern industrialization. The previous two sections have covered compensation and stimulation. This section covers simulation. This involves a discussion of the attempt to gain industrial development by pursuing a growth centre policy. It should become clear when the role and function of growth centres are discussed, why this section has been called simulation.

In broad terms there are two alternatives in regional development. The first is to spread development over the existing settlement structure, the second is to concentrate effort on a selected number of locations. Growth centre policy involves the concentration of development on selected areas which are considered capable of rapid growth. This policy, it is argued, will give faster growth for the region as a whole and/or enable development to be attained at a lower cost than would be the case if development was spread.[3] The arguments are usually couched largely in terms of faster growth with the aspect of lower development costs, e.g. in the provision of infrastructure, often being relegated to a relatively minor role. The faster growth is expected in as far as the concentration of industrial development in a few selected areas will create an industrial environment in which firms can enjoy greater external economies. In parti-

---

[1] Law 835, October 6, 1950.
[2] See page 92, below.
[3] For a detailed evaluation of the benefits from pursuing a growth centre policy, see *Regional Policy in EFTA: An Examination of the Growth Centre Idea*, Oliver & Boyd, Edinburgh, 1968. See also Chapter 13.

cular, there will be benefits to industry from being in proximity to other services and suppliers. A further external economy arising out of a policy of concentration is that it ensures a large and diversified labour market. These factors are currently of great importance in industrial location decisions. The increasing degree of industrial specialization, the increasing need for specialized services and the heavy demands on social infrastructure mean that the need to build up an environment which can provide these facilities is all the greater. If the South is to attract industry then it needs to provide an environment which at least resembles that of the North. The aim of growth centre policy is therefore to simulate the industrial conditions of the North and in particular to build up rapidly the external economies which are so essential for industry. If this can be done then the attractiveness of the South for industry will be increased or at least the deterrent to a southern location will be diminished.

The need for a growth centre policy was recognized fairly early by the Italian authorities, and introduced formally in 1957 with Law 634 authorizing the creation of growth centre consortia at the initiative of local bodies. The consortia were to have the role of stimulating and guiding the development of their areas. The rationale behind this step towards growth centre policy was well explained in the following terms:

'The primary and induced effects of public expenditure do not create *per se*, in the absence that is of an autonomous mechanism of development, a sufficient flow of private investment. Public infrastructure expenditure furnishes only part of the advantage that an entrepreneur gains by operating in a zone already economically developed: one can provide roads, bridges, rail junctions, water but one cannot bring about the external economies that the firm derives by being near complementary industry, by the availability of specialized, trained manpower, by the existence of a market for its products, etc.'[1]

Under Law 634 which authorized the setting up of consortia, the delineation of growth centres was left to the local bodies (Chamber of Commerce, local authorities, etc.) and not to the central authorities though, as we shall see, the criteria for acceptance were carefully laid down by the authorities. The role of the central authorities was more in modifying the areas and their plans rather than actual

[1] Comitato dei Ministri per il Mezzogiorno, *Relazione al Parlamento*, 1960, p. 5.

delineation. All the areas which have so far presented themselves for consideration have been accepted though often in a modified form. None have been totally rejected.[1]

Growth centre policy was, and is, pursued at two levels in Italy with two types of growth centre being considered and designated: the first is the Areas of Industrial Development (*Aree di Sviluppo Industriale*), the second is the Nuclei of Industrialization (*Nuclei di Industrializzazione*). The major difference between the two is size, the former being large with populations of at least 200,000, the latter usually having populations below 75,000. Twelve Areas and thirty Nuclei had, by early 1968, presented themselves for consideration.[2] Their geographical distribution is shown on Map 1.

Although, as mentioned above, Areas and Nuclei are created out of local initiative, requirements have been laid down by the central authorities which should ensure that only a limited number are created and that they conform with the requirements of the central authorities. The basic requirements for the Areas and Nuclei are discussed below with the Areas being treated first.

[1] The process whereby an area is designated officially, and thus accessible to the advantages which come through acceptance, is complicated and slow. The consortia must first draw up a '*piano regolatore*' for the area. This is in fact usually done by consultants. The basis for this plan are the directives and criteria laid down by the Committee of Ministers for the South Circular 2356 of March 1961. The '*piano regolatore preliminare*' (as it is then) is presented to the Committee of Ministers where it is considered by an inter-ministerial Commission. The Commission makes a detailed examination of the plan and relays its opinions and suggestions back to the consortia. The consortia, taking account of the points made by the Commission and other interested local bodies, then moves towards drawing up the final plan (*piano regolatore definitivo*). This is returned to the Committee of Ministers and passed again to the Commission who advise the Committee. If favourable, the plan gets a final vote, receives the appropriate decree and is legally accepted. For more details see, Comitato dei Ministri per il Mezzogiorno, *Relazione sulla Attività di Coordinamento*, 1965, Vol. I, pp. 77-80.

The number which had been officially designated, i.e. approved by decree, was, however, much smaller. By early 1968, only 6 Areas and 6 Nuclei had reached this stage. 3 Areas and 10 Nuclei were at the stage where they were only awaiting the decree. It is probable that the 42 Nuclei and Areas which have so far presented themselves represent the final list though it is conceivable that more Nuclei may appear. It is also possible that some of the Nuclei will be converted to Areas. For details on each of the Areas and Nuclei—their structure, area, population, and a variety of other economic and social characteristics—see IASM, *I Consorzi per le Aree di Sviluppo Industriale ed i Nuclei di Industrializzazione del Mezzogiorno*, 1966. For a more recent and more comprehensive study in the form of an introductory volume and 42 supplementary booklets (one for each Area and Nuclei) see Comitato Interministeriale per la Programmazione Economica, *Documentazione sulle Aree di Sviluppo Industriale ed i Nuclei di Industrializzazione del Mezzogiorno*, March 1968.

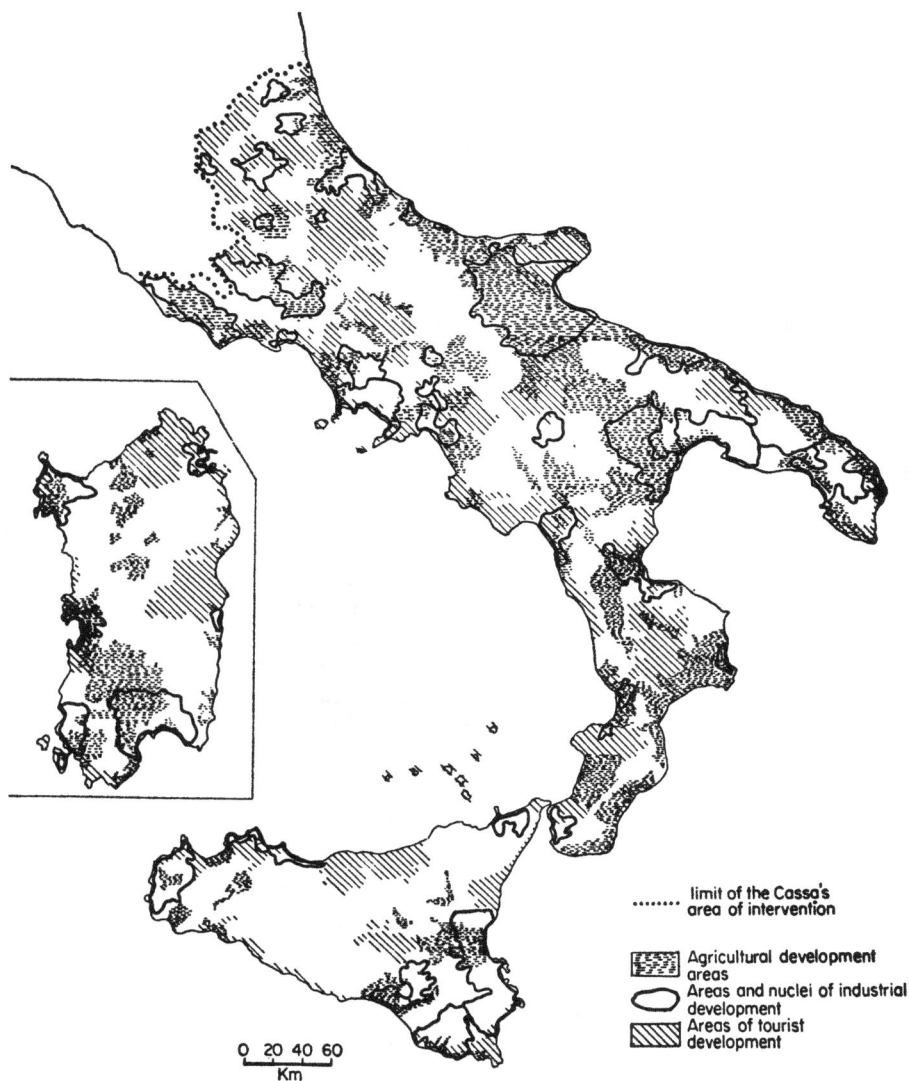

MAP 1: Areas of industrial, agricultural and tourist development
Source: Cassa per il Mezzogiorno, *Bilancio* 1968

Legend:

········· limit of the Cassa's area of intervention

Agricultural development areas

Areas and nuclei of industrial development

Areas of tourist development

0 20 40 60
Km

A basic requirement for an Area to be delineated is that it is characterized by a rapid development of industry. This is measured in simple but meaningful terms by the number of employees to be employed in plants being constructed or already firmly planned and in the course of being financed. In general, the number should not be less than 5 per cent of the industrial employees in the Area in 1951. However, in the absence of such verifiable conditions there can be substituted a visible tendency towards concentration in the Area after 1951 and that this tendency be expected to continue.

Evidence of rapid industrial development and the expectation that this will continue in the future represent the basic requirement for delineation, but there are also others which can be divided into 'necessary' and 'complementary' requirements.

The 'necessary' requirements include the following. First, the Area must include all the communes which border on the principal commune except where the topological conditions forbid this. Secondly, the population of the communes adjacent to the principal commune be at least 100,000 and that the Area in total must have a population of not less than 200,000 inhabitants. In general, the principal commune should have a population which is not less than one-third of the entire Area. Thirdly, the land in the Area must be reasonably flat and safe. Fourthly, the principal commune, at least, must be already well provided with basic infrastructure.

The complementary requirements include adequate supplies of water and energy, complementarity between principal and other communes, and generally favourable prospects and attitudes for industrial development. The Area must be reasonably well endowed with physical and other basic infrastructure: roads, educational facilities, rail and road connections, etc.

The Nuclei must comply with similar requirements to those demanded for the Area, the main difference being that the Nuclei are on a smaller scale and have more modest objectives. The population of the Nuclei should not normally exceed 75,000 inhabitants. No strict conditions have been laid down concerning industrial structure and trends though the Nuclei are expected to show a tendency for industry to concentrate and develop. It is expected that the firms setting up in the Nuclei will be relatively small—mainly exploiting local markets or local characteristics and materials.

The Nuclei, more so than the Areas, are a varied group. Some undoubtedly have considerable prospects for development and indeed, but for the smallness of the population, are similar to the Areas, e.g. Avellino. Others, however, and principally those in Calabria, seem to have only slight prospects and appear to have been accepted more to give an impression of reasonable balance of effort rather than reflecting concrete possibilities of development.

Both Nuclei and Areas need, as was mentioned above, *piani regolatori* which must be drawn up according to strict criteria laid down by the central authorities. The plans must not only aim at the promotion of an intensive process of development but must also select and plan a location for the industrial zones (*agglomerati*). Areas can have more than one *agglomerato*; Nuclei are restricted to one only.

There are now so many Areas and Nuclei that one must doubt the extent to which current policy can be really considered as being one of concentration. 'Dispersed concentration' rather than 'concentration' would be a better term. Areas and Nuclei cover virtually the whole of southern Italy capable of any industrial development on any reasonable scale and without exorbitant costs. They cover a not inconsiderable area of the South and include an even higher proportion of its population. Virtually all the industrial development which has taken place in southern Italy over the past fifteen years has been in the Areas and Nuclei.

The 12 Areas and 30 Nuclei which had presented themselves for consideration by early 1968, included almost 450 communes (about 15 per cent of the total number of communes in southern Italy), had an area equivalent to around 29 per cent of the South, and held about 45 per cent of the resident population. The Areas cover a larger proportion of the South and have a larger proportion of the population than the Nuclei in spite of the latter's numerical superiority. The total resident population in the Areas and Nuclei in 1961 was 8·9 million, of which 6·6 million were in the Areas.

It is, however, not the static but the dynamic picture of the Areas and Nuclei which is the most interesting; confirming the point above that these are the parts of the South where future development is likely to take place if past trends indicate anything about the future. They would, with some exceptions, be the main growth centres whether they were designated or not. Between 1951 and 1961, the resident population in the Areas and Nuclei increased by 14 per cent while the rest of the South saw a slight fall of 1 per cent. The expansion of population in the Areas and Nuclei was virtually the same as that in the North. Looking at active population, the favourable position of the Areas and Nuclei is again clear for while the active population in the South as a whole declined by 4 per cent between 1951 and 1961, the Areas and Nuclei saw an increase of 5·9 per cent. The active population outside the Areas and Nuclei fell by 9·9 per cent over the same period. The Areas and Nuclei gained virtually all the increase in manufacturing employment between 1951 and 1961 with a growth of 29·8 per cent[1] as against a fall of 1·2 per cent outside. The expansion of employees in manufacturing within the Areas and Nuclei was similar to that in the North.[2]

More than any other country in Europe, Italy has taken a positive line towards growth areas by using the incentive system to discriminate in their favour.[3] We shall see later that the preferential treatment becomes even stronger after 1965. Away from industrial incentives, *per se*, the Areas and Nuclei have also benefited by the fact that most of the state-controlled firms moving to the South have located in either an Area or Nuclei and particularly the former. The Areas and Nuclei are further favoured in as far as they receive assistance from the Cassa which is not normally available for other areas. For general infrastructure works in the *agglomerati*, grants of up to 85 per cent are available with further grants of up to 50 per cent for industrial waterways and drainage. They are eligible for the total reimbursement of expenditure on plans. Grants are available for the construction of workers' houses, while loans are available for the appropriation of land. Loans at favourable interest rates are available for parts of expenditure not covered by grants.

There can be little doubt that the major part of future industrial development is likely to take place in the Areas and Nuclei. Favourable incentives, the location of the state-controlled firms, better infrastructure and planning are all likely to reinforce the natural trend of industry to move into them.

The inevitable question which a growth centre policy provokes, and particularly one so strongly pursued as that in Italy, concerns what happens to those areas outside an Area or Nuclei or at least outside their sphere of influence. This is something to which we want to turn in detail later.[4] There are of course alternative prospects for employment beyond industry itself. Some parts of the South will be able to prosper perfectly well through agriculture and perhaps tourism. However, even in these sectors there has been a tendency to concentrate effort. Tourist and agricultural areas or zones have been set up.[5]

There remains, however, a considerable area of the South, and a not significant proportion of the population, which lies outisde a tourist, agricultural or industrial area. The population involved,

---

[1] There was also a slight reduction in the number of production units and thus a considerable increase in the number of employees per plant in the Areas and Nuclei.

[2] A good discussion of the Areas and Nuclei and their development vis-à-vis the rest of southern Italy between the two Census years of 1951 and 1961 can be found in Comitato dei Ministri per il Mezzogiorno, *Relazione sulla Attività di Coordinamento*, 1965, Vol. I, pp. 65-77.   [3] See pages 56-57 above.

[4] See pages 118-119 below.   [5] See pages 81-83 below.

though no official estimates are available, is probably about 2 million; living mainly in the inland central areas where the prospects for development of virtually any kind are small, and indeed where the current population is in excess of that which the present albeit labour-intensive and inefficient economic structure can support. These areas exhibit severe characteristics of depression, and the people live at an almost non-European living standard. They represent a serious problem and one which has been largely neglected. The strong pursuit of a growth centre policy neglects them still more. The underlying assumption, implicit if not explicit, is that these areas must be run down with the populations moving into the Areas and Nuclei. The justification for such a policy brings one back to the rationale of growth centre policy. In this particular context it would be two-fold. First, these areas do not offer prospects for long-term economic development. Second, by concentrating development one will secure, by building up external economies, an environment in the South that will give faster growth for the South as a whole than would be the case if the development was spread. A growth centre policy will thus give the people in the non-centre areas a greater opportunity of finding employment *within* the South rather than have to go to the North or abroad. Without a growth centre policy the long-term prospects for the South would be less and the solution to the problem would take longer. Most of the evidence would seem to support such arguments.

Even the supporters of growth centre policy in principle have criticized the manner in which it has been operated in the South.

First, the procedure for designation is long and complicated with the consequence that even now, more than ten years after it was first announced, few of the Areas and Nuclei have been officially accepted. By early 1968 only six Areas and six Nuclei had been officially designated by decree. In theory, the slow speed at which they have been created could have given greater rise to problems in as far as the Cassa is limited in the assistance that it can give prior to official designation. In practice, the difficulties have been reduced somewhat by giving assistance to what were termed 'urgent' works. The term 'urgent' seems to have been applied fairly liberally.

Second, and a strong criticism of the policy, is that there has not been sufficient co-ordination between the various Areas and Nuclei. A global approach has been lacking. The consortia have responsibility only for their own areas and have no obligation to take a more global view.[1] There is no body which has the ability to carry out this

---

[1] There has been some co-operation between individual areas, e.g. Bari, Taranto and Brindisi, see *Informazioni Svimez*, December 1961, pp. 1124-5.

co-ordination adequately. It can indeed be argued that the creation of the Areas and Nuclei has added yet another prong to the problem of co-ordination, for to the problem of co-ordinating the efforts of the Cassa and the ordinary Administration, there has now been added the consortia.[1]

Third, there is doubt as to whether the consortia are suitable for the role that they need to play. Although it is important to encourage local initiative and although they have access to outside help and advice, IASM being particularly important here, they do lack the objectivity which a more neutral industrial development board would possess. A rather contradictory argument, and one which we favour, is that the consortia have too little responsibility and have a role which is too restricted. Their responsibilities are confined almost wholly to industrial development and have a very limited urban planning role. Urban planning in the Areas and Nuclei, as in Italy in general, has unfortunately been very much neglected.

Finally, the question of proliferation. This has been a source of severe criticism. With forty-two Areas or Nuclei one must doubt the prospects of gaining sufficient industry to secure adequate development to create the required external economies in all of them. It could be argued that nothing is lost by designating an Area or Nuclei for political reasons even though in practice it has little prospect of development. However, an important aspect of growth centre policy is the preparation of sites and making provisions for industry before it actually arrives. There is therefore the danger of provisions being made by the consortia more on the basis of optimism than realism. There is, in brief, a great danger of duplication and waste of effort. The greater the number of areas involved, the greater is the danger. The lack of a global strategy makes the danger all the greater. The Cassa could, of course, restrain exorbitant waste by the careful vetting of projects, but one wonders whether the same political factors which allowed such a large number of Areas and Nuclei will also make for the provisioning of them in excess of their real prospects. Of all the criticism, this is probably the most serious; particularly in view of the limited funds at the disposal of the Cassa. There is a need in the South for policies for those parts without a feasible growth centre, but this policy should not be one of growth centres. The mere designation of a growth centre does not ensure growth. The designation of too many detracts from growth itself and makes development policy more costly.

[1] The problems of co-ordination are discussed by V. Apicella in *Realtà del Mezzogiorno*, N.3, 1961. A summary of the article can be found in *Informazioni Svimez*, June 1961, pp. 611-14.

CHAPTER 3

PRESENT POLICIES FOR SOUTHERN DEVELOPMENT

This chapter is in two main parts. First, there is a detailed discussion of Law 717 of August 1965, the basis of present southern policies, and the extent to which the measures involved differ from those contained in earlier legislation. The fact that the changes in policy reflect the problems of operating earlier policies is one good reason for discussing the Law in some detail. The second part is entitled 'The South and the Italian National Plan (1966-1970)' and involves an evaluation of the extent to which the objectives for the South, set out in the Italian National Plan, are likely to be fulfilled.

1965—A NEW POLICY FOR THE SOUTH

The mandate of the Cassa expired in mid-1965. Law 717 of that year prolonged its life up to 1980 and allocated funds to it for the five-year period 1965-69.[1] The law also introduced policy changes, and we shall look at these in more detail later. The funds allocated to the Cassa for the five-year period amounted to 1,640 milliard lire. Relative to the earlier fifteen-year period, this represented a considerable increase in the Cassa's funds. Its funds between 1950 and 1965 amounted to 2,216 milliard. The funds available to the Cassa, calculated on an annual basis, averaged 147 milliard lire between 1950 and 1965 as against an annual average of 328 milliard lire for the period 1965-69. Even so, the amounts involved are still not very large relative to, say, the United Kingdom expenditure on regional development. At the then current rate of exchange, 328 milliard lire

[1] In late 1968, the Cassa's planning period was stretched to 1970 in order to bring it into line with the National planning period (1966-70). At the same time, the Cassa was allocated a further 560 milliard lire. This was to cover the extra year and also to help it through 1969, for by late 1968 it had already spent or committed virtually the whole of the funds allocated to it for industrial development. The additional allocation was below that requested—800 milliard lire. For further details of the extension of the planning period and the increased funds made available to the Cassa, see *Informazioni Svimez*, October 1968, p. 718.

is equivalent to around £200 million.[1] This is well below United Kingdom expenditure on regional development. The Board of Trade industrial incentives *alone* cost around £300 million per annum. The Cassa's funds must, of course, also cover efforts in fields other than those of industry. The Cassa has the equivalent of about £70 million per annum for industrial development—less than one-quarter of the comparable British expenditure.

In point of fact, the funds available to the Cassa are not even as large as they seem at first sight. Four hundred and ten milliard lire was required for the completion of the 1950-65 programme, leaving 1,230 milliard (about 300 milliard per annum) for new effort in the four-year period 1966-69.[2]

Law 717 not only prolonged the life of the Cassa and increased the funds available for its work, but it also changed quite considerably the direction of southern policy. A quick, though rough, indication of the change of policy can be gained by looking at the decision on how the Cassa's funds are to be spent and comparing these with its expenditure in the period 1950-65. Table 3.1 below shows the division of expenditure 1950-65 and the Cassa's intentions for the period 1966-69.[3] The figures are annual averages.

The importance of industry in the new policy is clear; the annual allocation being ten times as large as that between 1950 and 1965. Industry takes over a third of the total funds and agriculture suffers a reduction in its funds. Industry alone takes almost as much as agriculture and infrastructure together—a considerable change from the earlier period when these two accounted for almost 80 per cent of the Cassa's annual expenditure.

Figures such as those above can only give the most general indication of the direction in which southern policy has moved. We now want to examine in some detail the proposals of Law 717 and the extent to which they represent a change of policy. The section headings approximate to these used in the Law itself.

[1] It is an open question as to which rate of exchange to use and neither the now current rate or the pre-devaluation rate is completely acceptable. The fact that the sterling equivalent of the Cassa's funds or of southern income have risen by 15 per cent as a result of the British devaluation must be very consoling to the Calabrian peasant! We have decided to use the pre-devaluation rate.

[2] As mentioned above, this period was in late 1968 extended to the end of 1970 and the Cassa was allocated a further 560 milliard lire. The general lines of the argument below are not disturbed by this change.

[3] At the time of writing, there was no evidence available as to how these divisions might change, if at all, following on from the decision to extend the Cassa's planning period to the end of 1970 and increase its funds by 560 milliard lire.

TABLE 3.1

SECTORIAL DIVISION OF THE CASSA'S ANNUAL EXPENDITURE
1950–65 AND ITS INTENTIONS 1966–69

	1950-65*		1966-69	
Sector	Value (milliard lire)	Percentage by sector	Value (milliard lire)	Percentage by sector
Industry	10·1	6·9	110·7	36·0
Agriculture	82·9	56·1	76·2	24·7
Tourism	6·2	4·2	24·8	8·1
General Infrastructure	33·1	22·4	60·3	19·6
Others†	15·3	10·4	35·8	11·6
Total	147·6	100·0	307·8	100·0

* Up to the end of June 1965. The figures do not include money available from the 1965-69 allocation for the completion of the 1950-65 programme.

† Technical assistance, management training, artisan and fishing incentives and 'others'.

Source: The figures above have been calculated from data in Comitato dei Ministri per il Mezzogiorno, *Piano di Coordinamento degli Interventi Pubblici nel Mezzogiorno*, Rome, 1966 and the *Italian National Plan*, chapter 16.

I. THE CO-ORDINATION OF INTERVENTION

The co-ordination of southern intervention has always been difficult even when the problem was basically one of co-ordinating the extraordinary intervention of the Cassa with the efforts of the ordinary administration. A new dimension has now been added with the need to co-ordinate southern policies with the National Plan. The addition of this further complication, and the need anyway to secure a better basis for co-ordination between ordinary and extraordinary intervention, is recognized by the new Law and new procedures are suggested which, it is hoped, will improve the situation.

The possible problem of co-ordination between ordinary and extraordinary intervention was recognized from the start of the Cassa's life but has never been satisfactorily resolved. The need to co-ordinate was written in general terms into the 1950 law creating the Cassa which demanded that its plans be on a long-term basis

(1950-60 in the first instance) and co-ordinated with the plans of work put forward by the ordinary administration.[1]

The fact that from the start the general lines of the Cassa's work were set out by an interministerial group should have ensured some success. In fact this was not the case. The general lines were too general to form the basis of co-ordination. The other ministries in their own efforts were not thinking long term and were certainly not thinking in terms of a co-ordinated effort with the Cassa. The resolving of the southern problem was but a small part of their interest. In consequence, the lack of more specific machinery or proposals for co-ordination, and in part the lack of inclination, meant that co-ordination was poor and this gave rise to considerable frustration and waste.

This vague situation was not much improved by Law 634 of 1957, which attempted to put co-ordination on a more formal level. The various ministries and the Cassa, through this Law, were required to submit programmes of work in the South to the Committee of Ministers for the South. It was the function of this group to co-ordinate the programme received and to communicate to the Cassa and the ministries involved the decisions adopted for the annual programmes of work which were to be fulfilled.

This again, however, did not prove to be very satisfactory. Lack of inclination is an important explanation, but the main problem was that the basis of co-ordination was still *ex-post*. It was difficult to change plans after they had been clearly worked out, particularly if many of these plans were in no way related. There was no reason why they should be related: the Cassa was concerned solely with the South, the other ministries had problems other than the South to worry them.

The current arrangements for co-ordination should result not only in greater co-ordination between ministries and bodies operating in the South, but also greater co-ordination between the National Plans and those for the South. The basis for the arrangements were laid down in Law 717. The Committee of Ministers for the South becomes the Interministerial Committee for southern Italy. The change of name is unimportant. The major change has been that the Committee now operates within the framework of CIPE (Interministerial Committee for National Economic Planning). In other words, the old Committee for the South has been integrated into the body responsible for economic planning and co-ordination. The Interministerial Committee for Southern Italy has the task of drawing up 'plurennial plans for the co-ordination of direct public interventions

[1] Article 1, Law 646, August 1950.

and to promote and aid the location and expansion of productive activity and that of a social character in the [South]'.[1] The plans are drawn up in consultation with, and the agreement of, other relevant ministries and bodies. The plans are then approved by CIPE and the ministries. The Cassa and other relevant bodies are then obliged to take such measures as is required to implement the plans. The first plan was drawn up in mid-1966 and was for the period 1966-69,[2] extended to 1970 in late 1968. The advantage of the current system of co-ordination, other than that it brings Southern Planning within the National Planning framework, is that it results in an *ex ante*, as opposed to the earlier *ex post*, formulation of plans and in this way should give rise to greater co-ordination. There are indications that the system is bringing better results—at least at the global level for, as we shall see in the next section, the expenditure of the 'ordinary administration' in the South has, as a proportion of its total expenditure, been rising after many years of decline.

II. THE ORGANIZATION OF INTERVENTION

This is an important section of the new Law. It covers two aspects of policy: first the responsibility of the ordinary administration in the South and, secondly, the extent to which the efforts of the Cassa are to be concentrated in selected areas as opposed to being spread over the whole of the South. These two aspects are treated in this order below.

There has always been a fear that the efforts of the Cassa would become a substitute for, rather than an addition to, the investments of the ordinary administration. In 1950 (Article 1, Law 634) it was laid down that the ordinary administration must continue to fulfil their role in the South and maintain what would be considered a normal level of activity. There was no quantification of 'normal' and the ordinary administration invested proportionately less and less of their budgets in the South. The original fear was being realized —the Cassa was becoming a substitute. Whether specific quantification of investments alone would have helped is dubious as is seen after 1957. With Law 634 of that year an attempt was made to lay down a qualified norm. The Law demanded that the expenditure on southern public works by the ordinary administration between 1957 and 1965 (the period of operation of Law 634) should not, as a proportion of their total expenditure be less than the proportion of

[1] Article 1, Law 717, 1965.
[2] *Piano di Coordinamento degli Interventi Pubblici nel Mezzogiorno*, op. cit.

the Italian population living in the South—about 38 per cent.[1] This, however, was not attained and by 1964-5 the proportion was lower than it had been in any other previous period. The trend in public works expenditure is illustrated by Table 3.2 which shows southern investments in public works by the ordinary administration.

TABLE 3.2

INVESTMENTS IN PUBLIC WORKS BY THE ORDINARY
ADMINISTRATION

	South		North	
Year	Absolute value (milliard lire)	Proportion in the South	Absolute value (milliard lire)	Proportion in the North
1951-55	709·4	40·0	1064·9	60·0
1956-60	875·3	32·3	1832·9	67·7
1961	205·5	30·1	477·3	69·9
1962	191·0	31·5	416·3	68·5
1963	189·3	32·2	398·3	67·8
1964	210·9	27·3	560·7	72·7
1965	267·2	29·6	636·2	70·4

Note: The figures cover expenditure on new buildings, reconstructions, extensions and maintenance. They thus cover virtually all expenditure on public works.

Source: Comitati dei Ministri per il Mezzogiorno e per Le Zone Depresse del Centro-Nord, *Relazione sull'Attuazione del Piano di Coordinamento degli Interventi Pubblici nel Mezzogiorno e sui Provvedimenti per le Aree Depresse del Centro-Nord*, 1968, p. 10.

To try to correct the situation, much needed in view of the optimistic objectives set for the South by the Italian National Plan and discussed later, Law 717 again fixed a proportion for the South. This time the proportion was fixed at 40 per cent and was to cover all investment expenditure by the various ministries. Between 1950 and 1959, southern investment expenditure by the ministries was about 39·6 per cent of their total investment expenditure and 37·7 per cent in the period 1959-65.[2]

[1] Article 3, Law 634, 1957.
[2] Comitati dei Ministri per il Mezzogiorno e per le Zone Depresse del Centro-Nord, p. 8, cited in Table 3·2. In point of fact the figures above do not cover all the ministries. They do not include the ministries of posts; health; shipping; industry and commerce; tourism and culture. The figures on which the calculations above were made cover a little more than 80 per cent of total annual investments.

Considering the failure of the 1957 legislation to secure increased proportions of expenditure by the ordinary administration in the South, it is surprising to report that the 1965 legislation appears to be having the desired results— perhaps a consequence of the improved planning procedures discussed above, perhaps a consequence of the changed political climate after 1965. From an average of 37·7 per cent for the period 1959-65 mentioned above, the proportion of investments in the South by the ordinary administration rose to 40·6 per cent in 1966 and 41·7 per cent in 1967.[1] Investments in public works in the South as a proportion of national investments in public works saw a reversal of the earlier trends shown in Table 3·2 above. The proportions rose to 36·2 per cent in 1966 and to an estimated 37·4 per cent in 1967.[2]

Law 717 continued the earlier policy of requiring the state-controlled firms to invest in the South specified proportions of their total investments The proportions laid down in 1950—60 per cent investments in new industrial plant and 40 per cent of all investments —was continued in the new Law. However, the National Plan 1966-70 went yet further and demanded that all new plant which was not tied in its location for 'technical reasons' must be located in the South or in the depressed areas of the North.[3] This should not make for any great difficulties. Since the late 1950s, the state-controlled firms have been pursuing just such a strategy on their own initiative.

Perhaps the most dramatic aspect of the new Law is the more explicit element of concentration of effort required by the Cassa. Although much of the Cassa's activity in the past had been concentrated in the so-called 'areas susceptible to fast economic growth', this is now made more explicit.

The majority of the Cassa's effort and expenditure will be in the 42 designated Areas and Nuclei of industrial development, 82 Agricultural Development and Connected Zones and 29 Areas of Tourist Development—merely called the Areas from now onwards. They are shown on Map 1 above. Many of the three types of Area do in point of fact overlap with each other because they are, for the greater part, plain land and near the sea and thus often suitable for agriculture and industry as well as tourism. There are five major areas in the South where the overlapping is extremely strong

---

[1] It is estimated that if the ministries mentioned in footnote 2 p. 80 are included then the proportion for 1967 is 48·5 per cent as against the 40 per cent laid down in Law 717; ibid., p. 9.

[2] ibid., p. 10.

[3] *Italian National Plan*, 1966-70, chapter 16, para. 13.

and these have been tentatively designated as 'Growth Poles'.[1]

Although the Law makes it clear that industrial and hotel incentives will be available in the whole of the South[2] (but not normally agricultural incentives), most of the Cassa's effort will be in the Areas and, as a consequence of this, most of the development also. Intervention outside the Areas can only be authorized by the Minister for Extraordinary Intervention in the South for five reasons which are either purely humanitarian or else indirectly to aid the Areas: first, for the safeguarding of irrigated and connected zones or for the indirect improvement of these; secondly, for roads to connect the Areas to autostradas and railway lines; thirdly (the humanitarian aspect), work for the improvement of services in restricted areas characterized by severe depression; fourthly, incentives are available for agricultural development outside the agricultural zones but only on condition that it is part of a special programme connected with the improvement of the zones; finally, the Cassa can provide water and sewerage facilities anywhere in the South.

In brief, the results of Law 717 are, more so than in the past, that the Cassa is to concentrate virtually all of its effort on, or for, a limited number of Areas. Although industrial and hotel incentives can be paid to establishments outside the Areas, it is not expected that the expenditure in this respect will be very high. Most industrial and tourist development in the past has been in the Areas while the incentive schemes now differentiate quite strongly in favour of them.[3] A considerable proportion of the southern area—though a smaller proportion of the population—lies outside the designated areas. Although no official estimates are available, it is probable that around 2 million people live outside the Areas and parts immediately contiguous to them. The area involved is for the greater part inland and largely hill and mountain country. This is the *osso* (bone) of the South—a fairly hopeless area from the viewpoint of long-term economic development. The Cassa does have funds available for this area but they are pitifully small in absolute terms (35 milliard lire) and relative to the Cassa's total budget, of which they account for around 2·5 per cent. The Cassa's efforts in these areas is to be

[1] The poles which have been tentatively identified are: the area around Chieti-Pescara; the area of lower Lazio and Campania; the area around Bari-Brindisi and Taranto; the area around Catania-Siracusa; the area around Palermo; the area around Cagliari, Sulcis-Iglesiente Oristano in Sardinia. See *Piano di coordinamento degli Interventi Pubblici nel Mezzogiorno*, op. cit.

[2] Though, as mentioned below, with discrimination in favour of the Areas.

[3] See pp. 93-94 below.

aimed largely at improving basic public services.[1] Considering the size of the problem and considering that the Cassa's funds amount to little more than £20 million for a five-year period, it is difficult to envisage any great results. It is of course true that these areas are not to be completely neglected. The ordinary administration operates in them as it does in the rest of the South. It needs to be recalled, however, that the current desperate plight of these areas is in spite of past efforts by the Cassa plus the ordinary administration. With the virtual withdrawal of the Cassa, their condition can but deteriorate yet further. We return again later to a discussion of these areas.[2]

III. INCENTIVES FOR THE DEVELOPMENT OF AGRICULTURE

We shall see later that southern agriculture is expected to see a fall in employment of 420,000 between 1965 and 1969. It is expected, however, that though employment will fall, output will grow rapidly. It is in this context that the provisions of the new Law for agriculture should be seen.

Agriculture gets fairly short treatment in the Law, taking only three Articles, and few of the proposals are new. Although it is not mentioned in the agricultural section *per se* of the Law, agricultural assistance through the Cassa is available only for the irrigated areas or in exceptional circumstances for areas outside, but only on condition that such effort is likely to improve the irrigated areas.[3]

There are basically three types of agricultural aid by the Cassa laid down in the new Law:

(*a*) Grants and loans at favourable rates for the implementation of farm improvement plans.

(*b*) Grants and loans at favourable rates for the construction of plants for the conserving, improvement and distribution of agricultural products.

(*c*) Shareholding by the Cassa in a financial company with the aim of helping organizations responsible for creating economically efficient agricultural units.

The grants for farm improvement plants have a maximum ceiling of 45 per cent of admissible expenditure including up to 60 per cent

[1] *Piano di Coordinamento degli Interventi Pubblici nel Mezzogiorno*, op. cit., pp. 225-9.
[2] See pp. 118-119 below.
[3] The size of the agricultural area within which the Cassa is to operate is around 3 million hectares. The total agriculturally productive area of the South is around 11·5 million hectares.

of the expenditure needed to hold adequate stocks. If, however, the improvement plan involves more than one unit, the grant can go up to 60 per cent—an attempt to encourage the creation of larger units. Loans are also available for improvement plans but limited to the expenditure not covered by grants. The rates of interest are subsidized and have been fixed at 3 per cent but can be reduced to 2·5 per cent for owner farmers.

The same grants and loans are available for plants for the conservation, improvement and distribution of agricultural products, *but* on condition that these are promoted by co-operatives of farmers even though in association with industrial firms and financial companies.[1] This condition is an attempt to give the farmer an interest and control in this aspect of agriculture and halt the division which had become fairly common in the South between small farmers and the processing side of agriculture with, indeed, occasional exploitation of the former. Where there is not sufficient local initiative available and where such a plant is considered essential for an area, the Cassa can assume for itself the task of building the plant and leave the running of it to local bodies, co-operatives or consortia. They later can, if they want, purchase the plant at cost less the grant which would have been available.

The processing side of agriculture is vital. Without attention to it, much of the effort of irrigation and farm improvement will have been wasted. The future demand for agricultural products will increasingly be towards better quality products. This can be attained only to a limited extent on the land itself and the rest can only be secured outside the farms. The new Laws seem to cover this need very well, ensuring that the processing is under the control of the farmers themselves but with the provision that the Cassa can step in where local initiative is absent.

Finally, the third aspect of agricultural intervention—the creation of a financial company—is a new departure. Its aim is to promote and develop agriculture through financial participation in co-operatives and other groups having the objective of creating economically efficient farm units. It should get round the continual complaint of shortage of funds by co-operatives and the like.

But the payment of incentives and the developments mentioned above will take a relatively small part of the Cassa's expenditure on agriculture. Land reform, soil conservation and irrigation schemes

---

[1] An interesting aspect here is that the grants and loans are available for plants involved in the distribution of southern agricultural produce even if located outside the South. They must, however, fulfil the same conditions as mentioned above and deal only with southern produce.

will, as in the past, take the bulk (well over three-quarters) of the Cassa's agricultural expenditure. Virtually all of this expenditure will be in the designated irrigated and connected zones.

IV. INCENTIVES FOR INDUSTRY

The growing importance of industry as a part of southern post-war policy has been discussed in Chapter 2. We shall see later that current objectives for the South as laid down in the Italian National Plan demand a massive expansion of industrial development with a concomitant need for increased industrial investment. The extent to which the southern objectives are likely to be attained is, of course, to a larger extent dependent upon the value and appropriateness of incentives available. It is worth while, therefore, to examine in some detail the decisions taken on industrial incentives as initially proposed in Law 717 and which are now in operation.

Three concessions previously mentioned in Chapter 2 in connection with the 1957 legislation remain unchanged and these, to avoid repetition, can be briefly mentioned immediately. They are: first, the exemption from company registration fees; second, the exemption from the IGE (turnover tax) on building materials and machinery for new and expanded plant[1]; third, the arrangements for the provision of risk capital.[2]

1. *Financial incentives*

Loans at reduced interest and grants continue to form an important part of the southern Italian industrial incentives though there are some important changes over previous legislation. In particular, there is a more open use of the incentives in order to secure two basic objectives. First, to further growth centre policy and secondly, to make greater efforts to attract the more dynamic and modern industries to the South. The criteria for awarding loans and grants reflect these aims.

Loans. In general terms, loans are available at low interest rates for new and expanding enterprises where the fixed investment involved is below 12 milliard lire. Such loans can cover up to 70 per cent of the investment. In the original provisions as set out in Law 717, fixed investments above 12 milliard lire could receive loans to cover the excess only to the extent of 50 per cent of the amount allocated for the first 12 milliard. This was changed, however, in March 1968 and fixed investments above 12 milliard can now

[1] The concession on turnover tax is still half the ruling rate though its value is now higher in as far as the ruling rate is 4 per cent as opposed to 3·3 per cent.
[2] See p. 59 above.

receive loans to cover up to 50 per cent of the total investment if certain conditions are fulfilled.[1] The interest rates on loans are 4 per cent for establishments with a fixed investment of up to 6 milliard and 5 or 6 per cent for investments above this figure. In special cases interest can be below these levels.

These are the general conditions and the maximum concessions available. The actual proportion of admissible expenditure covered by the loan and the actual interest charged are determined by a number of criteria. Limiting ourselves initially to the proportion of admissible expenditure, this is decided by three factors. The factors, and the maximum percentage allowed under each head, are: first, location (25 per cent); second, industrial sector (25 per cent); and third, size of the enterprise (20 per cent). An enterprise which fully satisfied the authorities on each criterion would receive a loan to the maximum extent of 70 per cent of admissible expenditure.

An enterprise receives the maximum percentage on each criterion only if it fulfils specified conditions, otherwise it receives lower specified percentages. The criteria, the conditions and percentages for each are outlined below.

(i) Location

The aim with respect to location is to secure as much development as possible inside the Areas and Nuclei and furthermore, in order to ensure fast and efficient use of infrastructure, inside the *agglomerati*.

(a) The maximum of 25 per cent is for enterprises
—inside the *agglomerato* of an Area or Nucleo
—inside an Area or Nucleo but outside the *agglomerato*, though only:

(i) if the enterprise is a big user of materials which lie outside the *agglomerato* and if it needs to be in close proximity to these materials,

[1] See Ministerial decree, March 23, 1968, *Gazzetta Ufficiale*, No. 112, 4/5/68. This represented a very important change of policy. The conditions required to be fulfilled include the following—that the sector is poorly represented in the South, that the plant increases direct and indirect employment considerably, that the plant be located in an *agglomerato*, and finally that the plant induces new complementary investment in the South. These conditions are so vague, and the bargaining power of a company investing above 12 milliard lire so great, that the maximums will doubtless become norms. One important development which undoubtedly caused the change of policy in favour of the big investments was the decision to locate the new Alfa-Sud car plant in the South. Without the changes, the incentives going to this plant would have been very small and well below those obtained by the British car firms when they moved to Scotland.

(ii) if it is a user of products from other plants outside the *agglomerato* which are not easily transportable by road, rail or sea,

(iii) if the enterprise existed before October 15, 1966 and is requesting a loan for the purpose of expansion.

(*b*) The next level of 15 per cent is for new or expanding enterprises in an Area or Nucleo though outside an *agglomerato*, but only on condition that the enterprise is of a limited size and can be set up or expanded without the financial help of the Cassa or any other public authority with respect to the provision of infrastructure specific to its needs.

(*c*) The lowest level of 5 per cent applies to enterprises outside an Area or Nucleo.

(ii) Industrial sector

The sectorial conditions give preference to modern growth industries like foods, chemicals and engineering; industries which satisfy the national demand for capital goods; and finally those which make heavy use of local resources. The sectorial conditions are the most vague of the three criteria. The percentage awarded and the conditions laid down are as follows:

(*a*) The maximum of 25 per cent is for
—foods, chemical and engineering industries
—capital goods industries
—heavy local resource users.

(*b*) The next level of 15 per cent is available for
—industries partially complying with the points above
—industries producing goods and services which are necessary for southern development either in as far as they use southern products or because they supply to other southern enterprises
—enterprises which are contributing to the modernization of southern, or national sectors which are characterized by decline, stagnation or backwardness, through radical innovation with respect to size, technology or techniques.

(*c*) The lowest figure of 5 per cent applies to establishments not considered to fulfil the above conditions.

(iii) Size of enterprise

This is the most complicated of the three criteria. Industries have been divided into technologically homogeneous groups.[1] For each

[1] *Informazioni Svimez* 1967, pp. 272-7.

of these groups (twelve in total), three categories of investment size are given. Category One receives the figure of 5 per cent, Category Two 15 per cent and Category Three the maximum of 20 per cent. Category One is the lowest investment size and Category Three is the highest. Thus, preferential treatment is given to the larger size of enterprise within each group. The investment required to secure admittance to a particular category varies with the industrial group, the broad aim being to favour enterprises which attain a size which the authorities deem appropriate for that group. An example may clarify these points. The production of paint (Group H) is in the same group as carbon paper production, agricultural machinery, chemical plant *inter alia* and has the following investment categories: (1) up to 1,200 million lire; (2) 1,200-3,000 million lire; (3) above 3,000 million lire. An enterprise in the investment Category Three would receive the maximum of 20 per cent; an enterprise in Category One would get 5 per cent. To continue the example, the weaving of artificial fibres is in Group G where the categories are: (1) up to 1,000 million lire; (2) 1,000-2,500 million lire; (3) above 2,500 million lire. These are lower investments than in Group H and reflect what is considered to be the lesser need for large-sized plants in this sector.

The total amount of loan at favourable interest that a firm receives is the sum percentage points it secures on each of the conditions above. The maximum would be 70 per cent of its admissible expenditure; the minimum would be 15 per cent.

Grants. The general picture for grants is as follows. The maximum grant is 20 per cent of admissible investment, on condition that the fixed investment is not above 6 milliard lire. For the part of investment in excess of this figure and below 12 milliard lire, the maximum grant is 10 per cent. The maximum grant for an enterprise with a fixed investment of 12 milliard lire would thus be 15 per cent of admissible expenditure. For enterprises with fixed investments above 12 milliard lire, the Law originally limited the grant for the amount above 12 milliard lire to 50 per cent of the grant conceded on the first 12 milliard lire. This was, however, amended in March 1968. The situation is now that enterprises with fixed investments in excess of 12 milliard lire can obtain grants equal to a maximum of 12 per cent of their admissible expenditure if certain conditions are fulfilled.[1]

[1] The conditions are identical to those mentioned above in the context of loans and indeed the change of policy with respect to grants is part of the same decree. See *Gazetta Ufficiale*, 4/6/68, op. cit.

The grants for all enterprises can be increased by 50 per cent for that part of the investment which involves expenditure on machinery produced in the South. This additional grant is a most useful measure. Not only is it an additional incentive for enterprises to locate in the South but it is also beneficial in as far as it encourages purchases from the South, thus expanding the markets available for existing and potential southern enterprises.

The criteria for the actual award of grants are similar to those for loans and again involve location, sector and size. The maximums and gradations for fixed investments up to 6 milliard lire are similarly proportioned and geared to give the maximums mentioned above.

	Maximum	Gradations		
	%	%	%	%
Location	6·5	6·5	3·5	0·5
Sector	6·5	6·5	3·5	0·5
Size	7·0	7·0	4·0	1·0

The conditions for each gradation are exactly the same as those set out above at length for favourable loans except with the criterion of size where, although the conditions themselves are the same, the gradations are such that the smaller, *not larger*, investment sizes are favoured.[1] The logic of this approach is that grants are more suitable for the smaller firms which do not wish, or cannot afford, to be burdened with debts.

There are a number of additional points to make to the scheme for loans and grants described above. First, the decision as to whether an enterprise with fixed investments above 6 milliard lire receives a loan at the 5 or 6 per cent mentioned above, depends on its location and sector. If an enterprise scores 50 percentage points on the criteria of location and sector, then it secures a loan at 5 per cent. Otherwise it pays 6 per cent. This obviously reflects again the point we made initially—the great stress on the two objectives of securing rapid development of growth centres and modern growth industries. Secondly, only new establishments investing over 80 milliard lire can benefit fully from the above incentives.

For new enterprises with investments between 30 million and 80

[1] Thus in our loan example of industry Group H above, an enterprise in Category One would receive a grant of 7 per cent; Category Two, 4 per cent and Category Three, 1 per cent—quite the reverse of the position with loans.

million lire, or if expanding by between 15 million and 40 million lire, the maximum amount of aid is lower than for the bigger establishments. Loans, as a proportion of admissible expenditure, cannot exceed 45 per cent and grants cannot exceed 15 per cent. The actual figure is determined by the same criteria listed above.

New establishments with an investment of less than 30 million lire or expanding by less than 10 million lire are not eligible for the incentives outlined above. However, they continue to benefit from the 1957 arrangements and are eligible for loans at 3 per cent interest rates. A serious shortcoming, however, is that they are not eligible for grants. The lack of small, efficient establishments in the South is a very serious problem. It is unfortunate that the incentives still do little to overcome the problem.

2. *Exemption from customs duties*
The alternative to taking a grant on machinery under the previous legislation had been exemption from customs duties on imported machinery. This concession was abolished by Law 717—a result of a number of factors but mainly pressure from Confindustria and for Balance of Payments reasons. Although the general lowering of world tariffs, and particularly those in Europe, meant that the concession was losing much of its weight, it did have a non-monetary value. Many foreign firms going to the South prefer to work with their own machinery. Furthermore, some of these firms used their national equipment if only to placate their own governments for their move. The removal of the concession will represent a deterrent, albeit slight, to foreign investment. It is a pity that this relatively inexpensive concession has now been removed.

3. *Fiscal incentives*
The fiscal incentives remain largely the same as before except for two aspects. First, the ten-year exemption from company income tax (*Richezza Mobile*) is prolonged until 1980 and to some extent expanded in as far as it now applies to the income arising from the commercial activities of new industrial firms. Second, companies in the South are now exempt from company tax (*imposta sulle società*) for ten years. The rates for this tax are 7·50 lire for every thousand of share capital and 15 per cent on the part of income in excess of 6 per cent of share capital. Thus a southern company with share capital of a milliard lire and a total income of 200 million would normally pay 7·50 lire per 1,000 lire on the milliard and 15 per cent on 140 million lire. It should pay 28·5 million lire—a sum from which,

under the present legislation, it is exempt.[1] A very important point concerning the eligibility for this concession is that it is only available for companies with their head office in the South. It does not therefore apply to branch factories. The aim of this is undoubtedly to encourage the location of the industrial decision centres in the South and avoid the increasingly branch characteristic of much of southern industry as well as to make for ease of administration. If the concession had been allowed for branch factories, it would have opened the way to considerable tax evasion.

4. Transport concessions

One of the major impediments to southern industrial development (and agricultural development also) is the peripheral position of the South relative to the prosperous countries of Western Europe. The new Law has attempted to ease this problem. Previous legislation gave rail and maritime transport concessions for machinery and materials required for the creation of new industrial plants in the South. This is a long-standing concession, being available in fact since 1947. The new Law aims at improving this position in two ways. First, the concessions are to be available for the modernization of plant, not only the creation of new plant. Secondly, and far more important, concessions were to be made available for the transport, by sea and rail, of materials and semi-finished products required for industrial production as well as the transport, outside the South, of finished products by southern industry.[2] This would reduce the disadvantage of distance from suppliers and markets often suffered by southern firms and make them more competitive. The transport concessions were to be paid by the Cassa.

The Law demanded that the extent and form of the concessions should be drawn up within ninety days. It was only in mid-1967 that the maritime concession was announced.[3] It amounts to 5 per cent of the transport cost. The rail concession still remains to be fixed.[4]

---

[1] The concession applies to firms in any productive sector: industry, agriculture and commerce.

[2] The concession also applies to agriculture.

[3] *Gazzetta Ufficiale*, Nos 171, and 172, July 11, 1967.

[4] It has been suggested that the slow speed with which the maritime concession was decided and the failure to introduce the rail concession is a result of difficulties encountered in the European Economic Commission. See 'Interventi d'Incentivazione e Squilibrio tra industria meridionale e industria centro-settentrionale' in *Bulletino Sicindustria*, 1967, No. 4; reprinted in *Informazioni Svimez*, No. 23-24, June 1967. It is more likely, however, that the Cassa's shortage of funds has been the main delaying factor. It now seems unlikely, because of this shortage, that the rail concessions will be introduced.

5. *The reserve of contracts and work by the public administration*
The law of *'quinto'* has already been discussed above.[1] It represents
an attempt to push demand into the South—the demand in this
case being the contracts and purchases made by the public administration.

The new Law extended the *quinto* in two ways. First, it widened
the public agencies which were required to adhere to it and, in
particular the state-controlled industries were included in the list.
This is in fact not so important as it might seem at first sight for,
after considerable debate in Parliament, it was decided that the
reserve should only apply to the management agencies and not to
the component firms, i.e. it would only apply to the IRI and not to
the companies within its control. It is obvious that the extension
in this instance is not of any great importance for the South. Second,
the reserve, set by earlier legislation at 20 per cent, was raised to
30 per cent. If adhered to, this should stimulate extra demand in
the South, making the area more attractive for existing industry
both directly as a result of the additional demand and indirectly
through the faster growth which it should allow the South to secure.

But the benefits for the South arising out of the reserve depend
upon it being respected. Most observers have been of the opinion
that the reserve was not being respected.[2] An attempt by De Luzenberger to quantify the extent of adherence to the reserve for the
year 1967 came to rather startling conclusions.[3] He found, in the
sectors where he was able to secure data, that less than 10 per cent
of the value of contracts and purchases subject to the reserve was
actually going to the South.

Law 717 recognized that control over the reserve had previously
been slight and demanded that interested parties should submit
each year to the Ministry of Extraordinary Intervention in the South,
the details of contracts and work awarded and how far these complied
with the requirements of the Law. The list is then passed on to a
commission, based within the Ministry of Industry and composed
of representatives from that Ministry and the Ministry for the South,
whose task it is to examine the extent of adherence by the various
parties and to make proposals as to how greater adherence can be
achieved.

[1] See page 66 above.
[2] F. Ventriglia, 'La Nuova Legge per il Mezzogiorno' in *Realtà del Mezzogiorno*, 1965.
[3] A. De Luzenberger, 'Le Reserve di Forniture alle Industrie del Mezzogiorno' in *Rassegna* Economica, 1969, No. 1; reprinted in *Informazioni Svimez*, May 30, 1969, pp. 364-9.

The figure mentioned for 1967 might seem to indicate that the procedure was not working. In point of fact, it was not until almost the end of 1967 that the Commission was fully constituted. It therefore remains to be seen as to whether the new procedure will be sufficiently influential as to secure greater respect of the reserve.

V. TOURISM

There are two important facets of the provision for tourism though perhaps the most important point is a general one—that tourism is recognized as an important sector which can contribute to southern development if encouraged in a similar manner to, say, industry. The two facets are: first, the direction of effort; second, the encouragement of tourist activity through financial incentives.

As with industry and agriculture, the intention is to concentrate tourist effort and development in selected Areas, though the usual proviso is added that the Cassa has the right to intervene in the whole of the South. Again, however, as with agriculture and industry, there can be little doubt that the majority of effort will be in the selected Areas, of which there are 29. The location of the Areas is shown in Map 1 above.[1]

The financial incentives for tourism are new and generous. Loans are available for the construction, modernization and expansion of hotels, hostels and tourist villages as well as local bodies involved in tourist development. The loans can go up to 70 per cent of the admissible expenditure at an interest rate of 3 per cent and duration of up to twenty years. Those concerns lacking the necessary guarantees can have these provided by the Cassa. Grants are also available but are lower than those for industry, being set at a maximum of 15 per cent.

The grants and loans are available outside the Tourist Areas except for one type of intervention activity—the promotion of investments which are complementary to tourism. These can only be aided if they are inside the Areas.

Although assistance is available outside the Areas as well as inside, the majority of the Cassa's activity and aid will be made

[1] Although not shown on the map, there are in fact three types of Tourist Area and with different policies for each: those not yet much developed but capable of being developed in a short time, Areas in the initial phase of development, and so-called Mature Areas which could, if care was not taken, become saturated. For more details of these types, the geographical areas involved and the broad approach set for policy, see *Piano di Coordinamento*, op. cit., pp. 164-6 and 179-97. For a discussion of policy implementation in 1968 see Cassa per il Mezzogiorno, *Bilancio* 1968, pp. 141-7.

inside the Areas. With assistance to hotels and the like, there are in fact criteria laid down which discriminate against regions outside the Areas. The criteria used as guidelines to the actual grant or loan given are similar to those for industry and determined by the location, size and character of the concern with percentages graded to favour the larger second- and lower-class hotels within the Tourist Areas.[1]

VI. MISCELLANEOUS

The points above represent the more important proposals of the 1965 Law for the South. There are, however, a few other proposals which should be mentioned at least for the sake of completeness, though changes over previous legislation are very slight. These concern the provisions for artisans and fishing and a group of measures concerned with technical and social assistance.

For the artisan and fishing sectors, there are no great changes in the incentives over previous legislation (mainly Law 634 of 1957). Assistance continues to be limited to grants.[2]

The grants available for artisans are generous, the maxima being slightly above those available for industry. Priority is given to applications which are likely to allow technological and/or organizational changes in the concern; to sectors which are linked by demand to larger firms; and finally to concerns of an artistic nature and producing 'regional' products. There is fairly strong discrimination in favour of concerns which are part of a consortia. For example, maximum grants for equipment and building are 25 per cent for single concerns and 35 per cent for consortia. On average, the maximum grants are between 25 and 30 per cent of admissible investments costs.

Grants for fishing-boats and equipment are above those for artisans, being set at an average maximum of about 40 per cent. Again there is some discrimination in favour of co-operatives and consortia though this is not as strong as it is with the artisans.

The proposals for social and technical assistance in the new Law are again largely a continuation of previous legislation.[3] Technical assistance for industry will continue to be given through IASM and

---

[1] For more details on the criteria, see *Piano di Coordinamento*, op. cit., pp. 174-5.

[2] For details of the current incentives and criteria for award in both the artisan and fishing sectors, see *Piano di Coordinamento*, ibid., Chapter VI.

[3] Details of the social and technical provisions can be found in Articles 19-21 of Law 717 and *Piano di Coordinamento*, Chapter V.

labour training schemes are to be continued. A new departure, however, concerns research. The South is particularly lacking in research institutes and bodies.[1] It is considered that an expansion of research could help in the development of the South. In consequence, similar grants and loans to those available for industry are to be allowed for university and other research institutes.

SUMMARY AND CONCLUSIONS

The present provisions for the South, outlined in Law 717 and described above, are on the whole a considerable improvement over previous legislation and provide a framework from which faster southern growth will undoubtedly be secured.

The Cassa has a much increased fund at its disposal while the arrangements for greater co-ordination between the ordinary and the extraordinary (Cassa) administration should ensure more efficient intervention and, in quantitative terms, already appear to have brought a halt to the past trends whereby the extraordinary intervention was becoming increasingly substitutive for, as opposed to being additive to, the efforts of the ordinary administration. The increased 'reserve' of public works and contracts is, on paper, a further useful measure for southern development. It remains to be seen as to whether better adherence to the requirements can be attained as a result of the new procedures for ensuring compliance. Increased adherence to the raised reserve plus the already evident increased quantitative co-ordination of ordinary and extraordinary intervention will push increased purchasing power into the South and give greater possibilities for increased southern output by industry, agriculture and services.

A major facet of the new policy introduced in Law 717 concerns the direction of policy. In all sectors there has been a move away from policy of a public works character—a trend which had already commenced in the early 1960s but which is now much clearer. In all fields, the key words are now to be concentration and growth. Effort is to be concentrated on those sectors and geographic areas which offer the greatest prospects for rapid growth. The geographic concentration in particular is well established. The Cassa, to a greater extent than before, will not be aiming its efforts at the whole of the South but at selected Tourist, Agricultural and Industrial Areas. It seems likely that the policy will leave considerable social problems in its wake. It is, however, probably the policy which will ensure the fastest and most economical southern growth.

[1] Only about 13 per cent of Italian research workers are in the South.

95

It is with industry that the most important changes have been made, a reflection of the recognition that industrial development must be the key to southern progress.

The funds allocated for industrial development are far greater than under previous legislation. The direction for industrial development, at which these funds are to be aimed, is clearly laid down in Law 717 and subsequent policy documents. Industrially, the direction through the discriminatory incentive system is towards growth industries and growth firms. Geographically, again through incentive discrimination, the stress is on growth centres. The Italians have gone further than any other country in developing a strongly growth centre oriented policy. The new Law and its supporting plans make it very clear that the southern policy is not being operated for humanitarian reasons but primarily to secure fast and economic development. The directions in which the incentives push, the location of the state-controlled firms as well as the growth centre concentration of infrastructure by the Cassa; all give new strength to the growth centre policy started in 1957.

Another important industrial aspect of the new legislation is that there has been an increase in the average value of the incentives. The continuance, and often increased value, of most of the earlier incentives plus the introduction of the company tax concession means that the incentives are now more attractive, though they also involve a greater element of discrimination. Firms which coincide fully with the location, sector and size criteria outlined above could receive incentives of more than double the value of those for a firm completely out of line. On the basis of a number of assumptions, but principally on assumed capital output ratio of one, a new plant with a total investment of 6 milliard lire or less, locating in the South, would be eligible for incentives having a value around 5·8 per cent of its total revenue if it coincided fully with the new criteria. A similar plant completely out of line could receive around 2·4 per cent. Plants with a total investment above 6 milliard lire but below 12 milliard lire could receive between 4·4 per cent and 5·8 per cent of their total revenue if coinciding fully, and between 1·9 per cent and 2.0 per cent if completely out of line.[1]

[1] The assumptions involved in the estimates above and the method of calculation were as follows: *Assumptions*—capital/output ratio of one; investment in stocks represent 30 per cent of total investment; share capital is one-third of total investment; profit amounts to 7 per cent of share capital net of taxes and 13 per cent gross of taxes; the rate of interest on a loan would normally be 8 per cent; plant starts producing 3 years after building commences; machinery and materials have a value of 50 per cent of the total investment and thus about 70 per cent of investment net of stocks; a 15-year period is used for the calculation

As noted, the estimates above are based on an assumed capital/ output ratio of one. The Italian industrial capital/output ratio between 1951 and 1967 was about 3·0. If this ratio currently holds in the South, then a medium-sized firm (investment below 6 milliard lire) with a capital/output ratio identical to the national average could, on the most favourable assumptions, receive incentives of

of the annual value for the incentives; the enterprise makes profits in its sixth year of operation.

Method of calculation: there are two ways in which incentives can reduce costs. First they can reduce the need for capital which would have had to be repaid and on which interest would also have had to be paid. Savings of this form apply to grants, concession on IGE (turnover tax) on machinery and building materials for construction and exemption from company tax during the construction period of the factory. Secondly, there are those incentives which directly reduce costs. These include loans at favourable interest rates and company income tax concessions.

A *hypothetical* example may clarify the scheme for the reader. In addition to the general assumptions above, we assume a total investment of £100 and that the incentives are given immediately building starts.

A. SAVINGS THROUGH A REDUCED NEED FOR CAPITAL

(a) Grants—assumed at 20 per cent of fixed investments of £70. £14·0

(b) Concession on IGE (turnover tax) reducing it from 4 per cent to 2 per cent. Assume that building materials and machinery have a value of £50 £1·0

(c) Registration fees—exemption from. Assume share capital of £33 3s. Fees are about 1 per cent of share capital £0·33

(d) *Imposta sulle società* (company tax) at 0·825 per cent per annum of share capital for the 3-year construction period is: £0·825

TOTAL

This is capital which would otherwise have needed to have been repaid and on which interest would have been paid at an assumed rate of 8 per cent per annum. Assuming that the money is repaid uniformly over 15 years and interest at 8 per cent charged on the declining balance, the total value per annum of £16 16s. is £1·77

B. INCENTIVES DIRECTLY REDUCING COSTS

(i) Assume that 70 per cent of the investment is financed with a loan at the favourable rate of interest of 4 per cent instead of the normal 8 per cent. Annual saving is £2·8

(ii) Assume that net of *Richezza Mobile* (company income tax) income is 7 per cent of share capital as against 13 per cent gross. Exemption from RM applies for 10 years. Averaged over the 15 years this would be an annual saving of £1·33

(iii) Exemption from *imposta sulle società* for the 7 years remaining after the construction period. This, averaged over 15 years, gives £0·128

TOTAL ANNUAL VALUE of incentives over the 15-year period is £5·88

On a capital output ratio of one, the incentives would therefore have a value equal to 5·88 per cent of total revenue.

D 97

an amount equal to about 17 per cent of total revenue. A similar firm in the most unfavourable assumptions would receive an amount equal to around 7·2 per cent of total revenue. The value for the large firm with investments above 6 milliard lire would vary between 5·7 and 17 per cent. The average of these four estimates is around 11 per cent though any such average figure must be treated with extreme caution. Within the context in which it was calculated, however, it is likely that it underestimates the average for a number of reasons. First, the Southern Industrial capital/output figure is slightly above the national average. Second, the Southern Industrial capital/output ratio in the 1960s had been above the average for 1951-67. The average for the period 1960-67 was quite close to 4 though this may be a short-run phenomenon associated with the large industrial investments in plants which had not attained full output. Third, most firms going to the South will be of an investment size below 6 milliard lire and for which the value of the incentives are higher than the average. Fourth, the average is probably an understatement in as far as firms, by their location choice, can edge towards the higher range of the incentives and must be expected to choose their location accordingly, i.e. move into the growth centres. Finally, it may be an underestimation in as far as the calculations exclude the concession introduced in late 1968 whereby southern industrial firms employing more than 35 employees enjoy a reduction of the social security costs which they are obliged to pay for their employees. The reduction amounts to 10 per cent of the social charges on existing employees and 20 per cent on newly engaged employees. The value of this concession was, however, probably offset by the moves in 1969 aimed at eliminating (by mid-1971) the regional differences in contractual wages in Italy. Contractual wages were, before 1969, generally lower in the South than in the North.

The value of the Italian incentives as a percentage of revenue is certainly above those in the United Kingdom which have been estimated at being around 5 per cent after tax.[1] But then the disadvantages and problems of southern Italy location are very much greater than a location in, say, Scotland. It is not possible to say whether the real value of the Italian incentives is higher or lower than in the United Kingdom. Staying within the Italian context, it will be remembered from Chapter 1 above that the difference in value added per employee in modern manufacturing industry between

[1] T. Wilson, 'Finance for Regional Industrial Development', *Three Banks Review*, September 1967. Considering that part of the Italian incentive scheme is exemption from tax, it seems more meaningful to compare their value with the UK estimates after tax.

North and South was around 10 per cent in favour of the North. Certainly, relative to this differential, the incentives are not over-generous.

Perhaps the most important point to keep in mind when considering the Italian industrial incentive schemes is the fact that, unlike the United Kingdom, the funds for the payment of incentives are not open-ended. The paucity of funds in the past has meant that not all applicants receive the incentives for which, on paper, they are eligible. The industrial funds allocated to the Cassa in 1965 were, by 1968, fully committed. Though more funds were, surprisingly, allocated in the latter half of 1968, it still seems unlikely that they are adequate for the task and the Cassa will need to pursue a more stringent policy towards applicants for aid. This is a point to which we return later.

On paper at least, however, the new industrial incentives for the South are higher than in the past. This is at a time when the difficulties of a southern location, though still considerable, are less than in the past. Southern infrastructure is closer to northern standards, there are better transport facilities to and from the North and a greater degree of industrialization exists, thus reducing the earlier lack of external economies. These changes should make the extended incentives all the more powerful. Whether or not the incentives have been sufficiently expanded to attain the levels of southern industrial development expected in the National Plan is discussed in the next section.

The power of incentives to attract industry is not, of course, dependent solely on their size. Some incentives have a greater psychological impact than others.[1] The probable damage done by the removal of the customs duty concession has already been mentioned. However, an important counterweight to this could have been the expanded transport concessions. Businessmen have a tendency to overrate the importance of transport costs. This is perhaps not surprising since transport costs represent one of the few easily measurable re-location costs and there is always a temptation to give greater weight to the quantifiable than the non-quantifiable. It is very unfortunate that the discussion on the rail concessions has been long delayed for they could have a greater influence on industrial location decisions than their size alone would suggest.

One final point on the industrial aspects of the new Law concerns a point of omission. No disincentives for industrial development

---

[1] Some, though seemingly important on paper, are less important in practice. The widespread tax evasion in Italy reduces, for example, the power of fiscal incentives.

in the North are included in the new policy. There had been a considerable amount of debate on these prior to the Bill getting to Parliament.[1] Their exclusion from the Bill was probably a result of three forces or arguments. First, the political problems of getting such legislation through Parliament would be very great and, if included in the Bill, would have jeopardized its chance of being passed quickly. Second, and related, Italian industry was strongly against such intervention. Lastly, the argument was frequently put forward that to restrict development in the North could send industry even further north and out of Italy altogether, closer to the heart of the Common Market.[2] Any system of disincentives would need more Common Market backing than was, or is, feasible. This latter argument does not augur well for the British Industrial Development Certificate.

THE SOUTH AND THE NATIONAL
PLAN (1966-1970)

The recent Italian National Plan presents quantified objectives for southern development—though not for the first time. The Vanoni Plan in 1955 similarly set out objectives for the South, though it had few concrete proposals tied to its regional objectives.[3] The whole plan was anyway rapidly overtaken by events. This is not to deny that the Vanoni Plan had enormous merits. It was one of the first attempts at detailed planning in Western Europe and if it did nothing else it illustrated the problems and sacrifices required for rapid southern development as well as the possible national benefits. However, southern policy did not gear itself to the Plan and the aim of policy in the South remained as it had been—a general effort

[1] 'Debate' is a rather genteel word for the polemic which took place on disincentives—particularly between some of the northern and southern newspapers.

[2] In spring 1969 a Bill on planning procedure was ready to be put before Parliament—one of a number of Bills preparing the way for the National Plan 1971-75. The Bill envisaged that companies with capital of more than 5 milliard lire would be required to inform the office for National Planning of their investment plans. On the basis of this information the planners would have a better idea of future industrial development and would also attempt to dissuade companies from expanding in the North when such expansion is possible in the South or other needy areas. Furthermore, it is intended that the planners will be able to withhold urban development permission where necessary. It will be interesting to see Parliament's reaction. For further details see the article by F. Forte reprinted in *Informazioni Svimez*, May 1969, pp. 375-9.

[3] *Elements of a Programme for Raising Income and Employment Levels in Italy over the Ten Years 1955-1964*, Rome, 1955. Also see *Reappraisal of the Vanoni Plan in the Fifth Year of Operation*, Rome, 1959.

to improve conditions without any specified targets. The current Italian National Plan 1966-70,[1] relative to the Vanoni Plan, involved more resources in its design and has more machinery available for its implementation.

The aim of this section is to examine the objectives for southern development set out in the National Plan and, in the light of the resources available, to evaluate their feasibility.

Although the possibility of fulfilling the southern objectives is naturally tied up with the possibility of attaining the Plan's national objectives, it is not intended to spend much time discussing the feasibility of these, but merely to list them in order to set the regional objectives in context.

There are four main objectives of the Plan. First to attain general full employment by 1970. This means reducing unemployment to 2·8-2·9 per cent of the labour force.[2] In order to do this and to employ the natural increase of the labour force as well as to absorb the expected large decrease in agricultural employment (a fall of 600,000), it will be necessary to create 1·4 million new non-agricultural jobs. Second, the aim is to attain a growth of national income of 5 per cent per annum. A third objective is to increase the percentage of Gross National Product going to social uses—housing, education, transport, etc.—to 26-27 per cent of Gross National Product[3] as against the 24 per cent attained in the period 1959-63. Last, and most important from our point of view, there is the objective of locating 40 per cent of new non-agricultural jobs in the South.

In order to attain these basic objectives, the effort involved will need to be very great. Industrial value added, for example, will need to rise by 7 per cent per annum while gross saleable agricultural output must increase by 3·3 per cent per annum.

The aspirations for the South are considerably higher than anything actually experienced in the past. The aim of locating 40 per cent of the nation's new non-agricultural jobs in the South is well above the ratio of 25 per cent secured between 1959 and 1963. An indication of the vast amount of resources which will need to move to the South if the Plan is to be fulfilled is best indicated by the

[1] The current plan covers the five years 1966-70. There was an earlier plan for 1965-69, but through a variety of political and economic problems, though mainly the former, it was out of date before it got through Parliament.

[2] Incidentally, this is far more pessimistic than the full employment objective set out in the 1965-69 Plan which was 1·5-1·6 per cent unemployed.

[3] Again this target is more pessimistic than set out in the 1965-1969 Plan when the aim was 27-27·5 per cent.

absolute value of net fixed industrial investments required. This is 3,000 milliard lire for the five-year period—equal to gross fixed investments around 4,500 milliard lire. This is an absolute level of investment 25 per cent above that realized in the entire fourteen years 1951-64.

It is hoped that this massive investment will help attain the proportion of 40 per cent of the nation's new non-agricultural jobs, amounting in absolute terms to about 590,000 in the five-year period. Even if this is achieved, there will still be the need for net emigration from the South. It is interesting to have a more careful look at the southern employment aspects of the Plan because they well illustrate the nature of the southern problem.

The natural increase in the southern labour force, together with the reduction of unemployment to the desired level over the Plan period, would require 570,000 new jobs in the South. Even this figure is an understatement, for it excludes those who are expected to emigrate abroad. It is expected that 300,000 Italians will emigrate abroad in the five years 1966-70 of which, based on past proportions, about 200,000 will be from the South. The number of new jobs required in order to employ the natural increase of the southern labour force, to reduce unemployment to the desired level and to halt overseas migration would thus be 770,000. Even this takes no account of the need to reduce the level of underemployment or to bring southern activity rates to northern levels. Confining ourselves to the 770,000, however, it is an obvious point that southern agriculture is not going to supply these jobs. Indeed, it is expected to continue declining and will put on to the labour market a further 350,000 people. The total number of jobs required, taking account of all the labour sources quantified above, is 1·12 million. The prospects of employing all these people in the South is quite out of the question. The total number of non-agricultural jobs expected to be created in the whole of Italy during the planning period is only 1·4 million. If all the southern labour coming on to the market was to be employed in the South, the region would need 80 per cent of Italy's new non-agricultural jobs. Even assuming that overseas migration reaches the expected level in the South, 200,000 for the five-year period, then 940,000 non-agricultural jobs would still be needed—about 65 per cent of total Italian non-agricultural new jobs. Even this lower figure is not feasible. In the period 1959-63 the South secured only 25 per cent of Italian new non-agricultural jobs. The 920,000 new jobs required is equal to the whole of the forecasted employment expansion in the South *and* the North-West of Italy. There is obviously a limit to the extent which jobs can be transferred from the North. The majority of employment growth is of course geographically immobile.[1]

In consequence, the Plan quite rightly sees the need for continued emigration from South to North. If the target of 570,000 non-agricultural jobs are in fact created in the South, then this will require net emigration from the South to the North of 350,000 workers. The majority will go to the North-West.[2]

The recognition that there must be continued net emigration from the South is a realistic element of the Plan. The validity of the forecasted net emigration of 350,000 workers from South to North does, however, depend on whether in fact 40 per cent of Italy's new non-agricultural jobs are located in the South. Whether this is feasible and whether therefore the emigration estimates are realistic is something to which we want to return shortly.

Some of the figures in the National Plan, with the addition of others culled from elsewhere, can be used to make what is to some extent a digression. It concerns two basic aspects of the southern problem: first, that the natural increase of the labour force is higher than elsewhere in Italy; and second, that the South has a higher weighting of agriculture. Without these, the South would not be nearly so much of a problem.

The natural increase of the southern labour force[3] according to the Plan is expected to be 570,000 between 1965 and 1970—an increase of 9·4 per cent over the labour force in 1965. This is well above the national average. If the South saw a percentage increase equal to the average for Italy, 4·1 per cent, the labour force expansion would not be 570,000 but 242,400. Using the northern rate (1·7 per cent) the expansion would be only 103,000. Even using the former figure there would be no need for emigration if the planned 570,000 new non-agricultural jobs materialized.

A high natural increase of the population is one of the *bêtes noires* of the South; the heavy weighting of agriculture is another. Southern agriculture is expected to shed 350,000 of its labour force over the period of the Plan—a percentage rate of decline 50 per cent above the national average. If the South had the same percentage decline as the North (9·2 per cent) it would need to shed only 200,000.

[1] Even in the North, a high proportion of the normally most mobile sector—manufacturing—is artisan activity.

[2] The shortage of labour in the North-West without this immigration would be impossibly acute. The source of labour for this region from the natural increase of the labour force and reduction of unemployment is *negative* (to the extent of 70,000). Net worker immigration is expected to be 310,000.

[3] In fact the natural increase plus the planned decrease in unemployment net of overseas emigration.

The difference between this and the expected decline would be sufficient to halve the required migration from the South. The problems arising out of a declining agriculture are likely to continue well into the future. Recent estimates by SVIMEZ anticipate that southern agriculture, between 1965 and 1980 will shed 930,000 labour units—66,000 per annum as against 74,000 per annum between 1965 and 1970.[1]

This has been something of a digression. Our aim has been merely to show that the structure in the South is such as to prevent a quick and easy solution. To overcome the need for any southern net emigration would require an unrealistic proportion of Italian new non-agricultural jobs going to the South. The planners therefore accept the need for emigration but at the same time, also anticipate a very high proportion of Italy's new non-agricultural jobs to be in the South—40 per cent. Is this realistic? Our conclusion will be that it is not. Laudable though the sentiment of putting such a proportion in the South may be, sentiment is not enough. Good plans should not be based on hope alone or pander to economically impossible political wishes.

How does this 40 per cent compare with earlier figures? It is well above the proportion in 1960-65, which was 18 per cent, and even this is biased in the South's favour in as far as 1965, being a year of recession, was a bad year for industrial employment in the North. The proportion for 1960-64 was 16·2 per cent. If the Plan's proportion of 40 per cent is to be secured then there must at least be a doubling over earlier attainments. Perhaps more serious is the fact that the trend is not even rising. The proportion of non-agricultural jobs going south was higher in 1954-60 (33 per cent) than in 1960-65. In order to secure the desired proportion then, it is not even a case of speeding up an existing trend but reversing it.

It is difficult to see why there should be any great change in the proportion. Admittedly, conditions in the South are now better than previously with better infrastructure and a more industrialized economic structure; both of which should give more indigenous growth and diminish the disadvantages of a southern location for new firms. On the other hand, greater international competition as tariffs continue to be reduced, and the fact that many of the potential firms have already gone South, may counterbalance these points.

The incentives available to encourage southern industrial development contained in Law 717 and discussed above are an improvement over earlier incentives but are unlikely to be sufficient to give

[1] *Ricera sui Costi d'Insediamento*, SVIMEZ, 1967.

the great shift of proportions required if the southern part of the Plan is to be fulfilled.

The enormity and improbability of attaining the job proportions required in the Plan can be illustrated by the size of industrial investments needed and its relation to that gained in earlier periods. It is estimated that the volume of gross industrial investment necessary in order to give the required industrial jobs in the South is 4,500 milliard lire. This is over twice as much as that experienced in the years 1960-64 (2,083 milliard at current prices) and indeed is almost 30 per cent above the total industrial investments in the South between 1951 and 1964 (3,388 milliard).

An important factor which will decide whether or not the required industrial investment is attained will be the action of the state-controlled firms. In the past they have been an important determinant of southern industrial investment and employment. By 1964 they were accounting for 54 per cent of southern industrial investment and in the five-year period 1960-64 were responsible for about 50 per cent of the new industrial investment. What they do in the Plan period will obviously be important in determining total southern industrial investment. Past trends would not give grounds for expecting a large expansion of their investments. The volume of *industrial* investments by the state-controlled firms in the South declined between 1963 and 1967 with 1963 at 286 milliard lire; 1964 at 285 milliard lire; 1965 at 230 milliard lire and 1966 and 1967 at 173 milliard and 206 milliard lire respectively.[1]

On the basis of figures presented in 1967 by the Ministry of State Holdings, there is no great grounds for optimism for the period 1967-71. The Ministry expect their total southern investments to be around 950 milliard lire, of which about 500 milliard lire will be industrial investments.[2] On an annual basis, this level of industrial investments is much lower than in the period 1960-66. It must be admitted immediately that these figures will be adjusted upwards. The recent Alfa-Sud decision, for example, was excluded from the estimates and this will add another 300 milliard lire to the industrial investment figure. It can be seen that investments by the Ministry of State Holdings are rather difficult to predict. One way of predicting over the period of the National Plan is to take the average

---

[1] Calculated from data in *Relazione sull'Attuazione del Piano di Coordinamento Degli Interventi Pubblici nel Mezzogiorno* op. cit., Vol. 1, 1967, pp. 84-5. Industrial investments have been taken to include investments in telephone services, autrostrade, radio and television services.

[2] *Informazioni Svimez*, May 1967, pp. 407-24. Industrial investments are again taken to exclude telephone, autostrade, radio and television investments.

annual industrial investments 1965-67 and multiply by five—crude though this might be. The annual average over the period 1965-67 was 200 milliard lire. This would then give a total industrial investment of 1,000 milliard lire over the quinquennium.

A generous view would allow the argument that this understates their likely investment.[1] If we assume an understatement of 50 per cent over the full five-year period, total southern industrial investments by the state-controlled firms will then be 1,500 milliard lire. Now, if their investments remain at 50 per cent of total southern industrial investments—probably they would rise on the assumptions above—total southern industrial investments will still be only 3,000 milliard lire. Even on these very generous assumptions then, we are still 30 per cent below the 4,500 milliard lire of industrial investment required to implement the Plan. If the investment target is to be attained, southern industrial investments other than those by the state-controlled firms would, on the assumptions above, need to be three times those of 1960-64.[2] It is difficult to see any reasons why this should occur.

Not only is the total southern industrial investment required by the Plan enormous, but it is doubtful whether the Cassa has sufficient funds to pay the necessary incentives if it came about. This would not be surprising. The decisions on the allocations to the Cassa were largely unrelated to the National Plan targets.

How far would the Cassa's 550 milliard lire for the industrial sector take it?[3] The 550 milliard lire must cover industrial incentives made by the Cassa as well as the provision of specific infrastructure for the Areas and Nuclei.

Grants alone would take up a sizeable proportion of this allocation. Of the 4,500 milliard lire gross industrial investment, about 55 per cent would be eligible for grants. The average grant is about 17 per

[1] Generous because it is not unknown for the state-controlled firms to scale their projections downwards as well as upwards as happened in 1965.

[2] 1960-64 industrial investments by state-controlled firms in industry were about 1,000 milliard lire and total southern industrial investments about 2,000 milliard lire.

[3] As mentioned elsewhere, this 550 milliard lire is not in fact the amount available for the fulfilment of the new programme since 107 milliard was needed to complete the earlier 1950-65 programme. The Cassa was thus left with 443 milliard lire for the 1966-69 programme. The period does not coincide with the National Plan period 1966-70. In 1968 the Cassa's funds were extended to carry it for the extra year to 1970. No indications were given, however, as to how much of the increased funds (560 milliard lire) were to go to industry. Taking into account the use of funds for the completion of the 1950-65 programme, plus the additional funds given in 1968, it seems likely that 550 milliard lire is probably somewhere near the actual funds for the five-year period 1966-70.

cent of eligible investment. On these figures, grants alone could cost the Cassa about 400 milliard lire. There would not be a lot left to do much else in the way of helping industry. Subsidized interest on loans to firms would, on such a large investment programme as 4,500 milliard lire, again be very costly to the Cassa, the sum involved probably being in the order of at least 150 milliard lire. Thus, grants and loans alone are likely to exhaust the Cassa's industrial funds.

The other major cost likely to be incurred by the Cassa on the industry front, and which is paid out of the industry allocation, is that of equipping the *agglomerati* in the Areas and Nuclei and helping financially in the provision of other specific infrastructure planned by the consortia. Under the existing allocation, only 70 milliard lire is available for these forms of expenditure. The Cassa is responsible for 85 per cent of these expenditures with the consequence that 70 milliard lire is sufficient for 82 milliard lire of expenditure. This is well below demands likely to be made on the funds. An early estimate of expenditure by the consortia during the Plan period was 354 milliard lire,[1] of which the Cassa would pay 85 per cent. This is probably a high figure and could be pared down with a more careful scrutiny of claims. Nevertheless, with *agglomerati* costing 30 million lire per hectare to equip, the allocation will allow few hectares to be equipped. Even the 30 million lire understates the costs in as far as it covers only the costs of the *agglomerati* themselves and excludes port plans, running and maintenance costs, as well as administration costs. Equipping of the 5,000 hectares of *agglomerati* in all the Areas and Nuclei, as well as the other costs, will need total resources of 200 milliard lire of which 170 milliard will be the responsibility of the Cassa.

We have limited ourselves to only a few aspects of the Cassa's industrial allocation but have tried to show that it is inadequate for its tasks. It is certainly inadequate to finance the vast expansion of industry which the National Plan envisages for the South. It is even doubtful whether the industry allocation would be sufficient to finance industrial investment equal to 60 per cent[2] of the Plan's industrial investment estimate.

In brief, our conclusions are rather pessimistic. The hopes for the South as set out in the National Plan are not very realistic, and even

---

[1] Sardinia alone anticipated spending 42 milliard lire on infrastructure works in the Areas and Nuclei in 1965-69. See *Informazioni Svimez*, No. 17-18, 1965.

[2] This is about the figure which would result if industrial investment in the South grew at 5-6 per cent over the five years 1966-70. This seems a more reasonable forecast than that in the National Plan.

less so in view of the unsatisfactory funds at the disposal of the Cassa. Even by the end of 1968, the Cassa had spent or committed virtually all of its funds. It was admittedly given more funds (560 milliard lire) but this was largely to allow it to stretch its planning programme to include 1970 and thus coincide with the National Plan. The annual allocations for the period 1966-69 had been around 300 milliard lire, so this leaves about 260 milliard to help rescue it from its obvious financial difficulties. The very need for such a rescue illustrates well the futility of allocating funds to the Cassa which are so much out of line with likely demands on its resources. There can be little doubt that the Cassa will again run into further difficulties before the end of 1970 unless it acts in a more stringent manner—but this can only be to the detriment of southern development.

CHAPTER 4

CONCLUSIONS

I. THE RESULTS OF POLICY IN THE SOUTH[1]

With all the money and effort which have been invested in the South, what have been the results? What has happened in the South, and have the results been worthy of the efforts? These are the questions to which we now want to turn our attention. Inevitably, what has happened in the South has not necessarily been solely the result of intervention. Some development would anyway have taken place even without intervention. It is not possible to isolate what has happened as a result of policy and what is autonomous development. In consequence, to try to assess what has happened in the South and to comment upon it in relation to the efforts expended is no easy task. The evidence is furthermore often of a contradictory nature giving plenty of opportunity for those of an optimistic, critical or laudatory turn of mind to indulge their prejudices.

The results in the South have not been spared commentary. The effort and money involved in southern development has been so great that it would be surprising if such attention had been lacking. Between 1950 and 1969, the Cassa alone spent about 4,000 milliard lire.

To start on a fairly obvious point, the South is still poor relative to the North (see Chapter 1). Income per head is low, emigration is heavy, underemployment is high, activity rates are low, etc. The South still relies for about 25 per cent of its gross product on agriculture as against 11 per cent in the North. Agriculture employs around 35 per cent of the labour force—about double the northern proportion. Industry accounts for only 35 per cent of southern gross product and employs 31 per cent of the labour force as against the northern proportions of 50 and 45 per cent respectively. The modern industrial sector is still very much lacking. In 1965, the South produced only around 10 per cent of Italy's output in the modern industrial sector. The South has an unfavourable economic structure —both between sectors and within them.

[1] For a very good brief discussion of Italian regional policy and its results, see P. Saraceno, 'La Politica di Sviluppo Regionale nella Esperienza Italiana', *Nord e Sud*, May 1968.

Conditions in the South are of course far better than they were in 1950 and, indeed, its development since 1950, measured by virtually any index, has been high. It now has far better infrastructure, private consumption at constant prices has more than doubled, infant mortality has been halved, illiteracy is lower by 40 per cent, the index of housing overcrowding has fallen by 20 per cent, income per head has risen by 4·2 per cent per annum while fixed capital investment at constant prices increased by around 280 per cent between 1951 and 1967. In the same period gross industrial output at factor prices increased by 215 per cent (1963 prices) while agricultural output on the same basis grew by 257 per cent. The growth of output in the tertiary sector was 127 per cent.

The economic structure of the South, though still backward relative to the North, has undergone an enormous change since 1951. The weight of southern agriculture both in terms of output and employment has fallen while the weight of industry has grown substantially. Employment in industry as a proportion of total southern employment increased from 20 per cent in 1951 to 31 per cent in 1967 while industrial output as a proportion of southern gross product rose from 24 to 35 per cent over the same period. Agriculture has seen a very considerable shedding of labour with one million workers leaving the sector between 1951 and 1967. While agricultural employment accounted for 57 per cent of total southern employment in 1951, it was down to 35 per cent by 1967.

The fact that there has been progress in the South is not very surprising considering the efforts involved. In order to judge its progress, however, a yardstick is needed against which the development can be compared. One such possible yardstick is the progress of the North over the same period. If the objective of policy has been to reduce the disparities between the two regions, then this is obviously the measure to use.

The picture from this yardstick is varied. The growth of southern gross output in agriculture and the tertiary sector has been faster than in the North though the differences have not been very great. The growth of industrial gross output has been virtually the same in both regions.[1] In all three sectors fixed gross investment has been substantially faster in the South than in the North.[2] Total gross

[1] With 1951 as 100, southern gross output at factor prices in the private sector for agriculture, industry and the tertiary sector in 1967 was 157, 315, 227 respectively. The comparable figures for the North were 135, 318 and 217.

[2] Again taking 1951 as 100, gross fixed investment in southern agriculture, industry and 'other activities' had, by 1967, reached levels of 277, 348 and 430 respectively. Comparable figures for the North were 243, 205 and 365.

investment in the South increased by 350 per cent between 1951 and 1967 as against only 180 per cent in the North. The rapidly growing capital output ratio in the South—a quite normal phenomenon in the early stage of development—has meant that the high rates of investment growth have not shown a similarly rapid employment growth. The numbers employed in industry in the South increased by only around 45 per cent (600,000 jobs) between 1951 and 1967. The percentage growth in the North was 30 per cent. The growth of industrial jobs in the South between 1951 and 1967 was well below the fall in agricultural jobs (about 1·5 million) and total employment fell by around half a million. In the North, agriculture saw an even more drastic fall (2·5 million) while industrial employment grew by around 1·5 million. Total northern employment fell by around 200,000.

In many ways, then, the South has done well relative to the North. However, in terms of the most important index of development, income per head, it has made disappointing progress relative to the North. The disparity in income per head was only slightly less in 1967 than it was in 1951. At current prices, southern income per head was around 53 per cent of northern income per head in 1967 as against 50 per cent in 1951. Similar proportions hold using constant prices.

An immediate question which arises, however, is whether the North is the best yardstick with which to compare the growth of southern income per head. The North has, over the period 1951-67, had an average rate of growth which is one of the highest in the world and it must be questionable as to whether it is fair to plot the progress of the South against it. Growth in the North has been so fast in the post-war period that perhaps the most surprising thing is that the South—virtually an underdeveloped country in 1950— has been able to keep pace. Perhaps a better yardstick than the North is the growth of other European countries in the Mediterranean basin. Here the South fares well and its rate of growth of income per head has been faster than any of these countries. The South fares well even relative to most Northern European countries —including Germany.

It is obviously no easy task to evaluate the success of southern development policy in global terms. The South has done well relative to most other countries in the world, yet the North-South disparity in the crucial measure of income per head has declined but slightly. If the aim of policy was to remove or substantially reduce this disparity then it has obviously failed.

The objective of southern policy has rarely been clearly set out.

111

In policy documents where the objective has been made explicit one remains in doubt as to how far political considerations have outweighed realism. In a most interesting article, Graziani makes the point that southern policy was never aimed at carrying the South to northern standards, even if 'for understandable strategic reasons this was the formulation in the Vanoni plan'[1]—one of the few occasions when an objective was explicitly given. This rings true. It would be unrealistic to have expected the South to catch up with the North in the short period of ten or fifteen years. A centuries-old disequilibrium cannot be removed in one generation. The prospects of attaining equilibrium, particularly in the 1950s and early 1960s were slight because of the North's rapid growth. But even if the North had stagnated completely and the South had enjoyed the income per head growth rates which it has seen between 1950 and 1964, the disequilibrium would still have remained (albeit slight) in 1964. Graziani suggests that the aim of policy has been to transfer a static economy into a dynamic one and to propel the South to a level where it can enjoy automatic and continuous development. It is difficult to judge how far this aim has been attained.

Inevitably, the efforts in the South have put it in a better economic position and placed it closer to a situation of take-off into self-sustained growth. The economic structure is now better geared to economic growth. There is a lower weighting of agriculture and a higher proportion of this is of good quality. There is more modern industry, a reasonably good infrastructure and a better trained labour force. However, whether the South is in any way ready to grow independently of any further external effort is a different point. Obviously the fact that the Cassa is still operating, and indeed that effort to help the South is being stepped up, indicates that nobody believes that the South is ready to be left to its own devices.

On the subject of dependence, Italy has data which allows an assessment to be made of the extent to which the South is still dependent on outside help. It is interesting to look briefly at these figures as they show the extent to which the South is still dependent on external assistance and indicate the extent to which past growth has been a result of outside assistance.

In 1966, southern net income (net of amortization and imports from the North and abroad) was 8,120 milliard lire at current prices. In the same year, net imports from the North and abroad amounted to 1,787 milliard lire, i.e. over 20 per cent of net income.[2] The

[1] A. Graziani, 'Le Due Italie', *Cassa per il Mezzogiorno: Dodici Anni* 1950-1962, op. cit.
[2] *Studi Monografici sul Mezzogiorno*, op. cit., 1967, pp. 50-1.

absolute deficit was almost equal to gross southern investment—around 2,000 milliard lire. Net imports amounted to about 17 per cent of gross southern income (10,753 milliard lire) and were equivalent to around 5 per cent of Italian net income as a whole (excluding amortization and imports). It is fairly obvious that the South is by no means in a self-supporting position—a large proportion of its present income arising from outside its own boundaries. This is not a new situation. Between 1951 and 1967, net imports averaged around 27 per cent of net southern income.[1] A large proportion of southern growth has thus been a result of outside help. Indeed, looking at the amount of outside help one wonders whether the region should have done better. Its growth rates may have exceeded other countries in the Mediterranean basin or even in Northern Europe but none of these countries has received anything approaching the amount of aid, as a proportion of national income, that has been seen in southern Italy. No independent country could afford to have what is tantamount to a Balance of Payments deficit equivalent to around 20 per cent of gross national income. No independent country would be able to import the equivalent of its gross investments. At a very minimum, around 20 per cent of the South's income growth between 1951 and 1966 can be explained by net imports.

Whether the South has now reached a situation of take-off into self-sustaining growth is a moot point. Certainly all the trends have been accelerating. Yet this can be put down either to a spontaneous development of the southern economy arising out of past long-term efforts or else one can be more pessimistic and see the speedier growth as being mainly a result of additional efforts in the South after 1959. This was the time after all when the industrialization policy became operative, when the law of 1957 was being enforced and when very large investments were being made by the state-controlled firms and finally when a big impetus was given to policy and expenditure through Law 717 in 1965. Our own feeling is inclined towards the more pessimistic view.

Certainly all the past efforts are going to ensure spontaneous growth eventually, but this point does not seem yet to have been reached, nor is it likely to be reached in the near future. The National Plan envisages continued emigration from the South and the need for continued, indeed increased, effort to keep the South moving. Even if the South was able to attain a growth rate equal to that of the North, emigration would still be required well beyond 1980.[2] It

[1] ibid., pp. 50-1; and *Relazione sulla Attività di Coordinamento*, op. cit., 1965, Vol. II, pp. 48-9.   [2] *Ricerca sui Costi d'Insediamento*, op. cit.

will be a long time before the South can be weaned off the vast amount of outside help upon which it still so heavily relies. Undoubtedly the southern economy will continue to improve and probably at an accelerated rate as the more static sectors lose weight and the more dynamic ones grow in importance; as the South increasingly enjoys an infrastructure comparable to that in the North; as increasing industrialization creates a base of external economies. There are also other potentially favourable factors which may help in the future and which have been barely operative in the past, e.g. the rapid development of tourism. Even so, it is more likely to be two generations rather than one before the South is fully integrated and at par with the North and able to operate without large scale assistance.

II. SOUTHERN POLICY—SOME GROUNDS FOR CONCERN, SOME GROUNDS FOR OPTIMISM

The past southern policies which have given the results described above do of course have their faults and can be criticized. One can question the wisdom of the early stress on infrastructure and the belated attention paid to industry; the early allocations of land under the land reform policy were in pieces which were too small; some of the resources have been misspent (though the stories frequently overtower the truth); there has often been poor planning and phasing; some of the resources have been spread too thinly; there has often been poor co-ordination between the Cassa and the ordinary administration. Mistakes are however inevitable in any intervention and particularly in a programme as large as that which has been operated in the South. Southern policy has probably had no more than its fair share of mistakes.

We want to use the space available in this concluding section not to discuss the past mistakes, many of which have anyway been discussed in preceding chapters, but rather to have a look briefly at a number of current issues and aspects of the southern problem and policy which arouse concern. There are six issues which we want to cover. First, the inadequate funds available to the Cassa, particularly in view of the high aspirations for the South in the National Plan. Second, the implications for the South of the development policies in the northern depressed regions. Third, the consequences of the growth centre policy being pursued in the South for the areas outside the selected centres. Fourth, and associated with our second point, the growing and strong disparities *within* the South. Fifth, the shortage of private industrial development, particularly in the medium and small size of firm. And lastly, the question of whether the South is likely to suffer in the future as Italy increasingly experiences the stop-go conditions of other Western Europe countries. These issues are treated in this order below.

Although the funds available to the Cassa are currently greater than in the past, they have not kept pace with the growth of income in Italy and thus the ability of Italy to aid southern development. The current annual allocations to the Cassa are lower, as a proportion of the Italian national income, than they were in the early 1950s. Italy at present spends more money reimbursing industrial exporters for turnover tax and on export credits than the Cassa spends on aiding southern industrial development. Italy is sacrificing proportionately less on southern development today than in the 1950s though the need for rapid growth in the South is as great today as it was then. Considering the problems likely to arise in the North through heavy immigration if greater development is not secured in the South, the need may now be even greater. Not only are the present funds for the Cassa out of line with Italy's ability to contribute such funds but, perhaps more important, the allocations are wildly out of line with what is required if the southern objectives in the National Plan are to be secured. The Cassa's funds are insufficient to finance the aspirations of the Plan for southern development.[1] Inevitably, the prospects of achieving the Plan's southern objectives are thus diminished. It is vital that the allocations to the Cassa for its next planning period (the early 1970s) are more generous.

Even in the North of Italy, there are of course problem areas— areas with high levels of unemployment, a heavy weighting of poor agriculture and high outward migration. The fear of those involved in southern development has always been that the provision of assistance for these areas would dilute the effectiveness of measures for the South. Recent legislation may appear to confirm these fears though there is a danger of exaggerating the likely impact on the South arising out of the level of assistance currently agreed for the North. Law 614 of July 22, 1966, decided the present level of assistance. Assistance for the depressed regions of the North is not novel. Assistance at a level lower than that available in the South has been a feature of post-war Italian regional policy. The areas in the North eligible for assistance under the new legislation are those experiencing depopulation, having a level of income below the national average, lacking in industry, and in a position where there seems little

[1] See Chapter 3.

115

prospect for spontaneous development. The areas are geographically large and usually involve more than one province.

The provisions for the northern depressed regions with respect to industry (the main concern of those who argue that the effectiveness of southern policy could be diluted) are not so comprehensive or so powerful as those for the South. There are no grants, and industrial assistance is limited to financial assistance and exemption from company income tax (*Richezza Mobile*). Medium term loans are available for up to 70 per cent of a firm's total investment at 4 per cent interest rate in Umbria, Marche and Lazio, and 4½ per cent in the remaining, less depressed, regions. On tax concessions there is exemption only from company income tax for new enterprises, and only if the total fixed investment is less than 2 milliard lire. In the case of expanded enterprises, the total investment in the whole plant must still not be in excess of 2 milliard lire. The exemption, as in the South, is for ten years. The incentives for industrial development in the North are thus less comprehensive and weaker than those for the South. Loans are available on slightly less favourable terms and, very important, are limited to small and medium sized firms while tax concessions are similarly limited to this size of enterprise. The maximum value of the northern industrial incentives is around 60 per cent of the southern incentives. Most important, however, is the fact that the funds available to finance extraordinary intervention in the North are extremely small and amount to 200 milliard lire for the five-year period 1966-70—about 12 per cent of the Cassa's funds. The 200 milliard must cover interventions in tourism and public works as well as industry. The sum available for industrial incentives amounts to a mere 12 milliard lire for the five-year period.

There is a danger of becoming too preoccupied about northern development policy as it exists at present. The danger is more that, *in the future*, the funds available for this policy will be greatly extended. Even at present, though not very important, the industrial incentives available for the northern depressed regions do represent some detraction, albeit slight, from southern development. They particularly cut back on the relative attractiveness of the South for the much-needed small and medium-sized firms. Whether the diversion of effort from the South to the northern depressed regions is justified represents more of a political than an economic question. There is certainly no more economic justification for helping the southern than the northern depressed regions. On the political front, it depends how much the northern depressed regions can be tolerated and what weight is given to the much poorer southern regions in the political mind. It needs to be remembered that no northern region has an income per head below that of a southern region. The poorest northern region in terms of income per head in 1967 was Marche, but the level was still about 8 per cent higher than the richest southern region of Puglia.[1]

One point concerning the northern incentives which has disturbed many observers involved in the southern question is the fact that, while a policy of concentration is being pursued for the South, the northern assistance is now to apply over very wide areas.[2] If concentration and concomitant faster growth and associated movements of labour are desirable for the South, one wonders whether they should not also have relevance for the North. Some of the designated northern depressed regions, furthermore, have their boundaries very close to quite large and prosperous northern towns.[3] One, for example, starts a mere four miles west of Ferrara while a particularly large depressed area lies between Ferrara and Bologna—both prosperous cities. Extended travel to work would appear to be a policy more reasonable than that of industrial development. If the existing size of incentives in the North was maintained and the funds to finance them increased, many of the northern depressed regions would, because of their location, be much more attractive to industry than the South in spite of its bigger incentives.

In brief, the areas selected as depressed in the North are large and often very close to major prosperous cities. The location of the areas, and the value of the incentives, could mean that the northern policy represented a considerable detraction to southern development. In practice it is no serious threat at present because the industrial incentives only apply to small and medium-sized firms and, most important, the funds available to pay the incentives are extremely limited. There is a real danger, however, that the funds will be increased and that the larger firms will be declared eligible for assistance. This would then be a very serious threat to southern industrialization policy.

[1] G. Tagliacarne, 'Misura delle Disuguaglianze Interprovinciali dei Redditi e dei Consumi', *Studi di Mercato*, Rome, 1968, No. 4; reprinted in *Informazioni Svimez*, No. 11, June 1969.

[2] In the past, aid has been available only to depressed communes having less than 10,000 inhabitants. About one-third of the total northern population and 95 per cent of communes with less than 10,000 population were eventually designated depressed and eligible for assistance. The new law probably covers a larger proportion of the northern population. See M. Annesi, *Aspetti Giuridici della Disciplina degli Interventi nel Mezzogiorno*, Svimez, Rome, 1966.

[3] For the areas covered see Comitato dei Ministri per gli Interventi Straordinari nelle zone Depresse del Centro-Nord, *Delimitazione delle Zone Depresse*, 1968.

The third of our points for concern arises out of the strong policy of concentration which at present forms such an important part of southern policy. As we have seen, the policy in all sectors is not one of dispersion but strong spatial concentration. The recent legislation (Law 717) has confirmed and strengthened this policy and indeed the Cassa is now directing its efforts for the most part not at the South but at selected areas of industrial, tourist and agricultural development. Even in the field of infrastructure the Cassa will operate mainly in the selected areas.

The areas selected are those which have seen above-average growth in the past and which would anyway probably grow spontaneously even without designation. The rationale behind the policy is that concentration, particularly in the industrial growth centres, will bring these areas closer to simulating the external economies of the North and also give economies in infrastructure provision. Unfortunately, however, the policy of concentration is reinforcing the existing disparities between the bone (*osso*) and the flesh (*polpa*) of the South and leaving large areas, and not insignificant proportions of the population, within the poor *osso*. Under present legislation, these areas are left largely to the ordinary administration. It will be remembered, of course, that the reason behind the creation of the Cassa was the inadequacy of the ordinary administration to deal with the southern problem. Although the ordinary administration is now much improved since the early days and although, as a result of Law 717, the ordinary administration has more clearly defined tasks in the South, there must still remain fear for the parts outside the selected areas. The population in the *osso* is probably around 10 per cent of the southern population. For these people prospects are very poor indeed and for most the only hope is migration which, on the scale required, will inevitably create many, and frequently long-standing, social and economic problems. Mr G. Pastore, during a recent interview, declared that the aim of southern industrial policy was 'concentration of interventions and diffusion of effects'.[1] The former is relatively easy but there is still no certainty as to how the latter can be attained.

That a growth centre policy is a sensible policy for the South there can be little doubt, yet at the same time one wonders whether too little attention has been paid to the outside areas, their problems and feasible policies. At least there is a need to prepare the population for migration and preferably also to guide it. This is not for humani-

---

[1] Interview given to 'Il sole—24 Ore' and reprinted in *Informazioni Svimez*, No. 2-3, January 1967, p. 62.

tarian reasons alone but also on grounds of economic efficiency. At the humanitarian level, however, there is a need to provide, in a co-ordinated and comprehensive fashion, the necessary infra-structure required to give a reasonable standard of life for those who remain. One cannot help feeling that the present *osso* may well be the problem areas with which the Cassa is wholly involved in the not too distant future. Some form of policy now, and at least detailed studies and analysis of these areas, may make the Cassa's possible future task easier.[1]

Our fourth cause for concern is the regional disequilibrium *within* the South. This is somewhat but not wholly related to our third point.

Considerable disparities exist within the South with a few regions, compared with the rest of the South, being well out of line with respect to both their present position and their past performance. The extent of the disparities has only recently been brought fully into the light by attempts to disaggregate data on income, consump-tion, investment, etc.[2] There are sizeable disparities between the poorer southern regions of Calabria, Molise and Basilicata and the richer regions like Campania, Puglia and even Sicily. In 1967 income per head in Calabria (the poorest of the southern regions) was around 70 per cent of income per head in the richest southern region of Puglia.[3]

Although such regional disparities are very high relative to most other European countries, they are not abnormal for Italy and even within the North there are sizeable differences: indeed percentage regional disparities are greater in the North. The poorest northern region of Marche has an income per head which is only 60 per cent of income per head in the three richest northern regions—Valle D'Aosta, Lombardia and Liguria. Italy as a whole is a country of great regional disparities. Our concern over the disparities within the South is not simply that they exist, but that the poorer regions are poor relative to an area which itself is poor, i.e. the South as a whole. Calabria and Basilicata, which contains large tracts of the *osso*, have economies which are more similar to underdeveloped than developed countries and some areas within these regions are

---

[1] Because the problems of the *osso* are so unique and so demanding of attention, it may be worth while for the authorities to consider creating a separate body with adequate funds and with special responsibility for these areas.

[2] *Alcuni Principale Aggregati dei Conti Economici Regionali per gli Anni,* 1963-1964-1965. Published by Unione Italiana delle Camere di Commercio, Industria e Agricultura. For more recent figures see G. Tagliacarne, op. cit.

[3] Tagliacarne, ibid.

distinctly underdeveloped. For humanitarian, social and political reasons, even if not economic, there is a need to take stronger measures to help these very backward regions.

The lack of private industrial development in the South is our fifth concern. About 45 per cent of southern gross industrial investment between 1957 and 1964 was accounted for by the state-controlled firms. A similar proportion holds for the period 1965-68. Without this intervention the progress of the South would obviously have been very much slower than that which has been attained. The development of private enterprise in the South has been very disappointing. It was always hoped that public enterprise would stimulate industrial development in the private sector—the public companies starting the process of industrialization and the private sector following. The figures above indicate the disappointing lack of response so far. There is a real danger of the South becoming the most public enterprise economy in Western Europe if the present trends continue.

The lack of small- and medium-sized enterprise is in spite of the generous incentives schemes; although it should be remembered that these incentives are diminished in value in as far as similar, though less powerful, incentives are available in the North. This size of firm, however, is frequently the most immobile and one cannot help feeling that their development must come from within the South itself. The lack of entrepreneural talent in the South makes one rather pessimistic about their rapid growth. It could be argued that the continuing industrialization of the South will increasingly make the South more attractive for the development of the smaller firm. This, however, will be a slow process.

The authorities are not of course blind to the lack of private enterprise in the smaller size range. The Italians not only have a large range of relevant incentives but also have more positive policy weapons—more so indeed than other Western European countries. IASM and INSUD are both forces which are being used to promote the small- and medium-sized firm. These organizations could be expanded with great benefit to the South.

One recently announced development which, if properly exploited, could give a great impetus to private industry in the South is the Alfa-Sud motor-car plant. With the positive encouragement of supplying industries there could be considerable ancillary development; particularly of the engineering industry which is at present very weak in the South. It would be unfortunate if the development of this plant did not give rise to more ancillary development than was the case when the motor-car industry moved to Scotland. With appropriate policies, the new plant could represent an enormous stimulus to southern industrial development.

Our final point of concern for the South arises out of the effects on the South of the recent Italian recession, 1964-5. In this period the South, relative to the North, did reasonably well and indeed in terms of income per head at current prices, the gap between North and South narrowed. Even so, the level of industrial investment fell seriously in both regions—slightly less in the South, though it could much less afford such a fall. In 1966 however, with the general revival of the economy, the North pulled away rapidly with gross income rising by around 9 per cent as against only 6 per cent in the South. This was almost sufficient to offset the slight reduction of income per head disparities which had taken place between 1963 and 1965. More important perhaps than the trends in the disequilibrium, southern industrial investment continued to fall. In part this might be explained by the delay and uncertainty concerning the final operational form of Law 717.

More important than the movement of income *differentials* between North and South is the fact that the southern growth rate slowed down considerably during the recession. One wonders whether this will be repeated in future years with a consequential reduction in southern growth prospects. Northern Italy is now very much a Western European country and is probably increasingly likely, in the future, to be subjected to the ills of stop-go and slower growth. This does not augur well for the South. Far better that the South grows rapidly, even though slower than the North, than that it grows slowly though faster than the North.

The points above have been what we see as causes of concern and pessimism for the South's future. But there are also optimistic aspects as mentioned above. The South is now on the whole in a much better position to secure faster growth than previously. Agriculture carries less weight while industry (sometimes of the modern type) carries more; tourism, as yet relatively unexploited, could be an important propulsive factor; infrastructure provisions are now more comparable with the North and educational standards are rising constantly. Many of the past efforts of the Cassa were of a long-term nature and they should soon start to pay off. On the credit side also there is the continuing and indeed to some extent increasing interest in the South by the Italian authorities; and there will be continuing pressure by the *meridionalisti*. The traditional spirit of *meridionalismo* is to some extent changing; its emotional character being replaced by more concrete and objective arguments.

The most important sign for optimism is perhaps the fact that

121

there is a growing recognition and acceptance of the national benefits that can arise out of southern development. In particular, recent estimates by SVIMEZ on future Italian population trends and public costs of alternative population distributions, have gained considerable currency and given, for virtually the first time, a quantified estimate of some of the national benefits of faster southern development.[1]

The SVIMEZ work estimates that the labour supply coming on to the Italian market from a variety of sources (natural increase, declining agriculture, declining traditional industries) between 1961 and 1981 will be 5·2 million. The geographical distribution of this supply will be predominantly in the South (66·3 per cent) with a mere 2·6 per cent in the North-West. If the employment growth rate in the South over this period was to be the same as that between 1951 and 1961, 2·37 million workers would need to leave the South. This level of emigration would have severe damaging effects on the South, particularly when added to the heavy emigrations of the period 1950-61. Emigration would take away the better qualified people and, on the scale forecasted, would give rise to considerable social as well as economic problems. If, however, the future southern rate of employment growth was to be the same as the North (as anticipated in the National Plan) the emigration required becomes 1·26 million workers—a high but more tolerable level. However, not only is this second approach more preferable from the southern viewpoint, it also has benefits on the national side. SVIMEZ estimates that the public cost of providing for the population under the first approach would be 6,344 milliard lire of which 1,378 milliard lire would be spent in the South. The second approach would give a lower total cost at 5,667 milliard lire with 2,071 milliard going to the South. Even these calculations underestimate the national saving in as far as more southern development will ease Italian inflationary pressures, many of which arise in the North and which would probably be exacerbated by high levels of immigration.

It is estimates of the SVIMEZ type which give most hope for the South's future. *Meridionalismo* will secure more southern development if it bases its case on such economic rather than emotional arguments. In fact, the new *Meridionalisti* do just that.

'We are not therefore *Meridionalisti* for reasons of birth or political belief, we are *meridionalisti* and have always been, because every day we become more certain that the development of the South represents a contribution to the faster growth of the whole economy.'[2]

[1] *Ricerca sui Costi d'Insediamento*, op. cit.
[2] Part of a speech by the Italian Minister of Finance, Colombo, reported in *Informazioni Svimez*, No. 26-27, 1967, p. 608.

PART II

REGIONAL PROBLEMS
AND POLICIES IN FRANCE

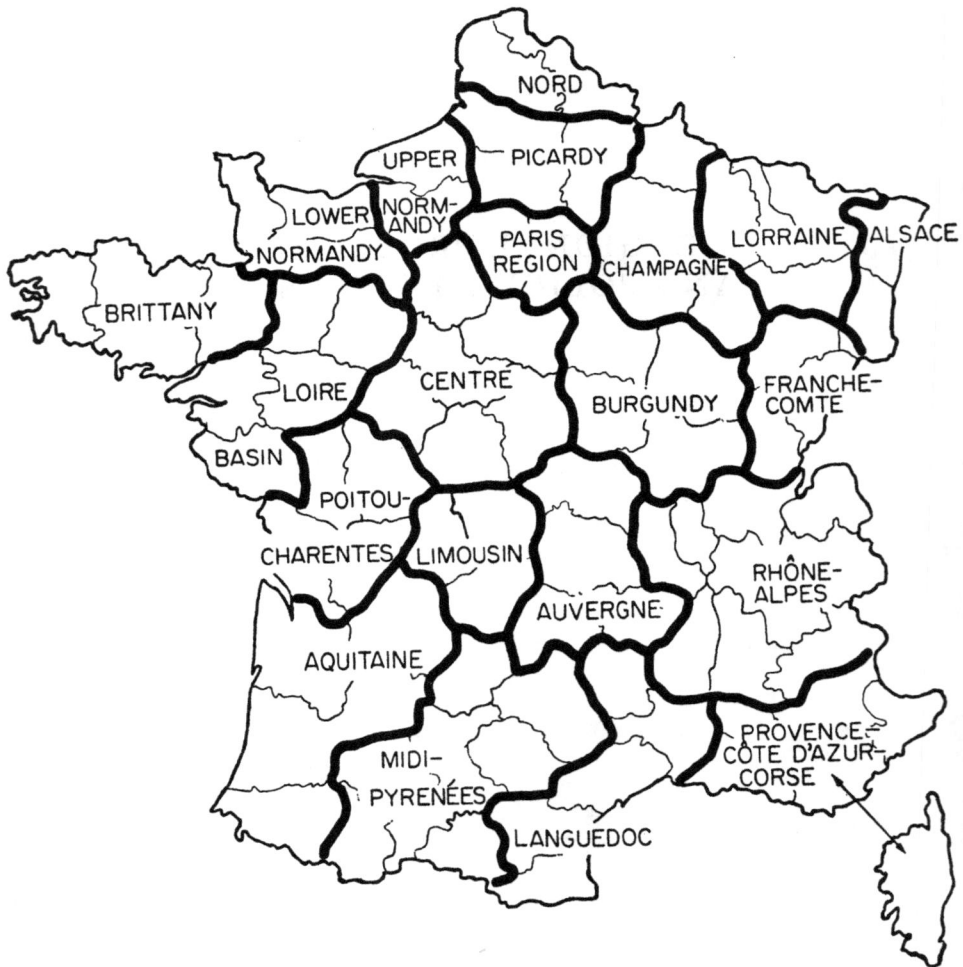

MAP 2: French planning regions

CHAPTER 5

THE REGIONAL PROBLEM
IN FRANCE

The regional problem in France can be expressed very generally in terms of the disparities in the standard of living between the regions in the north and east and those in the south and west. Any such line of demarcation must be to some extent arbitrary, but there are real differences between the 'comfortable' France north and east of a line from Mont-Saint-Michel to Arles, and the 'poor' France to the south and west.[1] By far the most important factor explaining this difference is the concentration of population and economic activity in the Paris region at the expense of the provinces.

While it is useful and important to formulate the regional problem in terms of the relationship between Paris and the rest of France, it is necessary also to distinguish the different forms which the regional problem takes in different parts of the provinces. The broad division between the north and east and the south and west was used by the regional planners in the preliminary regional studies for the Fifth National Plan (1966-70). This division has the merit of treating separately the industrialized and urban regions of the east and the predominantly agricultural regions of the west. In the former the regional problem is essentially one of redevelopment of areas whose economies are based mainly on the older heavy industries and textiles which are now facing a secular decline in demand; in the west the problem is one of introducing manufacturing industry and services to replace a shrinking and rapidly modernizing agricultural sector.

The work on the Fifth Plan moved on to a more refined breakdown which distinguished seven main economic regions each comprising several of the planning regions (*régions de programme*) which were established in 1959 as the basic units for regional planning.[2]

---

[1] For detailed statements of the problem see Claude Delmas, 'L'Aménagement du Territoire', *Que Sais-je?*, PUF, Paris, 1963, and Paul Romus, '*Aspects Européens. Expansion Economique Régionale et Communauté Européenne*, Chapter V.

[2] These were first outlined in the Fourth Plan (1962-65). See *Quatrième Plan*. The same divisions are used by P. Bauchet in his important article 'Regional Development Policies in France', *Area Redevelopment Policies in Britain and the Countries of the Common Market*, US Department of Commerce, Washington, January 1965.

There is, firstly, the *Paris basin* including the regions of Upper Normandy, Picardy, Champagne and Centre. This region is dominated by Paris. Its peripheral areas, particularly Champagne, have suffered as a result of the movement of population into the Paris region proper. This has been partly offset by the decentralization of industry from Paris, particularly in the north and west of the region, but there is still an increasing concentration of population, industry and services around the capital which imposes considerable costs on the economy. The problem of the region is, therefore, the need to halt the growth of Paris and the development of other centres of population to act as counterweights.

The economic region in the *north* of France, made up of two *départements*, Pas de Calais and Nord, is a heavily industrialized region with a high birth-rate, an industrial structure dominated by two declining industries, coal and textiles, and a highly urbanized population living in old and unattractive towns. This combination of circumstances has produced considerable migration and a lower than average income per head. The region poses the problem of redevelopment rather than underdevelopment and requires industrial and physical conversion.

The planning regions of Lorraine, Alsace and Franche-Comté form a natural socio-economic grouping in the *east* of France. This traditionally industrial area shares some of the problems of Nord. Although Lorraine has prosperous steel and metal working industries, Alsace and Franche-Comté, despite the growth of new industries in the latter which is well situated between the Rhine and the Rhône, are still too much dependent on textiles and small-scale artisan trades such as leather goods and furniture. The valleys of the Vosges are particularly backward. A large-scale programme of urban development is also required to modernize and develop heavily built-up and poorly serviced towns such as Metz and Thionville.

The *west* of France, comprising the geographically large planning regions of Brittany, Lower Normandy and the Loire basin, is part of the area known as the 'French desert'. Remote from the main centres of population and poorly endowed with natural resources, the west has for a long period been one of the poorest parts of France and has lost a large proportion of its active population, mainly to the Paris region. The increasing mechanization of agriculture has considerably increased the rate of migration in the last fifteen years. Despite this, underemployment and to a lesser extent unemployment are still serious problems. The problem of the west is, therefore, that of creating modern industrial groupings in a predominantly agricultural area. Progress, which in some individual cases has been quite spectacular, has been made as a result of regional policy measures but, given the inevitable further decline in the numbers employed in agriculture, the creation of industrial complexes adequately provided with the necessary infrastructure is still needed on a large scale if the region is not to become so depopulated as to make future development even more problematical.

The *south-west* is another large area. It includes the planning regions of Poitou-Charentes, Aquitaine and Midi-Pyrenées. Like the west, the main activity is agriculture but, despite a more favourable climate which gives greater scope for improvement, income per head remains low. The development of industry and services is required. There have been important industrial developments within the region, notably around the natural gas deposits at Lacq-Pau and in Toulouse where the French aero-space industry and its auxiliary services are concentrated. But further and more widespread expansion is required. Again, like the west, the south-west is a region where the regional problem will have to be solved by the successful implantation of modern industries in a remote area with a scattered population mainly engaged in agriculture.

The planning regions of Languedoc and Provence-Côte d'Azur constitute the *Mediterranean* region of France. It is a varied region. Languedoc is one of the poorest regions in France with high unemployment, and suffers from an almost exclusive concentration on viniculture, much of it on poorly irrigated land. Provence-Côte d'Azur is, on the other hand, among the more prosperous regions as a result of its highly developed tourist industry. The problems of the region are being tackled in several ways. There is a large-scale irrigation scheme in the Bas-Rhône-Languedoc and, more recently, tourist facilities have been developed along the Languedoc-Rouissillon coast. Industrial development in the region is concentrated around the port activities of Marseilles, and an important new urban and industrial complex is being constructed on the Gulf of Fos.

The planning regions of Limousin and Auvergne are situated in the *Massif Central* in the centre of France, where climatic conditions and infertile soil have led to widespread depopulation of large areas. There are, however, pockets of fertile land both in the north and the south of the region, where agriculture and forestry are being developed. Extensive agriculture is, however, impossible, and, to reduce the very heavy migration from the region, industrial development is necessary. The natural centres for industry are Clermont-Ferrand and St Etienne, but there is also an industrial tradition in the textile towns of Limoges and Saint-Junien and the coal-mining area around Decazeville, although these areas are faced with the problem of rapidly declining industries. Tourism, hitherto not as fully exploited as it could be, is also being expanded in the mountainous region of Puy-de-Dôme, and one of the first national park schemes in France is under way in the Cevennes.

The *south-east* of France is divided between the planning regions of Burgundy and Rhône-Alpes. There is a marked difference in prosperity between the predominantly agricultural region of Burgundy and Rhône-Alpes with its large and increasing concentration of population and modern industries along the Rhône valley centred mainly on Lyons and Grenoble. The development of Lyons as one of the main provincial counterforces to Paris is the key to regional development in the area. The Rhône-Alpes region is one of the three planning regions which have experienced net immigration concentrated almost entirely in the younger, active age groups.

This very brief and general description of the socio-economic regions in France indicates the varied nature of the regional problem. The remainder of this chapter will seek to examine the different aspects of the problem and its causes in more detail.

REGIONAL INCOME DIFFERENCES

Estimates of regional income are shown in Table 5.1.

The most striking feature in the table is of course the disparity between income levels in the Paris region and those in the rest of France. The difference is less when social security benefits in the form of cash payments are taken into account. Most of these latter payments vary with the size of the family, and the average size of family is smaller in the Paris region than in any other region—2·73 persons compared with a national average of 3·11 persons. This correction which, it should be noted, is largely the result of transfer payments from the Paris region and has nothing to do with the economic performance of the regions, still leaves the Paris region very much richer relative to the rest of France than London and the south-east is in relation to the rest of Britain. The gap is admittedly less than that between the North and the South of Italy but the size of the differentials between Paris and the regions of the west and the Massif Central suggests a similar problem of underdevelopment in these areas rather than merely differences in the rate of growth of industrial economies.

Almost equally striking is the absence of any region where incomes come at all near to the Paris level. The income figures, excluding social security benefits, show that every region apart from Paris has an income level below the national average, while those including

TABLE 5.1

HOUSEHOLD INCOMES[1]

Regions	Average annual household income in 1962 excluding social security benefits	Average annual household income in 1962 including social security benefits
1. France	100	100
2. *Paris basin*		
Paris region	151·2	128
Champagne	92·8	92
Picardy	104·0	90
Upper Normandy	99·4	95
Centre	78·7	85
3. *North*		
Nord	94·7	91
4. *East*		
Lorraine	104·0	94
Alsace	99·8	96
Franche-Comté	98·9	93
5. *West*		
Brittany	67·4	87
Lower Normandy	85·8	88
Loire basin	69·3	88
6. *South-west*		
Poitou-Charentes	65·9	87
Aquitaine	77·6	91
Midi-Pyrenées	78·7	90
7. *Mediterranean*		
Languedoc	87·9	91
Provence-Côte d'Azur	101·4	93
8. *Massif Central*		
Limousin	68·6	85
Auvergne	76·3	89
9. *South-east*		
Burgundy	76·5	85
Rhône-Alpes	95·9	96

Source: 'Essai de Régionalisation des Comptes de la Nation, 1962', *Etudes et Conjoncture. Numéro Spécial 1966*, p. 149; and 'Expansion Régionale', *Cahiers du Conseil National des Economies Régionales* No. 2, January 1967, p. 10.

[1] The income figures for each of the planning regions shown in the above table were obtained from the tax returns for the year 1962. They include the income from employment of the head of the household and that of his wife and children, retirement pensions and unearned income in the form of rents, capital gains, etc.

social security benefits show only three regions slightly above it. Of these, Picardy is within the Paris basin while Provence is in many ways an atypical region in terms both of its economic and demographic structure.

A breakdown of the income estimates, excluding social security payments, by socio-professional group allows a more detailed description of the supremacy of the Paris region.[1] As might be expected, the incomes of higher management (146·7) and middle management and the professions (113·6) are well above the national average (100) although in the latter group Lower Normandy has a higher figure (116·7). Apart from Lorraine (141·3), no other region comes anywhere near the Paris level for higher management incomes. The incomes of skilled industrial workers (114·8), office workers (113·3) and unskilled workers (130·7) are similarly high in the Paris region. Only Franche-Comté (124·5) shows a higher figure for skilled workers and Upper Normandy (119·8) is the only region where the income of office workers is higher. The Paris figure for unskilled workers is far above the next region, Upper Normandy (103·2). Paris also has the highest figure for the group 'other categories' (120·7), and for the category of retired persons it takes the third place (143). The high incomes of the managerial groups and the industrial and commercial workers have an important influence on the overall figure for the Paris region where the proportion of household income coming in the form of wages and salaries (net of social benefits) is 52·5 per cent as against an average for the whole of France of 41·0 per cent.[2] The existence of full employment and the range of well-paid jobs in industry and commerce help to explain the high number of women in employment in the Paris region and this in turn elevates the household income figures. Finally, although agriculture accounts for only a tiny fraction of employment in the Paris region it is enormously remunerative. The income of farmers stands at 701·4, seven times the national average and agricultural workers in the region (189·2) are easily the most highly paid.

The income figures suggest that the regions of the Paris basin are affected in differing degrees and in different ways by their proximity to the Paris region. Both estimates of total income show Centre to be the least prosperous region. This is true for all the socio-economic groupings except farmers and agricultural workers. This is associated with a low degree of industrialization in the region and is an example of the attractive power of the Paris region where wages and salaries

[1] *Cahiers du Conseil National des Economies Régionales*, op. cit., table on p. 10.
[2] *Etudes et Conjoncture*, op. cit., p. 144.

are much higher. Upper Normandy, on the other hand, is one of the richest regions outside Paris and wages and salaries in industry and commerce are particularly high. The figure for office workers (119·8) is the highest in France, including the Paris region. This pattern of income suggests that Upper Normandy, which contains the port facilities of the Seine, has the advantage of being near enough the Paris region to attract industrial and commercial firms able to provide a wide range of employment. It is in fact an extension of the Paris region proper. Picardy is less easy to classify. While wages and salaries in industry and commerce are much lower than in Upper Normandy, the figures for top management (117·2), distribution and services (119·7) and retired persons (151·2) are relatively very high. This suggests that Picardy benefits from its proximity to the Paris region by serving as an area where businessmen and wealthy retired people can live and be near Paris. A significant feature of all the regions in the Paris basin including Centre is the high levels of income of farmers. Centre (118·5) is the lowest and Picardy (226·1) is far and away the closest to the Paris region. The same situation holds for agricultural workers in Picardy and Champagne but not, interestingly enough, Upper Normandy (65·5), despite the presence there of a high demand for labour in the industrial sector.

The figures for the north of France reflect the difficulties of this predominantly industrial region. Wages and salaries are generally lower than the industrial regions of the Paris basin and Rhône-Alpes, and top management incomes (94·9), considering the economic structure of the region, are particularly low. Agriculture, as in the Paris region, is remunerative, farmers' income standing at 143·6.

The underdevelopment of the west, south-west and Massif Central regions emerges very clearly from the table. Industrial incomes are the lowest in France, in several cases less than half the Paris level. But agricultural incomes, taking both farmers and agricultural workers, with the exception of Languedoc and Lower Normandy (which can be regarded as part of the Paris basin), are relatively much lower. Since all these regions are heavily dependent on agriculture, this factor has a large influence on the total income figures. The contrast with agricultural incomes in the regions of the Paris basin is extremely marked. In the south-west and the Massif Central the position is improved by the existence of service incomes well above the national average (Limousin [173] has the highest figure in France). This is the case also in Lower Normandy, but in the rest of the west service incomes are extremely low (Loire basin 51·5). The other region where service incomes are high is Provence where the figure for retired persons is also high.

TABLE 5.2

REGIONAL DIFFERENCES IN WAGE AND SALARY INCOMES
(FRANCE = 100)

Regions	Wage and salary incomes in 1962 (net of social security benefits)	Average annual wages and salaries in industry and commerce in 1961 (net of social security benefits)[1]
1. France	100	100
2. *Paris basin*		
Paris region	128	132
Champagne	94	84
Picardy	96	87
Upper Normandy	106	92
Centre	85	78
3. *North*		
Nord	105	89
4. *East*		
Lorraine	118	93
Alsace	110	89
Franche-Comté	99	88
5. *West*		
Brittany	66	76
Lower Normandy	71	78
Loire basin	77	79
6. *South-west*		
Poitou-Charentes	67	76
Aquitaine	82	82
Midi-Pyrénées	74	82
7. *Mediterranean*		
Languedoc	77	81
Provence-Côte d'Azur	94	97
8. *Massif Central*		
Limousin	71	74
Auvergne	75	82
9. *South-east*		
Burgundy	84	84
Rhône-Alpes	109	97

Source: *Etudes et Conjoncture*, op. cit., p. 145, and P. Bauchet, op. cit., p. 158.

[1] These figures exclude farming, forestry and fishing, domestic service and public service. They do, however, include the nationalized industries.

The type of income which is most significant for regional policy is, of course, wages and salaries. Table 5·2 shows the regional differences in wages and salaries.

The two indices of regional wage and salary levels give markedly similar results. The gap between income levels in Paris and those in the rest of France remains large. The exclusion of the generally poorer paid agricultural workers and public service employees enhances the difference and indicates the predominant position which Paris has of high income industries. It is, however, significant that Rhône-Alpes moves from fourth to second place when the industrial measure is used, reflecting the growth of new and sophisticated industries in the region. At the other end of the spectrum the regions in the west, south-west and the Massif Central remain firmly in the lowest rankings, registering very low incomes in both agriculture and industry. Limousin in fact drops to the bottom of the list when industrial incomes only are considered. Midi-Pyrenées, on the other hand, shifts upwards, suggesting a higher level of industrial development.

The other ranking changes are not unexpected. Centre moves down from ninth to fourteenth place when its relatively prosperous agriculture is left out, and Provence moves from eighth to second on the strength mainly of its highly paid commercial sector.

UNEMPLOYMENT

From the end of the war until late in the 1950s the working population in France did not increase, and would indeed have declined but for immigration, and the demand for labour has been high. The level of unemployment has consequently been very low. There has been very considerable emigration from agriculture to industry and services, but the generally tight conditions of the labour market have normally allowed this to be absorbed without causing serious unemployment. In these circumstances it is not surprising that regional imbalance has not shown itself primarily in the form of heavy unemployment or underemployment as in Italy and, to a much lesser extent, in Britain.

There are, however, some regions where unemployment tends to be consistently higher than the national average. M. Bauchet has produced estimates of regional unemployment for each *département* in 1962, using as a measure the number of job-seekers per 10,000 of industrial working population.[1] The figure for France as a whole is 132 unemployed per 10,000 working population. The highest

[1] P. Bauchet, op. cit., p. 141.

unemployment rates registered were in Hérault, 637, Aude, 443, and Pyrenées Orientales, 422—all in the Languedoc region—Morbihan in Brittany, 476, and Alpes Maritimes in Provence, 519. The lowest rates are all concentrated in seven *départements* in the north-east where the lowest figure is Moselle, 13, and the highest Meurthe et Moselle, 36. M. Bauchet's figures are expressed in terms of the working population in 1954, since the 1962 Census results were not available to him. Since working population declined over the inter-censal period in some of the less prosperous regions, this method of calculation exaggerates the problem in these areas. Using the 1962 figures for working population, however, still produces results which are very low, even allowing for the unreliability and incompleteness of the figures, and which are at considerable variance with the very sizeable differences in income levels.

POPULATION GROWTH AND MIGRATION

Part of the explanation of the low regional unemployment figures is, of course, the emigration which has occurred from all but a very few regions.

Table 5.3 shows the very substantial immigration into the Paris region over the period 1954-62. In only four other regions was there net immigration and it was sizeable in only two of these: Rhône-Alpes and Provence-Côte d'Azur. Net emigration was highest in the poorest regions of the west and south, particularly in two regions of the Brittany peninsula, Brittany and Lower Normandy. The increasing concentration of population in the Paris region to which this pattern of migration has contributed has been strengthened by the low birth-rates in the west, south-west and the Massif Central. The population of Limousin has in fact declined absolutely over the period. These regions have also lost population due to migration overseas (not shown in the table). Conversely, the natural increase of the Paris region has been higher than at any time since the latter part of the nineteenth century and it has also attracted immigrants from overseas.

Apart from the Paris region, the other areas with net immigration have been Rhône-Alpes and Provence. The age structure of the immigrants in these two regions is, however, very different. In Rhône-Alpes almost the whole of the net immigration is evenly divided between the age-groups 'under 25' and '25 to 54'. In Provence, one-third of the immigrants are over 55. These figures reflect the different industrial structures of the two regions, Rhône-Alpes attracting younger active age-groups to its expanding new industries while in

TABLE 5.3

NET INTER-REGIONAL MIGRATION 1954–62[1]

Regions	Total net migration ('000s)	Total net migration as percentage of total population in 1954	Change in total population as percentage of total population in 1954	Percentage of total population in 1962
1. France	0	—	+8·1	100
2. *Paris basin*				
Paris region	+326·3	+4·5	+14·9	18·3
Champagne	−25·9	−2·3	+5·5	2·6
Picardy	−19·5	−1·4	+6·0	3·2
Upper Normandy	−10·2	−0·8	+8·0	3·0
Centre	+3·6	+0·2	+4·8	4·0
3. *North*				
Nord	−45·9	−1·4	+6·8	7·8
4. *East*				
Lorraine	−7·6	−0·4	+12·3	4·7
Alsace	+4·9	+0·4	+7·1	2·8
Franche-Comté	−1·4	−0·2	+8·1	2·0
5. *West*				
Brittany	−93·0	−4·0	+1·5	5·1
Lower Normandy	−52·2	−4·5	+2·8	2·6
Loire basin	−52·6	−2·3	+5·2	5·3
6. *South-west*				
Poitou-Charentes	−37·1	−2·7	+3·5	3·1
Aquitaine	−9·4	−0·4	+4·5	5·0
Midi-Pyrenées	−31·9	−1·6	+3·6	4·5
7. *Mediterranean*				
Languedoc	−35·1	−2·4	+6·7	3·4
Provence-Côte d'Azur	+78·3	+3·2	+16·4	6·6
8. *Massif Central*				
Limousin	−20·3	−2·7	−1·3	1·6
Auvergne	−15·0	−1·2	+1·8	2·7
9. *South-east*				
Burgundy	−5·1	−0·4	+3·9	3·1
Rhône-Alpes	+49·1	+1·3	+10·1	8·7

Source: Projet de Loi des Finances pour 1967, Vol. III, Imprimerie Nationale, Paris, 1966, p. 326.

[1] The period covered by this table excludes consideration of an important factor influencing internal migration since 1962, namely, the return from Algeria in that year of almost one million repatriates. For the most part these immigrants have settled in the south and west of France and the major cities.

Provence migration into retirement is much more important. This is not to say that Provence does not provide employment opportunities for younger age-groups. In fact 52,000 of the immigrants to the region were under 54 compared with 48,000 in Rhône-Alpes and, even if there had been no immigration at all in the over-55 age-group, Provence would have been the most attractive region next to Paris. The net immigration into Provence is explained mainly by the large positive balance with the Paris region; this accounts for 22 per cent of total net immigration into the region. The regions of Nord and Lorraine provide another 13 per cent as do Languedoc and Aquitaine. The major link is therefore still with the Paris region, in the form of a flow of retired persons to one of the most desirable parts of France. The exchanges with Languedoc and Aquitaine are more plausibly interpreted in terms of the employment opportunities offered in the tertiary sector and by the industrial developments around Marseilles.

The pattern of net immigration into Rhône-Alpes is of much greater economic significance. Here exchanges with Paris are unimportant. Almost 70 per cent of total net immigration results from positive balances with Limousin and, much more important, Auvergne in the Massif Central, the south-west and the neighbouring (mainly agricultural) regions of Burgundy and Languedoc. It is also interesting to note that 4·5 per cent is provided by Nord. These figures for Rhône-Alpes are important for they suggest that the southeast of France is beginning to emerge as a potentially important counterweight to the Paris region and that, for the first time in the twentieth century, there is the possibility that Paris may cease to be the only possible destination and source of employment for the vast majority of migrants.

The considerable net migration from west, south and central France is explained entirely by movements of the working population; all of these regions experienced net immigration in the over-55 age-group. This is very largely the obverse of the net emigration of 83,000 in this age-group from the Paris region. These regions, particularly the three in the west, are essentially tributaries to the Paris region and the regions of the Paris basin. Its negative balance with the Paris region alone accounts for 83 per cent of total net emigration from Lower Normandy, while the figures for Brittany and the Loire basin are 65 per cent and 64 per cent respectively.

The other region with a serious population loss is Nord. More than half of total net emigration is to the Paris region. The other important exchanges are between the neighbouring region of Lorraine and Rhône-Alpes and Provence.

Table 5.4 shows the movement of working population broken down into three broad categories. The regions where employment increased over the period are, predictably, the Paris region, Lorraine

TABLE 5.4

GROWTH OF WORKING POPULATION 1954-62

Regions	Working population (percentage change)				Net inter-regional migration of working population as percentage of working population in 1954
	Agriculture, forestry and fishing	Manufacturing and extractive industries (including construction)	Transport, distribution and services	Total	
1. France	−24·9	+7·1	+13·0	+0·4	0
2. *Paris basin*					
Paris region	−29·1	+8·3	+14·6	+10·7	+7·8
Champagne	−21·8	+7·7	+4·9	−1·1	−2·4
Picardy	−26·6	+13·7	+10·5	+1·3	−2·5
Upper Normandy	−21·4	+7·7	+7·8	+1·4	−1·0
Centre	−20·9	+17·1	+17·6	−0·7	−1·3
3. *North*					
Nord	−23·4	−4·6	+11·0	−2·1	−1·5
4. *East*					
Lorraine	−27·5	+1·5	+21·1	+3·3	−0·1
Alsace	−37·1	+0·9	+11·9	−3·4	+0·4
Franche-Comté	−29·1	+13·2	+5·7	−1·4	−0·3
5. *West*					
Brittany	−22·3	+0·9	+14·5	−7·6	−5·4
Lower Normandy	−17·1	+2·9	+10·5	−4·3	−5·8
Loire basin	−25·2	+6·1	+13·1	−6·0	−3·3
6. *South-west*					
Poitou-Charentes	−24·8	+4·5	+18·1	−5·4	−3·8
Aquitaine	−28·7	+10·8	+9·8	−6·7	−1·8
Midi-Pyrénées	−19·9	+6·4	+13·2	−4·2	−2·7
7. *Mediterranean*					
Languedoc	−18·5	+9·6	+13·0	0	−4·3
Provence-Côte d'Azur	−11·9	+22·9	+14·0	+9·6	+1·6
8. *Massif Central*					
Limousin	−26·8	+1·9	+4·4	−12·4	−4·3
Auvergne	−17·6	+1·9	+5·3	−9·8	−2·4
9. *South-east*					
Burgundy	−17·3	+11·7	+7·6	−3·9	−2·7
Rhône-Alpes	−18·7	+12·7	+15·5	+2·6	+1·4

Source: Projet de Loi des Finances pour 1967, op. cit., p. 326.

and the south-east. The migration figures show the same pattern, immigration being particularly important as a source of manpower in the Paris region and Rhône-Alpes. The indicators for the regions of the west, centre and south are again unfavourable, the effects of migration being most significant in Lower Normandy, Brittany,

Poitou-Charentes and Languedoc. The other region where net emigration has been significant is Nord, in contrast to the neighbouring industrial regions of Lorraine and Franche-Comté.

In all regions there has been a substantial reduction in the numbers employed in agriculture. It has been proportionately greatest in regions such as the Paris basin where agricultural productivity is rising most rapidly as a result of mechanization and reorganization and those like Franche-Comté and Aquitaine where employment opportunities in other sectors exist in the region.

By far the most rapid increase in employment in manufacturing has been in Provence. An important influence here is the high level of activity in the construction industry in that region. The other regions where manufacturing employment has expanded are in the Paris basin, Franche-Comté and the south-east. The large increase in Aquitaine is explained largely by the natural gas and petrochemical developments at Lacq. Manufacturing employment in the Paris region has grown just slightly faster than the national average, but this must be seen in the context of the controls put on development in the Paris region since 1955 and the rapid expansion in the neighbouring regions of Picardy, Centre and Burgundy. Nord is the only region where manufacturing employment has fallen. This reflects the acute problems posed by declining industries, notably the coal industry, in this predominantly industrial region. Lorraine and Alsace show similarly small increases which contrast sharply with the expansion that has taken place in Franche-Comté. There has, however, been a large increase in service employment in Lorraine. Expansion has also been very limited in the Massif Central, Lower Normandy and Brittany and also in Poitou-Charentes which has not benefited from the industrial development in other parts of the south-west. The figure for Brittany is very low indeed, the major source of expansion in the west being in the Loire basin where Nantes-St Nazaire is the main industrial area of the whole west coast.

Employment in transport and services has, over the whole economy, grown twice as fast as in the manufacturing sector. Regional variations have also been less. The most rapid increase has been in Lorraine and in regions with obvious service centres such as the Paris region, Provence and Rhône-Alpes. Service employment of a different kind has, however, also grown rapidly in the regions of the west and in Poitou-Charentes.

A recent study has attempted to test, for the period 1954-62, the relationship between inter-regional migration and employment growth in the different regions, using the concept of an 'in-migration' location quotient.[1] This ratio measures the importance of in-migration in a particular industrial sector of the economy into a particular region taking as unity the percentage of total inter-regional migration accounted for by persons in that sector. This is then compared firstly with the employment location quotient of that sector in the region concerned (i.e. the importance of total employment in that sector in the region, taking as unity the proportion of total national employment in the sector), and secondly with the growth of employment in the sector in the region. These three indicators can be used to identify which sectors in which regions are the most attractive to in-migrants, taking into account by means of the employment location quotient the initial importance of each sector in each region as well as the rates of growth of employment.

Mr Fielding applies this test to four different types of region—the Paris region, Nord, Brittany and Aquitaine—and draws some interesting conclusions. In the Paris region, relative to the initial size of the sectors, the highest in-migration occurred in agriculture, extractive industries, domestic service and transport. Apart from transport, where employment grew at about an average rate, these were sectors where employment fell during the period studied. In contrast, apart from building and public works, all the fast-growing sectors which were heavily represented in the Paris region had relatively lower in-migrant location quotients. Mr Fielding argues that in the case of Paris migrants come first to low-paid, relatively unskilled jobs and that vacancies in the sectors requiring higher qualifications are filled by Parisians. This is a different situation from that shown for Aquitaine where migration was heaviest in the previously small petroleum products and chemicals sector as a result of the development of the petro-chemical complex based on the natural gas find at Lacq. Here the type of labour required was in the main skilled and, in the absence of a suitably qualified indigenous workforce it has apparently been necessary to import skilled workers from other regions. Some of these may have come from the Paris region which, with Poitou-Charentes and Midi-Pyrénées, constituted the major source of immigration to Aquitaine. But since the latter two neighbouring regions, both offering limited employment opportunities, provided one-third of the immigration to Aquitaine there are grounds for supposing that the developments in Aquitaine attracted suitably qualified or quickly trainable workers from all over the south-west of France.

In Nord and Brittany the results confirm the impressions already

[1] A. J. Fielding, 'Internal Migration and Regional Economic Growth—A Case Study of France', *Urban Studies*, Vol. 3, No. 3, November 1966.

got from other indicators. Brittany has a very high concentration of employment in agriculture with relatively little in-migration. This reflects the predominance of small farms run by their owners and a sufficiently high birth-rate to provide for the succession. This is in marked contrast to the regions in the Paris basin which have experienced a sizeable inflow of farm workers to work in the large modernized farms. In-migration is highest in the more highly paid parts of the services sector, i.e. those parts other than domestic service. This phenomenon may be partly explained by the absence of employment opportunities for immigrants in these sectors in the Paris region which is suggested by the low in-migration figures there. The outstanding feature in Nord is its extremely large employment location quotients in coal and textiles and in consequence in-migration from other regions is low.

INDUSTRIAL STRUCTURE

Information on the industrial structures of the twenty-one planning regions has been made available as a result of the preparation of regional accounts relating to the year 1962. This is shown in Table 5.5. The major feature here is once again the massive dominance of the Paris region which accounts for 25 per cent of total national value added at factor cost. Next in rank comes Rhône-Alpes with 9 per cent and Nord with 8 per cent. Fourteen regions each account for less than 4 per cent of the national figure.

Table 5.5 shows the substantial importance of agriculture in all regions except the Paris region and the industrialized areas of the north and east. Manufacturing industry is predominant in the Paris basin, the north and east and in Rhône-Alpes and noticeably lacking in the three regions of the west as well as in Poitou-Charentes and Languedoc. The amount of manufacturing in the Paris region is high for an area dominated by the capital city of a highly centralized economy. In the rest of the Paris basin the difference between Centre and the more northerly regions is very marked. There is a significant difference, too, in the south-west between Poitou-Charentes and the rest of the region where some industrialization has occurred.

The pattern for the tertiary sector is more uniform, reflecting the widely differing activities falling within this heading and also the influence of the construction industry. Services are most important in Provence where the weight of construction is also significant. Next comes the Paris region. Services are much more heavily represented there than in Champagne, Picardy and Upper Normandy but they

TABLE 5.5

VALUE ADDED BY SECTOR (1962)   (percentage)

Regions	Agriculture	Manufacturing industry	Construction and services[1]
1. France	13·5	46·0	40·5
2. *Paris basin*			
Paris region	1·4	52·2	46·4
Champagne	21·5	43·8	34·7
Picardy	23·2	45·2	31·6
Upper Normandy	15·6	49·5	34·9
Centre	22·2	35·0	42·8
3. *North*			
Nord	10·3	59·5	30·2
4. *East*			
Lorraine	7·6	60·1	32·3
Alsace	9·5	51·3	39·2
Franche-Comté	12·4	57·9	29·7
5. *West*			
Brittany	30·2	24·8	45·0
Lower Normandy	33·8	27·4	38·8
Loire basin	24·3	36·6	39·1
6. *South-west*			
Poitou-Charentes	29·6	28·9	41·5
Aquitaine	19·0	38·6	42·4
Midi-Pyrenées	19·7	39·1	41·2
7. *Mediterranean*			
Languedoc	29·0	30·6	40·4
Provence-Côte d'Azur	10·4	35·5	54·1
8. *Massif Central*			
Limousin	22·5	38·8	38·7
Auvergne	19·3	42·3	38·4
9. *South-east*			
Burgundy	18·6	41·4	40·0
Rhône-Alpes	9·1	53·8	37·1

Source: Etudes et Conjoncture, op. cit., p. 131.

[1] Transport and communications are not included. No regional breakdown has been made for this sector.

are very significant in Centre as they are in most of the poorer agricultural regions.

A more precise measure of the importance of different industries in different regions can be obtained by using location quotients. The location quotient can be calculated in two ways. The first method is to express the proportion which the value added of industry X represents of the total value added in region Y as a fraction of the proportion which value added in industry X represents of the value added in the nation as a whole. The second is to express the proportionate contribution which value added in industry X in region Y makes to the total value added in region Y as a fraction of the contribution which the total value added of region Y makes to the value added in the nation as a whole. A location quotient (calculated in either of these ways) of unity indicates that the importance of industry X in region Y is the same as the importance of industry X in the nation as a whole. Location quotients (LQs) have been calculated for nineteen sectors of the economy for each of the twenty-one planning regions.[1] Some of the main results of this study are summarized below.

The Paris region has a high degree of specialization in all the service sectors (particularly the 'service' of providing housing, i.e. the counterpart of income from rent), mechanical and electrical engineering and motor-cars, chemicals and petro-chemicals, paper and printing and plastics. All these industries have shown rapid rates of growth of output over the period 1959-65.[2] Only Franche-Comté has a higher LQ in the varied, rapidly expanding sector electrical and mechanical engineering and motor-cars. The rest of the Paris basin excluding Centre shows a specialization in manufacturing industry, notably building materials, engineering (in Champagne), chemicals and food. Upper Normandy has a very high LQ in the oil and natural gas sector.

The regions of the north and east also have their highest LQs in the manufacturing sector but in different industries from the Paris region. Nord's greatest specialization is in coal, textiles, iron and steel and construction materials. In the east, Lorraine has a huge LQ in iron and steel (10·43) and is highly represented in coal and electricity. Alsace, on the other hand, shows a higher than average specialization in the fast-growing sectors of engineering and motor-cars and chemicals, which are not strongly represented in either Lorraine or Nord. It also has a high LQ in textiles. Franche-Comté has the distinction of having the highest LQ in engineering and

[1] *Etudes et Conjoncture*, op. cit., pp. 159-85.
[2] *Projet de Loi de Finances pour* 1967. Vol. II, pp. 234-51.

motor-cars (2·23) mainly due to the expansion of the motor-car industry there, and also has a high share (1·48) of the synthetics fibre industry. The other region emerging as specialized in the growth sectors of manufacturing is Rhône-Alpes. The region has, however, also a high representation in textiles although the growth of synthetic fibres is to some extent offsetting this.

The regions specializing in manufacturing industry are thus very different in structure. There is a large concentration of the modern, fast-growing industries in the Paris basin and particularly in the Paris region itself. These industries are also represented in Rhône-Alpes and to a more limited extent in Franche-Comté. The economies of Alsace and Lorraine are still based to a sizeable extent on coal, iron and steel and textiles, while Nord has the classic characteristics of an old, industrial area.

The three regions in the west have the highest LQs in agriculture and above-average representation in the services which here are mainly vehicle and machinery repair activities. Food processing is also highly represented. The Loire basin has an above-average share of the oil and natural gas sector and a much larger share (LQ of 0·78) of engineering and motor-cars than any of the other regions in which the growing sectors of manufacturing are poorly represented. This reflects the influence of the Nantes-St Nazaire area which is the only industrial area in the west. Much of the engineering sector here is in fact shipbuilding and related engineering activities.

The two regions of the Massif Central are, predictably, heavily under-represented in manufacturing industry. Limousin has some specialization in resource based activities such as electricity and wood, and the Michelin tyre plant at Clermont-Ferrand gives Auvergne a high LQ for the chemical and rubber industries. A similar pattern obtains in the south-west, where the natural gas find at Lacq is reflected in a high LQ for natural gas and a barely above-average share in the synthetics sector in Aquitaine. The main features in Provence-Côte d'Azur are high LQs in services and construction. The growth sectors of manufacturing industry are not heavily represented with the exception of non-ferrous metals, although the LQ for chemicals and rubber (0·97) is fairly high.

Table 5.6 gives a general indication of the concentration of industrial power in the different regions as measured by the head offices of large firms. It shows the very high proportion of industrial control exercised by Paris relative to its share of the working population and by implication its contribution to national production. The effects of this concentration in economic, social, administrative and political terms is observably large and as a result the area of influence of the

TABLE 5.6
HEAD OFFICES OF LARGE FIRMS[1]   (percentages)

Regions	Head offices of important firms in 1954	Working population in 1954	Head offices of important firms in 1962	Working population in 1962
1. France	100	100	100	100
2. *Paris basin*				
Paris region	54·7	18·9	51·9	20·1
Champagne	2·1	2·5	2·1	2·5
Picardy	1·6	2·9	1·6	2·9
Upper Normandy	2·9	2·9	2·5	2·9
Centre	1·0	4·1	1·6	4·0
3. *North*				
Nord	9·7	7·2	8·0	7·0
4. *East*				
Lorraine	3·0	4·2	3·4	4·3
Alsace	3·7	2·9	3·7	2·8
Franche-Comté	1·0	2·0	1·1	2·0
5. *West*				
Brittany	0·7	5·7	1·4	5·2
Lower Normandy	0·6	2·8	0·8	2·7
Loire basin	1·6	5·7	1·8	5·3
6. *South-west*				
Poitou-Charentes	0·8	3·1	0·9	2·9
Aquitaine	2·0	5·4	2·2	5·0
Midi-Pyrenées	0·9	4·6	1·3	4·4
7. *Mediterranean*				
Languedoc	1·0	2·8	1·6	2·8
Provence-Côte d'Azur	3·0	5·3	3·8	5·9
8. *Massif Central*				
Limousin	0·4	1·9	0·5	1·7
Auvergne	0·6	3·0	0·9	2·7
9. *South-east*				
Burgundy	1·3	3·1	1·2	3·0
Rhône-Alpes	7·5	8·9	8·0	9·1

Source: Projet de Loi de Finances pour 1967, Vol. III, op. cit., p. 368.

[1] The firms covered in the table are those which, according to tax returns, had a minimum annual turnover of £735,000 in 1955 and (to take account of the rise in prices) £1 million in 1962.

Paris region is vastly superior to that of any other urban centre in France.[1] To take an example from the table, Rhône-Alpes, with Lyons as its central focus, has half the Paris region's share of working population but only one-seventh of its share of the largest firms.

Of the other regions, only Nord and Alsace have a greater share of the largest firms than they have of working population, but the orders of magnitude are entirely different from those in the Paris region. The nature of these regions' economies suggests in addition that the large firms in them have a mainly regional influence, whereas the concentration in the Paris region is such that many of the large firms there exercise considerable influence in many other regions. There is the further point that the largest firms, particularly in Nord, are by the nature of what they produce expanding less rapidly than those in the Paris region. This further reduces the significance of the figures for that region. A contrast of some interest with Nord and Alsace is Rhône-Alpes. Here the industrial structure, at least in 1962, is more oriented towards the newer, growing industries, but its share of the largest firms is still below its share of employment. The interesting question here is whether this region, the main counterweight to Paris, is on the way to reversing this situation and producing or attracting large firms in the kind of numbers that will allow it to stimulate the subsequent induced development in its many aspects which currently makes Paris unique.

The development of the situation over the period 1954-62 has to be interpreted in the light of the various regional policy measures introduced during that time whose efficacy will be discussed in Chapter 11. The figures must also be treated with caution in view of the considerable changes in the structure, organization and ownership of industries which have taken place since 1954. It is, nevertheless, worth noting that relative to working population the only regions to reduce their share of the largest firms have been the Paris region and its industrial neighbours in the Paris basin (Centre has made a fairly definite gain) and, for quite different reasons, Nord.

CONCLUSION

The above description of the regional problem in France allows some general comments to be made. The first is that the problem is a large one no matter what indicator is used. The disparities in income levels between the richer and poorer regions and the differences in industrial structures are too large to be tolerated in a modern western industrialized economy. Any attempts to reduce these

[1] This point is discussed in Chapter 8 below.

differences must involve some reduction in the concentration of population and employment in the Paris region. It must also involve the expansion of one or more cities in the provinces to a size and form which will reduce the huge gap in size and economic and social influence which exists between Paris and the next largest French city. It can be argued that such a policy would ensure a more efficient allocation of resources by reducing the 'congestion costs' of the Paris region but in the French context this is a point that cannot be taken too much for granted.[1]

One of the reasons for the magnitude of the regional problem is the fact that in the west, south-west and centre of France the problem is broadly one of introducing modern industries and service activities, together with the necessary infrastructure, to areas which are predominantly agricultural and where full employment at a reasonable level of income cannot be provided by an agricultural industry which is becoming very rapidly highly mechanized and capital intensive. There are other regions in the north and east where the regional problem is one of converting regional economies dominated by old-established, declining industries. In some areas, notably the Nord region, the situation is acute but the success of policies to deal with regional inequalities will depend ultimately on their achievements in the west and south-west.

A feature of the French regional problem which is at first glance somewhat surprising, especially to the British observer, is the relatively low level of unemployment in the poorer regions. The problem presents itself rather in the form of heavy out-migration from the poorer regions in the south and west, mostly to the Paris region. The need in these regions is, therefore, not the creation of jobs in particular localities where unemployment is especially high but the provision of industrial employment on a sufficient scale to reduce migration significantly. This in turn suggests that development efforts should be concentrated in locations which have some prospect of sustaining industrial and service expansion of the size required. The following chapters will be concerned with the development of regional policy and its success in dealing with the problems discussed above.

---

[1] One estimate has put the cost of providing public services (roads, schools, hospitals, police, public transport) for an additional family in a Paris suburb at £3,676 as against £2,573 in a provincial town. See P. George *et al.*, *La Région Parisienne*, PUF, Paris 1964. But against this must be set the loss in efficiency which may arise if firms are persuaded or directed to expand in the poorer regions where a number of locational disadvantages may exist and persist for varying periods of time.

CHAPTER 6

THE DEVELOPMENT OF REGIONAL
POLICY IN FRANCE 1945-1958

Legislation to deal with the problems posed by the considerable disparities in the standard of living among the different regions of France was not introduced until the post-war period, and not until the middle of the 1950s was any serious effort made to control and influence economic development in the various regions. Since then, and particularly since the early 1960s, regional development has become an increasingly important aspect of national economic policy, and many far-reaching measures have been introduced to encourage and organize the expansion of all the regions of the country. It is important always to keep in mind that this considerable activity is very recent in origin and is the result of a definite evolution of thought about 'the regional problem' which has occurred during the post-war years. It is one of the interesting features of regional development policies in Western European economies that they have all, in differing degrees and forms, shown a similar growth from being a peripheral concern of the central government to one of its major preoccupations in the field of national economic policy.

The evolution of thought and action on the regional problem in France in the last twenty years can be broken down into three main phases.[1]

The first covers the period 1945-54. During this time the first pieces of legislation on regional policy were introduced. Most of the measures took the form of controls on the development of certain regions rather than incentives to encourage expansion. Professor Lajugie refers to this period as one of *aménagement ordonnateur* or 'controlled development'.

The second phase of regional policy lasted from 1954 to 1957. During this time the dominant concern of regional policy was to promote the decentralization of industry from the Paris region. A considerable number of incentives designed to encourage industry

[1] See Professor J. Lajugie, 'Aménagement du Territoire et Développement Economique Régionale en France (1945-1964),' *Revue d'Economie Politique,* Jan.-Feb. 1964, No. 1, p. 278.

to expand in the less prosperous regions were introduced at this time and these are usually considered as the first serious official steps actively to promote regional development.

By 1958, and certainly by 1960, a third phase can be detected. Regional development gradually came to be set more and more in the context of policies aimed at increasing national economic growth and as an integral and increasingly important aspect of the medium-term national plans for economic expansion. Regional policy and regional development thus became much more closely related to national economic policy and, as a result, were given much greater emphasis in the national plans. This, in turn, led to the development of a system of regional planning integrated into the framework of the national plans. These innovations provoked considerable conceptual and institutional changes. The emphasis on the contribution which regional development could make to national economic expansion encouraged examination of the necessary conditions for growth within the less prosperous regions. The difficulties of creating these conditions, while at the same time seeking to assist every locality where the symptoms of lagging development were present, quickly became apparent and led to a much more selective definition of the areas to which aid should be given. The larger role of regional development also required the establishment of new institutions and the reform of existing ones to carry it out, and from 1960 onwards extremely far-reaching administrative changes have been introduced with the specific objective of creating an administrative framework more suited to the needs of planned regional development.

The publication of the Fifth National Plan in 1966 may be said to mark the beginning of yet another phase of regional policy. The plan insists that efforts to develop the less prosperous regions must recognize the constraints which limit the expansion of the national economy and, most particularly, the need for increased competitiveness to meet the pressures of foreign competition which the Common Market has produced. Expenditure on regional development must, therefore, be required to yield a return in the form of increased national output, and the promotion of expansion in the less prosperous regions must not be carried to the point where it impedes or slows up expansion in the more prosperous and faster growing regions whose contribution to increased national productivity is of crucial importance.

To divide the evolution of regional policy in France into these stages is, of course, a simplification. But it does serve to highlight the very definite maturing of thought on the problem of regional imbalance and the growing extent to which regional development has become recognized as a necessary part of any policy aimed at increasing national output. This chapter will deal with the period up to 1958.

I. ORIGINS OF REGIONAL POLICY, 1945-54

Regional policy in France did not come into existence until the post-war period. Some decentralization from the Paris region to the south-west and Toulouse was encouraged and assisted in certain industries in the 1930s, but this was purely for strategic reasons. It was limited for the most part to the aircraft industry. The economic possibilities of such a policy for regional development were scarcely considered and, indeed, the firms concerned ran into serious diffi-culties over the recruitment, the housing and the rates of payment of workers. There was, moreover, little consideration of the problems of setting up a firm in a new location away from suppliers and ser-vices. Economically speaking, therefore, the experiment was a disappointment.

The first serious studies of the regional problem began with an analysis of the problem of decentralizing industry from established industrial centres, particularly the Paris region. These studies, which included several case studies, were undertaken by the Direction de l'Equipement National of the Ministère de l'Economie Nationale under the direction of M. Dessus in the years 1943-45. Regional initiatives began with the formation of a Comité d'Etudes et d'Aménagement de la Région de Reims in 1943 with the objective of producing an economic survey of the region and suggesting policies to deal with its economic problems.

In 1945 a special section was created in the Ministry of Recon-struction and Housing (Ministère de la Reconstruction et de l'Urbanisme) to deal with industrial decentralization and regional development.[1] But it was not until 1947 that regional development really became recognized as an important national issue. In that year, J. F. Gravier published his work *Paris et le désert français*[2] which drew attention in considerable detail to the disparities that existed between Paris and the regions of the south and west of France, which thereafter were known as 'the French desert'.

---

[1] This ministry has frequently been renamed. Its tasks, however, are basically part of a Ministry of Construction or Housing and Town and Country Planning. It was the Ministry which took responsibility for the first measures of regional policy and retained in large measure until fairly recently.

[2] J. F. Gravier, *Paris et le Désert Français*, Flammarion, Paris, 1947.

Official reaction came in February 1950 when M. Claudius Petit, Minister of Reconstruction and Housing, produced a document entitled *Pour un plan national d'aménagement du territoire.* This report, produced at a time when the reconstruction of the economy was the dominant concern, set out in broad terms the case for a policy of regional development which would bring about 'a better distribution of population in relation to natural resources and economic activity'. It stressed four main aspects of policy—industrial decentralization, the modernization of agriculture, the development of tourist facilities, particularly hotels, and the creation of cultural and intellectual centres in the provinces which would offer some of the attractions of Paris. It set the problem of regional development firmly in the context of national economic development. Regional development planning, it argued, was more than a series of land use plans for towns and conurbations. It was an attempt to organize the development of the economy in a way which would avoid the concentration of population and industry into a few huge urban centres, leaving large sections of the country under-populated and resources, both human and physical, under-utilized. The key element in the plan was the decentralization of industry from the Paris region. The emphasis was not so much on the transfer of established firms but the channelling of expansion, particularly in the newer industries such as motor-cars and electronics, away from the Paris region. These industries were, by their technical nature, much more mobile than the industries of the nineteenth century, and were able to operate in a much wider range of locations. The plan did not, however, advocate the indiscriminate distribution of industry. It emphasized the importance of selecting locations which could reasonably support industrial development. At the same time, it drew attention to the dangers of having a town or region too dependent on a single industry.

A number of measures were introduced to implement the plan. The officials in the regional development section of the Ministry of Reconstruction and Housing did their best to persuade firms whose premises were damaged during the war to expand out of the Paris region. They had, however, no legal or statutory powers. Construction permits, introduced in 1943 and confirmed in 1945, could be refused only in cases where the firms concerned were classified as dangerous or unsuited to operation in a residential area. Persuasion alone was scarcely a powerful enough weapon at a time when firms were concentrating on getting back to peace-time conditions of production. It should also be noted that the majority of war-damaged industrial premises in the Paris region were not wholly destroyed and the costs to the industrialist of moving to the provinces were frequently higher than rebuilding or repairing his premises on its original site.[1] It was not until 1955 that official restrictions were put on industrial building in the Paris region.

With this absence of control it is not surprising that the policy of decentralization had a limited impact.

Table 6.1 shows the disproportionate share of new industrial development which the Paris region obtained in the early post-war period, and how little the proportion changed over the period. Between 1950 and 1954 only forty-nine firms expanded out of the Paris region while around 270 *new* firms established themselves in it.[2] There was, in addition, considerable expansion of office building in Paris over which no control that had any direct bearing on decentralization was exercised.

In order to promote decentralization, the National Fund for Regional Development (*Fonds National d'Aménagement du Territoire* —FNAT) was established in 1950 as a result of pressure from M. Petit and his Ministry. The fund had powers to finance, either directly or by assisting local authorities, the creation of industrial estates which would offer industrial premises adequately supplied with the necessary services such as road links, water, energy, etc. The first of these estates were created at Chalon-sur-Saône, Châlons-sur-Marne and Rennes. By 1954 ten estates in all had been created, ranging in size from 10 to 140 hectares. The fund also gave financial help in the construction of houses which were required for the workers of firms setting up in the estates.

The Ministry of Reconstruction and Housing was the first to admit that the fund was not nearly as powerful as it needed to be. In the first place, its resources amounted to only £370,000, raised to £740,000 in 1951. Equally important, it did not possess any powers to expropriate land and this restricted the Ministry in its choice of industrial locations to those localities where suitable land could be purchased either from private owners or local authorities. In 1953 a Bill was passed which gave the government the right of compulsory purchase of land for industrial or housing purposes, but even then many problems remained which necessitated later legislation, particularly the effect of an industrial estate on the value of nearby land and the consequences of this for future industrial development.

The activities of the Ministry of Reconstruction and Housing

[1] See J. Faucheux, *La Décentralisation Industrielle*, Editions Berger-Levrault, Paris, 1959, p. 21.
[2] See J. Lajugie, op. cit., p. 289.

TABLE 6.1

CONSTRUCTION PERMITS GRANTED AND ESTIMATED FACTORY SPACE AND NUMBER OF JOBS CREATED

	1949			1950			1951			1952			1953			1954		
	No. of permits	Factory space (sq. metres)	Estimated no. of jobs	No. of permits	Factory space (sq. metres)	Estimated no. of jobs	No. of permits	Factory space (sq. metres)	Estimated no. of jobs	No. of permits	Factory space (sq. metres)	Estimated no. of jobs	No. of permits	Factory space (sq. metres)	Estimated no. of jobs	No. of permits	Factory space (sq. metres)	Estimated no. of jobs
Paris region[1]	182	321	6,350	153	256	5,250	137	215	4,000	128	319	6,910	160	270	5,130	147	342	5,310
Rest of France	334	560	14,370	254	499	11,360	265	668	10,850	312	579	12,790	295	598	9,320	354	688	12,030
Total	516	881	20,720	407	755	16,610	402	883	14,850	440	898	19,700	455	868	14,450	501	1,030	17,340
Percentage of total in:																		
Paris region	35	36	31	38	34	32	34	24	27	29	36	35	35	31	36	29	33	31
Rest of France	65	64	69	62	66	68	66	76	73	71	64	65	65	69	64	71	67	69

Source: Décentralisation et Localisation Industrielle, Ministère de la Construction, Paris, 1961.

1 The Paris region includes the *départements* of Seine, Seine-et-Marne, Seine-et-Oise and five cantons of the *département* of Oise.

extended beyond the field of urban development which was its traditional responsibility. In 1953 the decentralization of industry, particularly the engineering industry which was considered to be sufficiently 'footloose', was recognized by the government as an important aspect of national economic development which required direct financial help. In February 1953, a special fund, the Conversion and Development Fund (Fonds d'Adaptation et de Développement), was set up within the framework of the Modernization and Equipment Fund (Fonds de Modernisation et d'Equipement), the special Treasury fund which was responsible for financing the major part of the investment programmes in the First National Plan. The new fund, whose managing body included a representative of the National Planning Commission (Commissariat du Plan), was able to grant, in the case of firms in the engineering industry, loans and, more generally, partial rebates of the land transfer tax and local taxes (*la patente*). The fund was also given the power to subsidize interest repayments on loans raised by firms in 1953 to finance a decentralization operation. This last measure was, however, never applied.

The Ministry of Reconstruction and Housing sought also to aid regional development by having transport charges manipulated so as to favour the less prosperous regions. Even without this pressure the pricing policies of the nationalized industries had a definite influence on regional development. This was particularly true in the case of transport. The system of railway tariffs which existed before the war was based on the principle of *ad valorem* charges which levied tariffs according to the value of the commodities carried. Raw materials could, therefore, be transported fairly cheaply and this favoured manufacturing industries in the Paris region who could import raw materials at a cost less than the real cost of transporting them. The low passenger fares charged on the suburban lines in the Paris region was another subsidy to industries in the region in so far as they were able to pay lower wages as a result of the subsidized transport enjoyed by their workers. After the war, the authorities, concerned about the loss of traffic to road transport which the high rail-tariffs on certain goods were causing, introduced a more uniform system of charging which tended to make the charge per mile the same on all lines. This favoured the less prosperous regions with their less dense populations, and removed the bias in favour of the Paris region. In 1951, however, a further reform was introduced which moved in the direction of charging lower rates on the heavily used lines and something nearer the real costs of operating those with a smaller volume of traffic. This, of course, operated to the disadvantage of the less prosperous regions and it was this measure which the Ministry sought to alter by having special provision made for some of the most obviously affected regions, such as Brittany. Some concessions were made but both the government and the railway authorities were extremely reluctant to concede them or to extend their application too widely.[1]

One other aspect of regional development in this period must be mentioned. That is, the beginning of large-scale regional projects financed and carried out by combinations of central and local government, nationalized industries and private enterprise, known as 'mixed-economy' companies (*sociétés d'économie mixte*).[2] The first of these companies to be directed specifically towards regional development was the Compagnie Nationale d'Aménagement du Bas-Rhône-Languedoc. The company was formed as the result of a law passed in May 1951 which provided for the establishment of companies financed for the greater part by state loans and subsidies and with the task of carrying out projects at the regional level which required the co-operation of government departments, local authorities and private enterprise. The above company was established to carry out schemes of irrigation, agricultural conversion and diversification, and industrial development in the predominantly wine-growing region of Languedoc. The scheme involved three *départements* with a total population of 600,000 persons and covered an area of 210,000 hectares. The company was financed to the extent of 60 per cent by straightforward subsidy and the remainder by long-term loans, originally at a very low rate of interest. Other companies were created later for a variety of regional development schemes and this kind of regional project has continued to play a very important role in some of the most backward regions in France.

It should be noted that until 1953, when the first financial aids were introduced, the National Planning Commission played little or no role in regional development policy, which remained definitely the responsibility of the Ministry of Reconstruction and Housing. The First Plan, 1946-52, understandably concentrated on the task of reconstructing the basic industries in the economy. The development of manufacturing industry and the location of industry was treated very much as a secondary issue. There was no attempt at all to 'regionalize' the Plan. Concern about the regional problem, however, increased in the regions themselves and a number of

[1] For a discussion of this point, see J. Faucheux, op. cit., p. 31, and P. Bauchet, *Propriété Publique et Planification*, Editions Cujas, Paris, 1962, p. 167 *et seq.*

[2] There is a considerable literature on the *sociétés d'économie mixte*. See A. Chazel et H. Poyet, 'L'Economie mixte' *Que Sais-Je.* PUF, Paris, 1963.

regional expansion committees came into being, comprising the various interest groups in the region who sought to analyse and publicize their problems. Among the first in the field were the Comité d'Etudes et d'Aménagement de la Région de Rennes, in Brittany, created in 1946, and in 1950 the well-known Institut d'Économie Régionale du Sud-Ouest was established as a regional research centre in Bordeaux.

This growth in awareness of, and interest in, the regional problem accelerated after 1952 with the advent of the recession of 1952-54. This struck particularly hard at those regions whose industrial structures were dominated by the older industries which were facing a secular as well as a cyclical fall in demand. This, combined with the increasing concentration of the newer industries such as electronics, chemicals and some of the newer mechanical and engineering industries in the Paris region, compelled the government to act. In 1954 and 1955, a very considerable range of measures were introduced to promote regional development, and the consequences for the national economy of continued regional imbalance quite suddenly became the subject of widespread official and unofficial studies.

II. THE DECENTRALIZATION OF INDUSTRY, 1954-57

Between 1954 and 1956 a flood of legislation was passed dealing with regional policy. Most of the measures were concerned with establishing for the first time in France means of persuasion and control which could be used to promote the development of the less prosperous regions. These measures will be discussed later, but before doing so, it is important to examine the principles upon which they were based and the kind of regional development they were to encourage.

The basic aim of the exercise was the control of industrial (but not commercial) development in the Paris region. The costs to the nation of continued, uncontrolled expansion of the Paris region were clearly recognized, particularly in view of the increase in population which would come as a result of the large number of births in the years immediately after the war and the large-scale exodus from agriculture as a consequence of increasing mechanization. Thus, despite the very heavy concentration of industry in the Paris region, much of it being in the rapidly expanding sectors, the government was concerned about the costs to which their location there gave rise. Discussing the establishment of the Fonds d'Adaptation et de Développement in February 1953, M. Barangé, chairman of the finance committee of the National Assembly, gave a vigorous and comprehensive statement of the economic case for industrial decentralization: 'The gregarious instinct which attracts many firms towards the large urban centres and especially to the Paris region, gives rise to unprofitable migration, which leads, in turn, to an inefficient use of our housing stock, our schools and universities, and our communications network, etc. . . . This attraction is due, in large measure, to the fact that industrialists can transfer to the public authorities the responsibility of providing housing, transport and, indeed, employment for workers.'[1] M. Barangé went on to point out the economic and social cost of these obligations which have to be borne by the Paris authorities, and indirectly the state, and estimated that the cost per inhabitant of providing what would now be called social infrastructure (*équipements collectifs*) was four or five times greater in Paris (in 1951) than in an average-sized town in the provinces without taking account of the purely social costs such as congestion, noise, distance from place of work, etc.

A second important issue was the manner in which financial aid should be given to the less prosperous regions. The measures introduced in 1955 provided for preferential treatment in the form of supplementary financial benefits to be given to firms expanding in certain 'critical areas' (*zones critiques*), of which twenty-six were scheduled by 1956. There were three criteria according to which these areas were selected. The first was the existence in the area of a permanently high level of unemployment or a permanently high number of unsatisfied job seekers. The second was the imminent danger of large-scale unemployment due to the closure or the substantial run-down in activity of firms in the area. The third was the existence of a surplus of agricultural manpower of 'exceptional significance' indicating that full employment in the area could not be maintained by the development of agriculture.[2]

The idea of critical zones was conceived solely in terms of local unemployment. Examination of the list of zones shows that they were created partly to deal with the effects of the recession of 1952-54 on certain industries upon which certain localities were heavily dependent. These industries—coal, leather, textiles being the most important—were also facing the much more serious problems of a secular decline in demand and the threat of severe competition as a result of the projected Common Market. This latter problem dominated the Second Plan (1954-57) and industrial decentralization

---

[1] Cited in Faucheux, op. cit., p. 33. The same argument is set out in the *Décret*, No. 55-36, January 5, 1955, *Journal Officiel*, January 8, 1955, imposing restraints on industrial expansion within the Paris region.
[2] P. Bauchet, 'Regional Development Policies in France', op. cit., p. 112.

was seized upon as a convenient way of offsetting the unemployment which would be inevitable in certain areas if French manufacturing industry carried through the rationalization schemes and structural changes essential to increased productivity. In other areas the problem was the local unemployment caused by the termination of construction works in the area.

The selection of the critical areas was, therefore, based on the need to 'rescue' certain localities particularly affected by, or prone to, cyclical and structural unemployment. In this sense they were very similar to the Development Districts introduced in the United Kingdom in 1958.

Finally, and in many ways in contradiction to the previous point, an attempt was made to integrate the development of the different regions of France into the national economic plan. France was divided into twenty-two planning regions, for each of which a regional plan was to be prepared. This was a conscious attempt to co-ordinate regional development by relating each region's problems and prospects to those of the others and to the national plan. This exercise in regional planning will be discussed in more detail later. The point that should be noted here is that the decision to draw up these plans meant a recognition that regional development required more than a series of *ad hoc* measures directed towards particular areas where economic development for various reasons was lagging, and that the development of the different regions, and the measures used to promote it, had to be co-ordinated and made compatible with the objectives of the national economic plan. This approach to the regional problem is not easily reconciled with the short-term approach exemplified by the critical areas. But it does indicate that the government was coming to recognize that a lasting solution to the regional problem required the establishment of conditions which would allow the various regions to achieve economic expansion which would serve the national as well as their own interest. It was natural that it should seek to extend the planning procedures used to guide national economic policies to the regional level.

III. REGIONAL POLICY MEASURES 1954-57

In January 1955, a decree was issued which was aimed at ensuring 'a better distribution of industry throughout the country'.[1] To this end it imposed a control on the construction or extension of

---

[1] *Décret* No. 55-36, January 5, 1955, *Journal Officiel*, January 8, 1955.

industrial buildings employing more than fifty persons or occupying a surface area greater than 500 square metres in the Paris region or exceeding 10 per cent of the existing surface area. In July 1955, the control was extended to privately owned technical and scientific research establishments, including office space as well as laboratories.

This control was introduced to slow down the concentration of industry in the Paris region. The decree drew attention to the growing number of factories falling vacant in the less prosperous regions while new factories continued to be built in the Paris region, imposing increasingly heavy social costs. At the same time the control was deliberately not made too severe. The decree argued that what was required was a 'filtering process' which would prohibit the establishment in the Paris region of firms 'whose activities are not directly linked to the life of great urban centres and can be set up elsewhere'. It went on to stress that the control did not mean an automatic refusal to every expansion project but would be operated with 'all necessary flexibility'.

The task of implementing the control was given to a committee on which were represented the Ministers of Industry and Commerce, Interior, Finance, Economic Affairs and Planning,[1] Labour and Social Security, and Agriculture. This committee was to report its judgment on all applications for a construction permit above the prescribed maximum to the Ministry of Reconstruction and Housing, whose responsibility it was to grant or refuse permits.

The criteria to be applied by the committee were not published although its widely based membership suggests that they were broad rather than narrow. M. Faucheux, however, speaking with practical experience of the scheme, indicates some of the main points that were considered.[2] Extensions were generally regarded with more suspicion than new establishments, careful consideration being given to the possibility of the firm opening a new branch in the provinces. Estimates were made of the manpower needs of the applicant firm and the technical nature of its products and its link with clients and suppliers, which determined the multiplier effect of its expansion both in the Paris region and in other regions. The Ministry of Reconstruction and Housing was asked on this point to furnish details of the various areas in other regions where the firm could reasonably be expected to find adequate manpower, industrial land, vacant factories, or an industrial estate and the necessary infrastructure services. Attention was also given to the ability of the firm

[1] At this time the National Planning Commission was, for a brief period, under the authority of a new Ministry of Economic Affairs.
[2] Faucheux, op. cit., p. 62.

to finance a transfer out of the Paris region and the effect of a refusal of a permit on its competitive position in international markets.

The control was not, therefore, by any means intended to be watertight. This is scarcely surprising in view of the concentration of the fast-growing industries in the Paris region. Nevertheless, it was the first serious attempt to limit the growth of the Paris region and actively to promote industrial decentralization.

The government was, however, well aware that limiting industrial expansion in Paris could not, in itself, ensure regional development. Indeed, the criteria used to determine the award of permits would, in many cases, make it difficult to refuse a firm the right to expand in Paris in view of the absence of the conditions necessary for industrial growth in many of the most needy regions. Accordingly, a wide range of incentives was introduced to remedy these deficiencies.

In April 1955, the government acquired special powers to encourage the development of regions suffering from high unemployment or 'insufficient' economic development. These powers allowed the government to legislate by decree, and in June 1955 a 'package' of fourteen decrees was published which marked the first serious commitment by the state to a policy of aiding regional development.[1]

A series of decrees instituted a system of financial aid to firms establishing outside Paris. Certain areas were scheduled as critical areas, selected according to criteria discussed above, and firms establishing or expanding within these areas were eligible to receive a special investment grant (*prime spéciale d'équipement*) which could amount to a maximum of 20 per cent of the capital costs involved in the expansion. As indicated above, the critical areas were chosen on the basis of local unemployment or the imminent threat of it. By January 1956, twenty-six such areas had been scheduled.[2] They were all geographically small areas grouping several communes within *départements* and in some cases single towns. They were scattered widely over the country, including the north and east, although most were in the poorer regions of the south and west. They were, as regards concept, size and geographical relationship to each other, very similar to the Development Districts in the United Kingdom.

As well as investment grants, the legislation of June 1955 introduced a system of loans, interest subsidies, tax concessions and manpower training and mobility grants to firms decentralizing anywhere outside the Paris region, not necessarily into one of the critical areas.

[1] These decrees were issued on June 30, 1955, and were all published in *Journal Officiel*, July 2, 1955.
[2] The areas are defined in Faucheux, op. cit., pp. 218-21.

The administration of these aids was vested in a special interdepartmental committee with specially voted funds at its disposal. This was the Economic and Social Development Fund (Fonds de Développement Economique et Social—FDES[1]). The FDES was established 'to ensure the financing of projects in the (national) modernization and equipment plan and the regional action programmes (to be discussed later), particularly construction works, rural equipment and economic expansion, schemes for increasing productivity, industrial and agricultural conversion, retraining of manpower and industrial decentralization'. It replaced several other bodies which had the responsibility of financing and managing various aspects of national and regional development. At the national level it replaced the Modernization and Equipment Fund which had financed the investment projects in the First Plan (1946-52) and the interministerial Investment Committee which, since 1948, had supervised the spending of all public investment funds voted by Parliament. The Directing Council of the FDES was further given the responsibility of 'advising on the order of priority and the rhythm of the execution of the projects as well as the method of financing applicable to them . . . taking into account the directives of the plan'. It had, therefore, considerable control over all publicly financed investment.

In the sphere of regional development, the FDES took over the functions of an increasing number of bodies created since 1950 to manage the many-sided job of regional development. The most important of these were the funds financing construction and rural equipment, productivity schemes and the fund created in September 1954, to assist the retraining of workers made unemployed as a result of conversion operations and of workers employed by decentralizing firms.[2] Although these funds had all been placed under the management of a single committee, it quickly became apparent that they should be combined in a single agency.

The Directing Council of the FDES included representatives of every department concerned with economic policy, the Bank of France, the National Planning Commission and the special financial institutions such as the Deposits and Consignments Office (Caisse des Dépôts et Consignations). It divided itself into several sub-committees. The two most heavily concerned with regional development were those dealing with operations of agricultural conversion and industrial conversion and decentralization, and investment in agricultural, industrial and tourist promotion schemes approved by

[1] Established by *Décret* No. 55-875, June 30, 1955, *Journal Officiel*, July 2, 1955.
[2] Labour Retraining Fund (Fonds de Reclassement de la Main d'Oeuvre) *Décret* No. 54-951, September 14, 1954, *Journal Officiel*, September 23, 1954.

the National Planning Commission or written into the regional action programmes.

The FDES gave various forms of aid. Firstly, it granted loans to decentralizing firms for a maximum period of twenty years at a rate of interest fixed in 1955 at 5·5 per cent, with the possibility of a moratorium on repayments of two or three years. In practice, the duration of the loans averaged between eight and twelve years. The rate of interest charged was less (by 2 or 3 percentage points) than the firm would have had to pay on the capital market or to the special financial institutions, to finance a project bearing rather less risks than an operation of decentralization. Secondly, the FDES could bear a part of the interest payments on borrowings by firms either on the capital market or from the banks and other institutions to finance, either in whole or in part, an operation of decentralization. This type of assistance was normally reserved for projects involving a large loan by firms able to raise capital on the open market. The amount of subsidy given could reduce the interest rate by 2½ percentage points to a minimum of 4½ per cent, but in some cases it would be rather less than this. A third form of aid was the provision of underwriting facilities for a debenture issue by firms, but this was rarely employed.

The FDES also had the powers to vet requests for certain fiscal advantages which were introduced in June 1955. Decentralizing firms, subject to approval, were partially exempted from the tax on the transfer of buildings acquired for industrial purposes (*droits de mutation*). In 1955, the reductions meant a tax of 4·7 per cent on the value of the buildings acquired instead of 16·5 per cent. In addition, decentralizing firms who had already received aid of some kind from the FDES were granted partial or total exemption from local taxes for a period of five years.

As well as aids to capital expenditure, the FDES took over responsibility of financing labour-retraining schemes and the rehousing of workers moving to a new place of work. Originally conceived in 1954 as part of the policy of promoting industrial reconversion, the retraining aids were adapted to help decentralizing firms defray the costs of training the labour force in the region in which they were settling in the skills necessary for their particular operations. This was often necessary in localities where the local unemployed were either agricultural workers or trained in the skills of declining industries such as coal and textiles, and where retraining involved sending the workers to courses provided in the Paris region or bringing qualified personnel from Paris.

The FDES was prepared to pay by means of reimbursement, the

wages of workers during their period of retraining for a period of up to six months. The firm had to show that the retraining was necessary to their manpower needs and that the programmes of instruction met the required standards. The state was also ready to meet the salaries of instructors and other expenses involved in setting up training courses.

The task of retraining was initially borne largely by regional centres of the Association Nationale Interprofessionelle pour la Formation Rationelle de la Main d'Oeuvre (ANIFRMO). These regional training centres, operating in co-operation with the regional divisions of the Ministry of Labour, were originally financed before the war by trade unions and employers' associations but were now taken over by the State.

As a further aid to labour mobility, a measure was introduced which reimbursed a worker the cost of transporting his family and possessions as a result of his moving to take up a job with an approved decentralizing firm. A relocation allowance, varying with wages and family situation, was also paid.

The effectiveness of these various financial incentives will be discussed later. The decrees of June 1955[1] did not, however, limit themselves to giving financial help to decentralizing firms. A number of measures were taken aimed at creating conditions in the less prosperous regions which would attract and sustain new economic activity. Inevitably, this was a much longer-term exercise and required detailed information about the economies of the different regions. Experience since 1950 had also shown that, despite the very limited nature of regional policy and the means of implementing it, there was already an obvious lack of co-ordination among the departments and specially created agencies involved. The additional measures of June 1955 made some kind of co-ordination of policy at the national level a matter of obvious urgency.

The first step towards this was the creation in June 1955 of twenty-two regional action programmes (*programmes d'action régionale*) covering the whole of France. These programmes or plans were intended to 'extend and complete' the national plan. They would serve as a framework within which the economic problems of the region could be exposed and analysed, and the public investment programmes in the different departments in the different regions co-ordinated. They would also provide information for bodies like the FDES to aid them in their assessment of applications for construction permits in the Paris region and for the various financial aids available.

[1] *Décret* No. 55-873, June 30, 1955, *Journal Officiel*, July 2, 1955.

The programmes were designed to be 'integrated' with the Third Plan (1958-61) but it is scarcely possible to call them regional plans in any strict sense. They were not plans for a definite time period, their scope being left to the various authors. They were not, therefore, regional sections of the national four-year plan. Neither was there any commitment by the government to them as there was in the case of certain public investment projects in the national plan.

Perhaps the most striking evidence of the tentative nature of the programmes was the introduction, in August 1957, of a Bill providing for land-use plans to be prepared in each programme region. These physical plans, drawn up under the supervision of the Ministry of Housing, were to organize all construction projects, both public and private, in order to 'ensure a harmonious distribution of population and economic activity'. They were to 'take account of' the regional programmes, but since they were the responsibility of a separate Ministry, and since the form of the regional programmes, was by no means specifically defined, the chances of overlap and contradiction were considerable. The separation of physical and economic planning in this way is a clear indication that the nature and function of a regional plan as a means of promoting regional development was still not fully thought through or, if it was, that the changes in traditional administrative structures and responsibilities which it required had not been carried through.[1]

The task of drafting the regional programmes was entrusted to civil servants based in Paris but with regional duties. They consulted the various government departments concerned with developments in the region and the prefects of each *département*. Consultation with regional interests, notably the Committees for Economic Expansion (Comités d'Expansion Economique) for each *département*, whose composition had been regulated by another of the decrees of June 1955 to ensure representation of all interest groups in the region, was carried out by the prefect. When completed the draft programme was to be submitted to a 'synthesis group', including a senior member of the National Planning Commission, before being finally approved by an interministerial committee.

The programmes were, therefore, very much the creation of centrally appointed civil servants (the prefect is the representative of the Ministry of the Interior in the *département*) and regional consultations were carried out at the level of the *département*. There was no officially responsible representation of the region for which the programme was being prepared. The role of the National

[1] For a fuller discussion of this point see Chapter 10.

Planning Commission in the formative stages of the programmes was also limited despite the intention that the regional programmes should become the extension of the national plan into the regions.

Concern with the promotion of sound long-term expansion in the regions led the government to take steps to remove obstacles which the financial incentives outlined above were inadequate to deal with. One of these was the inability of the banking and financial institutions to meet the demand for credit by the small and medium-sized firms, most of them family concerns, which were very important in France. The credit policy of French banks was traditionally conservative and borrowers required sizeable collateral security. The capital market did not offer a satisfactory alternative. It was inadequate to meet the demand for investment funds and, as a result, the cost of raising money was beyond the resources of the average small business, quite apart from the loss of control which could result from this manner of raising funds. Moreover, the administration of the credit institutions was overwhelmingly concentrated in Paris, and credit policy tended, as a result, to be to the considerable advantage of firms in the Paris region where, in any case, there was a high concentration of firms. Regional savings were thus diverted to Paris and lent to firms in Paris. Regional banks did exist but many of these had closed down in the inter-war years and had not reappeared.

To fill this gap, Regional Development Companies (Sociétés de Développement Régional—SDR) were created in June 1955, with the function of acquiring shares in firms located in regions suffering from unemployment or inadequate economic development. The SDRS could acquire up to a 35 per cent share in any eligible firm and could invest up to 25 per cent of its capital in a single firm. In 1957, they were given further powers to grant loans of over five years' duration[1] to firms in which they had a share and to underwrite long term borrowing by such firms. The SDRS had to have a minimum paid up capital of £185,000. The capital was subscribed very largely by the large banks, both private and nationalized, most of which were Parisian. A few large private firms contributed and, to an even less extent, local authorities and other bodies such as the Committees for Economic Expansion.

The SDRS were not expected to apply the tests of profitability normally employed as this would clearly reduce their efficacy as lenders of risk capital in areas where it was most required. To encourage an enterprising lending policy they were totally exempted

[1] *Décret* No. 55-876, June 30, 1955.

from taxes on any capital gains and interest received, and the State guaranteed a minimum dividend to shareholders, provided the projects invested in were granted approval by the FDES as useful for the development of the region concerned.

An even more important obstacle to regional expansion which emerged very clearly from the applications for a construction permit in the Paris region was the absence of industrial and other services in almost the whole of the provinces. These services were one of the most crucial external economies of a location in Paris and it became clear that a policy of industrial decentralization could not hope to succeed unless an effort was made to make these services available in the regions. This point was taken in the legislation of 1955 and a special committee was set up attached to the National Planning Commission to look into the problem. It was to prepare an inventory of all civil and military establishments providing industrial, commercial, scientific, cultural or social services in the Paris region whose location there was not technically necessary. Once this survey was carried out, the committee was to prepare a programme to transfer or decentralize the activities of such establishments over a ten-year period.

Finally, there was the problem of creating an adequate infrastructure in the less prosperous regions. The FNAT had begun to act in this field but with very limited powers and resources. The measures of 1955 recognized that this was perhaps the most important of all aspects of regional development. By decrees of November 1954 and June 1955 the formula of mixed-economy companies, which were responsible for large-scale public development projects, was adapted to provide a suitable agency for managing, and partly financing, the construction and reconstruction of housing and industrial buildings and, in some cases, aiding agricultural improvement schemes in certain approved localities, particularly the critical areas.[1] The maximum participation of local authorities in these companies was raised from 40 to 65 per cent and they were considered eligible for the various financial aids administered by the FDES. Similar organizations had operated in the 1930s but they were now specifically oriented towards promoting regional development and were not simply housebuilding agencies.

In addition to these schemes, the government created the Central Agency for Regional Infrastructure (Société Centrale pour l'Equipement du Territoire—SCET) financed and managed by the nationalized banks and special financial institutions such as the Deposits and Consignments Office. Its function was to aid local authorities or

[1] Chazel et Poyet, op. cit., p. 11.

165

'mixed-economy' companies by helping to finance the infrastructure investment—power supplies, water, schools, roads—necessary to stimulate industrial development in a region. It also undertook to provide skilled technical advisers to assist local authorities in the task of planning and construction. As well as being a source of finance, the SCET was conceived as a means of ensuring a more rational use of infrastructure than would emerge if local authorities competed with each other to create industrial estates in order to attract industry.

CONCLUSION

By 1958 regional development in France was on the point of being recognized in official circles as an issue of national concern which had to be taken into account in the formulation of the medium-term national plans into which some kind of regional planning system had to be inserted. This approach was a sophisticated one at the time because it implied a regional policy which was directed at getting a faster rate of growth of regional outputs and incomes and not simply at reducing the unemployment rate in localities where this had risen to levels which were socially and politically undesirable. It implied, too, an awareness of the national character of the regional problem, regional development conferring both benefits and costs (measured in terms of actual and potential national output) which national economic policy had to take into account. On the other hand, the implementation of regional policy and planning was still in the process of being cautiously, pragmatically and unevenly related to the new approach. New institutions and policies were introduced as new problems were uncovered and old ones, like local unemployment, reappeared, their scope and power varying according to assessments of the relevance, riskiness and feasibility of the new attitude to regional development to the particular matter in hand at the particular time. It is possible to review this period of French regional policy in terms of its slow and unco-ordinated adjustment to currently accepted notions. But this would be to ignore the valuable and at times far-seeing measures (in contrast to other countries) that were at least initiated. It is to the development of these that the next chapter turns.

CHAPTER 7

TOWARDS A NATIONAL POLICY FOR REGIONAL DEVELOPMENT 1958-1966

By 1958, a wide range of measures existed which allowed an active policy of regional development to be pursued. There was, however, little evidence that the objectives of regional policy and the strategy it was to follow had been worked out with similar thoroughness. From 1958 onwards, it is possible to see the main points of such a strategy emerging and the policy measures adapted accordingly. This evolution in attitudes was neither rapid nor continuous and there were many contradictory moves, but three main features of regional policy became increasingly accepted by both the central government and the regions.

Firstly, it was recognized that the problem of uneven regional development had far-reaching implications for the national economy. Regional policy was not simply a matter of aiding particular localities where unemployment was above the national average, or of controlling the growth of population and industry in the congested Paris region. Its task was the much wider one of evening out the large disparities in resource utilization and living standards which existed among the different regions of the economy in order that all regions could make the maximum contribution to, and reap the maximum benefits from, economic and social development. Regional policy thus became inevitably an integral part of national economic policy and its objectives required to be consistent with the aims of national economic policy.

Secondly, regional policy came increasingly to be based on the creation of a limited number of growth centres. Once integrated with a national economic policy aimed at achieving a fast rate of growth of national output (not necessarily the maximum rate), regional policy had, by definition, to be directed towards creating self-sustaining development in the less prosperous regions, thus utilizing under-used or unused resources in these regions and utilizing them in a way which would increase productivity both in the regions and in the economy as a whole. Such a policy is very different from socially motivated attempts to 'rescue' localities in which a labour surplus appears by encouraging or directing industry there. It is much more selective requiring development to be concentrated in pre-selected areas within the less prosperous regions where the conditions for self-sustaining growth can be created at the least cost to the national economy.

Thirdly, the methods of organization and promoting regional development had to be considerably changed and extended in order to meet the new conditions of regional policy. This involved far-reaching reforms of the traditional administrative and planning structures and machinery to serve the needs of a nationally co-ordinated regional policy based on the promotion of a small number of growth centres and a similar reshaping of the incentives and controls used to implement regional policy.

REGIONAL DEVELOPMENT AND NATIONAL ECONOMIC POLICY

The Third Plan (1958-61) was the first to devote a specific section to regional problems and to include regional development as one of its general objectives. The aim of its regional development policy was stated in the following terms. 'To allow a country as highly diversified as ours to achieve full economic and social development, it is necessary that all regions contribute to, and benefit from, such development. A balanced distribution of population, industry and incomes is thus one of the conditions for the achievement of the plan's objectives.'[1] The plan went on to argue the benefits whch would result from this more balanced regional development.

There was first, and by far the most important, the need to reduce the growth of the Paris region. The plan emphasized the undesirable social consequences of the high concentration of industry, commerce and cultural activities in the Paris region, and the loss of active population to which it gave rise in the less prosperous regions. If allowed to go on unchecked, this emigration threatened to leave large areas of France in a worsening state of relative poverty and economic backwardness and inadequately provided with public services and amenities of all kinds. Such an outcome was politically and socially intolerable. On these grounds alone, therefore, regional development was a necessity whatever the more narrowly economic arguments about the future of the Paris region might be. The case for regional development in France is thus rather different in emphasis from that in the United Kingdom, where the economic conditions in the less prosperous regions are such that it can be

[1] *Troisième Plan, Journal Officiel*, March 22, 1959, p. 3447.

argued that the social aims of regional policy can frequently be achieved as a consequence and by-product of policies which are justified in terms of the economic development they may produce in these regions, thereby increasing the rate of national economic growth.

The plan, however, also produced more detailed economic arguments for limiting the growth of Paris. It drew attention to the financial burden on the national economy of providing the necessary infrastructure and services for an urban agglomeration above a certain size. It estimated the total cost of providing essential services, including housing, for each new family establishing itself in the Paris region in 1958 at 4,200,000 francs, as against 2,800,000 francs in a provincial city. Unless the growth of Paris was checked, these disparities would increase. This, the plan warned, was particularly undesirable since none of France's competitors in the EEC incurred social costs to the same degree because of the existence of effective provincial counterweights to their capitals provided by cities such as Milan, Munich and Antwerp.

A further undesirable consequence of the high concentration of industry in Paris was the inflationary pressures which it produced as the demands on scarce supplies of land and labour in that region increased, despite and indeed to some extent because of the large-scale immigration from the provinces. It was natural for the plan to emphasize the dangers of inflation resulting from the uneven pattern of demand for labour in the economy, for one of its principal objectives was to improve the balance on external payments which had shown large deficits in 1957 and 1958 and led eventually to the devaluation of the franc in December 1958. France's entry to the EEC made the halting of inflation and the restoration of equilibrium in the balance of payments a matter of urgency.

The removal of regional unemployment was not a major concern of regional policy in the third plan. Unemployment in the less prosperous regions was not, generally, a serious problem. The economy as a whole was, on conventional definitions, fully employed, and the estimated manpower needs over the period of the plan could be met only on the assumption of increased participation of women in the labour force and increased immigration, since the increase in the birth-rate in the immediate post-war years would not affect the size of the working population until after 1961. Although there were pockets of local unemployment in certain regions, mainly those affected by the decline in older industries such as coal or textiles on which they were heavily dependent, unemployment was generally kept down as a result of migration, very largely into the Paris region.

It was the reduction of this flow which was the central aim of regional policy and the main means of providing a reserve of labour in the regions for the firms encouraged to expand outside the Paris region. The contribution of regional development to national economic growth, however, lay not so much in the activation of unutilized manpower resources in the less prosperous regions as in the widening of the constraints of price stability and the balance of payments by shifting demand and output away from the Paris region.

The measures to implement this policy concentrated, not unnaturally, on promoting the decentralization from Paris of industry, services and administration. The plan did, however, recognize that the encouragement and inducement of decentralization was not, in itself, likely to be effective and had to be complemented by efforts to simulate in the less prosperous regions the conditions normally classified as external economies and the possibilities of achieving economies of scale, which attract industry to the Paris region and allow it to operate there efficiently, while avoiding the diseconomies of congestion. The creation of these conditions was the task of the regional programmes which the plan argued should be coterminous with the national plan and give it a regional dimension. The plan explicitly recognized that the traditional administrative structures would have to be radically altered to allow them to cope with the tasks of regional economic planning of this kind and the co-ordination of regional plans with the national plan.

Although available data on the regional economies was very inadequate and the plans for the regions in no sense quantitatively linked to the targets of the national plan, the Third Plan did attempt to sketch out, in very broad terms, the strategy of development to be followed in different broadly defined regions during the period of the plan. Despite its limitations, this exercise is important. It meant that regional policy was defined in terms of all the regions in the economy and their economic and social interrelationships, and was not limited to temporary rescue operations in a few localities in economic difficulties. It had to consider the implications of action within one region upon all the others and upon the objectives of the national plan. This would inevitably involve conflict between the claims and aspirations of different regions and between regional and national needs and objectives in any given period of time, which would have to be settled by a process of discussion and negotiation at the national level between central and regional planners. Secondly, the problems and prospects of the regions were discussed in terms of how most effectively to promote growth in the regional economies. Particularly in the discussion of Brittany

170

and the other predominantly agricultural areas in the west of France, the plan recognized the need to base industrial development on certain deliberately chosen growth poles within different regions.

The Fourth Plan (1962-65)

The Fourth Plan continued to give prominence to regional policy and stated its basic aims in terms very similar to those used in the Third Plan, although it stressed the economic as well as the social importance of a more even regional development. It restated the need to view regional development as a means of promoting expansion in all regions and not simply jacking up the less prosperous ones. The growth of the Paris region was still recognized as a major problem but the plan did not advocate indiscriminate control over it. It argued that improvements in communications and the impact of the EEC compelled a reappreciation of the economic role and prospects of the different regions in France. The Paris region, with its high concentration of the most rapidly growing industries, was one of the natural growth points within the EEC economy. Any policy of controls over its development, therefore, must distinguish between industries and services for which Paris, in its role as European centre, is a necessary and reasonable location, and those which could, at less cost to the nation, operate as profitably elsewhere. This distinction is particularly important in the rapidly growing services sector, and the plan recommended the establishment of service areas within Paris where those operations essential and natural to the city could operate. It also made the point that the regional economies were in many respects complementary and a policy aimed at arresting the development of any single region might well prejudice expansion in client and supplier regions.

The plan is more explicit than its predecessor about the strategy of regional development. It came down strongly in favour of a selective approach to regional development and drew two important distinctions. It distinguished first of all between regions where agricultural, industrial and commercial expansion are proceeding at a satisfactory rate, and those where growth is slower. In the former, a policy of 'accompaniment' (*politique d'accompagnement*) should be pursued which would develop infrastructure as required by the growth of their economies. Investment in infrastructure or other 'substantial aid' would not be used to force the pace of growth. In the slower growing regions, a policy of 'stimulation' (*politique d'entrainement*) should be followed. This would involve the use of aid in various forms directed towards speeding up the rate of growth and the creation of infrastructure in anticipation of needs and demands upon it in order to create the conditions for this faster growth.[1]

The policy of stimulation involved a second exercise in selection. The plan states firmly that such a policy will be both wasteful and ineffective if it attempts to promote development simultaneously in a large number of points throughout the regions. 'To achieve its objective it must concentrate on well-chosen locations. This will create poles of growth in which preferential action by the government will develop infrastructure and educational and training establishments in order to encourage large firms to decentralize and locate in them. The expansion of these main centres will have a stimulating effect on their hinterlands and induce the development of a network of secondary poles where components and service industries can expand.'[2] The growth area approach is thus clearly stated as the basis of regional policy. The expressed aim of the Fourth Plan to integrate regional development with the objectives and policies of the national plan and to operate a selective policy of development both between and within regions, made it a logical necessity to formulate definite policies on the distribution and movement of labour between regions and the regional pattern of public expenditure. The Fourth Plan introduced extensive new proposals in both these fields.

The preparatory work on the plan included much more detailed assessments of regional manpower resources and inter-regional migration than had hitherto been done. The Manpower Commission of the plan and the industrial modernization commissions were asked to supply the data for a regional breakdown of estimated manpower needs and resources. Table 7.1 indicates the two main areas of regional imbalance in the labour market to which the planners directed their attention. Firstly, the Paris region was likely to be short of labour during the Fourth Plan. The manpower gap of 174,000 would have been over 300,000 in the absence of immigration to the region from overseas. Alsace was the only other region where a shortage of any magnitude was likely. On the other side of the problem, a sizeable labour surplus appeared likely in the three western regions of the Loire basin, Lower Normandy and most especially Brittany. In the rest of the country demand and supply were more or less in balance, although the influence of the declining industries in the region of Nord produced a surplus that was considered sufficiently serious to require special action.

The planners' reaction to these forecasts was that the imbalances

---

[1] *Quatrième Plan de Développement Economique et Social (1962-65), Journal Officiel*, August 7, 1962, p. 45.
[2] *Quatrième Plan*, op. cit., p. 46.

TABLE 7.1

ESTIMATED MANPOWER RESOURCES AND NEEDS IN NON-AGRICULTURAL OCCUPATIONS, 1960–65

(in thousands)

Programme region	1 Estimated total working population January 1, 1960	2 Growth of manpower without migration	3 Growth of manpower with immigration	4 Estimated growth of manpower needs	5 Manpower surplus or deficit (Col. 3—Col. 4)	6 Surplus or deficit as percentage of total working population
Nord	1,330	+64	+81	+57	+24	+1·9
Paris region	3,899	−25	+124	+298	−174	−4·5
Picardy	540	+29	+37	+36	+1	—
Champagne	473	+22	+27	+26	+1	—
Centre	757	+28	+35	+35	0	—
Upper Normandy	565	+28	+37	+40	−3	—
Lower Normandy	526	+41	+42	+24	+18	+3·4
Loire basin	1,054	+74	+80	+49	+31	+2·9
Brittany	1,016	+71	+73	+34	+39	+3·8
Lorraine	838	+54	+64	+55	+9	—
Alsace	546	+10	+19	+37	−18	−3·0
Franche Comté	374	+17	+23	+27	−4	—
Burgundy	570	+19	+26	+28	−2	—
Rhône-Alpes	1,718	+65	+100	+98	+2	—
Auvergne	537	+23	+26	+18	+8	+1·5
Limousin	334	+11	+12	+7	+5	+1·5
Poitou-Charentes	572	+30	+31	+22	+9	+1·6
Aquitaine	1,005	+41	+56	+38	+18	+1·8
Midi-Pyrenées	855	+26	+45	+24	+21	+2·5
Languedoc	536	+6	+26	+12	+14	+2·6
Provence	1,064	+26	+74	+73	+1	—
France	19,109	+660	1,038			—

Source: *Rapport Général de la Commission de la Main d'Oeuvre. Quatrième Plan.* Table 24, p. 171.

173

were not large enough to pose a serious obstacle to the attainments of the plan's objectives. The Manpower Commission argued that the risk of serious unemployment in some regions and serious labour shortages in others was not very great, and went on to show that, on the basis of past trends, the rate of internal migration required to bring the regions into balance was not infeasible. In the extreme case of Brittany, the labour surplus likely to appear during the Fourth Plan was less than the volume of net migration from the region to other parts of France between 1955 and 1960. The regional disequilibria could, therefore, be corrected by spontaneous or unplanned migration. The planners made the additional point that the 'propensity to migrate' was likely to rise rather than fall during the period of the plan as the large number of births in the immediate post-war years increased the proportion of young, and therefore more mobile, people in the labour force.[1] Regional policy was not, therefore, justified as a corrective to a situation which natural forces were inadequate to handle. The nature and extent of its role depended rather on whether inter-regional migration on the required scale would have undesirable economic effects. The planners noted various situations where migration was not the economically preferable solution.

Firstly, they distinguished between emigration which resulted in a slower rate of growth of population in a region and that which caused an actual fall in the population of a large region, such as one of the programme regions. In the latter case, which threatened to occur in the Massif Central, migration would reduce the size of the regional factor and product markets and deprive the region of its most valuable manpower to its own and the national detriment.

Secondly, the planners insisted on the varied nature of the problems created by the continuing fall in the numbers employed in agriculture. In some regions, such as Brittany, there was a genuine surplus of agricultural manpower; in others, such as Champagne and Lorraine, there was, in fact, the danger that the numbers employed in agriculture, particularly in the younger age-groups, would fall below the minimum level required to utilize full available resources of good agricultural land. In order to encourage a faster rate of transfer from Brittany alternative employment opportunities in industry had to be created.

Thirdly, there was the exceptional problem posed by the influx of repatriates from Algeria. The planners feared that the immigrants would concentrate in the Mediterranean regions of France where

[1] *Rapport Général de la Commission de la Main d'Oeuvre. Quatrième Plan,* p. 173.

there was already a surplus of agricultural manpower, and recommended that industrial development be encouraged in these areas to prevent the economic and social difficulties that this would create.

Finally, there was the question of the projected labour shortage in the Paris region. The Manpower Commission recommended that the policy of decentralization and controls on factory building be continued but did not suggest that the halting of immigration to the region was either necessary or feasible. Indeed, in line with the nuanced attitude of the plan towards the development of the Paris region the Commission accepted such immigration as was necessary for the expansion of industries, many of them among the fastest growing, in the Paris basin to the south of the capital.

Even more significant than this first exercise in regional manpower forecasting were the innovations introduced by the Fourth Plan in the methods of allocating public investment funds both between and within the different regions. The regional development programmes begun in 1955 laid heavy emphasis on the improvements in infrastructure required if the regional economies were to expand. There was, however, neither a timetable of concrete projects nor any commitment by the central government to specific operations. But if regional development were to be integrated with the national plan, a decision had to be made about the amount and type of infrastructure which each region required to achieve its planned development and could be permitted to have, taking account of the other objectives and constraints in the national plan.

As a first step towards meeting these conditions, the Fourth Plan included a new procedure for 'regionalizing' the public investment programmes of the national plan. This was the preparation by the various central and regional authorities of 'operational sections' (*tranches opératoires*) of the regional programmes.[1] These documents contained two main elements. Firstly, they presented a four-year forecast of the region's development, i.e. over the period of the national plan, and on the basis of this a list of actions to be taken involving public investment expenditure. The second part translated these actions into specific projects with a timetable for their execution, an estimate of their cost and proposals as to how they should be financed. In the Fourth Plan the *tranches* covered housing, urban development, agriculture, communications, energy, education and research, and health and social welfare.

The projects included in the *tranches* were divided into three kinds. There were individual projects which, because of their size, nature and importance, had to be decided at the national level as key

[1] *Quatrième Plan*, op. cit., p. 42.

175

actions of the national plan, e.g. motorway construction, the expansion of university and research establishments, and the power station programme. Secondly, there were projects which could be left to the regional authorities to work out in consultation with the relevant central authorities. Thirdly, there were projects which had to be worked out at the level of the *département*, or even commune, rather than the programme region, e.g. housing, sporting facilities, forestry and water, non-trunk roads.

The introduction of the *tranches* meant that the expenditure on capital account in the annual budget now had to be divided not only as between sectors but as between regions. This was specifically recognized in the law relating to the Fourth Plan, Article 3 of which stated, 'The Finance Bill will, in addition, be accompanied by a general appendix stating the financial outlay estimated in the state budget as necessary for the execution of the operational sections'.[1] This document was to contain, 'firstly, the statement of credits granted, projects approved and credits paid broken down according to economic and social sector; further, a statement of these credits broken down by programme region'. The first application of this law occurred in the Finance Bill for 1964. As well as the normal budget estimates there were two documents appended totalling some 200 pages outlining the regional and sectorial breakdown of public investment credits for the eight sectors mentioned above. This first exercise was, perhaps inevitably, incomplete and imperfect but the report did raise frankly some very important issues. It pointed out that not all public investment could be 'regionalized' at will. Examples given were motorways and particular kinds of research. It emphasized, too, the need for more information about the different regional economies if the programme regions were 'to be rigorously classified according to their needs and vocation'.[2] Finally, the report made the point that the regionalization of the budget would require a considerable change of attitudes and working practices on the part of government departments at both their central and regional levels. The introduction of a regional dimension to their activities would compel them to be less narrow in their outlook and to take account of the fact that in order to play an effective part in regional development policy they would have to take more account of the high degree of interdependence that existed between their various

[1] *Loi No. 62-900* of August 4, 1962. *Journal Officiel*, August 7, 1962.

[2] *Projet de Loi des Finances pour 1964. Document Annexe. Régionalisation du budget d'équipement pour l'année 1964 et coordination des investissements publics au regard des objectifs de l'aménagement du territoire.* Imprimerie Nationale, Paris, 1965.

activities. In the budgets for 1965 and 1966 the procedures for distributing credits between the different regions were very much improved, but the 1964 exercise is extremely important as it marks the first time that regional development was formally and specifically considered in the traditionally centralist process of making annual budgetary allocations.

The Fifth Plan (1966-70)

The Fifth Plan saw a very much fuller integration of regional policy into the national planning framework and the adoption of a national view of the various regions' problems. The statement of regional policy in the plan was based on a much greater amount of preparatory work on the regional problem than had previously been done. It leant particularly heavily on a long-term study of regional development in France prepared by the National Commission for Regional Planning (Commission Nationale de l'Aménagement du Territoire—CNAT), a special commission created within the Planning Commission in 1963. This report sought to trace out the probable development of the different regions in France up to 1985. It divided France into three regions—the west, the east and the Paris region—and examined the main features of development likely to take place in each. The planners admitted that this was an extremely simple division and the analysis full of uncertainties. But it was none the less necessary. Regional development was by its nature a long-term job which required forecasts over a considerably longer period than the five-year national plans. A second and more detailed source of information were the reports provided by the prefects of each of the programme regions analysing the problems and prospects of their regions during the period of the Fifth Plan and indicating in some detail and in order of priority the public investment they wished to see carried out. The usefulness of these reports was greatly enhanced by the fact that they were prepared before the plan was completed and could be taken into account in the final 'synthesis' discussions at the Planning Commission where many important changes are made. Regional policy in the Fifth Plan was not, therefore, added on as some kind of corrective after the broad national objectives of the plan had been worked out but was considered as an important issue in the determination of these aims. The point was also established that the objectives of regional policy written into any medium-term national plan were merely a phase of the much longer term operation of planning or adapting to the changing distribution of people and employments in the light of technical, economic and social changes.

The direction to be taken by regional policy during the Fifth Plan was influenced by three main factors. The first, and in the planners' eyes by far the most important, was the need to change the form and structure of many French industries to make them competitive in the context of complete freedom of trade within the EEC; a corollary of this aim is an increase in the amount of resources going into productive investment. The implications for regional policy were far reaching. 'It must, in a highly competitive situation give every opportunity to the "strong" regions whose economic potential can benefit the whole economy. On the other hand, it must seek in the "weak" regions to promote development which will become self-sustaining so that these regions can play a part in the schemes for modernization and expansion.'[1] This kind of argument is in marked contrast to recent British approaches to regional development which have stressed the benefits accruing from a fuller utilization of underemployed resources in the poorer regions. There is, of course, something of this in the French planners' view but their main concern is to ensure that regional development will help increase or, at the very least, not hinder the rate of growth of *productivity*. It is this rather than increased production or employment which must be the criterion by which regional policy is judged.

Such an austere attitude to regional development poses particularly awkward problems in the case of the west of France and the Paris region. The key feature of regional policy in the west of France is the commitment to provide in that region 143,000 jobs or 35 to 40 per cent of the estimated number of new jobs in industry over the period 1962-70.[2] This is a very ambitious target. It is almost double the proportion of industrial jobs created in these regions between 1954 and 1962. If it is to have any hope of being achieved, the west must get a large share of the new jobs created in the rapidly growing industries such as engineering and electronics. This, in turn, means that the planners must create the conditions in which a small number of industrial complexes will be created which will provide the kind of location required to attract these newer industries and allow them to operate profitably. All this, however, requires a large-scale investment effort for even in reasonably established industrial centres such as Nantes-St Nazaire, Pau and Toulouse, much is lacking in the way of communications, suitable housing and amenities, industrial services and educational or training establishments.

[1] *Cinquième Plan*, Vol. I, p. 118.
[2] The west of France in this context comprises the programme regions of Aquitaine, Auvergne, Brittany, Centre, Languedoc-Rousillon, Limousin, the Loire basin, Midi-Pyrénées, Lower Normandy and Poitou-Charentes.

Although much of this investment is, on the particular short-term definition adopted by the Fifth Plan, unproductive, it must be provided if growth industries are to be attracted to the west and, equally important, to operate there without a serious fall in productivity. Regional policy towards the west of France will, therefore, to an extent which is bound to raise social and political issues, have to be extremely selective and based to a greater extent than in the Fourth Plan on the development of three or four growth areas so planned as to yield the maximum in economies of scale and external economies.

The exigencies of national economic policy have also significantly influenced policy towards the Paris region. The move away from a regime of tight controls on industrial and commercial expansion begun in the Fourth Plan is continued. The emphasis in the Fifth Plan is to organize the development of the Paris region in such a way that it can most effectively fulfil its role as a major growth centre in the European economy. This has involved a debate between the central planners and the Paris planners about the future expansion of the region, and there is evidence of a difference of view on this point which naturally has important implications for the development of the rest of France. There is very little in the Fifth Plan about extending physical controls on industrial expansion, although the area around Paris within which firms receive no financial aid with expansion or extensions has been increased. The plan concentrates rather on the physical planning of the Paris region and especially the creation of three new towns around the capital, so as to minimize the economic and social costs of its expansion, and advocates the introduction of measures aimed at making residents of the Paris region meet a larger part of the costs which they cause to be incurred by choosing to live in the region. In all the agencies of the public sector the need for a Paris location is to be more closely investigated. This is a point of quite crucial importance given the unique dominance which Paris has in these activities, their growing importance as growth industries of the future and the decision to create provincial counterweights to Paris into which some at least of the 'tertiary' activities presently concentrated in the capital must be transferred and extended. In the private sector measures are to be taken to establish *vérite des coûts*. Part of a much wider drive to bring prices more into line with 'true' costs, the aim here is to charge residents in the region somewhere nearer the total cost to the nation of location in the Paris region. Some of the main measures envisaged include a reform of the system of local taxation which varies very greatly from region to region, and in certain cases acts as a disincentive to firms expanding into poorer regions, since the local taxes there are frequently very much higher than in the richer areas. The pricing of various public services in the Paris region, including public transport, car-parking facilities, water supply and sewerage, is also under review and the Fifth Plan is in favour of an increase in the prices of these services in order to make users take more account of the social costs of their location in the capital. If this is done, the planners claim it will let them 'form a more accurate appreciation of the relationship between the policy adopted towards the location of industries in the Paris region and the modifications made to it in the new towns and the need to step up decentralization towards the regions which have to be industrialized'.[1]

The second major decision about regional policy in the Fifth Plan concerned the regional distribution of manpower needs and resources. The problem isolated in the plan as crucial is the continued lack of growth of employment in the regions in the west of France. Between the Census years 1954 and 1962, the west's share of industrial jobs remained stationary at 23·8 per cent. In its long-term study the CNAT estimated that, even if the west got half the total number of new industrial jobs created between 1962 and 1985, the numbers employed in agriculture (despite a projected decline of one million in the labour force in that sector) would still be much higher than the average for the whole country and the proportions in industry and the services sector much lower.[2] If the trend established up to 1964 were to continue, the west would have only 25 per cent of industrial jobs by 1970 and, if the migration from the area were to continue at the same rate as in the period 1954-62, the loss of active population through migration by 1970 would be around 250,000. The aim of the Fifth Plan is to create in the west between 35 and 40 per cent of new industrial jobs. This target would require the creation of 145,000 jobs over the five-year period of the plan, giving a net figure, after deduction of estimated job losses in industry, of around 110,000. If these figures were achieved, the planners reckon that migration would be cut by about one-third to 170,000. The planners are acutely aware of the costs of this policy and admit that it may well limit the national rate of growth in the *medium term* (their italics). But they go on to assert that this price is a reasonable one to pay in order to avoid the costs which an increase in regional disparities would impose in the long term. 'The criterion

1 *Cinquième Plan*, Vol. I, p. 130.
2 *Premier Rapport de la Commission Nationale de l'Aménagement du Territoire*, *Commissariat du Plan*, Paris, 1964, p. 40.

of national efficiency implies too narrow a conception of growth. An unfair distribution of the benefits of growth resulting from geographical differences gives rise to a whole range of social problems and eventually undermines the very basis of economic development.'[1] Regional development must not, therefore, be expected to justify itself immediately. The balance to be struck in regional policy is between an allocation of investment which will deliberately create excess capacity in anticipation of and as a means of inducing self-sustaining growth in the less-developed regions but which will not place unreasonable strain on the physical and financial constraints on national growth.

Since the Paris region is by far the main attraction for emigrants from the west, the above commitment clearly implies a reduction in the growth of the Paris region. The CNAT report made two forecasts of the population of the Paris region in 1985. The first exercise (*hypothèse fort*) estimated an increase in total population from 8·6 million in 1963 to 12·1 million in 1985; a second forecast (*hypothèse faible*) gave a figure of 11·1 million. The difference is due entirely to assumptions about migration. The first forecast assumes constant annual net immigration of 80,000; the second a flow of immigration falling to nil in 1985. The Fifth Plan adopted as a benchmark an intermediate figure of 11·6 million in 1985 as being consistent with its job target for the regions in the west.

The compromise forecast is not a target in the same sense as the job creation figure for the west. It is a forecast based on definitely optimistic assumptions about the ability of regional policy to create an industrial base in the west far more extensive than anything achieved in the past. It poses problems and choices. The first concerns the economic role of the Paris region. The point has already been made that the Fifth Plan does not recommend draconian restrictions on the Paris region; its acceptance of a 1985 population of 11·6 million is clear evidence of this. The influence of the Paris planners here is significant. The forecasts made by CNAT and used in the Fifth Plan are based on their estimates of the population of the Paris region in the year 2000.[2] More important, their view of the future of the Paris region has undoubtedly influenced, if not entirely convinced, the central planners. The Paris planners point out in their study that their estimates are made not on the assumption of a *laissez-faire* economy, but are set in the context of a nationally

[1] CNAT, op. cit., p. 19.
[2] *Avant-Project de Programme Duodécennal pour la Région de Paris. Délégation Général au District de la Région de Paris*, Imprimerie Municipal, Paris, 1963.

organized regional policy. They do, however, add the strong *caveat* that in their view it would be 'stupid' and 'negligent' to plan the future of the Paris region on too optimistic assessments of the effectiveness of regional policy. In particular, they stress the magnitude of the problems involved in creating really effective provincial counterweights to Paris. In the light of these doubts they are emphatically confident that their estimates of the expansion of the Paris region are reasonable and feasible. Their case, however, does not rest solely on a judgment about the efficacy of regional policy. They proceed to the very important statement that a Paris region of the size suggested by their calculations is far from being against the interests of the French economy and the French nation as a whole. Paris is a natural centre of growth in France, and indeed in Europe, and is thus a suitable and in some cases the best possible location for the rapidly expanding industries. The offsetting social costs which are so frequently emphasized can be considerably reduced by sensible long-range physical planning of the Paris region. The planners are convinced that there is scope for this. The Paris basin is a relatively 'empty' region capable of absorbing both people and industry in an environment much more agreeable than that which exists, and is so frequently deplored, within the present limits of the *city* of Paris, and one which they frankly consider to be more attractive to the newer industries than a problematic new location in the west. To this end, plans are already in existence for the construction of eight new 'satellite' cities of between 300,000 and 1 million inhabitants along two axes running east-west to the north and south of Paris.[1] The Fifth Plan forecasts for the Paris region and the west thus do no more than meet the minimum estimates of the Paris planners, and there is every evidence that unless regional policy can quickly and effectively create provincial counter-influences to Paris the superior planning efforts of the Paris planners will serve to increase the attractiveness of that region.

The French regional problem is not, however, a simple dialogue between Paris and the west. The south-east of France, particularly the Rhône-Alpes region, has been attracting an increasing number of immigrants, and together with the rather different region of Provence-Côte d'Azur has been establishing itself as the most rapidly growing and powerful counter-attraction to Paris. In the north and north-east the reverse tendency has developed to the point where potentially serious losses of younger, skilled labour are being

[1] For a good short account in English of these developments, see Michel Piquard, 'Regional Planning in France', *Town and Country Planning Summer School*, Belfast, 1967.

experienced. The open frontiers with Belgium and Germany have aggravated the already considerable problems posed by the decline of the older industries concentrated in these regions. The accumulated industrial experience and the established and concentrated urban nature of these regions make the creation of a new infrastructure, the large-scale modernization of towns and cities and the introduction of new industires a national imperative. The proposed reduction of emigration from the west and the high forecasts of growth in the Paris region could well become incompatible with the continued development of these other regions. This fear is expressed in the Fifth Plan, but no conclusion is drawn except a restatement of the need for regional development to be viewed in a national and not a regional context. The clear implication, however, is that the real incompatibility at present lies in the attempt to bring about a significant reduction in migration from the west, and to allow the Paris region to expand as the present forecasts suggest.

The regional distribution of manpower proposed by the Fifth Plan is not likely to be achieved without considerable efforts by the regional planners. But the way in which the problem has been tackled yields some interesting and important lessons. The most important of these is that the regional manpower policy of the Plan was consciously organized at the national as well as the regional level. The prospects for each programme region were considered in relation to developments in all the others before the objectives of the national plan were finalized and the results of these exercises brought into confrontation. They were furthermore worked out in the context of a long-term forecast of regional development which provided a set of guidelines for the planners in each region to follow. This long term exercise is bound to be inaccurate and the guidelines to some extent arbitrary. They do, however, provide a framework of reference against which the various regional forecasts can be checked and which provides an outline of what the distribution of population and employment might on certain assumptions look like a generation hence. Such a framework is crucial if regional policy is not to become simply a series of marginal *ex post* correctives to situations created by the workings of the (by no means perfect) market economy and the different short- and medium-term priorities of a series of national plans exposed to the uncertainties inherent in an open economy. In the case of the Fifth Plan, this procedure led to substantial modifications of the various regional manpower forecasts and exposed areas of potential incompatibility during the course of the Plan. At the very least this means that when measures to increase productivity and to improve the performance of export industries are being considered, their effects on regional development will be one of the issues raised as a matter of course. Similarly, the effects of a deflationary reduction in public investment, which may be considered as unproductive at least in the short term, on the development of infrastructure in the west of France will be able to be taken into account.

One of the conditions for the success of the Fifth Plan's regional policy is an active and sophisticated manpower policy. Athough the aim of regional policy is to reduce internal migration from the west and the north and north-east, the planners consider it neither feasible nor desirable to halt migration completely. Indeed, in certain respects regional policy requires considerable mobility of labour, both geographical and occupational. The far-reaching structural reforms which are required in French industry, and which are being forced on it, bring with them the need for considerable changes in occupational structures. In the north and north-east regions such changes are essential to the future development of the region and are the only effective means of reducing the debilitating emigration of workers and the increasing number of school leavers and technical college and university graduates. The increasing importance of the services sector in the economy has made these industries of fundamental importance to the development of the less-developed regions. This must involve the transfer and extension of both public and private establishments away from the Paris region as well as the development of services in the regions themselves. For this to be achieved conditions must be created in the provinces which will attract or at least not deter the movement out of Paris of professional and managerial personnel and their families and halt the emigration of people with such training to Paris.

Geographical mobility within regions is also a key element in the Fifth Plan's regional policy. The acceptance of the principle of concentration of both industrial and agricultural activities in centres where they can operate competitively must involve both permanent migration and commuting on a large scale. In the sparsely populated regions of the west the former is likely to be the more important. The difficulties of promoting this kind of mobility are likely to be considerable, and much more knowledge of the factors influencing mobility is required so that the costly investment in communications, housing and urban development to which it gives rise will be most effectively undertaken. Mobility over shorter distances has an important role to play as well. The provincial centres selected as counterweights to the Paris region and the new cities around Paris must develop sophisticated labour markets independent of the influence of Paris. This will require provision to be made for extensive travel to work into these centres.

There is, finally, the increasingly significant role of the services or 'tertiary' sector. The manpower forecasts of the Fifth Plan showed that it is in this sector that the disparities between Paris and the rest of France are greatest. Employment in service industries is also a crucial part of the strategy of creating centres of growth outside Paris. There is, however, even less known about the influences governing the growth of this type of employment than about industrial employment. With France becoming rapidly a more urban society, the Plan presses for more research on the relationship between the growth of employment in services and the growth of towns. Another area to be explored should be the development of services in relation to the growth of employment in agriculture and industry. It is particularly important to have more detailed information about this relationship, since the continued rundown of manpower in agriculture and the growth of towns is a feature of many French regions and one which it is the aim of regional policy to promote and organize in the form of centres of growth in both industrial and agricultural areas.

The third major influence in the Fifth Plan is the increase in the proportion of people living in areas classified as urban. In 1962, 74 per cent of the French population lived in urban areas as against 70·7 per cent in 1954. Over the same period the urban population grew by 13·8 per cent, while the total population increased by only 8·1 per cent. The need to provide the facilities and infrastructure required by this expansion and to use it as a means of promoting economic growth will require considerable investment, and important choices will have to be made about its distribution among and within the various regions. As the Fifth Plan puts it: 'For ten years economic growth has been able to proceed within the limits of infrastructure already in existence and largely written off. Now this infrastructure is utilized nearly to saturation point especially in the fast growing, densely populated regions.'[1] In the less-developed regions the concentration of development in selected centres similarly requires sizeable new investment in infrastructure.

In this situation the regionalization of public investment begun during the Fourth Plan assumes central importance in regional policy and the Fifth Plan introduced some important improvements in the process. Although the *tranches opératoires* for the period of the Plan were not worked out until after the first budget of the plan (1966), the long-term studies of the CNAT and the co-ordinated

[1] *Cinquième Plan*, Vol. I, p. 119.

regional reports provided a much firmer base for decisions about the regional distribution of investment. Advances were made, too, in the preparation of regional breakdowns of investment within government departments, particularly in the Ministries of Education, Housing, Agriculture, and Youth and Sport.

The regionalization of the 1966 budget was therefore done on the basis of more carefully thought-out allocation criteria (*clés de répartition*). The Fifth Plan distinguishes between public expenditure designed to bring a region into some kind of parity with other regions and the more selective action designed to promote economic growth in certain chosen centres.[1] The former objective is particularly important in the distribution of 'social infrastructure' investment in housing, water, hospitals, telecommunications, and primary and secondary education. In housing, the 1966 budget took overcrowding and inhabitability formally into account in the regional distribution of expenditure as well as the normal criteria of population size, natural population growth and immigration. The principle of parity is a simple and an obvious one, but it is of great importance for regional policy. Since infrastructure defined in the broadest terms is basic to the development of an area, the existence of a system aimed at achieving parity of conditions ensures that the less prosperous and thus less well-endowed regions are more or less *automatically* assured of a fair share of public investment. It also means that the creation of facilities in areas where they are absent, and the improvement or replacement of them in areas where they have become inadequate and obsolete, are not postponed or left out of account in the face of the pressing quantitative needs of the rapidly growing prosperous areas.

The Fifth Plan's regional strategy required, however, a selective as well as an egalitarian approach to public expenditure. This was applied in two ways. The first concerned the location of individual projects such as universities, training colleges, national parks, government departments or extensions or branches of them, and collective efforts such as the tourist centre on the Languedoc-Roussillon coast. The location of these projects had to be decided in the context of the varying possibilities offered by different regions and by different locations within these regions. The second type of selection concerned the use of more general public goods (e.g. housing, water, etc.) to promote economic development in certain areas. There are a number of essential preconditions for this kind of operation. Firstly, it pre-

---

[1] See 'La Régionalisation du Budget de l'Etat et l'Aménagement du Territoire, 1966', *La Documentation Française. Notes et Etudes Documentaires*, December 7, 1965, No. 3243.

supposes that a decision at the national level has been made about the areas of the economy where the growth of population and employment is going to be encouraged to concentrate over a reasonably long period, certainly long enough to justify the creation in them or around them of assets which are relatively long-lived and whose very existence will have a significant influence on the regional pattern of activity. The designation in the Fifth Plan of eight counterweight cities (*métropoles d'équilibre*) marks one of the most clearcut decisions on this point that any Western Europe country has taken. A second requirement is that the regional planners 'at the centre' or the national level should possess as full information as possible about the different regional economies, the areas within them where development can most effectively be centred, and the size and nature of the public investment needed in these areas to provide the physical environment which will encourage growth. This information can be provided only through the collaboration of experts in differing disciplines and particularly by an integration of physical planning with economic and social planning. The policy of *métropoles d'équilibre* in the Fifth Plan emphasizes the crucial role that the physical planning of cities and regions has to play in regional development. A further requirement is that individual government departments should prepare their estimates and plan their programmes in a way which distinguishes between the equalizing and stimulating functions of their expenditure so that the expenditure finally agreed on, and any cuts which may be required as part of short term economic policy, will be decided in the fullest possible knowledge of their effects on regional development.

The regional distribution of capital spending is dependent not only on conscious decisions about the needs of each region but upon the conditions under which the annual budget is prepared. Expenditure on regional development is, therefore, not favoured by any longer term assurances like those that were provided by the programme laws (*lois-programmes*) voted for certain public projects in the Third Plan. The need to protect public investment in the less prosperous regions from the rigours of the annual budgetary vote was, however, recognized in 1963 when a special fund, the Regional Development Fund (Fonds d'Intervention pour l'Aménagement du Territoire—FIAT), was established. This fund was placed under the control of a newly appointed official, the Délégué Général de l'Aménagement du Territoire. The object of the Fund is to give short-term supplementary finance to projects which cannot be financed adequately in any financial year by budget credits or local authority contributions. The scope of the fund is strictly limited by the size of its resources and the restriction of its activities to operations which are assured of budgetary approval in the following financial year and to whose financing local authorities make a contribution of at least one-third. The annual credits voted the fund have never exceeded 175 million francs. It cannot, therefore, do more than provide bridging finance and then only for projects already approved. The fund has so far concentrated its aid in Brittany and the south-west and in the *métropoles d'équilibre*. Over a third of its aid has been devoted to financing road programmes and the remainder to urban development schemes, industrial estates, technical education and training, and agricultural improvement schemes. Around 10 per cent of FIAT's funds has been used to finance certain regional research projects. It has given financial support to research on urban development and planning in the *métropoles d'équilibre* and feasibility studies of the proposed Rhône-Rhine canal system linking the North Sea with the Mediterranean. It is also contributing to the financing of the land purchases necessary for the implementation of this latter operation.

FIAT is therefore no more than a useful instrument of adjustment and continuity in French regional policy, at least so far. The key factor is without doubt the regional distribution of budget credits. The French arrangements here are extremely interesting and important. But however extensively and carefully regional development needs are written into the process of allocating public credits, the object of the exercise, the integration of regional and national development, will not be achieved until a decision is made at the national level about where the public investment effort is to be concentrated. It is with this important question of selection that the next chapter is concerned.

.

CHAPTER 8

GROWTH AREAS AND FRENCH REGIONAL POLICY

As explained in Chapter 7, the legislation of 1955 listed a number of critical areas which were to be given certain special assistance. These areas were selected according to the criterion of above-average local unemployment or the imminent threat of it. The aim of policy was frankly to 'rescue' these areas by creating new jobs in them. This approach to regional policy quickly came under criticism. In a report to the Conseil Economique et Social, Prof. Maurice Byé was sharply critical of the system of critical areas and the regime of incentives related to them.[1] He argued instead that a distinction should be made between 'depressed areas' as they were defined in Britain, where a rescue operation was required, and 'development areas' where there was a reasonable chance of economic development. Policy towards depressed areas must aim at creating conditions in which industry could operate competitively without reliance on a *continuing* subsidy. An initial grant or subsidy could be given but it should be directed towards offsetting the costs of transfer and 'settling-in' and should on no account be permanent. An area unable to sustain industry under these circumstances ought not to be scheduled as eligible for special advantages. M. Byé went on to argue that development areas need not be areas with economic problems. It was much more important that they should be able to provide a sufficient supply of suitably trained or trainable manpower, industrial land and infrastructure to sustain efficient industrial growth. M. Byé pressed the point that it is these factors rather than financial inducements which are the most powerful and decisive attractions to a firm. A development area must also be able to support a complex of firms rather than just an isolated factory. It is much easier to attract industry to an area if the external economies provided by the presence of other firms are present. The selection of areas fulfilling these conditions should form the basis of the

[1] *Avis et Rapports du Conseil Economique et Social. Les Objectifs et les Principes d'une Politique des Economies Régionales. Rapport presenté par M. M. Byé, Journal Officiel*, May 7, 1957.

regional programmes. Substantially similar points were made in a later report by M. Jules Milhau.[1]

This line of criticism of regional policy was not without effect. In March 1959, in addition to the 'zones critiques', seven areas within them were scheduled as special conversion areas (zones speciales de conversion)—Avesnes-Fourmies in the north, Calais and Béthune in the *département* of Pas-de-Calais, the Vosges valleys in the north-east, Nantes-St-Nazaire in the west, the three towns of Montpellier, Sète and Bèziers in the extreme south-east, and Limoges. All these areas were chosen because of a recession in the dominant industry of the locality and because they were considered to be at a particular disadvantage in the face of competition from the other Common Market countries. They were given two privileges. Firms establishing in them were eligible for investment grants at the maximum rates, 20 per cent for a new firm entering the area and 15 per cent for an operation of extension, concentration or specialization by a firm already in the area. Second, and by no means less important, the formalities required to obtain these grants were considerably streamlined.

Although the newly scheduled areas were all relatively small in area, and despite the fact that unemployment was still the criterion of selection, they were singled out as areas *within* existing critical areas where aid should be concentrated. To this extent the scheduling of the new areas could be represented as a move away from, or forward from, the original policy of diffusion of aid to all areas with local unemployment problems towards one of concentration on selected areas.

Almost immediately, however, there was another switch of direction in policy. In April 1959 a decree was issued extending the benefits available in the critical areas and the special conversion areas to localities outside these areas 'in which there existed exceptionally serious total or partial unemployment or a particularly large number of job seekers or where such a situation could arise in the near future because of the likely or actual closure of factories or of a significant reduction in the level of their activity'.[2] This measure was aimed at dealing with the consequences of the recession of 1959 in certain localities without having to schedule new critical areas. Flexibility was again preferred to the creation of new industrial

[1] *Avis et Rapports du Conseil Economique et Social. Problèmes de l'Elaboration et de l'Exécution des Plans Régionaux. Rapport présenté par M. Jules Milhau Journal Officiel*, May 15, 1960.

[2] *Décret No.* 59-483, April 2, 1959, *Journal Officiel* April 3, 1959, quoted in P. Bauchet 'Regional Development Policies in France,' op. cit., p. 112.

structures in the regions affected based on the promotion of new industrial development in preselected areas able to induce and sustain it.

In April 1960 a further change was introduced.[1] The regional manpower studies for the Fourth Plan had by 1960 produced estimates of the probable future demand for and supplies of labour in the different programme regions. These indicated that throughout the west, south-west and, in a rather different category, parts of the north and centre of France, a labour surplus was likely which, if left alone, would lead to sizeable emigration, mainly to Paris. The decree of April 15, 1960, reorganized regional policy in order to stimulate industrial development in these areas and bring their labour markets more into balance. The seven special conversion areas scheduled in 1959 were reduced to four: Nantes-St Nazaire, Limoges, Montpellier and Bordeaux. In 1961 virtually the whole of Brittany was added to this list. To deal with the problems of agricultural development, certain rural areas (*zones spéciales d'action rurale*) were scheduled again in Brittany and the Loire basin. These areas were to be given priority in respect of agricultural research and training establishments, road building programmes, electric power supply, housing and tourist facilities. Capital grants were made available to farmers to aid mechanization and other modernization schemes and reductions in railway tariffs were authorized for farmers if the distance from their suppliers and customers significantly affected their operations. The system of designating areas where and when the need arose (the *coup par coup* policy) was still applied, but the 1960 measures did mark something of a move towards promoting development in certain areas as a long-term operation aimed at halting the flow of migration to Paris. This is a very different aim and implies very different policies from a strategy concerned principally to alleviate short-term unemployment in particular localities.

The regional policy of the Fourth Plan developed this difference. It began by making the basic distinction between regions whose development required a policy of 'accompaniment' and those where a policy of 'impulsion' was required. Particularly in the latter the Plan argued that 'regional policy would be wasteful and ineffective if it took the form of a general "scattering" of resources (*saupoudrage*). To be successful it must concentrate its efforts on well-chosen points of application. In this way effective poles of development would be created. Preferential treatment by the State in the development of infrastructure and educational and training establishments must be

[1] *Décret No.* 60-370, April 15, 1960.

given to these centres to encourage large firms to expand there. The growth of these principal centres would have a stimulating effect on their environment and encourage the growth of a system of secondary poles where components and maintenance activities could establish themselves.'[1] The argument for growth areas is thus fully taken. This was an important advance in French regional policy, but it is very much easier to accept and expound the concept of growth areas than to implement it. The Fourth Plan did, however, go on to outline a series of concrete proposals aimed at doing this.

It first of all indicated the particular areas which were to act as development poles or growth areas. For this purpose it divided France into seven regions (defined in terms of the twenty-two programme regions)—Paris and the Paris basin, the north, the east, the west, the Massif Central, the Midi aquitain et pyrénéen, the Midi méditerranéen and the Rhône basin—and on the basis of information supplied by the regional plans for each programme region, sketched out a strategy of development for each of these seven larger regions based on the development of a number of areas of growth in each. The Plan did not formally indicate such areas in the manner adopted in Italy although certain localities were specified as crucial to the regions' economies. Generally speaking, the growth areas were those parts of the regions where economic growth had already taken place and which had the basic requirements for future growth and areas where natural resource endowment provided a feasible base for new economic development such as the large-scale tourist playground project on the Languedoc-Roussillon coast, the agricultural development scheme in the Landes and Gascogne regions, the project to build a national park in the Cevennes, the large irrigation schemes in the Bas-Rhône-Languedoc areas and the exploitation of the natural gas deposits at Lacq in the south-west. The Plan emphasized the need for improved communications both within and between regions as a basic factor in any development strategy. An effective communications system within a region was a crucial factor in the creation of a wide and varied labour market and was the means of linking major growth areas with other parts of the region. Or more accurately, it allowed the growth area to become geographically more extensive. Good intra-regional communications allowed the benefits of external economies due to the presence of a complex of firms with related activities to be enjoyed without the need for close physical proximity of plants. For most of the seven regions mentioned above the Plan singled out one or two towns or cities which were to be the foci of development in the

[1] *Quatrième Plan*, op. cit., p. 46.

region, but these were seen as the centres of a development strategy involving a larger number of communities. It did not envisage a regional development policy which relied solely on sucking population and industry into the main centres.

A second feature of the Plan's growth area strategy was its concentration on publicly provided infrastructure as the main force making for development, using the regionalization of public investment within the framework of the *tranches opératoires* as the means of implementing this policy. The vital role of communications has already been mentioned. The Plan also outlined schemes for decentralizing the programmes of school building and the expansion of university and research establishments in the light of the different regional development needs. Particular attention was paid to the west of France, where the provision of training centres for workers leaving agriculture and for school leavers with no prospects of finding employment in agriculture and the more general provision of university-level education and research institutes were considered major necessities if the newer industries in the manufacturing sector were to be attracted to the region and if it was to have its share of the rapidly expanding educational sector. Urban development and redevelopment schemes and the decentralization of all types of government establishment were two other areas where regional development needs were given first claim. The Plan makes it very clear that infrastructure is the key to regional development and more important than financial aid to private industry.

There is here a marked similarity between French policy and British regional policy. In one sense this is curious for, in the preparation of the Fourth Plan, the Modernization Commissions which supply the industrial data for the central planners were asked specifically to indicate the regional distribution of each industry's activities and its locational preferences and requirements. This information was used in the preparation of the *tranches opératoires*. But there is no hint in the Plan's section on regional policy of a willingness to supplement the regionalization of public investment with any schemes which would indicate in a systematic and detailed way the kind of industries which a particular region ought to have. Certain general lines of approach are recommended. The Plan set out in broad terms the kind of industries which are required in each of the seven regions in the light of its existing industrial structure, the changes taking place in it, the size and nature of its labour force and significant natural or created advantages. Particularly in the west, the Plan stressed the importance of having several firms which could, by their need for suppliers and maintenance services relatively

G 193

close at hand, act as the principal units of industrial groups or complexes of a technically interrelated nature. What is not specified is how such groupings are to be created.

The task of encouraging the relevant firms to locate in certain localities rests mainly on the industrial incentive policy and the creation of *infrastructure* external economies through the implementation of the *tranches opératoires*. The term 'infrastructure external economies' is one which has assumed increasing importance in both French and British regional policies. External economies are traditionally defined as cost reductions accruing to a firm as a result of the close proximity to it of other firms preferably with technically related production processes. This includes many items normally subsumed under the heading infrastructure—roads, port facilities, rail links, housing, commercial, industrial and personal services including educational and training facilities. These are the result of government action to provide for the needs of industrial development in the region concerned; they are the *consequences* of industrial development. The distinction between the infrastructure aspects of external economies and the industrial aspects is in this situation simply a matter of timing. If, however, in an effort to promote regional development infrastructure is created *in anticipation of* industrial development and in excess of current demands, a firm establishing in that region may enjoy the external economies provided by the infrastructure although there may be little in the way of industrial external economies, at least for the first firms coming to the region, if expansion there involves them moving away from their suppliers and sales outlets. It is this latter model on which the regional policy of the Fourth Plan is based. The direction of particular firms to particular areas, the operation being phased so that several firms would establish themselves in the region at the same time, thus ensuring industrial external economies for each other, is not anywhere recommended.

The implementation of 'growth area' policy was very considerably extended in the regional policy of the Fifth Plan. It centred on the selection of eight provincial cities which were designated as counterweight cities (métropoles d'équilibre) whose function was to act as counterweights to the economic and social pull of Paris and as the focal points of development in the different regions. These cities, or in some cases city regions, are Lyons-St Etienne, Marseilles-Aix-Delta du Rhône, Bordeaux, Lille-Roubaix-Tourcoing, Toulouse, Strasbourg, Nantes-St Nazaire and Nancy-Metz-Thionville.

Two major factors underlay the decision to create the *métropoles*. The first was the rapid growth of the urban population in France which was uncovered by the 1962 Census of population. It is quite clear from the planners' reports that the results came as a shock. In 1962, 74 per cent of the population lived in areas classified as urban compared with 70·7 per cent in 1954. Between 1954 and 1962 the urban population increased by 13·8 per cent compared with an increase in total population of 8·1 per cent. The outstanding feature of urban growth was the increase in the number of people living in large towns. In 1954, 33 per cent of the population lived in communities of 5,000 to 100,000 persons; in 1962 this figure had fallen to 22·7 per cent. This was almost entirely due to the growth of communities of 100,000 persons and above. These accounted for 36 per cent of the population in 1962 as against 17 per cent in 1954. In 1954 there were thirty-three urban agglomerations with more than 100,000 persons; in 1962 there were forty. This represents a very rapid increase; in 1901 communities of over 100,000 persons accounted for 14 per cent of the population.

The planners do not accept that the developments in the period from 1954 to 1962 are abnormal and that the growth of large communities will slow down in the future. They see them rather as the beginning of a process of increasing concentration of population in large centres which will continue. They are therefore not prepared to accept the idea of 'a France of average-sized towns'. Equally, they recognize the disadvantages of large cities but they argue that these are an inevitable urban form and that the real problem, and the potential crisis, is the inadequacy of the present urban structure both over the economy as a whole and within individual towns.[1] This conclusion has extremely significant implications for regional policy. The forecast pattern of urban development 'does represent not only quantitative growth but a profound economic transformation. This is due to the increasing role which the tertiary or "quartiary" (*quaternaire*) sectors are playing in the national economy.'[2] The planners take the view that regional policy has paid too little attention to this transformation and has been too exclusively concerned with industrial decentralization. It is no longer the case that the regional distribution of population and activities is influenced solely by the location of manufacturing industry. The influence of the facilities and services which large urban concentrations provide, both in themselves and for industry, has made the economic growth of regional economies dependent on the growth of its towns

[1] CNAT, op. cit., p. 81 *et seq.* and 'La Croissance Urbaine et les Problèmes d'Urbanisation'. *La Documentation Française. Notes et Etudes Docementaires*, July 16, 1965, No. 3210.
[2] *Notes et Etudes Documentaires*, No. 3210, op. cit.

and not the other way round as formerly. The construction of a nationally organized urban framework (*armature urbaine*) based on the assumption of increasing urban concentration is thus basic to regional development policy. The designation of the *métropoles d'équilibre* is the first step in this operation.

Even if urban concentration was not made inevitable by changes in the structure of industry and occupations, the creation of several large urban centres would be a *sine qua non* for French regional development policy in order to lessen the tremendous dominance of the Paris region in the economy. Although the 1962 Census showed that Paris grew less rapidly between 1954 and 1962 than many other French towns, the fact remains that there is no other urban centre which exercises anything like the attractive power of the capital. In this respect France is much more centralized than any other European economy. To redress the balance required the creation in the provinces of a small number of centres which can offer to their residents, both as consumers and producers, advantages comparable to those provided in Paris and which as a result will act as a centre of attraction for their region and be competitive with Paris.

Both these factors lead naturally to the selection of few rather than many *métropoles*. The planners accepted this point and named eight cities to fulfil the role. These are shown on Map 3.

This may seem the only obvious starting-point for policy, but it is the first time in the history of French regional policy that there has been a clear delineation of the areas to which regional policy in all its aspects is to concentrate its efforts. The definition of the *métropoles* represents an extremely important decision about the future regional distribution of population in France. Such a clear choice is fraught with political difficulties and poses many awkward social and economic problems, but it does make plain the basic objective of regional policy and the criterion by which it is to be judged. There are few other countries in which the aims of regional policy have been spelled out in such detail and the need for policies to be selective so openly admitted.

The eight *métropoles* were selected according to three main criteria. They had firstly to have a population large enough to provide a labour market sufficiently wide and varied to offer attractive employment opportunities in most occupations and to serve as an attraction to both indigenous and immigrant firms. The size of the product market was also critical. The investment in infrastructure which would be undertaken in the *métropoles* could show reasonable returns only if there were a sufficient demand for the facilities and

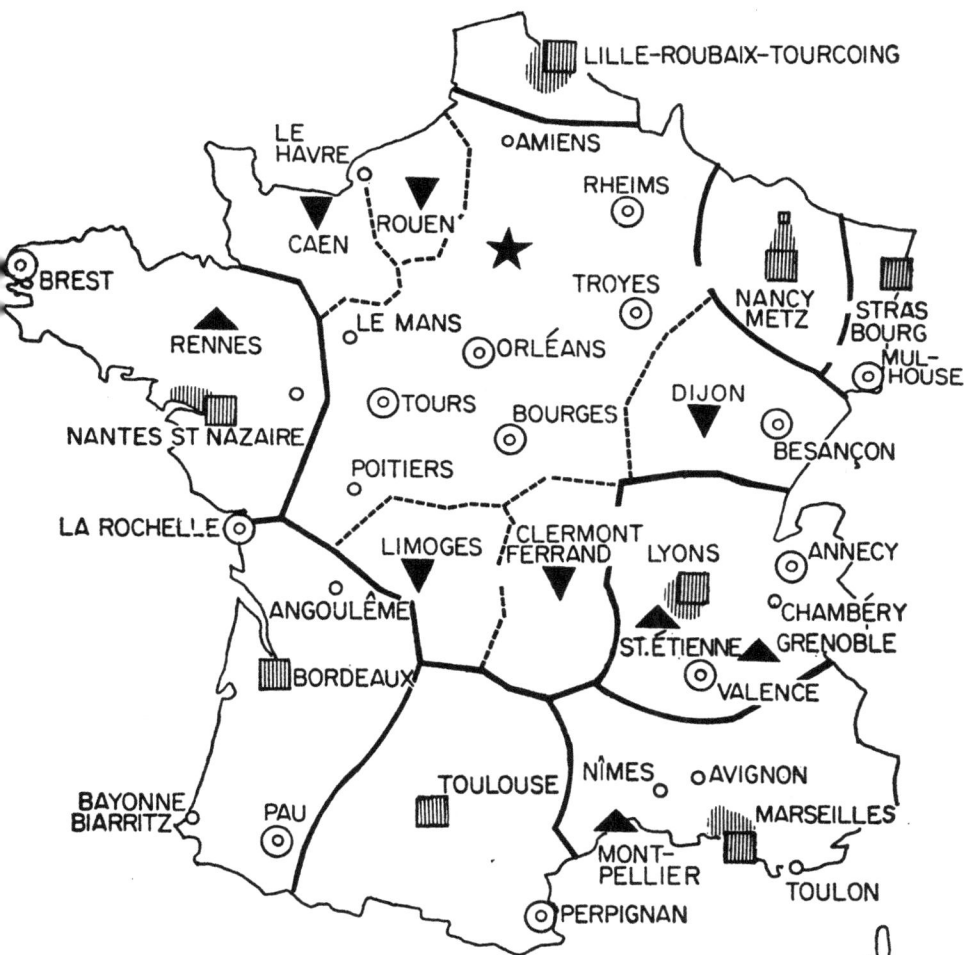

Map legend:

— Boundaries of the areas of influence of métropole

--- Boundaries of areas of influence of regional centres which are dependent on Paris

▲ Regional centres within the area of influence of a métropole

▼ Regional centres dependent on Paris

⊙ Regional centres for specific purposes

○ Regional centres of lesser importance

▥ Métropoles and metropolitan areas

MAP 3: The regional function of certain towns in France
Source: La Croissance Urbaine, op. cit., p. 20

if it were large enough to permit significant economies of scale in their construction.

Secondly, the cities chosen as *métropoles* had to possess a sufficiently wide range of activities to allow them to become seriously competitive with Paris. The features stressed by the planners were 'a fully developed commercial network including wholesale establishments and rare or specialized and luxury retail trades; a sophisticated banking system and a powerful financial sector drawing its strength not only from the banks but from the number of large firms with head offices in the city; large-scale provision of the usual services (administration, higher education, hospital and medical services, cultural facilities) and specialized professions'.[1] A town or city might have a large enough population to qualify as a *métropole*, but if its activities were too narrow and specialized, e.g. predominantly concerned with a university, industry or tourism, it could not be considered as a potential regional Paris. This principle marks a total victory for the school of thought which considers regional development possible only if efforts and privileges are concentrated in those parts of the region where growth is feasible. All the *métropoles* are towns which have been selected on the basis of their importance to the economies of their region and not to their need, whether of employment, increased income, etc.

Finally, the *métropoles* were judged according to what was termed their area of influence. This was a point of much significance if they were to play the part of counter-attractions to Paris and act as the focal points of regional growth. The limits of these areas are shown on the map on page 197. A number of different indicators were used to measure this area of influence. Once again attention was focused on the range of activities for which the town or city acted as a centre. To fulfil the function of a *métropole* a city had to be the regional centre for a wide range of activities and not simply an intellectual centre or a central place of employment. M. Olivier Guichard analyses the areas of influence of the eight *métropoles* in terms of three types of activity: intellectual activity, commercial relations, and direct suburban and travel to work functions.[2] This division shows up considerable differences in the proportionate importance of the three types of influence exercised by the *métropoles*.

[1] CNAT, op. cit., p. 82. The planners considered twenty-two professions as specialized and divided them into three categories: those serving consumers; those serving firms (engineering consultants, chartered accountants and advertising agencies); those serving both firms and individuals (lawyers, credit institutions, etc.).

[2] O. Guichard, *Aménager la France*, Laffont Gonthier, Paris, 1965, pp. 69-74 and map on p. 72.

The detailed task of selection was undertaken by the CNAT. The three criteria discussed above were applied to all towns which had the status of *préfecture* (capital of a *département*) and/or which had a population of over 20,000. The range of activities in the town were divided into economic services and personal services (*services a l'usage de l'économie* and *services a l'usage des particuliers*). The zone of influence of the town was measured in several ways. The main indicators used were: migration flows, including daily travel to work, into the town; telephone calls, both outward and inward, in so far as automatic exchanges permit this calculation; rail and road traffic for all purposes into and out of town. An estimate was also made of the number of wage earners working outside the town in branches of businesses whose head offices were located in the town. Different weights were given to these different criteria and a final ranking produced on a points system. Diagram 1 shows the final result of the calculations.

Diagram 1 shows the clear separation which exists between the first eight towns, those chosen as *métropoles*, and all the others; no similar discontinuity appears among the other towns. The planners do, however, divide them into groups again on the growth point model. After the *métropoles* come ten towns which, although less independent of each other and Paris than the *métropoles*, do act as the focal points of particular activities in their region. Below these is a group of twenty-four towns with what the planners term an 'incomplete regional function' and a further group of twenty-five towns with reasonable facilities. These are followed by a large number of towns of the *sub-préfecture* type which have a certain local dominance. There is finally the system of villages and small country towns whose functions are being altered by the rapid changes in the organization of agriculture and by the government's concern to reduce the disparities in living standards between rural and urban areas. The planners see these changes as leading towards the development of certain towns as rural centres acting as service centres for their agricultural hinterlands.

The acceptance of the growth area principle in the context of widely scattered rural populations is a response to a number of different factors. The first is simply the cost of providing in rural communities those social infrastructure facilities which, in many cases, are not only inadequate but totally lacking and which are essential if the aim of social parity between the rural and urban populations is to be achieved. Dispersion here is ruled out on grounds of cost. The developments within agriculture point in the same direction. Increasing demand for personal services as a result of increased

199

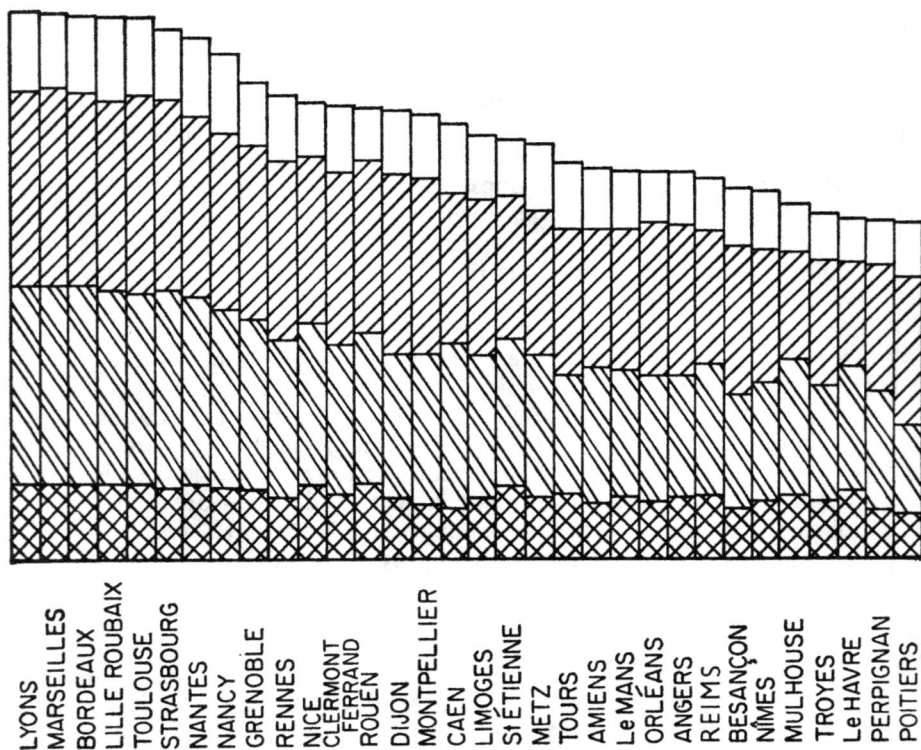

Key

☐ External influence

▨ Personal services

▧ Services to industry and commerce

▩ Population

LYONS
MARSEILLES
BORDEAUX
LILLE ROUBAIX
TOULOUSE
STRASBOURG
NANTES
NANCY
GRENOBLE
RENNES
NICE
CLERMONT FERRAND
ROUEN
DIJON
MONTPELLIER
CAEN
LIMOGES
St ÉTIENNE
METZ
TOURS
AMIENS
Le MANS
ORLÉANS
ANGERS
REIMS
BESANÇON
NÎMES
MULHOUSE
TROYES
Le HAVRE
PERPIGNAN
POITIERS

DIAGRAM 1

Importance of various towns to regional development.
Source: 'La Croissance Urbaine et les Problèmes d'Urbanisation,' *La Documentation Française. Notes et Etudes Documentaires,* July 1965, No. 3210.

incomes and the increasing contact with urban life which improved communications have brought, coupled with the growth of specialization and mechanization in the production process, has led to the emergence of certain towns as centres where these different facilities can be found together. The parallel increase in the numbers of agricultural workers continuing with higher education both at secondary school and post-school training colleges requires the construction of new establishments which cannot like primary schools be dispersed throughout a large number of villages.

This specification of different levels of urban organization is deliberate. The planners go to considerable lengths to emphasize that the creation of *métropoles d'équilibre* does not mean that the *métropole* should be allowed to spread like a grease stain over the map of its area of influence. Its function is rather to act as the central place of a highly developed communications network linking regional centres and rural centres. The growth area strategy implied by the *métropoles* is the encouragement of development over a large geographical area with the different centres playing their particular specialized roles at different levels. This strategy is well founded and feasible in regions like Lyons, Marseilles and Lille-Tourcoing-Roubaix, where an established communications network exists even if in an outdated form and to an inadequate degree. In less-developed regions, however, the problem is to lay down this infrastructure for the first time and, as in the west of France, to create quite new communications patterns. This problem arises in acute form in the cases of Toulouse, Bordeaux and Brest. If these towns are to fulfil the role of a *métropole* there must be a rapid and substantial improvement in their liaison with other regional centres. If this is not done, the traditional migration flow to Paris will continue with its adverse effects on the development of the region.

While the *métropoles* are regarded as part of a system of regional development it remains none the less true that they are to house considerable concentrations of population and activities—particularly service industries. This raises the question of the size of the *métropoles*.

The notion of a minimum and maximum size of community runs throughout the discussions of the *métropoles* and indeed minimum size was one of the main criteria in their selection. Table 8.1 suggests that a city region of less than 300,000 persons is unlikely to be capable of playing the part of a *métropole* which can act as the centre of development for a wide area. This same figure has been accepted by the Paris planners as the minimum size for the eight new cities around which the Paris region is planned. This is a deliberate choice, as M. Piquard makes clear. 'The master plan dismisses the idea of vast single-purpose housing developments with from 30,000 to 100,000 inhabitants. Instead, it maps out new urban hubs capable of serving from 300,000 to a million inhabitants and providing them with almost everything they need.'[1] The ceiling size beyond which diseconomies of scale and external diseconomies occur would appear to be around 1,500,000. The question of size, however, is inextricably bound up with that of structure, and both the Paris planners and those in charge of regional planning at the national level are convinced that the internal structure of the new population centres must be subject to extensive controls by planning authorities able to consider and plan the *métropole* or the new city as a whole and

TABLE 8.1
TOTAL POPULATION OF PARIS AND THE MÉTROPOLES IN 1962

Paris	7,664,000
Lyons-St Etienne	1,459,000
Marseilles-Aix	920,000
Lille-Tourcoing-Roubaix	864,000
Nancy-Metz-Thionville	1,085,000
Strasbourg	417,000
Nantes-St Nazaire	505,000
Bordeaux	524,000
Toulouse	357,000

Source: *Notes et Etudes Documentaires*,
No. 3243, p. 14.

not as a series of semi-autonomous local authority areas. Already some quite far-reaching reforms in regional and city administration have been made to create the kind of planning machinery required by the new regional development strategy. These are discussed in the next and final part of this chapter.

The success of the *métropoles* as the major agents of regional development policy will depend to a large extent on whether they can reduce the influence of the Paris region. The figures in Table 8.1 indicate the very large disparities in size between Paris and the largest of the *métropoles*, Lyons-St Etienne. More important, for regional policy, however, is the difference in size between Paris and the much smaller *métropoles* in the west and south-west where the cost of creating a really powerful regional centre is much greater than in the industrialized north and east. The problem in the west and south-west is further complicated by the existence of several

[1] M. Piquard, op. cit., p. 10.

towns of relatively similar size and importance to the *métropoles* of Bordeaux, Nantes-St Nazaire and Toulouse. In one sense this might be considered a benefit since the development of this vast area could be organized round these towns on the basis of a large, well-planned expansion in communications. Such a strategy, however, is scarcely compatible with the *métropoles* policy, and would fail on the crucial point that it would not give these regions the kind of focal point which is required to counterbalance Paris in the context of an industrial structure which is becoming increasingly dominated by service industries whose natural environment is a large city. What the *métropoles* require is not a number of related centres of equal importance to them but a series of satellite towns providing reasonable employment opportunities and income prospects while leaving the essentially metropolitan activities to the *métropole*. Given the already small size of the western and southwestern *métropoles*, the creation of this kind of urban network is going to pose many awkward choices for the planners and the government. This problem was raised in the regional report on Brittany which stressed the need for a clarification of the functions of Rennes in relation to the *métropole* Nantes-St Nazaire. This is a particularly interesting case since Rennes, which is the site of the large Citroën plant (moved there in 1957), has always been considered the main centre of growth in the Brittany peninsula. The relationship of Angers and Le Mans to the *métropole* was also raised in the report on the Loire basin.

Another obvious criticism of the *métropoles* strategy is its neglect of the centre of France. It is possible to attribute this to a sound economic judgment about the extent to which regional development can be pushed without coming seriously into conflict with the objective of increasing the competitiveness of the national economy. The locations of the *métropoles* of Lille-Tourcoing-Roubaix, Nancy-Metz-Thionville, Strasbourg and Lyons-St Etienne while peripheral in the context of France are in natural growth areas of the EEC economy. It could also be argued that given the large amounts of infrastructure investment required to promote the other *métropoles*, the addition of a further centre such as Clermont-Ferrand would impose unacceptable additional costs to the economy or diffuse and delay the development of the other *métropoles*. More serious, however, is the criticism that it is simply not feasible to create a *métropole* in the centre of France because neither Clermont-Ferrand nor Limoges possesses the necessary initial facilities.[1] This attitude implies leaving

[1] J. Hautreux, 'Le Rôle des Métropoles d'Equilibre dans l'Armature Urbaine', *Revue Juridique et Economique du Sud-Ouest*, No. 4, 1966, p. 805.

the whole of the centre of France and Burgundy within the zone of influence of Paris. The population of this area is too large to justify such an approach, which could conceivably be accepted if the area in question had no future other than more or less gradual depopulation tempered by the development of tourism and related activities. But an alternative strategy, in the absence of a *métropole*, may be very difficult to implement successfully.

There is finally the extremely important question of whether the policy of *métropoles* is compatible with the present plans for the development for the Paris region. The map on page 197 indicates the large area of influence which the planners have accepted for Paris, even excluding the cases of Clermont-Ferrand and Limoges. Towns like Rouen and Dijon have not been named as *métropoles* in the main because of their dependence on Paris for metropolitan services and their consequent small areas of influence, and the eight projected satellite cities round Paris are all planned to have populations of the same order of magnitude as the *métropoles*. This must necessarily involve a diffusion of effort in the building up of infrastructure in the *métropoles* and in the case of some individual projects a choice between a location in one of the new cities in the Paris region and one of the *métropoles*. It is generally agreed that the development of the Paris region must be planned in order to ensure that it fulfils its role as the major growth area in France as effectively as possible; the construction of the *métropoles* is seen as a complementary operation. This is a reasonable approach, but it does mean that the *métropoles* will have to compete from the start with the attractions of a Paris region becoming in physical terms progressively better planned and organized. It is true that the cost of residence in the Paris region will increase as measures are introduced to distribute the burden of social costs on to those who create them. But given the practical difficulties in this field, it is still possible that particularly in the private sector the net external economies of a Paris location may still appear to be positive.

If it is assumed that the attractive power of the Paris region will grow as that of the *métropoles* increases there will then be a kind of competition to extend the areas of influence. Here it is important to note that the areas of influence of the *métropoles* shown on page 197 have been estimated leaving Paris out of account. The boundaries of the eight *métropoles* measure the limits of each in relation to the seven others but not in relation to Paris. The area shown as the zone of influence of Paris is in fact in the nature of a residual. It represents the area *entirely* conceded to the influence of Paris whereas the other areas measure the attractive power of the *métro-*

pole without taking account of the influence of Paris. It is therefore possible that Paris may be more attractive than a *métropole* within its own area of influence as presently drawn. The competitive power of Paris is thus much greater than is depicted in the map on page 197. An illustration of this point is given by Prof. J.-R. Boudeville. Table 8.2 shows that within several cities which act as *métropoles* in their region the volume of employment controlled by firms with head offices in Paris is of the same order of magnitude as that controlled by firms whose head offices are in the regional centre.

TABLE 8.2

	Employment controlled by the *métropole* in 1962	Employment controlled within the *métropole* in 1962	
		Total	Paris
Lyons	50,763	61,437	53,158
Marseilles	15,452	28,578	13,222
Bordeaux	7,514	31,478	28,345
Nantes	10,161	26,014	23,382
St Etienne	18,598	9,319	6,806
Grenoble	5,651	11,184	8,237
Clermont-Ferrand	8,319	4,409	2,730

Source: J.-R. Boudeville, *Problems of Regional Economic Planning*, Edinburgh University Press, 1966, pp. 59-60.

INDUSTRY AND GROWTH AREAS

The Fifth Plan's ambitious targets of job creation in the west of France imply and require a vigorous policy of industrial decentralization, and the decision to centre regional development policy on the eight *métropoles* marks the complete abandonment of the former policies of industrial dispersal. Despite the ambitious objectives the approach adopted to regional industrial development in the Plan is in the circumstances extremely cautious and farsighted. There is first of all a warning against placing too much emphasis on industrial development and the movement of industry in regional policy. Between 1962 and 1985 the planners estimate there will be more than two new jobs created in the services sector for every one in industry and draw attention to the fact that technical developments in industry have considerably altered the relationship between

205

industry and services. The presence of a suitable range of service trades has in many industries replaced access to raw materials as a major factor influencing the locational decision.

The planners go on to argue that the degree of mobility of industry must not be exaggerated. Movement or decentralization of industry means effectively the redistribution of *new* jobs; transfers of existing jobs are very rare and since the planners estimate that employment in industry will increase by only 1 per cent annually up to 1985 the number of 'shiftable' jobs even assuming reasonably continuous expansion is very limited. Furthermore, the nature of industrial expansion does not encourage industrial movement. As M. Guichard puts it, 'It is difficult to change the industrial map for existing investment forms a base for new equipment and it is usually more economical to increase the capacity of an existing plant than to build a separate plant. Besides, a factory expands continuously, modernizes by stages and the replacement of an asset frequently involves the expansion of capacity. Finally, even in the case of the construction of new establishments, it is advantageous for the firm to group its plants in a relatively restricted geographical area.'[1]

A further factor which may limit the scope of industrial movement is the increasing concentration of industry which has occurred in France since the 1950s and is continuing.[2] This has several implications for regional policy. Firstly, it could reduce the total number of plants or establishments, particularly those of reasonable size, which are available for 'distribution' among the regions. Secondly, the growth of mergers and amalgamations and the trend towards large assembly plants served by specialized components suppliers encourages centralization of direction and administration in a single centre, thus reducing the amount and range of employment opportunities provided by its branches in other regions. Finally, many of the industries which are growing fastest and undergoing these technical and organizational changes require specialized services, both material and human, which can only be made available in large urban centres. All of these factors, therefore, limit industrial mobility and offset the locational freedom given by the independence of raw material sources.

Two other limiting factors should be mentioned. The first is the traditional one of transport costs. To arrive at an estimate of a desirable and feasible regional distribution of new jobs over the period to 1985, the CNAT carried out a study of locational advantages and disadvantages in different regions. It concluded that many of

---

[1] O. Guichard, op. cit., pp. 84-5.
[2] See O. Guichard, op. cit., pp. 80-3, and CNAT, op. cit., p. 28.

the disadvantages 'are directly or indirectly connected with transport costs to which firms are becoming increasingly sensitive as competition becomes more acute. Although the reduction in the weight of products widens the locational constraints, transport costs are still an important factor in the locational decision.'[1] The reference to competition here reflects the concern expressed frequently in official discussions of regional policy that regional development must not be promoted at the expense of competitiveness. More generally, it is important to note that, despite a tendency in some countries, notably the UK, to treat transport costs as of little importance in influencing locational decisions, the French consider them very significant. Apart from the much greater distances which are involved in France, this divergence of opinion can be largely explained in terms of the definition of transport costs. The CNAT study refers to indirect as well as direct transport costs, thus taking into account the various costs resulting from remoteness from suppliers and outlets and other necessary services. A recent British study has suggested that if transport costs are defined to include these costs then they do have a significant bearing on location decisions even in a small country like the UK.[2]

The cost of energy is another important influence on locational decisions in France, since it varies considerably from one region to another. These differences are likely to narrow in the future as a result of the introduction of more extensive and efficient distribution systems for natural gas and oil. The distribution of electricity is also to be improved and this will further reduce regional disparities in costs.

The other side of this very realistic assessment of the possibilities of industrial mobility is the attractive power of low earnings in some of the less prosperous regions. Earnings differentials in France are much greater than in the UK; earnings in some western regions are no more than half those in the Paris region and two-thirds of the national average.[3] The planners take the view that regional development must not rely on the advantages provided by low regional earnings. Within a policy aimed at reducing the regional income differentials such benefits can only be temporary and there is the risk that firms may be induced to locate in a region where labour costs are low only to find themselves unable to operate

[1] CNAT, op. cit., p. 64.
[2] G. C. Cameron and B. D. Clark, *Industrial Movement and the Regional Problem*, University of Glasgow, Social and Economic Studies, Occasional Papers No. 5, Oliver & Boyd, Edinburgh.
[3] See Chapter 5, pp. 128-133.

competitively when earnings begin to rise as a consequence, perhaps, of other firms entering the region. This is harmful to the development of the region, to the national economy and, if the firm has required infrastructure to be provided for it, wasteful of scarce public funds.

There are three kinds of areas where industrial development is likely and will be encouraged to take place during the Fifth Plan.[1] There are, firstly, port areas, notably Marseilles and the Gulf of Fos, Bordeaux, Nantes-St Nazaire and Dunkirk. The stimulus to these areas will come from the growth in imports of raw materials and as landing and processing areas for oil and natural gas. They will offer advantageous sites for industries like steel, non-ferrous metals and chemicals which have considerable powers of attraction over ancillary industries. This kind of development is particularly vital for Bordeaux and Nantes-St Nazaire which have no comparative advantage other than their port facilities which have been declining in importance.

A second type of growth area is the regional *métropole*. These areas have to offer the services which are in increasing demand as a result of the changing structure of industry—technical and financial expertize, proximity to airports, etc.

Finally, there are what are called 'industrial groupings and complexes'. The argument here is the familiar one of the creation, more or less simultaneously, of technically interrelated industries giving industrial external economies. A study of the mechanics of an industrial complex is being undertaken as part of the industrial development scheme on the Gulf of Fos near Marseilles.

There is, however, no suggestion that the planners should seek to direct particular industries to particular regions. Apart from the controls on development in the Paris region, measures to encourage the movement of industry have all been in the form of financial incentives to manufacturing industry and recently to service establishments as well, It is with this aspect of policy that the next chapter will deal.

[1] See *Projet de Loi des Finances pour 1965*, op. cit., pp. 27 and 28.

CHAPTER 9

INDUSTRIAL INCENTIVES
AND CONTROLS

In May 1964, sweeping changes were made in the system of incentives and controls used to persuade industry to establish in the less prosperous regions.[1] The control over the issue of construction permits was tightened. This had in fact been provided for in 1961 but had not been implemented. A decree in November 1961 allowed a construction permit to be refused where the proposed expansion 'ran counter to policies for regional and urban development'.[2] The 1964 measures required all requests for permits in respect of industrial building of more than 2,000 square metres to be submitted to the Regional Planning Office (Délégation à l'Aménagement du Territoire—DATAR) and the Ministry of Industry. This marked an extension of the controls beyond the Paris region and was modelled on the Industrial Development Certificate procedure used in Britain. It was felt necessary to do this because an increasing proportion of new industrial development taking place outside Paris had been concentrating in particular areas, mainly those within 200 kilometres of Paris. Control over development within Paris was not, therefore, benefiting some of the more distant regions.

The system of financial incentives was also considerably reformed. For the purpose of the new scheme, France was divided into five areas (see map on page 210). Area 1 covers the whole of the west and south-west of France where the regional problem was defined as one of long-term development. Area 2 covers those areas dominated by declining industries where the problem is the creation of new industrial structures. Area 3 is made up of a number of localities where there are no acute problems but where expansion is not taking place. Area 4 consists of regions in the east of France enjoying some expansion. Taken together, Areas 3 and 4 form what are termed in Britain 'grey areas'. Area 5 is the Paris region and a surrounding area.

The nature and amount of financial assistance given to firms varies

---

[1] *Décret* No. 64-440, *Journal Officiel*, May 26, 1964.
[2] *Décret* No. 61-1298, *Journal Officiel*, November 30, 1961.

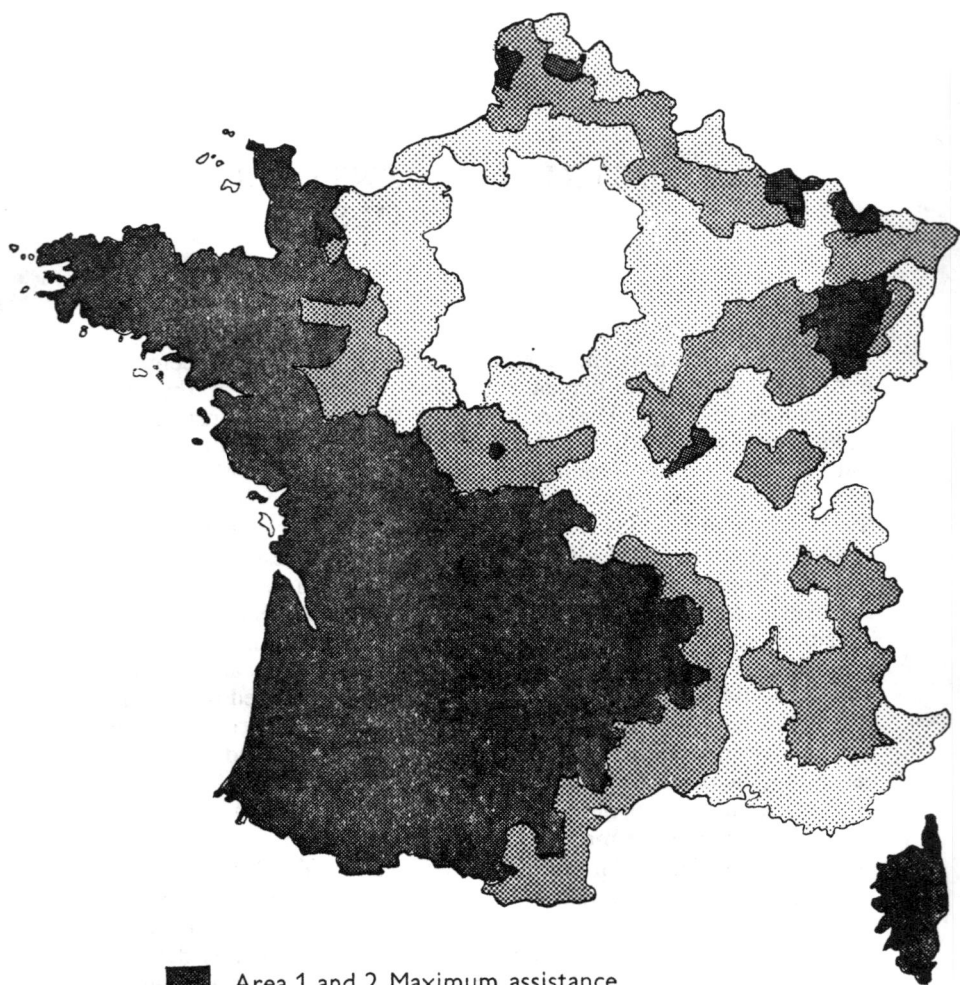

Area 1 and 2 Maximum assistance

Area 3 Average assistance

Area 4 Minimum assistance

Area 5 No assistance

MAP 4: Areas in which firms are eligible for financial assistance
Source: Aides au Développement Régional, DATAR, Paris, 1965.

according to the area in which they expand or establish themselves. There are currently seven kinds of financial incentive available:

1. Investment grants.
2. Reduction in the tax on land purchases (*droit de mutation*).
3. Total or partial exemption from local taxation (*la patente*).
4. An initial allowance on investment of 25 per cent (*amortissement exceptionnel*).
5. Reductions in the tax levied on capital gains made as a result of the sale of industrial land (*non-imposition des plus-values foncières*).
6. Reductions in the contributions towards expenses incurred in the transfer of equipment by firms vacating industrial premises in the Paris region (*indemnité de decéntralisation*).
7. Various forms of financial assistance with the movement and training of manpower in connection with the establishment of a factory outside the Paris region (*aides en faveur de la main d'oeuvre*).[1]

The major aim of the 1964 reforms was to replace the increasingly complex range of incentives by a simpler system designed to meet the different needs of the five areas specified above. The incentives available in the different areas are shown in Table 9.1.

The new measures distinguished between the regions in Area 1 where the industrial development grant is to be available over an indefinitely long period, and the much less extensive regions in Area 2 where the industrial adaptation grant is to be made available only so long as structural problems persist and on the condition that each operation creates a minimum of twenty new jobs. Within Area 1 there are eight urban areas where the grant is 20 per cent for new establishments and 12 per cent for extensions, as against 10 per cent for new establishments and 5 per cent for extensions in the rest of the Area. In another sense, however, the reforms have made the regime of incentives less selective than before. Area 1 is a continuous area covering the whole of the west and south-west of France and Areas 3 and 4—the 'grey areas'—are also extensive. Financial aid is, therefore, available automatically and without negotiation anywhere over vast tracts of the country and not in a more or less large number of particular localities. Indeed, it is admitted that the extent of the areas eligible for assistance is probably as large as it could be if the aid is to achieve its objectives.

The reforms are very similar to the redrawing of the Development

---

[1] '*Aides au Développement Régional*', *Délégation à l'Aménagement du Territoire et à l'Action Régionale*, Paris, no date.

Areas in Britain in 1966 and the accompanying switch to investment grants. Both policies would appear to be based on the view that it is undesirable to limit financial aid to a few growth areas within the wider development areas. There will always be an unforeseeable

TABLE 9.1

FINANCIAL AID AVAILABLE IN DIFFERENT AREAS

Area	Creation or extension of plant	Decentralization from the Paris region	Structural reform
Area 1	*a.* Industrial development grant *b.* Reduction in tax on land purchase *c.* Initial allowance *d.* Reduction in local taxation *e.* Reduction in tax on capital gains resulting from the sale of industrial land *f.* Reduction in transfer expenses *g.* Manpower aid		Reduction in tax on land purchase
Area 2	*a.* Industrial adaptation grant *b.* Reduction in tax on land purchase *c.* Reduction in local taxation *d.* Reduction in tax on capital gains *e.* Reduction in transfer expenses *f.* Manpower aid		Reduction in tax on land purchase
Area 3	*a.* Reduction in tax on land purchase *b.* Reduction in local taxation *c.* Reduction in tax on capital gains *d.* Reduction in transfer expenses *e.* Manpower aid		Reduction in tax on land purchase
Area 4	Nil	*a.* Reduction in tax on land purchase *b.* Reduction in local taxation *in the case of a transfer from the Paris region*	Reduction in tax on land purchase
Area 5	Nil	Nil	Nil

Source: 'Aides au Développement Régional,' op. cit.

212

number of firms of varying types which will for a variety of reasons choose to locate near to but not within the limits of a growth area. There is no reason for denying such a firm incentives particularly if there are additional financial advantages to increase the attractiveness of the growth area. The growth areas, moreover, have the further advantage of being those parts of a wider development area where growth is most likely to take place and, even more significant, in which infrastructure works are concentrated. This last type of attraction or incentive is in fact at least as important in France as any cash payment or fiscal benefits and the 1964 reforms included important alterations in the arrangements for the provision of infrastructure in the less prosperous regions.

Since 1964 there have been some alterations in the form and scope of the incentives. There are firstly the increases in the investment grants available in Areas 1 and 2. The position as at October 1967 is shown in Table 9.2.

The main reason offered for the increases in the value of the grants was the need to stimulate industrial investment in the west in line with the new job target for that region adopted as one of the main regional policy objectives in the Fifth Plan. The increases were also designed to offset the potential disadvantages of a location in the west following the final reduction of tariffs in the Common Market. The creation of a new privileged subdivision of Area 1—the 'extreme-west'—covering the whole of the Brittany peninsula, was a response to the particular need for new industries in Brittany and more particularly the problems posed by the impending closure of the iron-works at Hennebont in the *département* of Morbihan. The closure of the iron-works employing 1,350 workers is to be phased out to allow displaced workers to find alternative employment. The increased investment grants is one of a series of measures to attract several new firms to the area. This latter exercise is obviously in part a rescue operation, but Hennebont lies within the industrial complex already being built up around Lorient, and the considerable sum involved in providing alternative jobs is still well short of half the considerable subsidies (£6·5 million) which have been paid out since 1952 to keep the uneconomically small Hennebont works in operation. It does not, therefore, mark a reversion to the *coup par coup* policy.

Several other changes were made, two of which are of some interest. One of the innovations of the 1964 reforms was a 60 per cent rebate on transfer expenses incurred by firms moving anywhere outside the Paris region (defined as Area 5) provided it vacated 500 square metres of land. It was found that some firms were including items of transfer expenditure in their reckoning of capital expenditure

TABLE 9.2
INVESTMENT GRANTS

Area	Grant	Type of operation	Geographical scope	Rate Old	Rate New	Maximum amount of grant per job created Old	Maximum amount of grant per job created New
				%	%	£	£
Area 1	Industrial development grant[3]	Creation of new plant or re-opening of existing plant	a. Special urban areas b. Areas in the 'extreme-west' c. Rest of Area 1	20 12 10	25 15 12	809	956[1]
		Extension	a. Special urban areas b. Rest of Area 1	12 5	15 6	441	515[2]
Area 2	Industrial adaptation grant	Creation of new plant or total conversion of existing plant	Whole Area	20	25	809	956
		Extension or partial conversion of existing plant	Whole Area	12	15	441	515

Source: 'Que Sera la Politique de l'Aménagement du Territoire en 1968?,' *Délégation à l'Aménagement du Territoire et à l'Action Régionale.* Paris, December 3967.

[1] In the case of the special urban areas these figures may be reduced if the application of the maximum results in the firm contributing less than 12 per cent of the total capital costs involved.
[2] The conditions noted in (1) apply if the firm contributes less than 7 per cent of the total capital costs involved.
[3] In the case of projects involving investment expenditure greater than £73,500 the rate of grant available in Area 1 is 25 per cent.

on which they were eligible for investment grants. A ruling was passed in 1966 defining transfer expenditure to include all transport costs, all costs of movement from the original site and 50 per cent of reassembly costs. A second development was the extension to the Lyons conurbation of the legislation limiting industrial and commercial expansion in the Paris region in order to limit expansion within a radius of seven miles from Lyons city centre. The objective here is to preserve the green belt around Lyons which is considered essential to the 'balanced growth' of the city. This practical extension beyond Paris of the comprehensive IDC system created in 1961 is an important development, expecially since it is linked with a planning decision concerning one of the *métropoles d'équilibre*.

The most important addition to the 1964 measures, however, was the extension of controls and incentives to the 'services' sector. This was a logical action, in view of the heavy emphasis laid on this part of the economy in the Fifth Plan. The problem in the services sector is the disproportionate concentration of new jobs in the fastest growing sector of the economy in the Paris region. It is estimated that Paris gets one in every three new jobs in services (60,000-80,000 per year since 1962) and that the growth of the working population in the Paris region between 1962 and 1966 is therefore almost entirely explained by the rise in employment in services.[1] The problem has a qualitative side too. The Paris region tends to attract a more than proportionate share of what the planners term 'superior' services, e.g. research organizations, laboratories, industrial consultancy services for both the public and the private sectors. These trends are particularly unfavourable to the policy of building up the *métropoles d'équilibre* as regional centres of growth, and in an attempt to reverse them two measures were introduced in December 1967.

The first was a consolidation of the legislation introduced in 1955 and 1958 limiting the expansion in the Paris region of service establishments in the public sector and, later and less stringently, those in the private sector. There was particular concern about a loophole in the controls over private establishments which allowed the reoccupation of existing premises used for service activities and the conversion of premises used for other purposes to service use. This latter escape-route was becoming increasingly important as the movement of industry out of Paris left vacant premises which could be occupied by service establishments. The action taken by the government was to devolve upon a single committee the task of

[1] See 'Que Sera la Politique de l'Aménagement du Territoire en 1968?', op. cit., Chapter 3.

keeping a permanent watching brief on all service activities, both public and private, in the Paris region.

This by now typically cautious approach to any form of control over the economic structure of the Paris region, particularly in industries for which Paris was frequently the natural best location, was relaxed by the introduction of a new form of financial aid. An investment grant of between 5 and 15 per cent (20 per cent in exceptional cases) is to be made available to industrial firms who create, extend or transfer out of the Paris region those sections of their operations that fall within the services sector, e.g. management activities, administration and research and development. Where the new operations involve general administration it must provide at least 100 new jobs to qualify for a grant; in the case of research and development 50 new jobs are required. The new grant is to be available only in the eight *métropoles* and in seven other towns with 'an important regional function'. These are Rennes, Poitiers, Limoges, Clermont-Ferrand, Dijon, Besançon and Montpellier, none of which lies within the Paris basin.

This highly selective incentive is a further underwriting of the *métropoles* and another practical recognition of the growing importance of the service sector as the fastest growing area of employment opportunity and a crucial component of the external economies influencing location decisions in manufacturing industry. The limitation of the grant to service activities attached to industrial firms is not serious in terms of the services in the private sector which are most important to economic growth, and it has the additional benefit of encouraging in the growth areas the expansion of those activities of firms which will lead them to view their operations in these regions as important and permanent rather than flexible, marginal units. Finally, the exclusion of all towns nearer Paris than Dijon, including the putative new satellite cities around Paris itself, from the new benefit can only be to the advantage of the other centres and must have been contested by the Paris region planners.

The need to build up infrastructure, particularly in the south and west, which led to the creation in the mid-1950s of various financing and operating agencies such as the National Fund for Regional Development (FNAT) and the Central Agency for Regional Infrastructure (SCET) had, by the time of the Fourth and Fifth Plans, become the key factor in regional policy. The 1964 reforms were concerned to improve the co-ordination of efforts in this field and prevent wasteful duplication of infrastructure facilities. To this end the operations of the FNAT, which in February 1963 was renamed the Land Development Fund (Fonds National d'Aménagement

Foncier et d'Urbanisme—FNAFU) in the financing of industrial estates and related housing operations, were brought under the control of the DATAR as well as the Ministry of Housing. This was aimed at ensuring that FNAFU's activities would conform to the needs and aims of regional policy. It was further ruled that FNAFU should give priority to projects in the newly defined Area 1 and that no projects would be started in the region around Paris where no incentives were available. A limit was set on the amount of land to be zoned for industrial estates which would take account of the number of new industrial jobs likely to be created in the regions where they were to be concentrated.

A similarly selective policy was laid down for the SCET and the 'mixed-economy companies' (*sociétés d'économie mixte*). These agencies had been given the main responsibilities, in conjunction with local authorities, for building advance factories either for lease or sale. The 1964 reforms were intended to limit the number created and thus prevent wasteful and costly competition for industry by different localities and the hindering of regional policy as a result of excessive dispersion or an excessive concentration of factories in already favoured areas.

Finally, to deal with particular cases where an especially important industrial development is involved or where a firm is considering setting up in a region which is on the priority list for development, the 1964 measures introduced the formula of *conventions d'implantation industrielle*. These are agreements or contracts between the firm concerned and the DATAR.

In return for an undertaking from the firm to carry out an agreed type of operation in an agreed location, the DATAR will, together with the relevant ministries, ensure the provision of housing, telecommunications and manpower training facilities and personnel. Such agreements are to be negotiated on a case by case basis and are modelled on the *quasi-contrats*, the agreements by which the Planning Commission provided various financial advantages to firms or groups of firms willing to undertake projects in the context of the national plans.

The system of industrial incentives and controls has been reshaped so that it does broadly conform to the principle of selectivity which now governs all regional policy actions. One clear and significant conclusion, however, is that French regional policy does not interpret selectivity to mean the detailed categorization of industries in terms of their suitability for certain regions as has been done in Professor Tosco's exercise in Italy.[1] This may appear to be at odds

[1] See Chapter 13.

with the tradition of industrial planning built up in France over the post-war years but in fact it is not. Rather it reflects the strong streak of pragmatism which close examination shows to be central to the French planning approach and methods. The industrial development of the less prosperous regions in France is being encouraged by the very definite and by no means arbitrary selection of areas where the growth of population and employment could most feasibly take place and the creation in advance in these locations of the external economies which are considered to be the major influence on costs and therefore the location decision. Subsidies to direct costs of production such as labour, capital and transport costs are granted but they are of secondary importance. Given this approach the creation and location of interrelated industrial groupings is left to individual industrialists' decisions made in the light of these measures. The essence of French regional development strategy is the definition of a limited number of localities where the external economies available in the main centre of growth in the economy, Paris, can be and are deliberately simulated. Once a firm (or firms) moves into one of these areas its presence there, together with the *infrastructure* external economies, will serve to attract other firms who, when they come, will add the *industrial* external economies of an interrelated group of industries.

CHAPTER 10

REGIONAL PLANNING AND ADMINISTRATION

The increasing integration of regional and national economic policies and the movement of regional policy towards increased selectivity brought the need for changes in the traditional administrative and planning structures. The changes actually introduced are sufficiently radical and sufficiently similar to those projected and implemented in other European countries to make them of considerable general interest. Of particular interest is the French experience, since 1955, of operating a system of regional economic plans aimed at promoting the growth of income per head in the different regions of the economy and adding a regional dimension to the national economic plans.

THE BEGINNINGS OF REGIONAL PLANNING 1955-63

The origins of regional planning in France are to be found in the package of measures introduced in 1955 to implement regional policy discussed in Chapter 6. These measures marked the beginnings of a realization that, if regional policy were to be concerned with the growth of income and output and changes in the industrial structure in the different regions and not simply the *ad hoc* provision of jobs in localities suffering from higher than average unemployment at particular times, it would be necessary to prepare some kind of long-term plan or development programme for each region of the economy. It was clear, too, that given the existence of a national economic plan these regional plans would somehow have to be related to each other and to the allocation of national resources implied in the objectives of the national plan. Accordingly the various measures to encourage the movement of industry out of Paris were accompanied by the designation of twenty-two regional divisions (*circonscriptions d'action régionale*) for which regional programmes (*programmes d'action régionale*) were to be prepared. The programmes were to serve four main functions:

(a) to provide a diagnosis of the problems facing the region;

219

(b) to prepare recommendations which would indicate the contribution the region could make to the expansion of the national economy and the action required to improve the situation in the region;

(c) to act as a framework within which a co-ordinated distribution of public investment by region could be developed;

(d) to serve as a reference dossier for the regional authorities' and private firms' claims for aid from the government.

The programmes were to be prepared within the context of the Third Plan (1958-61) and were to 'extend and complete' the Plan by giving it a regional dimension.

These objectives, while very grand and ambitious, made incontrovertible economic sense and indicated an awareness of the link between the growth of regional and national output which was nowhere recognized in British regional policy at that time. But there were many problems.[1] The twenty-two regions were at first simply superimposed on some thirty other regional administrative divisions already in use, with the result that the regional work of government departments continued in many cases within a framework different from that of the new planning divisions. Serious lack of co-ordination arose in other ways. The preparation of the programmes was entrusted to general civil servants (not economic or financial specialists) with a special regional mission known as *Inspecteurs Généraux de l'Economie Nationale* (IGEN). They were to consult representatives of the various regional interests, notably the Committees for Economic Expansion for each *département*, which had been formed out of a number of regional interest groups and officially recognized in December 1954. The nature of these consultations was, however, only partly and rather curiously defined. The decree in June 1955 authorizing the programmes (which preceded the designation of the twenty-two new regional divisions by eighteen months) left to individual discretion the precise regional boundaries to be used by the IGENs. Even when the divisions were announced there were no statistics relating to them available and the IGENs had perforce to fall back on material prepared according

[1] For extremely critical assessments of the way in which the regional programmes were conceived and implemented see M. Jules Milhau, 'Problèmes de l'Elaboration et de l'Exécution des Plans Régionaux', *Avis et Rapports du Conseil Economique et Social, Journal Officiel*, May 15, 1960, and Prof. M. Byé, 'Les Moyens d'une Politique des Economies Régionales', *Avis et Rapports du Conseil Economique et Social, Journal Officiel*, May 16, 1957. See also J. Lajugie, 'Aménagement du Territoire et Développement Economique Régional en France 1945-1964', *Revue d'Economie Politique*, Jan.-Feb. 1964.

to other boundaries. The process of consultation was to take place, too, after the IGENs had prepared a draft programme in order to avoid the possibility of collusion.[1]

The implementation of the programmes was also fraught with difficulty. The idea of co-ordinated regional action ran into direct conflict with the traditional organization of French administration. At the regional level the basic unit is the *département*, while at central government level departments of state were organized on a rigidly vertical basis. The representatives of the central government in the regions are the prefects whose responsibilities are defined in terms of the *département*. They were in consequence ill-fitted to carry out the task of co-ordination beween *départements* and between government departments at the regional level which the new regional planning required. Although he is theoretically the representative of the government in the regions, the prefect is essentially a civil servant responsible to the Minister of the Interior for a particular *département*. He has no links with the economic Ministries, need not have any economic expertize and his primary loyalty to the Ministry of the Interior makes him not the most suitable person to co-ordinate the work of other government departments. Moreover, his term of office in a *département* is of limited duration and is considered simply as one of the stages of a civil-service career. Again this may not be the most effective arrangement in the context of a continuous long-term task such as regional development.[2]

Perhaps the most serious criticism of the programmes, however, was their very tenuous relationship with the national plan. They were designed to add a regional content to the Third Plan, but in no real sense did they do this. The drafts of the programmes had to be vetted by a 'synthesis' group which included a senior member of the staff of the Planning Commission, but the nature of the programmes themselves precluded any effective integration. They did not cover any specific time-period; they had no starting or terminal dates. Nor was there any commitment by the government to any of the projects and actions which the programmes included in their recommendations. As an attempt to 'regionalize' the national plan the programmes were clearly bound to fall far short of their objective.

The lack of co-ordination between the various authorities was further illustrated when in August 1957 the Ministry of Housing was instructed to produce a series of regional development plans (*plans d'aménagement régional*). These plans were to work out 'a harmonious distribution of population and employment and to

---

[1] This point is made by P. Bauchet, op. cit., p. 106.
[2] See J. Milhau, op. cit., p. 360.

guide the location of public and private investment taking account of the regional programmes'. There is here some suggestion of duplication of activity. But more important is the separation of the economic and physical aspects of regional planning implied in the statement. The 1957 plans were intended to be a national *physical* planning exercise conducted as a parallel exercise to the economic work of the regional programmes. Since the provision of infrastructure had been recognized in the 1955 measures as an important and integral element of regional policy, this clean-cut separation of the economic and the physical aspects of planning seems rather simple-minded. It was, however, not all that surprising for the precise scope and meaning of regional economic planning had not been fully clarified by the Planning Commission, and the Ministry of Housing was traditionally and naturally reluctant to abandon its responsibilities for regional development in favour of what was still a very vague and general alternative. It could quite plausibly be argued that thinking about the economics of regional planning had not progressed to the point where it was obvious that the physical planning work of the Ministry of Housing should play only a service role to the economic models and priorities of the Planning Commission. However, in December 1958, a decree ordered the two sets of plans to be fused into a single *plan régionale de développement économique et social d'aménagement du territoire*. To ensure that co-ordination did in fact take place a special committee (Comité des Plans Régionaux) was established at the Planning Commission with the task of assessing the new combined plans in the context of the national plan and the general objectives of regional policy.

But before any real operative system of regional planning could come into being, the problem of regional boundaries and institutions had to be tackled. A start was made in January 1959, when a decree ordered that there should be a definitive grouping of *départements* into regions which would be the generally accepted units for regional planning. The job of supervising the plans for these regions should be devolved upon one of the prefects of the *départements* involved, and the numerous other regional divisions used by government departments and other agencies should within a year be brought into conformity with the new regions. This proposal sparked off considerable controversy. One of the severest critics of the old system, Professor Lajugie, commented: 'The interested agencies were systematically hostile to the application of a measure which could compromise direct relations between the central administrations and their regional delegates or agents and make them more subordinate to the co-ordinating prefects and the time allowed ran out without any harmonisation being achieved'.[1] The Conseil Economique et Social then took up the issue and recommended strongly that the 1959 decree should be ratified and applied. This was done by a further decree in June 1960.

The new measures first of all divided France into twenty-one divisions known as planning regions (*régions de programme*) each grouping from two to eight *départements* with an average population of 1·5 million inhabitants. These regions (see map on page 124) were to be the basic regional divisions of France and all other regional divisions were to be brought into harmony with them.[2] Thirty administrative agencies were immediately to adopt their classifications to the new framework. This marked a definite step forward. The new regional pattern was not defended as ideal—there is a case to be made that 21 regions are too many and proposals have been made for 7, 9 or 16 regions—but it did greatly facilitate regional policy actions and marked a break to some extent at least from the *département*-based divisions which were becoming less relevant to the economic problems of many areas of the economy. For each of the planning regions a plan was to be prepared where possible building on the work done on the former regional programmes but adding to them a physical or land-use planning content.

To co-ordinate the preparation and implementation of the new regional plans a new administrative agency called a *conférence interdépartemental* was established. This was a standing committee of the prefects of the *départements* within the planning region and the IGEN with responsibilities in the region. One of the prefects was named chairman with the title of co-ordinating prefect (*préfet coordonnateur*), but the extent of his powers was strictly limited. He was not *primus inter pares* and a circular explaining the functions of the conference made it clear that it was not a second-tier regional authority. 'It must be emphasized that the creation of the *conférences interdépartementales* of the prefects in no way reduces the autonomy of each prefect within his own *département*. The *département* remains the basic unit of French local administration . . . . the co-ordinating prefect has no hierarchic authority over the other prefects in the conference. Any conflicts arising will be submitted for Governmental arbitration.'[3] This very cautious and limited co-ordination

[1] Lajugie, op. cit., p. 315.

[2] For a detailed description of the main regional divisions (with maps) and the texts of decrees and circulars relating to them see 'L'Harmonisation des Circonscriptions Administratives Françaises', *Recueils et Monographies* No. 24, *La Documentation Française*, Paris, 1962.

[3] Circular of January 26, 1961, quoted in J. de Lanversin, *L'Aménagement du Territoire*, Librairies Techniques, Paris, 1965.

of activities aroused much debate between those who opposed what they saw as a technocratic regionalism and those like M. Milhau who argued the need for a more definite regional authority with the powers necessary to promote active planning at an economically meaningful regional level.[1]

Despite the limited nature of their powers, the *conférences* did constitute a new form of regional administration and they were assigned tasks which marked an advance in the techniques of regional planning. By far the most important of these was the responsibility for preparing the *tranches opératoires* for the Fourth Plan, i.e. the public investment programmes to be undertaken in the regions during the period of the plan. When these were finally approved by the Comité des Plans Régionaux at the Planning Commission they then had the responsibility of ensuring their implementation, details of which were to be given in annual reports. By this arrangement the planning of regional development was formally integrated with the national plan and at least a semi-permanent official body established to supervise the execution of the regional plans. The absence of a definite time reference and financial commitment by the government which deprived the earlier regional programmes of any real influence was now, in theory anyhow, corrected.

Although these reforms improved the efficiency and rationality of regional planning, fears were expressed about the danger of regional development policy being determined by the administration with too little regard for the views of regional interest groups and elected representatives. These complaints were more than the anti-Government reflex of disaffected minorities. There were important points of principle. M. Bloch-Lainé stressed the underdeveloped and uncertain nature of what might be called regional economics and argued that in these circumstances the 'expert's love of secrecy' was inappropriate and suspect.[2] Prof. J. Rivero made the point that in any exercise of economic planning success depended upon the acceptance by all the main decision-taking agents of the objectives and actions of the planners.[3] Finally, Prof. Lajugie argued that regional development was a many-sided operation and warned against the adoption of too narrow a set of objectives: 'The extra-economic aspects of development are more important than the striving to attain maximum economic efficiency and development

[1] See J. de Lanversin, op. cit., pp. 63-85.
[2] F. Bloch-Lainé, 'Pouvoir Economique et Démocratie', *Revue de l'Action Populaire*, 1961, p. 567.
[3] J. Rivero, 'Action Economique de l'Etat et Evolution Administrative', *Revue Economique*, November 1962, p. 895.

plans must be assessed not only from a technical, economic viewpoint but in terms of their effect on regional structures which they must shift in the direction of economic and social progress'.[1]

These arguments were recognized by the appointment of two bodies designed to involve regional representatives in both the preparation and execution of the regional plans. The first of these was the Commission Départementale d'Equipement, established in December 1961. These commissions were to be chaired by the prefect of the *département* and membership included the chairman of the county council (conseil général) and one or more mayors of towns in the *département*. The function of the commissions was to act as a consultancy and information agency for the *conférences* and to supervise and co-ordinate the carrying out of the *tranches opératoires* at the level of the *département*. More directly representative were the Committees for Economic Expansion. These committees had been officially recognized as representing regional interests since 1954 but, as was pointed out above, the nature of their consultancy was never made clear and remained uneven and unsatisfactory. In January 1961 a decree ordered that the committees had to be consulted, during the preparation of the new regional plans, on any changes in the drafts of the plans and should have similar rights in respect of the preparation of the *tranches opératoires* and the implementation of them.

One of the consequences of the new regional planning procedures was the increasing importance of regional development in the work of the Planning Commission. The growth in its influence was largely at the expense of the Ministry of Housing, whose activities in the field of regional development were being channelled into the provision of housing and infrastructure for industrial estates and areas where industrial development was planned. In January 1962, however, it published a *Plan National d'Aménagement du Territoire* outlining the broad strategies of regional development for the next twenty years. The importance of this study lay in the fact that it was prepared without consultation with the Planning Commission which in the same month had launched the Fourth Plan and incorporated in it for the first time a definite regional strategy to be implemented by the new regional organizations. The long-term plan was criticized as an example of the lack of co-ordination which had so bedevilled regional policy in the past. It was criticized also as being too general in its approach in contrast to the regional

[1] J. Lajugie, 'Politique de développement régional pour les pays du Marché Commun', *Revue d'Economie Politique*, May 1959, p. 333.

policy of the Fourth Plan, clearly defined and made operational through the *tranches opératoires*.

The first of these objections undoubtedly has point. The rivalry of the Ministry of Housing and the Planning Commission is not defensible. But the need for a regional plan formulated at the national level over a period long enough to allow the necessarily slow process of changing regional structures to have gone some reasonable distance is difficult to deny. In a sense the long-term plan got the relationship between the regional and national plan right. Crucial though organized short-term and medium-term actions are in regional policy, they must be regarded as stages in a process of creating a pattern of population settlement and employment better than those already existing. The long-term plan had the merit of drawing attention to this point whereas the various reforms and the activities of the Planning Commission concentrated on improving the regionalization of the national plan. This latter concern tended to produce procedures according to which the translation of the national plan into regional projects took place *after* the objectives of the national plan had been finally decided and without reference to any long-term view of the future functions of the different regions in the economy.

In fact, after 1963 developments took place in regional planning which were directed towards constructing a system of national planning which would have as one of its long-term aims the creation of a particular pattern of population, employment and land use through the medium of a succession of integrated national and regional medium-term plans.

TOWARDS A SYSTEM OF NATIONAL REGIONAL PLANNING

In February 1963, what amounted to a Ministry of Regional Development was created.[1] This quite new agency was known as the Délégation à l'Aménagement du Territoire—DATAR, headed by a director (Délégué à l'Aménagement du Territoire et à l'Action Régionale) responsible directly to the Prime Minister and formally attached to the Prime Minister's Office. The wide-ranging functions of the DATAR were spelled out at some length. It was to be 'an agency with the tasks of co-ordination and promotion'. It was to prepare and co-ordinate the elements necessary for government decisions about regional planning and policy, and to ensure that the technical administrations adapt their activities in this field and co-ordinate

[1] *Décret* No. 63-112, February 14, 1963, *Journal Officiel*, February 15, 1963.

the measures at their disposal towards the attainment of objectives which are beyond their own individual policies and responsibilities. This interministerial function requires that it can at any time appeal to the Prime Minister for arbitration and authority. The creation of such a body was an explicit attempt to unify the efforts of regional planning and policy and remove the wasteful duplication of work by the Planning Commission and the Ministry of Housing and similarly to bring the ever-growing range of regional policy measures under the control and guidance of a body powerful enough to over-rule individual government departments.

In practice the DATAR has three types of function. The first is to be consulted by and represented on all bodies concerned in any way with regional development. In particular, its director is to submit to an inter-ministerial committee on regional development an annual report, established after discussion with other departments, outlining the problems involved in harmonizing the initial departmental estimates with the objectives of regional policy and the *tranches opératoires*. The DATAR is, therefore, engaged in a dialogue with the Treasury and the spending Ministries. This is the kind of influence which the Planning Commission has exercised most effectively at the national level and with an able director the DATAR could become a powerful, recognized lobby for regional development in the areas where decisions affecting it are being taken.

As well as co-ordinating the activities of different departments the DATAR has assumed the supervision of a number of special regional development projects involving the co-operation of national and local administrations and private agencies. Examples of this specific co-operation on the ground are the creation of interministerial groups to co-ordinate the zoning and construction of industrial estates, to manage water resources and the national and regional parks scheme. Other schemes in hand include the tourist developments along the Languedoc-Roussillon and Aquitaine coasts, the creation of a new urban industrial area on the Gulf of Fos near Marseilles and agricultural and tourist development schemes in Corsica.[1]

DATAR also had put at its disposal the Regional Development Fund (FIAT) which it can use to supplement public investment programmes which it considers important but which cannot be fully financed by budgetary allocation. FIAT is not large; it is voted only

---

[1] For details of these schemes, see *Projet de Loi des Finances pour 1967*, Appendix, *Exécution du Plan en 1965 en 1966*, Vol. *T*, Paris, 1966, Chapter V, and *Que Sera la Politique de l'Aménagement du Territoire en 1968?*, DATAR, Paris, December 1967, Chapter 6.

£20 million annually. Any aid given is short-term, normally for one year, with assurances required that the project concerned will be voted credits at the next budget and that the local authorities are prepared to contribute at least one-third of the total cost of the project.

The second function of the DATAR is to act as liaison between the regional *conférences* and the central administrations in connection with the implementation of the *tranches opératoires*. Finally, the DATAR was made responsible for co-ordinating the numerous controls and incentives which had been introduced since 1955 to encourage industry and commerce to move out of the Paris region and to produce an annual assessment of results for the interministerial committee.

The same decree which established the DATAR created a new committee of the Planning Commission with special regional responsibilities, the National Committee for Regional Development (Commission Nationale d'Aménagement du Territoire—CNAT). The CNAT had fifty members, all officials, appointed on the grounds of their interests and expertize in regional matters. The role of CNAT was to produce studies of regional development whose conclusions were to be written into the national plans. 'The studies of the plan will from now on extend beyond the four-year framework and take a longer-term view. The aim is not to give special attention to the regional aspects of development nor to its technical, economic or social aspects but to undertake a long-term, global, predictive study establishing the essential unity of the national plan and regional development.'[1] This is an extremely important statement, however grand sounding. There is here an explicit recognition that regional development is a national concern and that it is impossible to discuss future national economic and social development without forming a view about the regional consequences of any decisions taken. The task of the CNAT was to examine the probable pattern of regional development in the future and thus provide a framework within which the ensuing national plans could be set, each containing stages of regional actions implemented by the DATAR. The CNAT's work was divided among six sub-committees dealing with regional demographic tendencies up to 1985, the problems of the industrialization in certain regions, rural development, the regional pattern of growth of the services sector, the pattern of urban growth and communications. Its first general report was published in September 1964 discussing regional development in general terms and proceeding to an outline of the *grandes options* of regional policy in the Fifth

[1] *Décret* No. 63-112, op. cit.

Plan which significantly was proposed as the first stage in a long-term effort to achieve a particular regional allocation of resources.

These innovations at the national level were complemented by further changes in the regional organizations. In May 1964 the prefect presiding over the regional *conférences* was given the title of regional prefect.[1] His task is to 'stimulate and control' the activities of the prefects in the *départements* of his region, the work of government services and those of public agencies which are not national bodies and whose responsibilities extend over more than one *département*. These powers are conferred only in respect of economic affairs, and education, fiscal matters, labour legislation and the preparation of statistics are specifically excluded from his remit.[2] The regional prefect is responsible directly to the Prime Minister via the DATAR.

The new prefects have attached to them a small mission of young civil servants chosen for their competence in technical and economic questions. These aides concern themselves solely with regional development in a way which would be impossible for civil servants working in the regional service of a particular ministry. There are also deputy prefects with special responsibilities in economic affairs. Finally, despite various recommendations to the contrary, the regional prefect retains his position as prefect of his own *département*.

These new arrangements mark a further very cautious step towards a new regional framework and a new system of regional administration oriented towards the needs of regional economic development considered as an integral part of the national plans. The new regional prefects have a more extensive role than the co-ordinating prefects of the 1961 reforms and the need for technically competent staff dealing solely with questions of regional development has been recognized. But they are not yet possessed of any executive powers. As Mrs James points out, 'the economic planning region is not a new layer in the administrative hierarchy. It is not a legal entity in the way that communes and *départements* are. The role of the Regional Prefect is precisely defined so as not to encroach on the role of the Departmental Prefect.'[3] It should be added that it has also been defined so as to encroach as little as possible on the autonomy of individual government departments in the regions. The success of regional development policy will thus depend to a large

[1] *Décret* No. 67-251, *Journal Officiel*, March 14, 1964.
[2] See J. de Lanversin, op. cit., p. 63 *et seq.*, and Mrs P. B. M. James, 'The Organization of Regional Economic Planning in France', *Public Administration*, Vol. 45, Winter 1967.
[3] Mrs James, ibid., p. 357.

extent on the ability of the regional prefect and his staff to achieve by persuasive co-ordination what they cannot by authority.

The tasks of the regional prefect are quite explicitly defined. They are all centred round the preparation and execution of the *tranches opératoires*. The first stage is the preparation of detailed reports on the long-term economic prospects of each region. In the Fifth Plan these reports were prepared in the light of a preliminary outline by the CNAT of the probable growth up to 1970 in population, manpower and employment and migration flows in the twenty-one programme regions. This study was based largely on extrapolation from past trends corrected for the effects of certain broad policy assumptions, most particularly the creation of a certain proportion of industrial jobs in the west. The CNAT also set out the main lines of the regional policy proposed for the Fifth Plan. The regional organizations were asked to comment on this outline (the regional prefects had not yet been appointed) and after some retouching the main options of regional policy were approved by parliament in December 1964. It was at this juncture that the new prefects were asked to submit their reports. The nature of these documents had been fairly carefully defined. They fell into three distinct parts.

The first part was an analysis of the prospects of development in the region up to 1985 in the light of the general outline prepared by the CNAT and the broad objectives of regional policy approved by parliament. The reports were required to analyse the growth of population and manpower, the consequences of a continued reduction in the agricultural labour force, the problems posed by the geographical and occupational mobility of labour, the possibilities of attracting manufacturing industry to the region, the pattern of urban development within the region, education and training requirements and communications.

The second part of the report dealt with the period up to 1970 (the period of the Fifth Plan). The main task here was to get estimates of the supply of labour and the demand for labour in the region, again working from the initial outline by the CNAT. The preparation of such figures involves an attempt to forecast the growth of industrial output in each region. Although work is being done there was at the time of the Fifth Plan no comprehensive regional accounting system available and in many regions the growth of regional output depended to a considerable extent upon what industries could be brought into the region from elsewhere.

The estimates were obtained using the industrial breakdowns of the national plan and hurried investigations by the prefect's staff into the region's industrial structure. Despite the serious absence of statistical information, the report had also to indicate the kind of industries which it considered most necessary and suitable for the region's development given its existing industrial structure, labour force and available land, and the problems which were likely to arise in getting the right types of firm actually to set up in the region. Any conclusions here were bound to be highly incomplete and uncertain, but some appreciation of these issues was a necessary precursor of the third part of the report in which the prefect makes recommendations about the public investment programmes required in his region during the period of the plan and which should make up the *tranche opératoire* for the region.

The third part of the report was to indicate firstly the public investment necessary to bring the standard of public services in the region up to some national average level (*équipement de couverture*). This involved the compilation by the prefects of 'situation indices' for each region measuring its *per capita* share of public services. A list of public investment priorities was then drawn up in terms of broad sectors such as housing, hospitals, industrial infrastructure, roads, etc., and within each sector the report was required to indicate the particular operations which should have priority.

The prefects' reports when completed were then reviewed and synthesized in the familiar way by the CNAT in the light of the national priorities of regional policy and the forecasts of production, employment and investment prepared by the Planning Commission in conjunction with the various industrial committees. This review formed the basis of the regional policy section in the Fifth Plan.

The next stage of the prefect's work is to participate in the preparation of the *tranches opératoires* and the regional distribution of capital spending in the budget for the first financial year of the plan. The role and powers of the prefect are defined in significantly different ways according to the type of investment under discussion. In the first category are those projects whose location is decided at the national level. Examples are the siting of new universities or research establishments, power stations, motorways, agricultural improvement schemes. Here the prefect is held informed of the processes of decision and invited to offer his opinion either in writing or in person. He does not, however, have a major influence in the decision and his function is to argue the case for his region rather than to consider as an independent official the best (if there is a single best) location in terms of national policy objectives.

The second category of investments are those whose precise nature and location is important to the region's economy but are not directly matters of national concern. There projects will already have been outlined in the prefect's report and an 'envelope' of credits granted to the region as part of its *tranche opératoire*. Within the limits of this envelope the prefect has the power to decide on the nature and location of projects within the *départements* of his region. It is on this point that the regional prefect comes nearest to being a new tier of administration allocating resources according to the priorities of an economically relevant region. He has, however, no authority actually to carry out projects. This is done by the *départements* and other agencies such as the 'mixed-economy' companies. The prefect has to negotiate with these bodies in order to get his regional projects undertaken.

The third category of investment covers those operations of a mainly local character affecting and interesting individual *départements*. Here the prefect reverts to his role of consultant to the individual ministries involved. He can express an opinion about the priorities of the different projects but the final decision is not his.

The powers of the regional prefect are, therefore, severely limited. He and his small staff are no more than the beginnings of regional administration able to act in the context of regions which are suitable and relevant to the economic and technical facts of the present time. He is able, particularly in the case of regional investments (second category), to take a broader view than the traditional *département*-based organization, but he has no powers of execution. He is further limited by his obligation to consult about all significant decisions with two bodies established for this purpose in March 1964. The first is the *conférence administrative régionale* comprising the prefects of the *départements* in the region, the IGEN responsible for the region and the representatives of the regional services of the different ministries including a representative of the Treasury. In addition to this purely administrative body, the prefect is obliged to consult other regional interests. This consultation was formally organized by the creation of an Economic Development Committee (Commission de Développement Economique—CODER) in each region. The CODERs replaced and extended the former committees for economic expansion. Their membership was put at fifty persons. One-quarter of these were to be locally elected office-holders— county councillors, mayors, MPs. One-half of the members were to be regional representatives of industry, commerce, agriculture. The rest of the members were to represent other organizations in the scientific, economic, social or cultural fields including individuals chosen by the prefect because of particular qualifications. The CODERs were to be consulted at all stages of the preparation and implementation of the regional plans and the *tranches opératoires*.

This concern to establish an efficient and organized system of consultations with regional interest groups came in for severe criticism. The CODERs were essentially consultative bodies and in the execution of the regional plans this amounted to not much more than the right to be held *au courant* with decisions. Decisions about regional development were still firmly defined as the responsibility of the central government acting through the DATAR and the prefects. There was very little decentralization of authority. The formal organization of the CODERs was also objected to. It was felt that the integration of the CODERs into the administrative machinery would lead to their acceptance of policies decided by the prefects and to a tendency to assess regional policies and projects in terms of what could be done in practice rather than what had to be done.[1] Finally, the point was made that the CODERs, despite their representative nature, could not be said to introduce a democratic element into decisions about regional development. As Prof. M. Duverger argues: 'Although the CODERs are more representative and more modern than the county councils (*conseils généraux*) the fact remains that the former are essentially appointed bodies while the latter are elected'.[2]

SUB-REGIONAL ADMINISTRATION

The discussion so far has been conducted in terms of the twenty-one-region framework established in 1961. While there have been proposals for a smaller number of larger regions, this new breakdown has been generally accepted as an improvement bringing administrative boundaries into harmony with those of areas which are capable of justification in economic terms. There are, however, two issues which require more detailed analysis. The first, already referred to, is the regional prefect's notable lack of executive powers. Projects may be decided in regional terms but their implementation depends on the authorities in the *département* and the main smaller unit of local government, the commune.[3] The size and nature of the divisions within the *département* do not make for the co-ordinated administration required if projects are to be carried out on a truly regional basis. This problem became acute when the selection of the *métropoles d'équilibre* singled out certain newly defined areas within the

[1] L. Sweetman, 'Prefects and Planning. France's New Regionalism', *Public Administration*, Vol. 43, Spring 1965, p. 26.
[2] M. Duverger, 'La Democratie Régionale', Article in *Le Monde*, June 9, 1966.
[3] There are 90 *départements* and 38,000 communes.

regions for special treatment. Neither the regional nor the communal administrative machine was geared to handle the comprehensive planning which was necessary if the *métropoles* were to be developed both physically and economically to fulfil their role as balancing cities to Paris. The problem was even more urgent in view of the fact that the *métropoles* were to be the growth areas of the regions upon whose development the success of regional development policy would to a large extent depend.

Accordingly, in June 1966 the government introduced a reform which grouped the existing communes into urban communities (*communautés urbaines*) in four of the *métropoles*—Lille, Lyons, Bordeaux and Strasbourg.[1] The communities range in size from 300,000 persons in the case of Strasbourg to almost 1 million in Lyons and Lille. These new communities are to be administered by councils of fifty or sixty members depending on their size, elected or appointed by agreement by the local councils (*conseils municipaux*) of the communes involved, the number of representatives from each commune being proportional to the population of the commune. These second-tier councils will be responsible for urban and land-use planning, the zoning and creation of industrial estates, housing, public transport, secondary education and the provision of water, gas and electricity. Similar organizations will be created in all towns with a population of more than 100,000 persons if a majority of the local councils request them. This reorganization will enable the planning of the four *métropoles* to take place in a more co-ordinated way within the framework of a natural conurbation. For planning purposes, that is, the relevant units will be 'Greater Lyons' and 'Greater Lille'. The reason why the legislation was not extended to include the other four *métropoles* was that most of their population already fell within the existing town or city limits and the need for co-ordination was consequently less.

The increasing degree of interconnection of urban and regional planning has led to the creation of a number of new agencies with responsibilities for preparing long-term urban plans. Special groups have been set up to produce metropolitan area plans to the year 2000 for five of the *métropoles*—Nantes-St Nazaire, Metz-Thionville, Lyons-St Etienne, Marseilles and Lille—where the metropolitan area involves the co-ordinated growth of twin-cities.[2] The work of these groups and others is co-ordinated by a central study group at

[1] See *Le Monde*, June 12-13, 1966.
[2] These groups are known as *Organismes d'Etudes d'Aménagement d'Aires Métropolitaines*—OREAM. This may be translated as 'Environmental planning organisations for metropolitan areas'. See M. Piquard, op. cit., p. 12.

the DATAR which acts as a liaison with the government in the matter of raising funds for projects included in the plans. It is worth noting the degree to which the work of urban planning is conducted by groups like the OREAM appointed and financed by the national government or, in smaller towns, by local organizations under the oversight of the DATAR. This, on paper at least ensures better co-ordination between the various city plans and their easier integration with regional policy objectives. Once again, however, local influence is clearly subordinate.

The movement towards greater co-ordination and comprehensiveness in urban planning has an already operative model in the planning machinery for the Paris region. In 1961, for the purpose of comprehensive planning, a new agency was created known as the District de la Région de Paris headed by a director (*Délégué-Général*) appointed by the Prime Minister. Since 1966 he has also been the regional prefect for the Paris region (which is one of the twenty-one regions but is treated independently as a special case). The District is at present an amalgamation of eight new *départements*, with a total population of 8 million people, of which the city of Paris is one. It is governed by a board of twenty-eight members, half of whom are municipal and county councillors and half elected by the special Paris Council and the county councils of the seven other *départements*. A consultative assembly comprising the various interest groups is appointed by the board to be consulted by it.

The board is responsible for the preparation, co-ordination and execution of physical planning and infrastructure investment in the Paris region. Its director supervises the implementation of the board's decisions and co-ordinates the activities of other ministries when they affect the Paris region. The District has the right to levy special taxes which provide it with limited funds which it uses in the same manner as the FIAT to supplement the financing of capital projects to which the central government or the local authorities have agreed to contribute.[1]

The creation of the District was accompanied by the familiar protestations that it was not designed as a new authority superseding existing local authorities nor as an executive organization with powers to carry out projects. At the same time it is a unique institution which has no analogue in the twenty other regions. Its director is a more powerful figure than any of the other regional prefects and he has at his disposal funds which, though small, do allow him

[1] See 'Organisation et Aménagement de la Région de Paris', *Receuils et Monographies, La Documentation Française* No. 39, 1962, and 'Planning and Development of the Paris Region,' *French Embassy Broadsheet* A47/3/7, 1967.

to employ more than simple persuasion in negotiation with the central government over projects. It is significant, too, that the problems of the Paris region are handled by direct discussions between the director and the central government. This is different from the procedure for the other regions where the regional prefect's recommendations are collated and represented by the DATAR whose function is to pursue as effective a *national* regional policy as possible and to suggest regional allocations which will serve to bring this about. In contrast it has been pointed out that the draft plan for the Paris region and the role assigned it in the Fifth Plan not only argued a vigorous economic case for selective expansion in the region but proceeded on the assumption that the planning of the region should not be based on an optimistic assessment of the future development of the *métropoles d'équilibre* and of regional policy as a whole. If the consequences of this view can be traced in the Fifth Plan, one of the explanations is that the Paris region plan was more advanced both chronologically and technically than that of any other region or of any of the *métropoles*. The relationship between the development of the Paris region and the other regions of France will, therefore, be decided to a not insubstantial degree by the relative efficacy and power of their planning institutions. At the present time Paris would certainly appear to have the advantage.

CONCLUSION

At the present time regional development is probably more rationally thought out and formally organized in France than in any other Western economy with a recognized regional problem. The changes made in the traditional administrative structures and the new agencies introduced in response to changing technical and economic pressures have been considerable and important and, generally speaking, in the right direction. It is therefore natural that the French organization should be looked to as a model by other countries, particularly Britain, who are actively seeking to bring more order and rigour into their regional development policies. There are indeed important lessons to be learned from the French changes, but it should be recognized that not all of them are immediately (and some not at all) exportable.

The most important development in French regional planning is undoubtedly the integration of a number of clearly defined and comparable regional plans with the national planning framework. The pattern of regional development, defined in the broadest sense to include the distribution of population, the degree of urbanization of the population and the distribution of employment, is recognized as a major issue of policy about which any national planning or policy exercise must make assumptions and choices within a time horizon measured in generations rather than years. The scale of this task and the scarcity of resources makes it imperative that the long-term objectives of regional policy be conducted in successive stages, each of which is compatible in its demands on the economy's resources with the objectives and constraints of medium-term national plans or policies. This is what is meant by the regionalization of the national plan. It is not the division of resources between regions after what are regarded as purely national objectives have been planned and budgeted for without any longer term regional strategy having been decided. The French authorities' concern to consult the regional organizations earlier and more fully about the regional stage of the Sixth Plan, utilizing the hoped-for improvements in statistics and regional accounting techniques, indicates their acceptance of the value of this approach. The practical and the pragmatic may point out that it is impossible and undesirable to talk of the pattern of regional growth as far ahead as the CNAT exercises do. But the difficulties and errors that are bound to arise are not sufficient reasons for refusing to make at least some broad choices. If these are not made, regional policy runs the risk of being an expensive exercise in *ad hoc* tinkering on too small a scale ever to yield reasonable returns.

An essential precondition of this approach to regional planning is a system of regional plans co-ordinated and made compatible with each other by a national agency responsible for a long-term regional development policy. The plans prepared for the twenty-one programme regions and their co-ordination by the DATAR is certainly an impressively rigorous and coherent way of achieving this end. It is difficult to avoid the conclusion that it is also superior to the current very tentative efforts to create a regional planning system in Britain and Italy. Fears have been expressed, notably by Professor Lajugie, about the possibility of a lack of co-ordination between the Planning Commission and the DATAR. However well founded these may be, there is still a powerful case for having a DATAR in Britain. The existence of such a body as the apex of a system of regional planning authorities would have many advantages over the present arrangements where responsibility for regional development is diffused among several government departments each acting according to its own criteria and unco-ordinated regional pressures. The DATAR would not be a Ministry of Regional Development but rather an officially manned and recognized agency responsible for co-ordination and planning, preferably under the aegis of the Prime Minister, with a ubiquitous head represented on all committees dealing with matters affecting regional development.

Another feature of the French arrangements of relevance and applicability to other countries is the growing interconnection between regional and urban planning. One of the most obvious changes in direction of French regional policy is the recognition that a policy aimed at promoting development in certain pre-selected areas must essentially be based around a system of large, comprehensively planned city regions. From the top down this has been reflected in the administrative changes. The overlapping of functions of the Planning Commission and the Ministry of Housing has been removed; new planning and administrative agencies have been created to prepare and carry out the many-sided environmental planning operations which will determine the outcome of the 'bet' on the *métropoles d'équilibre* as new growth areas for provincial France and the DATAR's remit of co-ordination has been firmly extended to cover urban as well as regional planning. The system is incomplete and not without faults and problems, but it is a remarkable and swift development in a country where town and country planning was until the late fifties scarcely renowned for its success and certainly very little connected with national economic policy. The situation where the national economic plan contains a long section on the national strategy of urban development and the problems involved is one that could profitably be copied.

While acknowledging the merits of the French administrative reshaping, it is necessary to take account of history. The whole regional planning edifice in France is erected around the new regional prefect. It is important to note firstly that he is not as powerful as the organization chart would suggest. He is on one hand the servant of the central decision makers, and on the other dependent upon persuasion at the level of the *département, métropole* and commune to carry out projects planned in the context of the wider planning regions. In another sense, however, the prefectoral system of regional administration makes the construction of an intellectually satisfying and practically co-ordinated system of planning very much easier than it is in the British system of elected local governments. Much of the apparent purposiveness of the French effort derives from the easy and established channels through which a centralized administration can control its regional parts. The concessions to democratic participation that have been made are not impressive or probably even adequate by British standards. The British system would probably demand and need a more directly democratic agency than the CODERS with consequential additional constraints on the actions of any counterparts of the regional prefects and at the central level the DATAR, although it should be noted that the CODERS are more directly involved in and integrated into the planning process than similar existing bodies in Britain.[1] The absence of a prefectoral corps is therefore a very important difference between the British and French administrative procedures which cannot easily be overcome. The superstructure built on the prefect does, however, have considerable economic and administrative advantages. Regional planners in Britain and other countries have much to learn from it even if they are precluded from equalling its elegance.

[1] Mr Sweetman, op. cit., p. 28, puts much stress on this point and suggests that a study of how the CODERS operate would be of direct relevance to British planning efforts.

CHAPTER 11

THE RESULTS OF FRENCH
REGIONAL POLICY

I

The aim of this chapter is to assess the effectiveness of the regional policy measures discussed in the last six chapters. The basic criterion of effectiveness must be the extent to which the regional disparities outlined in Chapter 5 have been removed or reduced. This is difficult to express with any accuracy in quantitative terms for several reasons.

First, the time scale involved in regional policy is necessarily long. Serious efforts to remove the considerable regional imbalances in the French economy (the origins of which date back centuries) have been in operation for no more than fifteen years. It is early, therefore, to expect the problems to have been substantially removed. All that can be expected is that the policies should be showing signs, which are often difficult to detect and to interpret, of nudging the distribution of resources some way in the direction of greater regional equality.

A second difficulty arises out of the changes in the objectives of regional policy which have occurred in France over the period considered in this volume. Up to 1958, policy measures were directed essentially towards removing unemployment in a large and frequently changing number of relatively small localities. After 1958, policy veered towards the much longer term task of promoting the growth of output and incomes as well as jobs in widely defined regions. The reduction of unemployment in two communes of a certain *département* in 1957 cannot therefore be claimed in 1967 as an earnest of the success of regional policy. The relevant indicators are in fact in many cases not available. There are as yet, for example, no data on regional gross domestic products, nor is private gross fixed capital formation broken down by region.

A further complication is the attribution of identifiable improvements in a region's situation to this or that aspect of regional policy. An increase in a region's income per head over a specified period could be entirely unrelated to regional policy, e.g. the discovery of a new resource such as natural gas, or due to policy actions not specifically intended to promote regional development, e.g. particular investments in infrastructure or an alteration in the relative regional costs and prices of transport or energy. It may on the other hand be due directly to the existence of loans, grants, tax concessions or the availability of credit as a result of special regional arrangements. This particular problem becomes the more intractable the more extensive the scope of regional policy and its objectives, and when regional policy becomes officially recognized as a major and permanent aspect of the government's economic policy almost any action which increases employment, output or incomes within a region not designated as one in which positively no such increase is desirable can be said to be an achievement of regional policy. This untidiness is, however, to be expected in a many-sided operation such as regional development and indeed it can be argued that the situation described above in which all economic policy actions are examined in the light of regional policy objectives is in itself an indication of the success of those concerned to promote regional development.

Despite these difficulties there are a number of regional policy measures whose effect and suitability can be put to some measurable test and it is with these that the next section of this chapter will be concerned.

II

One general indicator of the effect of regional policies is the number of industrial building permits issued. The regional distribution of these is shown in Table 11.1. The figures show a definite reduction in the share of industrial building going to the Paris region and the Paris basin from the levels of 1955-60 and this suggests that the control imposed on industrial and commercial expansion introduced in 1958 had some effect. Between 1961 and 1965, however, when these controls were being progressively tightened the decline appears to have halted, the proportion of permits granted in the Paris basin remaining more or less constant at around 30 per cent of the total.

Within the Paris basin the decline in permits issued has been concentrated in the Paris region itself. The rest of the Paris basin has maintained its share of development at the level registered in 1955-60, and in 1963 increased it considerably. This tendency is consistent with the fact that the controls on development were limited to the Paris region and did not extend to the neighbouring regions. The controls have, therefore, probably had the effect of mitigating the influence of the various forms of official encouragement to firms to decentralize into the more remote areas scheduled for particular assistance, and have contributed to the growth of incomes and employment observable throughout the Paris basin.

Despite this rather perverse influence there has been a definite increase in industrial development outside the Paris basin. While the Paris basin has maintained its share of permits, since 1960 the number awarded in the regions of the west has been, on average, at least 60 per cent higher than in the period 1955-60. The west has been by a long way the main beneficiary of the transfer from the Paris

TABLE 11.1

INDUSTRIAL BUILDING PERMITS AWARDED (square metres)[1]

	1955–60	1961	1962	1963	1964	1965
Paris region	20·0	12·4	10·0	8·8	10·3	10·5
Rest of Paris basin	20·2	20·5	22·9	24·1	20·0	19·5
North	6·1	7·6	6·9	6·8	8·4	5·4
East	12·7	12·2	15·6	11·7	10·1	10·1
West	8·8	12·8	10·4	15·5	14·2	14·8
Massif Central	3·4	3·7	3·5	3·8	3·2	2·2
South-west	8·3	12·6	7·6	8·9	11·1	12·7
South-east	15·7	14·2	17·3	16·2	16·7	18·7
Mediterranean	4·8	4·1	6·0	4·2	5·9	6·2

Source: Projet de Loi des Finances pour 1967, op. cit., Vol. III, p. 367.

1 The figures all relate to building operations of more than 500 square metres.

region. The south-west has also gained but not to the same extent and in 1962 its share actually fell below the figure for 1955-60.

The situation in the Massif Central is very different. There has been scarcely any improvement in these regions and the 1964 and 1965 figures are particularly gloomy. The trend in the north is only slightly more encouraging.

Another indicator which perhaps gives a more direct measure of the efficacy of regional policy is the number of firms 'decentralizing' from the Paris region and which have successfully applied for financial assistance available for such operations. The term 'decentralization' here means the creation of an establishment outside the Paris region by firms which previously operated entirely within it. It does not cover the creation of further establishments in the provinces by such firms or extensions to the original operation. In the past few years decentralizations have accounted for around 15 per cent of the industrial building permits granted outside the Paris region. Over the period 1950-63 just under 50 per cent of the decentralizations have been to an area within a radius of 200 kilometres around the city of Paris. Between 1950 and 1962, 60 per cent of the jobs created by decentralizing firms were in the regions of the Paris basin and the contiguous regions of Burgundy and Lower Normandy.[1] Over the inter-censal period 1954-62 when the working population in manufacturing industry (excluding housing and public works) grew by 4·6 per cent, the figures for the regions in the Paris basin were 15·2 per cent in Centre, 18·6 per cent in Picardy, 11·0 per cent in Champagne and 13·7 per cent in Upper Normandy. In Burgundy and Lower Normandy employment grew by 12·9 per cent and 17·4 per cent respectively.[2] There is little evidence to suggest that this concentration in the Paris basin is being reduced.

Nor is this surprising. Even without financial aids the Paris basin and neighbouring regions like Burgundy and Lower Normandy offer many of the advantages of decentralization while minimizing its disadvantages. Wages are lower, land is cheaper, congestion and its attendant costs are less, infrastructure, if less developed than in the Paris region, is adequate, while the metropolitan services of Paris are still reasonably accessible. There are good reasons, therefore, why regions such as Centre, which has attracted by far the largest number of decentralizations, should be preferred to more remote and less developed locations.

The other main beneficiary has been the west. If Lower Normandy is included, the west received 15·1 per cent of the decentralizations between 1950 and 1962 and 19·7 per cent of the estimated number of jobs created by them. This compares very favourably with the much more attractive south-east which got 16 per cent of the firms and 15·1 per cent of the jobs. On the other hand, only one-fifth of the firms went to Brittany (the Loire basin and Lower Normandy sharing the rest equally), and the number of jobs created is small relative to the needs of the area. While decentralization operations created 46,000 jobs between 1950 and 1962, *net* migration of working population from the west over the shorter period 1954-62 was 124,000. At the same time decentralization alone produced 100,000 jobs in the Paris basin where only the region of Centre could claim to have problems on anything like the scale of the west.

The west, however, was a favoured location in comparison with the south-west and the Massif Central. The south-west got 4·7 per

[1] *Projet de Loi de Finances pour* 1967, Appendix, Vol. I, p. 27.
[2] *Projet de Loi de Finances pour* 1965, Appendix, Vol. I, p. 17.

cent of the firms and 4·5 per cent of the jobs while the Massif Central received only 3·8 per cent of the firms and 2·7 per cent of the jobs. 10,500 jobs were created by decentralizations to the southwest, but net migration of working population from the region was 65,000. In the Massif Central 6,000 jobs were created while net migration was of the order of 30,000.

The north received 4·8 per cent of the 11,300 jobs created by decentralizations. Decentralization has had a larger impact on the employment situation in this region than in the other problem areas, net migration from Nord being 19,000.

The most direct measure of French regional policy has been the investment grants and loans awarded by the FDES to firms expanding or extending their operations in particular areas. This financial aid is therefore available to a wider range of firms than the decentralization operations discussed above. It is clearly important to assess the effectiveness of this basic weapon of regional policy, but this is not easy to do. The areas where firms can claim assistance have changed frequently since 1955 as have the other conditions which applicants for aid have to meet. The amount of aid granted in different areas has also been adjusted several times. Nevertheless, some general conclusions can be extracted from the information set out in Table 11.2.

It is obvious at a glance that financial assistance has by no means been confined to the most severely deprived regions. Once again the regions of the Paris basin, notably Centre, have benefited considerably. So, too, have the north and east and Rhône-Alpes in the south-east. Although aid to the regions of the west and southwest has been far from negligible it has fallen far short of the levels required to make any sizeable inroads into the flow of migration from these regions. With the possible exception of Aquitaine, the southwest and the Massif Central have gained much less from the assistance than the west.

The limited impact of the incentives in the most needy areas is partly explained by the nature of regional policy. Until 1962 a considerable number of the areas eligible for assistance did not lie within the most backward of the planning regions but were scattered throughout the north and east. Many of these locations were preferred by industrialists to remoter areas in the west, south-west and the Massif Central, and regional policy did little to discourage them although rather higher grants were available in particular areas in the latter regions, and, generally speaking, firms in the more prosperous regions were given loans rather than straight subsidies. It was not until the 1960s that a deliberate effort was made to attract

TABLE 11.2

GRANTS AND LOANS AWARDED AND JOBS CREATED 1955–66

1	2		3		4
	Operations aided		Jobs created		Jobs created as percentage of net inter-regional migration of working population
Regions	No.	%	No.	%	1954-62
1. France[1]	1,926	100	177,218	100	
2. *Paris basin*					
Paris region	4	0·2	21	—	—
Champagne	43	2·2	3,846	2·2	33
Picardy	67	3·5	8,703	4·4	64
Upper Normandy	23	1·2	1,268	0·7	22
Centre	106	5·5	9,144	5·2	93
3. *North*					
Nord	121	6·3	15,498	8·7	80
4. *East*					
Lorraine	116	6·0	11,803	6·7	107
Alsace	47	2·4	3,932	2·2	(+)187[2]
Franche-Comté	21	1·1	1,323	0·7	110
5. *West*					
Brittany	191	9·9	26,140	14.8	45
Lower Normandy	46	2·4	5,273	2·0	17
Loire basin	207	10·7	23,576	13·3	68
6. *South-west*					
Poitou-Charentes	85	4·4	9,758	5·5	44
Aquitaine	163	8·5	12,947	7·3	70
Midi-Pyrenées	122	6·3	10,041	5·7	42
7. *Mediterranean*					
Languedoc	129	6·7	7,853	4·4	34
Provence-Côte d'Azur-Corse	65	3·4	1,931	1·1	(+)116
8. *Massif Central*					
Limousin	105	5·5	5,865	3·3	38
Auvergne	82	4·3	3,820	2·2	28
9 .*South-east*					
Burgundy	52	2·7	5,413	3·1	34
Rhône-Alpes	131	6·8	8,824	5·0	(+)39

Source: Cols. 1, 2 and 3, *Douzième Rapport du Conseil de Direction du FDES, Statistiques et Etudes Financières No. 222*, June 1967, Supplement, p. 874.

Col. 4, the figures for net inter-regional migration of working population are taken from *Projet de Loi des Finances pour 1967*, Annexe, Vol. III, p. 328.

[1] 374 operations and 23,086 jobs have to be deducted from the totals for France as a whole but since there is no means of ascertaining from the published figures in what regions the reductions occurred the gross figures have been retained as the basis for all the regional figures.

[2] The (+) sign indicates that there was net immigration into the region.

industrialists beyond the 200-kilometre circle round Paris by increasing the value of incentives in a limited number of localities and introducing a more selective public investment programme.

A comparison of each region's share of operations and jobs created gives a rough indication of the nature of the operations in each region. The west, particularly Brittany and the Loire basin, has been able to attract more large firms than either the south-west or the Massif Central. The pattern in the 'prosperous' regions of the south-east and the Mediterranean coast also suggests that few really sizeable concerns received assistance there. The situation is, however, different in the Paris basin and the regions of the north and east. In all of these regions some fair-sized firms have expanded as a result of regional policy. This pattern is in line with the general conclusion emerging from the figures examined so far, that up to 1966 the effect of financial aid has been to underpin industrial expansion in regions whose economies were reasonably healthy and latterly to encourage some substantial if still inadequate industrialization in the three western regions. The south-west and the Massif Central, on the other hand, have benefited to a much smaller extent.

A measure of the selectivity of financial assistance is given in Table 11.3.

The share of total financial assistance going to the priority areas has fluctuated considerably in the four years considered but no rising trend is discernible. The 1966 figures do suggest a considerable movement in favour of the *départements* in the west after a definite falling-off in activity there in the previous two years. This is in keeping with the ambitious target of new job creation in manufacturing industry in the western regions accepted in the Fifth Plan. The channelling of 50 per cent of aid to around one-fifth of the number of assisted firms located in what is effectively the Brittany peninsula and four city regions outside it can be said to be a fairly selective policy when account is taken of the fact that on average another 25 per cent of firms received small amounts of aid directly from the *conférences administratives régionales* and later from the regional prefects in the context of their regional plans.

The limited effect of financial incentives on development in some of the less prosperous regions leads naturally to a consideration of the effectiveness of the various financial aids as means of influencing businessmen's decisions about where to locate. This is not easy to measure or assess. Knowledge about the factors influencing location decisions in the private sector is far from adequate and in most cases the outcome is determined by a number of influences which are not easily separated or ranked.[1] French regional policy fully recognizes these difficulties and the distortions which can be created by a misuse of incentives, and the reforms introduced in 1964 were an attempt to make them more effective.[2]

The reforms were designed to meet a number of frequently raised criticisms. The most serious of these concerned the uncertainty

TABLE 11.3

GRANTS AND LOANS AWARDED IN PRIORITY AREAS AS A PERCENTAGE OF TOTAL AID GRANTED

Region	Operations aided				Grants and loans awarded			
	1963	1964	1965	1966	1963	1964	1965	1966
Special urban areas eligible for maximum assistance[1]	11·2	10·6	12·1	12·1	45·7	34·7	63·2	28·9
Départements in the west[2]	12·6	9·5	6·7	13·0	15·2	12·2	3·0	21·5
Total for Priority Areas	23·8	20·1	18·8	25·1	60·9	46·9	66·2	50·4

Source: Douzième Rapport du FDES, op. cit., p. 856.

[1] The areas are Cherbourg, Brest, Lorient and Nantes, St Nazaire in the west; La Rochelle, Rochefort, Bordeaux and Toulouse in the south-west; Limoges and Brive-la-Gaillarde in the Massif Central.
[2] The départements with the exception of Manche all fall within the regions of Brittany and the Loire basin.

created by the policy of *coup par coup* under which the list of areas in which aid was available was constantly being changed. Clearer and more automatic procedures were required concerning the amounts and forms of assistance obtainable in different areas. The new system was also meant to concentrate assistance more in those areas where it was most necessary to promote development, although it was stated explicitly that the provision of infrastructure, advance factories and privileged credit arrangements were frequently considered by businessmen to be more valuable than straight subsidies.

[1] See G. C. Cameron and B. D. Clark, op. cit.
[2] See Chapter 9.

This raises the question of the level of financial assistance given and the amount of subsidy which it is reasonable to give in order to help regional development.

The calculation of the value of regional incentives is far from straightforward. So much depends on the nature of the firm receiving assistance—the structure of its costs, its profitability, the nature and length of life of its assets and, of course, the area in which its expansion is located. In these circumstances all that can be done is to construct a number of hypothetical cases. These may be of limited value in indicating to any particular firm how much it can expect to benefit from the incentives but they do at least suggest orders of magnitude.

A recent study by the DATAR has attempted such an evaluation of incentives. The value of various incentives is shown in Table 11.4.

The incentives considered here do not include loans, the special provision of housing and telecommunications under the system of *conventions d'implantation industrielle*, the reductions in transfer expenses available to firms decentralizing from the Paris region nor the contribution towards training and retraining expenses. Similarly, no account is taken of the financial assistance provided by the Regional Development Companies (SDR). The only incentives considered are the grants and loans and fiscal concessions made available to reduce the capital costs of expansion.

Using the information in Table 11.4 the study proceeded to work out the value of incentives in the case of firms setting up a new plant in five different localities. These were: Paris, where no incentives are available and the firm is liable for the levy on any industrial or commercial development there; Chartres, in the Paris basin, where no incentives are available but no levy is charged; Angers, in the Loire basin, which is scheduled with Area 3 of the incentives system as an area without any acute problems but where no rapid expansion is taking place; the whole *département* of Mayenne in the Loire basin, which falls within Area 1; and, finally, Nantes which is within Area 1 and is in addition one of the special urban areas singled out for maximum assistance.

The following assumptions were made about the firms receiving assistance:

1. They make profits each year on which they pay profits tax after making full use of the provisions for accelerated depreciation.
2. The new plant fulfils all the technical and financial conditions (e.g. the cost per job is below the permitted maximum) required in each area to obtain the maximum level of aid.

3. Investment expenditure is allocated in the following way: 5 per cent on land purchase, 50 per cent on building, 45 per cent on plant and machinery. The average life of buildings is twenty years, and plant and machinery five years. Investment per square metre

TABLE 11.4

Form of assistance	Average value of assistance as percentage of investment undertaken
A. *Tax Concessions*	
—reduction in tax on land purchase	0·3
—reduction in local taxation	Very variable. A survey of 40 firms showed that a reduction of 100 per cent for a period of 5 years was equal on average, in 1964, to 5·7 per cent of investment
—accelerated depreciation	2·5
—reduction in tax on capital gains from the sale of industrial land	Very variable. A maximum of 5 per cent
B. *Grants*	
—industrial development grant 20 per cent	13·3
12 per cent	7·9
10 per cent	6·6
—industrial adaptation grant	0 to 13·3
—grant and levy relating to the construction and removal of buildings in the Paris region	Very variable. The savings enjoyed by a firm setting up in the provinces rather than the Paris region where it would be liable for a levy of £7 5s per square metre amounted to, on average, 12 per cent of investment
C. Reduction in the price of industrial land in certain industrial areas in the west	1·6

Source: *Effet Cumulé des Aides Financières Accordées Pour une Implantation Industrielle en Province*, DATAR, Paris, May 1966, p. 12. This document contains a full explanation of the assumptions on which the calculations in the table were based.

of factory floor space is £60. These figures are based on the results of several surveys of firms receiving assistance.

4. In the case where the plant is located in Paris, a levy of £7 5s per square metre is paid. When it is established in Nantes, in an industrial estate benefiting from government assistance, the price of factory space is 8s 9d per square metre compared with 11s 8d in other urban areas where the government does not subsidize the construction of industrial estates.

5. Local taxation in each locality is assumed to be 2·8 per cent of the new investment undertaken. In Angers, Mayenne and Nantes there is complete exemption from local taxation for five years.

6. In Mayenne the industrial development grant is 10 per cent of investment and in Nantes 20 per cent. These grants, however, constitute cash inflows which are liable to profits tax. The value of the grant is spread evenly year by year over the profits made during the life of the asset for which it was granted. Where accelerated depreciation has been applied, a proportionately larger share of the grant is imputed to the profits made in the years when the amount set aside for depreciation is greater than that under the normal procedure of writing off assets on a linear basis. As a result of this procedure, the part of the grant liable to tax becomes in effect a loan by the government to the firm repayable in yearly instalments over a period equal to the life of the asset. The net value of the development grant can be calculated by adding together that part of the grant not liable to tax and the discounted present value of the loan which the part liable to tax can be considered to represent.

On the basis of these assumptions the value of the incentives in the five areas is shown in Table 11.5.

Table 11.5 shows that in the extreme case of a firm deciding to establish in Nantes rather than Paris it would receive assistance equal to 34·9 per cent of its investment outlay. Since this study was published, the gross value of the grant has been increased to 25 per cent in the regions of Area 1, including both Mayenne and Nantes. The net value in Nantes would now therefore be around 38 per cent of investment outlay. Assuming that on average the capital costs of the firm which the incentives are designed to offset account for around 12 per cent of total production costs, the overall reduction in costs would be 4·5 per cent in Nantes and 3·2 per cent in a less privileged location such as Mayenne.[1] In Angers, assistance would be just over 2 per cent of total costs.

1 The figure of 12 per cent represents the proportion of Gross Domestic Product in France accounted for in recent years by the two items depreciation of capital stock and interest and dividend payments.

The important question is, of course, whether these subsidies are sufficient to offset the net additional costs of location in a less prosperous region. One possible approach would be to compare the value of incentives with the extra transport costs incurred in a new location. It has, however, already been argued that transport costs are only one part of what can be termed 'accessibility costs' and this latter item is not readily quantified. Even the wider interpre-

TABLE 11.5

Incentives	Value of incentives as a percentage of investment carried out				
	Paris	Chartres	Angers	Mayenne	Nantes
1. Reduction in the tax on land purchase	—	—	+0·3	+0·3	+0·3
2. Exemption from local taxation	—	—	+5·7	+5·7	+5·7
3. Accelerated depreciation	—	—	—	+2·5	+2·5
4. Industrial development grant	—	—	—	+6·4[1]	+12·8[1]
5. Special reduction in the price of factory space in selected areas in the west	—	—	—	—	+1·6
6. Levy on industrial and commercial building in the Paris region	−12	—	—	—	—

Source: Effet Cumulé des Aides Financières, op. cit., p. 14.

[1] This is the net value of the grants of 10 per cent and 20 per cent of investment expenditure using a rate of discount of 7 per cent and taking account of accelerated depreciation.

tation of the costs imposed by distance from suppliers and markets takes no account of the lower productivity which a firm may have to tolerate while both management and labour settle into a new location. These productivity losses may reduce or remove altogether the gains resulting from lower labour costs. One rough measure of the adequacy of the incentives would, therefore, be the extent to which they offset the differences in the level of productivity in the prosperous and less prosperous regions.

A number of measures of productivity all suggest that even the maximum incentive is far from adequate according to this criterion. The average value added per head in the Loire basin (the region in which Angers, Mayenne and Nantes are situated) is only 84·2 per cent of the national average. The difference between this and the national level is thus more than three times greater than the value of the offsetting incentives. This measure of productivity suggests that the maximum incentive would be inadequate in all the regions in the west, south-west and the Massif Central and in Burgundy and Centre. Very similar conclusions are reached if differences in regional wage and salary levels are taken as a measure of productivity differentials.

Such rough comparisons must, of course, be made with caution. The productivity figures used in the preceding paragraph refer to *average* productivity in the region whereas a new firm might reasonably be expected to be more efficient since it is emigrating from a region where productivity levels are higher. Moreover, the fact that it is expanding indicates that it has been able to compete successfully in its original location and considers its prospects sufficiently bright to justify movement to a new and uncertain location. It is possible to argue further that because of this an incentive which totally offset the difference between productivity levels in the economy as a whole and the less prosperous regions would wastefully over-compensate emigrant or decentralizing firms and run the risk of condoning inefficiency. None the less, the incentives under discussion are in the nature of temporary, once-for-all assistance and the average productivity levels in the less prosperous regions might reasonably be claimed to be a rough measure of the *initial* productivity performance of a more efficient firm during its settling-in period in one of the latter areas and, therefore, the relevant indicator of how large *temporary* aid should be.

In assessing the effectiveness of incentives it is interesting to note that the value of incentives in France would appear not to be very different from those granted to firms moving into development areas in Britain where the levels of productivity and living standards are much nearer the national average than is the case in France.[1] When the incentives provide an overall reduction in costs of the order of 3 to 4 per cent it is difficult to argue that the British measures are excessive. It is more likely that the French incentives are on the low side. This would certainly appear to be the case so far as the investment grants are concerned. The maximum grant obtainable in France is 25 per cent, while in Britain grants of up to 45 per cent are available

[1] One estimate puts the value of assistance with capital expenditure in development areas in Britain at between 2·5 to 3 per cent of total costs. See T. Wilson, 'Finance for Regional Industrial Development', *Three Banks Review*, September 1967.

in very extensively defined development areas. It might be argued that the element of risk involved in aiding private investment in the less prosperous regions is greater in France than in Britain because of the very unpropitious nature of many of the most needy regions in France. This could account for some unwillingness on the part of the authorities to be too generous in their aid to private investments lest it should encourage firms to move without realistically examining what their situation would be after the aid has ceased. This argument is, however, rather at odds with the facts of *public* investment policy, which expends much larger sums on setting up infrastructure in the less prosperous regions at the risk of its being underutilized or inefficiently employed if it is not accompanied by a flow of private investment. Parsimony with investment incentives could in such circumstances be an extremely short-sighted and wasteful strategy.

III

While financial incentives are important, it can reasonably be said that the key element in French regional policy is the creation of infrastructure in the less prosperous regions, which will give their economies a base from which growth can take place. There is, as has been pointed out in Chapter 9, very little emphasis in French regional policy on the planned creation of inter-industry groupings of the kind being developed in Italy. The essence of regional development is seen rather as the creation in selected areas, in particular in the *métropoles d'équilibre* and in other regional growth centres, of the external economies which are considered to be the most important factor in influencing location decisions in manufacturing industry. This approach is also compatible with ensuring the less prosperous regions a reasonable share of the most rapidly expanding sector of the economy—the services industries. It takes account too of the need to accommodate the trend in France towards a greater degree of urbanization by some means other than an excessive expansion of population within the Paris region.

In order to facilitate the planning of infrastructure in the regions the traditional budgetary processes were reformed to allow considerations of regional development articulated by the DATAR to be taken explicitly into account when budget credits are being voted. The Fifth Plan developed the criteria to be used in assessing regional needs by distinguishing between the equalizing and stimulating (or developmental) aims of regional expenditure. It should be noted that this regionalization of the budget is not an *ex post facto* division of credits among the different regions; it is ideally at least, a forecast of the public expenditures 'required' in the different regions which satisfies or compromises between the aims of regional policy and budgetary policy.

Such a formal integration of regional and national economic policy marks a very considerable advance in regional policy-making. It means that at both the decision-making and implementation stages of publicly financed projects the aims of regional development policy have to be brought into confrontation with the aims of national economic policy. More precisely and practically, any decisions about the promotion of a certain rate of growth of national output, the distribution of the increments and any reductions in the rate of growth objectives required to achieve consistency with the related objectives of price stability and a particular state of the balance on external payments must take account also of the aims of regional development. There need not always be a conflict but, if there is, the new procedures must be expected to produce a more informed and consistent resolution. In any economy in which regional policy is not a priority objective in the strict sense of the term, such arrangements must represent an upgrading of the status of regional policy in the range of policy aims.

Since the process of regionalizing the budget was only introduced in 1964 and is still being developed and reformed, it is early yet to judge the system on its results. Table 11.6, however, does enable some tentative comments to be made.

The table shows the regional distribution of most of the major items of public expenditure as it actually turned out in 1965 and relates each region's share to its share of total population. To draw firm conclusions from such a comparison is difficult for obvious reasons. The table deals with only a single year; the expenditures shown under each head are large aggregates which mask important differences; and total population may not be the relevant criterion in some cases. The norm or ideal distribution which is implied in the very presentation of the table is an equal expenditure a head throughout all the regions in the economy. The question must be asked whether this is a sensible and proper aim of regional development policy.

Such a norm can be defended on grounds of equity. Each region should receive the same amount of expenditure a head in respect of those public goods and services which the state has decided should be provided on a communal basis. This ensures that each region has an equal claim on a limited amount of funds. In another sense, however, such a distribution may not be equitable. If the costs of providing public goods and services are higher in the less favoured

TABLE 11.6

REGIONAL DISTRIBUTION OF PUBLIC EXPENDITURE

Regions	Percentage share of population	Housing 1966	Health and Population (Ministry of Social Affairs)	Posts and Tele-communications 1965	Education 1965	Urban Equipment and Rural Roads (Ministry of the Interior) 1965	National Road Network 1965	Scientific and Technical Research
1. *Paris basin*	31·1	39·1	40·8	47·7	31·6	31·9	42·9	49·9
Paris region	18·3	27·5	32·6	35·3	21·6	22·8	33·4	48·9
Champagne	2·6	2·1	2·3	1·9	2·4	1·7	2·1	—
Picardy	3·2	2·7	0·7	2·9	1·6	1·9	3·5	—
Upper Normandy	3·0	3·1	3·1	1·9	2·3	1·8	2·0	—
Centre	4·0	3·7	2·1	5·7	3·7	3·7	1·9	1·0
2. *North*	7·8	6·8	2·4	3·0	9·1	5·8	4·5	—
Nord	7·8	6·8	2·4	3·0	9·1	5·8	4·5	—
3. *East*	9·5	7·9	5·6	5·1	9·5	7·2	5·8	2·4
Lorraine	4·7	4·0	2·9	1·8	6·4	3·1	3·3	0·5
Alsace	2·8	2·2	1·3	2·2	1·8	2·2	0·6	1·9
Franche-Comté	2·0	1·7	1·4	1·1	1·3	1·9	1·9	—
4. *West*	13·0	11·2	20·3	9·0	15·7	13·8	8·3	4·3
Brittany	5·1	4·6	6·3	3·4	3·3	6·0	5·8	1·1
Lower Normandy	2·6	2·1	11·1	1·7	3·3	3·2	1·7	1·5
Loire basin	5·3	4·5	2·9	3·9	9·1	4·6	0·8	1·7
5. *South-west*	12·6	9·8	8·8	10·8	11·1	12·9	10·8	2·2
Poitou-Charentes	3·1	1·9	1·7	2·4	2·0	2·3	3·0	0·1
Aquitaine	5·0	4·0	4·5	5·0	5·8	4·7	5·9	0·6
Midi-Pyrénées	4·5	3·9	2·6	3·4	3·3	5·9	1·9	1·5
6. *Mediterranean*	10·0	10·4	8·4	10·9	9·8	12·5	13·6	22·1
Languedoc	3·4	2·7	3·1	3·2	2·3	5·3	4·8	9·6
Provence-Côte d'Azur	6·6	7·7	5·3	7·7	7·5	7·2	8·8	12·5
7. *Massif Central*	4·3	3·0	3·1	3·4	2·0	3·8	4·6	2·6
Limousin	1·6	1·1	1·5	2·1	0·9	1·8	0·8	2·3
Auvergne	2·7	1·9	1·6	1·3	1·1	2·0	3·8	0·3
8. *South-east*	11·8	12·2	10·9	10·1	11·1	12·1	9·5	16·7
Burgundy	3·1	2·3	2·8	1·7	2·1	2·7	0·5	0·3
Rhône-Alpes	8·7	9·9	8·1	8·4	9·0	9·4	9·0	16·4
Percentage of expenditure not broken down by region	—	10·1	0	59·6	50·0	0[1]	10·6	36·9

Source: Projet de Loi des Finances pour 1967, Appendix, Vol. III, passim.

[1] Only 57 per cent of the credits were regionalized in advance.

regions, it can be argued that equity demands that they be given a share of available funds greater than their share of population in order that they can be provided with the same amount of real, physical facilities as other regions.[1] The principle of providing equal facilities which was announced as one of the criteria to be used in France to determine the regional distribution of budgetary credits would suggest that some of the poorer regions should receive more expenditure a head than the more prosperous regions.

There are, however, two other different and conflicting criteria governing the regional distribution of public expenditure. The first is the principle of selecting development which involves deliberately building up infrastructure in certain selected regions with a view to creating the pre-conditions for an increase in regional output which will become self-sustaining without further privileged treatment. This approach is obviously bound to conflict with the 'equal expenditure a head' notion of equity. It may, however, produce the same general pattern of resource allocation as the alternative formulation of the equity rule if the decision is made to use public expenditure to create in the less prosperous regions the possibilities for long-term improvement in the rate of growth of output and therefore the level of incomes. Where the difference in motive is likely to show is in the concentration of expenditure in those areas within the region judged most capable of becoming centres of economic expansion which the development approach would almost inevitably produce.

There remains the criterion of national efficiency. The application of this rule may encourage a more than proportionate share of credits being devoted to those regions where costs are lowest and the possibilities of economies of scale and external economies greatest—exactly the opposite case to the second definition of equity. On this reasoning the Paris region, say, should have a larger share of credits than its population share warrants, and the west of France a lower share because the rate of return on expenditure is higher in the former than in the latter. On the other hand, an equal share of credits could be justified strictly on efficiency grounds if the external diseconomies

---

[1] It should, however, be noted that this definition of equity may in certain circumstances favour the prosperous regions. This would occur where the real standard of facilities and amenities had fallen as a result of a low priority being given to their replacement (due, perhaps, to a preference for more directly 'productive' investment) or the pressure put upon them as a result of immigration into the region. There is, of course, a difference between the case of public facilities which are virtually non-existent or of low quality—the situation likely to occur in poor regions—and the shortage of modern facilities which may occur in richer regions. But inadequate quantity can very quickly come to mean the same as low quality.

caused by the concentration of resources in the Paris region are at least sufficient to offset the higher costs, lack of opportunities to exploit economies of scale and absence of external economies in the west. Such calculations are of course extremely awkward and become more so if even the simplest of dynamic views is taken. Might it not be less costly to reduce by means of better planning (involving public expenditure) the external diseconomies in Paris than to seek to create external economies in the west?

At the present time, French regional policy is founded on an admixture of the second equity approach and the principle of selective development. It emphasizes the need to raise the level of incomes in some regions even if this means achieving less than maximum returns on inputs for a certain period of time and therefore infringing the efficiency rule. It does, too, in basing regional development strategy around the creation of *métropoles d'équilibre*, assume that by building up such centres a situation will be reached where the costs of producing a good or service, whether public or private, in each region with such a centre or its near equivalent will not be significantly different from the costs in the Paris region.

The implications of this argument for the present distribution of credits must be that the less prosperous regions should receive more public expenditure a head than the prosperous regions, since in the vast majority of instances they are worse off both in terms of equal standards and development possibilities. In practice, therefore, the regionalization of the budget should be nudging expenditure a head in Paris downwards to the benefit of the less prosperous regions. This expenditure should in the majority of cases be concentrated in the areas around or linked with the *métropoles d'équilibre*.

Table 11.6 shows the more than proportionate share of expenditure taken by the Paris region, particularly in the fields of Health, Posts and Communications, National Roads and Research. The south-east, especially Rhône-Alpes, has received more or less its proper allocation, while Provence-Côte d'Azur has exceeded it in most fields. It is probable that these regions have further benefited by getting a large share of the sizeable amounts of expenditure which have not been regionalized.

The distributional pattern shown in the table is a further instance of the ambivalent attitude of the authorities towards the continued expansion of the Paris region. It is difficult to reconcile the figures for the Paris region with a serious effort at building up infrastructure in the less prosperous areas. Similarly, the figures for Rhônes-Alpes and Provence-Côte d'Azur indicate the importance attached to the expansion taking place in these regions. These judgments must,

I

however, be qualified. Firstly, in some fields such as housing, the Paris region has a relatively more severe problem of standards than many other regions and the expenditure figures naturally reflect this. Again, the share of expenditure on Education and Urban Equipment and Rural Roads going to the Paris region is only a percentage point or two greater than its population share and these particular items of public expenditure constitute important parts of infra-structure.

Turning to the less prosperous regions, it is apparent that an effort of some magnitude is being made to remedy the disadvantages of the regions in the west. Each of the three large regions there has benefited in varying ways from expenditures sufficiently above the population norm to suggest a definite policy of assistance. There are at the same time serious shortfalls in Posts and Telecommunications and National Roads, both types of expenditure of considerable economic importance to geographically remote regions. But on balance the signs indicate that the long process of bringing the west into social and economic parity with the rest of France is under way.

A gloomier picture emerges for the Massif Central and the north, while in the east and Poitou-Charentes in the south-west the short-falls are not insignificant. Considering the small population of the Massif Central, it is remarkable that under none of the expenditure heads except, marginally, National Roads does this region get a share of public spending commensurate with its population. With no *métropole* and poor prospects for both agriculture and industry, it is now clearly the least favoured part of France, and the figures in the table suggest it may now be very late to improve the situation without still further emigration.

Nord presents a disturbing prospect of a rather different kind. It is at first sight rather surprising that this region, faced with the problem of declining industries and an extensive but outdated infra-structure, should not have benefited more from public expenditure. Bearing in mind the limitations of the figures, this would appear to be further evidence of a certain tendency in France to view the regional problem in terms of the west and the prosperous areas. In the south-west there is a fairly clear difference in treatment between Aquitaine and Midi-Pyrenées with their industrial complexes and the less developed Poitou-Charentes.

One particularly significant item of expenditure is Scientific and Technical Research. Expenditure of this kind is of great value to a region since it is both a provider of high income employment and an increasingly valuable external economy. The figures in the table call for two comments. The first is the extent to which the declared policy, now more than a decade old, of decentralizing research establishments from the Paris region has worked. Even allowing it a large share of the non-regionalized expenditure, the Paris region is no longer as dominant as it used to be. The problem is that the decentralization has concentrated in the prosperous, expanding regions of Provence-Côte d'Azur and Rhône-Alpes. The share of the other regions is tiny by comparison. Particularly disquieting is the apparent absence of any research expenditure in the north. Since the economic future of the north is inevitably dependent on its ability to attract new industries this is a most serious omission.

In addition to the regionalization of the general budget an important aspect of French regional policy are the various funds set up to give special additional assistance with infrastructure works in the less prosperous areas. One particularly important type of expenditure are the loans for capital projects granted to local authorities through the medium of the Deposits and Consignments Office. Capital expenditure by local authorities in France accounts for almost 60 per cent of civil public expenditure on capital account and most of it goes on the infrastructure works which are so important to regional development. The tax receipts of local authorities are nowhere near adequate to finance such expenditure. In 1965, for instance, 66 per cent of local authorities' capital spending was financed by loans mostly from the *Caisse des Dépôts*. The regional distribution of these loans is shown in Table 11.7.

The pattern emerging from the table is not discouraging. While the Paris basin and the south-east exceed the population norm, it would appear that an effort has been made to help local authorities in the west and south-west. The most significant disparity occurs in the north which, with 7·8 per cent of total population, receives only 4·9 per cent of loans. It should be said in mitigation that the low figure is partly explained by a delay in spending previous loans. But this in itself is scarcely a favourable sign in a region where the existing infrastructure is badly in need of modernization and replacement in order to attract the new industries which are required to offset the decline in employment in the older industries.

The distribution of loans granted by the two other agencies concerned with the promotion of regional development, the Land Development Fund (FNAFU) and the Regional Development Fund (FIAT), are shown in Tables 11.8 and 11.9.

The distribution of expenditure by FNAFU on land for priority housing and the construction and renovation of dwellings indicates the efforts being made to alleviate the shortage of reasonable housing accommodation in the Paris region. The much smaller sums spent

TABLE 11.7

REGIONAL DISTRIBUTION OF LOANS TO LOCAL AUTHORITIES
BY THE CAISSE DES DÉPÔTS ET CONSIGNATIONS, CRÉDIT
FONCIER, AND CRÉDIT AGRICOLE IN RESPECT OF CAPITAL
EXPENDITURE IN 1965

Regions	Percentage
Paris basin	35·5
Paris region	23·1
Champagne	2·5
Picardy	2·6
Upper Normandy	3·3
Centre	4·0
North	4·9
Nord	4·9
East	6·8
Lorraine	2·9
Alsace	1·9
Franche-Comté	2·0
West	13·3
Brittany	5·4
Lower Normandy	2·7
Loire basin	5·2
South-west	11·4
Poitou-Charentes	2·7
Aquitaine	4·6
Midi-Pyrenées	4·1
Mediterranean	10·3
Languedoc	3·3
Provence-Côte d'Azur	7·0
Massif Central	3·8
Limousin	1·3
Auvergne	2·5
South-east	13·8
Burgundy	2·9
Rhône-Alpes	10·9

Source: Projet de Loi des Finances pour 1967, op. cit., pp. 275–8.

TABLE 11.8

FINANCING OF INDUSTRIAL AREAS, LAND PURCHASE AND
HOUSING CONSTRUCTION BY FNAFU IN 1965

Regions	Industrial Areas (percentage)	Housing (percentage)
Paris basin	9·3	38·2
Paris region	—	26·3
Champagne	2·4	3·6
Picardy	0·8	1·1
Upper Normandy	1·6	3·3
Centre	4·5	3·9
North	2·2	5·1
Nord	2·2	5·1
East	7·1	8·9
Lorraine	3·5	5·3
Alsace	1·3	1·1
Franche-Comté	2·3	2·5
West	43·5	9·6
Brittany	16·0	3·3
Lower Normandy	11·4	1·9
Loire basin	16·1	4·4
South-west	19·9	9·7
Poitou-Charentes	3·0	0·9
Aquitaine	8·0	3·9
Midi-Pyrénées	8·9	4·9
Mediterranean	—	9·6
Languedoc	—	5·0
Provence-Côte d'Azur-Corse	—	4·6
Massif Central	4·4	0·3
Limousin	1·4	0·2
Auvergne	3·0	0·1
South-east	12·8	12·8
Burgundy	1·8	4·0
Rhône-Alpes	11·0	8·8

Source: *Projet de Loi des Finances pour 1967*, op. cit., pp. 105–15.

TABLE 11.9

INFRASTRUCTURE INVESTMENT GRANTS AWARDED BY FIAT,
1963–66

Regions	Percentage
Paris basin	3·9
Paris region	—
Champagne	3·2
Picardy	0·2
Upper Normandy	0·3
Centre	0·2
North	7·1
Nord	7·1
East	10·1
Lorraine	4·9
Alsace	5·2
Franche-Comté	1·0
West	26·7
Brittany	16·3
Lower Normandy	2·5
Loire basin	7·9
South-west	23·1
Poitou-Charentes	4·2
Aquitaine	7·4
Midi-Pyrenées	11·5
Mediterranean	15·9
Languedoc	5·4
Provence-Côte d'Azur-Corse	10·5
Massif Central	6·9
Limousin	2·1
Auvergne	4·8
South-east	5·6
Burgundy	1·2
Rhône-Alpes	4·4

Source: *Projet de Loi des Finances pour 1967*,
op. cit., pp. 259–65.

on the construction of industrial estates have been very heavily concentrated in the west and the south-west. This is in line with the policy of attracting industry to these areas and selectively limiting the number of industrial estates created by local authorities each year. A similar concentration on the west and south-west can be seen from an examination of FIAT's activities in the first three years of its existence.

IV

The various bits of evidence collected in this chapter allow the judgment that French regional policy has had some qualified success although it is still early for any assessment of the effectiveness of the regionalization of public expenditure. Awkward problems, however, remain. The understandably ambivalent attitude to the Paris region introduces a major element of uncertainty into the new, policy of selective regional development based on the *métropoles d'équilibre*. Apart from the metropolitan area of Lyons and the adjacent area around Grenoble, the *métropoles* will require a considerable share of public expenditure, swift, effective planning and equally effective lobbying if they are to get on the way to becoming counterweights to Paris. They have, however, been formally designated as the priority areas of growth in the economy and there are signs that both public investment and financial aid are being specially channelled towards them. The question is whether this will be done with sufficient speed to prevent further migration to Paris upon which regional policy to date has had only a limited effect.

It is fairly clear that despite the interest in promoting development in the Paris region and the south-east, regional policy is making some serious efforts to create both manufacturing and service employment in the west and south-west. Indeed, given the concern not to hinder population and employment growth in the Paris region too much, the programmes outlined for the west are remarkably ambitious. One consequence of this has been a tendency to relegate to a lower priority the problems of the north and parts of the east. The Massif Central presents a picture of almost unmitigated gloom unless further migration from the region is accepted as a reasonable element in any solution.

It is reasonable to conclude that the financial incentives available to industrial firms moving into areas outside the Paris basin are not excessively generous considering the disparities in productivity between the different regions. On the other hand, the system is sensibly selective and the new incentives to firms transferring their 'service' activities outside the Paris region are an interesting and potentially important development. The effectiveness of incentives as a means of influencing businessmen's location decisions is as difficult to gauge in France as elsewhere. It would appear, however, that the policy makers consider that the presence of external economies is probably of greater significance. Certainly, apart from Paris and areas within reasonably close travelling distance of it and the areas around Lyons and Marseilles, the level of infrastructure facilities of all kinds is inadequate and outdated. Public investment is, therefore, probably a more potent aid to development than any cash benefits.

It is in the arrangements for distributing public expenditure among the regions that French regional policy is at its most impressive. However embryonic this regionalization may be in concept and implementation, it has established the principle that the public investment decisions which will influence the distribution of population and employment must be taken with formal regard to a national strategy of regional development and in the context of the information supplied by an organized system of regional plans. Within this framework the possibilities for developing more penetrating and effective criteria for the distribution of credits and more effective methods of overseeing their utilization can fruitfully proceed.

PART III

REGIONAL POLICY:
THREE ISSUES

CHAPTER 12

REGIONAL PLANNING

I

The term regional economic planning is now widely employed in a great number of economies of very different types, and the last decade has seen the growth of a large number of new administrative agencies charged with the preparation and implementation of these regional plans. Indeed, it can be argued that in some cases more thought and effort has gone into the creation of such administrative frameworks than to working out the precise function and contribution of regional plans. What this chapter will seek to do is to pose what appear to be some of the central questions about regional planning and to see how the French and Italian experiences help to answer them. These two countries may not be the best models for such an exercise, but they have certain characteristics which form an interesting context within which regional planning can be investigated. They both have a 'regional problem' of serious dimensions which at least since 1950 has become a major concern of their governments. This concern has been reflected in the increasingly comprehensive regional policies which have been brought into operation to promote regional development. The growing importance of regional development in the economic policies of the two countries inevitably raised the issue of how regional policy should be formulated and implemented at both the central and regional levels. On this point the two countries present very different cases. In France a system of national economic plans was in existence before any comprehensive regional policy was formulated. Regional planning when it developed had therefore quite naturally to be related to the national plans because the latter were already operating. In Italy, on the other hand, the idea of a national economic plan did not develop until the mid-1950s, by which time regional policy or a 'policy for the South' was firmly established as a major responsibility of the government.

It is possible to distinguish three basic issues which naturally present themselves in any discussion of regional planning. The first concerns the objectives which a regional plan is intended to achieve.

The second question concerns the nature of the relationship between regional plans and national economic plans or policies. Thirdly, no discussion of regional planning is complete without an examination of the administrative arrangements for the preparation and implementation of the plans.

Regional plans can have a number of possible objectives which, although closely related to each other, are significantly different. The first can be expressed in terms of the creation of a specified number of jobs over the period of the plan with a view to reducing regional unemployment, raising participation rates and holding regional emigration at some desired level. A second possible objective is to maximize the rate of growth of output per head in the region over the period of the plan. This is sometimes expressed more precisely in terms of increasing output per head in a region so as to bring it into equality with other regions within a specified time. Finally, the objective of a regional plan for a region may be expressed in terms of the relationship between the region and the economy of which it is a part. In this case the regional plan may seek to achieve the fastest rate of growth of regional output per head consistent with the attainment of a particular national rate of growth of output per head. The formulation of the objective in this way draws attention to the relationship between regional and national growth. It might be possible to achieve a very rapid rate of growth of output per head in one region by transferring to it resources employed in other regions. But one of the costs of such an operation might be a lower rate of national growth than would otherwise have been achieved or, according to the objective stated above, a rate of national growth inferior to some desired or normative rate if the resources are used less efficiently in the region to which they have been transferred than in other regions. On the other hand, the promotion of regional growth may serve to facilitate a faster rate of national growth than would otherwise have occurred. This situation would arise when there exists in the region concerned unutilized or under-utilized resources which can be brought into employment within the region but which cannot as efficiently be transferred to other regions where resources are already being used fully and with maximum efficiency.

The most important distinction to be made is between a plan to reduce unemployment and a plan to increase output per head. Of course, the objectives of the plan may be expressed or measured in terms of either employment or output per head and in the case of regional plans where estimates of regional gross domestic product are not available employment is in fact commonly used. The strategies lying beneath the two types of plan do, however, differ significantly. A plan whose prime objective is to increase regional output per head creates jobs as a consequence of productivity growth. It does not promote activities simply because they are labour-intensive; it may indeed give priority to extremely capital-intensive projects on the grounds that they are necessary if the region is to increase or maintain its share of high productivity and fast-growing industries which can generate and attract related activities. The number of jobs created will depend on the income and employment multiplier effects of the increased output, the elasticity of demand for the products comprising the increased output and the extent to which it stimulates the growth of technically related activities.

The two types of plan differ also in their assumptions about labour mobility within the region. Where increased output per head is the aim, the plan will seek to encourage the development of industry in areas where the conditions for the growth of output and productivity are most favourable or are capable of being created at the least possible cost. It is very unlikely that areas meeting these criteria will coincide with localities where unemployment is particularly high and participation rates low. The plan will, therefore, have to include measures to encourage and provide for a greater amount of travel to work over longer distances and even for permanent migration within the region. Such measures may well involve intervention in a wide range of matters from the price of housing to the construction of new patterns and modes of communication. A plan aimed at increasing regional output per head may also wish to promote the transfer of labour from declining industries into newer industries even if this means temporarily increasing unemployment. It may have to oppose protection of declining industries in order not to lock into these industries reserves of skilled labour which new and immigrant industries in the region require. This approach is very different from that of schemes aimed simply at reducing unemployment which would concentrate much more on providing jobs in localities where unemployment was particularly high and possibly maintaining employment at least for a time in declining industries by some form of subsidy. There may well be considerable controversy and conflict over which strategy to adopt, and may eventually have to be resolved by some kind of political arbitration resulting in a plan with a hybrid objective.

The second main question which must be raised in any regional planning exercise is the relationship between the regional plan and national economic policies or, as the case may be, national economic plans. There clearly has to be some link between the two. Any policy or plan for managing a national economy demands a knowledge of the degree of utilization of resources, which will differ from region to region, and the effects of movements or manipulations of aggregate demand in the light of these differences. At the regional level any plan must take into account the flow of resources between the different regions. These interrelations between the regional and national economies become particularly important when at both levels plans are seeking to achieve a faster rate of growth of output per head. The preparation of a national plan compels a more comprehensive and detailed analysis of the different contributions each region can make to the desired increase in national output and provides both a framework and a constraint which any regional plans must respect. The objectives of the regional plans must therefore be consistent with the national plan and with each other.

In order to fulfil this condition it is necessary for regional plans to be co-ordinated at the national level. If this is not done, the sum of additional resources required by all the regional plans may bear little relation to the increase provided for in the national plans. A national view is required, too, to ensure that each regional plan properly takes account of its effect on other regional plans. This approach leads to the plausible proposition that plans following the model of a national plan with numerical targets for the main macro-economic variables and output targets for industry groupings should be prepared for the regions. These plans could be checked for consistency with the national plan and the publication of targets would allow both industry and the government to be informed in more detail about the possibilities of expansion and the role of the different sectors and groups in the regional economies. The favourable effect on the expectations of producers and investors concerning the future rate of growth of demand, which is frequently imputed to such national indicative plans, would thus operate at the regional level as well.

The major weakness of this argument lies in the fact that regional economies are generally more open to external influences than national economies and data is very often lacking on inter-regional flows of goods, expenditures and savings. The preparation of quantitative regional plans would require information about the future levels and pattern of *extra-regional* demand for regional products. In order to obtain this it would be necessary to construct an inter-regional input-output table and use it as the basis of a projection over the period of the national plan. Ideally it would be desirable also to have information about the flows of savings between regions in order to establish the feasibility and expose the problems of financing the investment required to produce the desired increases in regional outputs. Such information would also be of great usefulness to the central government in enabling it to assess both the regional and national effects of policies aimed at stimulating regional growth by transferring demand from some regions to others. The effectiveness of such measures must always rest to a greater or less extent on hunch and faith unless some estimates are available of regional propensities to import, the dependence of regions on extra-regional savings and investment and the values and probable stability of the technical coefficients in the inter-regional input-output table. If the hunches on these points are wrong, policies aimed at creating the basis of self-sustaining growth of output in particular regions may fail to achieve their objective. Moreover, in an effort to transfer production to particular regions they may interfere with efficient technical and geographical linkages between industries and stimulate demand in regions where resources are fully utilized as a result of underestimating the propensities to import of the less prosperous regions.

At the same time the difficulties and costs of providing such data must be clearly recognized. An inter-regional input-output table is open to the familiar objections that once constructed it would be out of date and of limited usefulness for forecasting purposes. This criticism has special point in the regional context. Most regional policies or plans are directed towards changing the industrial structure of the regions, by introducing industry to an agricultural area or replacing declining industries with newer industries and service trades. The emphasis is therefore on changing the technical co-efficients of the input-output table. The increase in investment and output brought about by target plans through their effect on expectations is probably much less important at the regional than at the national level. It is by altering the structure of supply and production rather than promoting confidence in the growth of demand that regional output will be increased. The level and growth of demand in the region is in most cases determined to an important extent by the ability of the region's industries to compete in markets outside the region.

Having said this it must be admitted that even a limited and partial knowledge of inter-industry linkages can be of considerable help in regional planning and policy. If it is intended to channel a new large plant or firm to a region as the putative base of a new group of related industries, it would be most valuable to know the nature of the links between the 'parent' firm and its ancillaries. This could be done on a partial basis even if some of the elements, notably the regional destination of final demand, which a full-scale input-output table would have identified are not taken account of. This partial approach would have the advantage of allowing additional questions to be posed which would not be dealt with in an input-output exercise at accustomed levels of disaggregation. What is the critical size of the parent firm necessary to offer a large enough market to induce components producers to move into the region or to induce existing producers to switch or expand their production to serve the parent firm? Under what circumstances will components producers consider it more profitable to move or expand into the region rather than transport their products to it? What particular demands will the parent firm make on component firms within the region in the way of technical standards, production runs, high-quality finish which may make it difficult, insufficiently profitable or uncongenial for the latter to organize its labour force and production processes to deal with it? These are all questions central to any regional planning exercise which could be answered without recourse to a comprehensive inter-regional input-output table, although the information required would involve detailed studies which few countries have yet attempted.

It is perhaps necessary at this point to insert a cautionary word about the use to which the information discussed above is to be put. There is sometimes implicit in the argument for more detailed knowledge about the relationship between firms and industries a suggestion that it might be used as the basis of a policy of directing particular types of firms at particular times to particular locations. This is a perfectly possible option, given enough success in data collection, but it involves far-reaching assumptions about the permissible degree of state intervention in pursuit of planning objectives. The information can, on the other hand, be used simply in an analytical and diagnostic capacity to point out the activities to which less compulsory measures might be directed. But even in economies such as the British economy, where direct intervention in firms' affairs is not generally practised, there do exist particular forms of direction. One of these, the system of Industrial Development Certificates, could conceivably be used to ensure that firms considered suitable for a deliberately engineered industrial complex in a region are not permitted to expand elsewhere.

Even if a complete inter-regional input-output table cannot be got, there remains the possibility of estimating regional imports and exports and inter-regional savings flows. These could be valuable in giving some guidance as to the multiplier effects of expenditure in a region and in shedding some light on the problems of financing regional investment. The introduction of a Regional Employment Premium in Britain is a good illustration of how the former information might be used, for one of the arguments about this measure centred on whether it would stimulate expenditure on consumer and capital goods mainly within the Development Areas in Britain or whether this expenditure would in significant measure spill over into the more prosperous regions and thus give rise to inflationary pressures. The point still remains, however, that it is not the demand or income effects of expenditure which is crucial for regional development but the extent to which new types of industries are induced to expand in the region. This brings the argument back again to the linkages effect which the expansion of certain industries creates.

As well as co-ordinating and synthesizing the different regional plans, the national planning body has to form a view about the objectives of regional policy. One guideline will be provided by the objectives set for the national plan. As argued above, the establishment of a national growth target will involve an assessment of the contribution which the different regions can make to an increase in national productivity and to a consideration of the measures required to achieve it. It is, however, misleading to think of regional plans simply as *post hoc* divisions of a national plan. Any regional plan which seeks to promote the growth of output must create the necessary economic and physical conditions for it. A regional plan is necessarily concerned with the distribution of population and employment in the region—the provision of external economies, the size and structure of labour markets, intra- and inter-regional transport links, the structure of the housing market and its relationship to population shifts and short and long-distance labour mobility, and the provision of other infrastructure requirements. It is, therefore, of necessity a physical as well as an economic plan, the two aspects complementing each other. This feature of regional plans means that they have to contain a genuinely long-term strategy, for the expansion of communities or the creation of new communities and the setting down of new infrastructure are necessarily long-term operations. If regional planning is taken seriously by the central government, the central planning agencies face the problem not simply of dividing the extra employment and output to be created over the period of the national plan between the different regions and giving each region some reasonable share of general public expenditure and of large projects capable of stimulating economic development, but also of reconciling a number of regional plans

273

which when taken together may involve a considerable change in the distribution of population and employment in the national economy. The central planning agency must therefore form a view about the distribution of population and employment it wishes to see come about and ensure that it is written into the regional plans. Regional plans, therefore, have to cover a period of time much longer than the four or five years which is usual for a medium-term national plan.

The question of timing raises some important problems. The long-term job of creating a desired distribution of economic activity may require the laying down of infrastructure in advance of its utilization, and the adoption of other measures involving public expenditure to encourage firms to locate away from areas which, rightly or wrongly, depending on how much account they take of social as well as private costs, they would consider preferred locations. Such expenditures may well be considered unproductive within a certain time-period if during it publicly provided facilities are under-utilized or firms have to be persuaded to move to locations in which for a time their productivity is lower than it might have been elsewhere. Such a situation could arise when the authorities are attempting to improve an adverse balance of payments which is proving to be a major constraint on the growth of national output. In these circumstances, regional development, in so far as it involves even a temporary risk of lower productivity as a result of the movement of firms to less prosperous regions, may cease to be a priority and may even be neglected or abandoned. On the other hand, the possibilities of expanding output in the less prosperous regions, without creating inflationary pressures and without a serious sacrifice of increases in productivity, could result in regional policy being considered as a means of breaking the balance of payments constraint on national growth. Whichever way the argument goes there is clearly a need for the broad, long-term objectives of regional policy to be firmly outlined and represented at the national level. If this is not done, the national and regional distribution of population and employment will be determined, not by a considered view of the necessary and desirable changes that could be brought about in it, but as a by-product of the exigencies of successive medium-term plans.

Such an outcome could be costly. If regional development is severely restricted or simply ignored, there are several possible consequences. The problems of the less prosperous regions may be left increasingly to solve themselves through migration. But such a solution may be far from satisfactory (leaving aside the social and political problems to which it would inevitably give rise). The movement of labour from regions in which it was under-utilized to others in which it can be used fully, and probably also more productively, will obviously yield increased output. Against this, however, must be set the costs of the extra infrastructure which may have to be created for the immigrant workers and their families. Assuming that the infrastructure in the regions exporting labour was so outdated that its under-utilization as a result of migration imposed no substantial opportunity costs, the costs of creating infrastructure in prosperous regions may still be greater than in the less prosperous regions because factor prices will generally be higher in the former areas. (Relatively higher productivity in the constriction industries in the more prosperous regions would of course reduce the disparity in costs.)

There is next the question of the phasing of costs and outputs. The inflow of immigrant labour may permit and encourage new investment in the more prosperous regions. The consequent additional demand for capital goods added to the new infrastructure needs may then create a situation where the demand for labour exceeds the available supply, even including the immigrant labour, and demand will thus rise faster than output until the newly created capacity is fully utilized and yields increased output. Immigration to the prosperous regions will also create additional social costs, the alleviation of which will constitute a further claim on resources.

At the other extreme it is possible to imagine a situation in which the problem of regional unemployment remained considerable due to the immobility of some sections of the population of the regions concerned despite a lack of employment opportunities. The government may be obliged to intervene and alleviate the problem by means of transfer payments to the regions concerned. Assuming that migration patterns remained unchanged and no development occurred to alter the prospects of the regional economies, these payments might have to continue for a long time. In such circumstances a government may be led to weigh the costs represented by such continuing unproductive expenditure against the costs of creating the possibilities of self-sustaining economic growth in the less prosperous regions which would make the transfer payments unnecessary.

This decision may be very pressing and difficult if the competitiveness of the national economy is related to a changing geographical pattern of trade which renders the less-prosperous regions more distant from the major domestic and foreign markets. The problem then is to avoid, on the one hand, the danger of neglecting these regions in order to increase national competitiveness and, on the other, mounting a regional development effort which diverts resources to temporarily less-productive uses and locations but offers the possibility (although not the certainty) of self-sustaining growth in the former regions. Such a strategy clearly requires both a central view of the regional problem and long-term regional planning.

The third main issue of regional planning concerns its administration and the means employed to implement the plans. This chapter began by arguing that too much attention has been paid in some countries to the institutions of regional planning. This is not to say, however, that institutions are unimportant; it is indeed possible to argue that setting up the wrong kind of institutions has been as much the trouble as concentrating too much on them.

The point has already been made that there must be some central body concerned with the broad strategy of regional development and the co-ordination and synthesizing of regional plans and the policies employed to implement them. This probably has to be a government department because it must have the right to be consulted on all major economic policy issues and the power to ensure that the national strategy of regional development is not ignored under the pressure of more immediate problems. One central issue on which this central body must have a say is the allocation of public expenditure between regions. The provision of public expenditure is the most important way in which the governments of Western economies can influence regional development, and it is crucial that the annual budgetary allocations should take account of this. The principles which should govern the regional distribution of credits are still rightly the subject of debates, but one point can be made here. Promoting development in a region may require, in any year or years, that the region concerned should have more than some definition of its 'fair' share of funds, if some large-scale project such as the creation of a new city, a new port, or a new industrial grouping central to the regional plan is to get under way. It may also be necessary to accept that investment in regional development will not yield returns immediately, but that the construction of facilities ahead of demands upon them may permit cost savings as a result of economies of scale in construction and enable related facilities to be built at the same time rather than piecemeal, thus presenting industry with the possibility of external economies.

The central regional planning agency must encompass both economic and physical planning. This means that housing, transport and recreational facilities in particular must be regarded as integral parts

276

of regional development and regional plans. The integration of economic and physical planning is vital if on both the national and regional level some desired distribution of population and industry is to be brought about. The problem of measuring social costs, and devising means of minimizing them and charging those who cause them, is one area requiring further work before proposals to shift population from existing centres and concentrate them in others can be formulated with any confidence. The different costs associated with different sizes and patterns of urban centres and a more precise analysis of the external economies which such centres are reputed to provide is another. The provision of various types of housing and the prices charged for them and their relationship to a freely working regional labour market is yet another. If regional development is to become a serious objective of national policy, the various traditionally separate departments dealing with these matters must be brought into closer co-operation.

The question of the definition of regions now arises. If the objective of regional planning is a more rapid growth of regional output per head, the most effective regional unit is likely to be larger than in the case of a policy of reducing unemployment in particular localities. It will probably also be larger than existing regional divisions which are the result of past economic and political circumstances. The need to have larger regions is a consequence of the nature of the conditions required for more rapid growth in a region. These will almost always include: the provision of infrastructure works either for the first time or more or less extensive replacement of existing facilities; the 'creation' of a labour market of sufficient size to meet the needs of the most rapidly expanding and the most technologically advanced industries, and to satisfy the demands of all sections of the labour force including the highly skilled and professional groups; the concentration of the population in, at most, a few centres capable of providing an adequate local market and housing the range of amenities and service industries which constitute external economies for both manufacturing industries and the service industries themselves. The mere statement of these relatively uncontroversial conditions points to the need for regional units which are almost bound to be more extensive than those relating to a past time when economic development was left more to the free play of economic forces and when the opportunities to achieve economies of scale were less widespread and less important. It is reasonable also to suppose that they will be larger than the regional units relevant to the administration of a policy of removing local unemployment by relatively small-scale, *ad hoc* transfers of resources.

The importance of the notion of centres of growth in regional development suggests that the delimitation of the new regions must be done essentially with reference to these centres. The region, therefore, becomes defined in terms of an area whose economy is dominated by one or more growth centres. The boundaries of the different regions will be established at those points where the influence of one centre or combination of centres becomes superseded by that of another.

The new regions will naturally call forth new institutional forms. It is likely that some new unit of regional administration will have to be created which is intermediate between local authorities and the national parliament and the central administration. Its area of responsibility will be coterminous with the new regions, and its functions will relate primarily to those activities which have to be organized at the regional level. To establish an effective relationship between this new authority and both the local and national authorities will require changes of some significance in local and national patterns of administration.

It is likely first of all to reduce the powers and responsibilities of local authorities. This is bound to occur as more decisions become essentially regional in scope. However much the individual citizen may consider his neighbourhood to be the next natural loyalty to the family unit, his existence as a member of society may become more dependent on decisions which have to be taken in the context of a more remote and perhaps more nebulous level—the region. Further, if the rate and forms of development of different regional economies have to be made consistent with some national view of the desirable distribution of population and employment, the natural locus of decisions may become even more distant from individual experience. Changes will also be necessary in national administration. The essentially vertical system of administration usual in a unitary state with a central government will have to be adapted to make possible the horizontal co-operation between government departments which is essential to regional development. In particular it will be necessary to ensure close collaboration between the economic and physical sides of the planning process. It must be emphasized that this introduction of a regional approach is no once-for-all or marginal exercise. It would involve every government department taking account of regional development in the working out and implementation of every major policy decision in its field. At the centre this could very well require the creation of some kind of Ministry of Regional Development which would represent, uphold and be consulted about the continuing strategy of regional development in the same manner as the Treasury in regard to the management of the national economy. At the regional level, representatives of government departments would have to be continuously in co-operation with each other and with the new regional authorities. These are no small demands and would require a considerable degree of innovation and change in administrative habits and expertize.

This discussion leads naturally and quickly on to the problem of whether the new regional authority should be democratically elected or in some other way appointed. There is a conflict here between the need for a permanent regional executive and the desire to ensure that power does not pass from elected local authorities to a more remote regional body not directly responsible to the inhabitants of the region. Some kind of compromise involving an executive regional board acting for and responsible to a democratically elected regional council or assembly might be worked out, but there then arises the question of the powers which the latter body might have. In the context of a unitary state these must be limited, the more so if regional development in its broad outlines is to be organized from the centre, and the various regional plans made compatible with national regional policy.

If the foregoing argument is accepted, certain broad conclusions can be drawn about the nature and function of regional plans designed to promote the growth of output per head. Perhaps the most important point to be made is the need to relate the development of any one region to that of the other regions and to the policies or plans for the economy as a whole. Since regional economies are, in the majority of cases, even more open to external influences and dependent upon them for development than the national economies of modern, industrialized states, it is essential that regional development plans should seek to extract the maximum advantage of such exchanges while maintaining a realistic attitude about what is compatible with the needs of other regions and the nation as a whole. In order to do this it will be necessary to obtain more information than is currently available in most countries about inter-regional flows of goods and factors and inter-regional input-output relationships in industry and services. The acquiring of such data is, however, a difficult and expensive business and, even when obtained, the information does no more than describe the situation existing at a given time. When many of the problems of regional development consist of changing these existing relationships, this is a considerable limitation. Regional planning cannot rely on forecasts which are basically extrapolations of the present. A more dynamic, developmental approach has to be adopted both in respect of policies aimed at encouraging changes in the private sector and decisions about public expenditure in the regions. It is of course valuable to be able to assess the impact of new firms or particular public expenditures on the region receiving them and on other regions. But such measures should not have to await the construction of a static system of regional accounts. A more partial assessment of the income and employment multiplier effects of particularly important actions and their effect on existing inter-industry linkages might usefully be attempted.

A further consequence of the interdependence of regional economies is the need for some form of co-ordination of regional plans at the national level. No serious attempt to alter the industrial structures and income levels of particular regions can be made unless some reasonably long-term view is taken about the kind of distribution of population and employment which is desirable in the national economy. Failure to have such a 'national regional plan' is almost bound to lead to caution, compromise and a diffusion of effort which may seriously hamper development in an age when concentration and size are becoming increasingly the pre-conditions for efficiency both in the private and public sectors. Moreover, many of the most important elements of regional development programmes in Western economies consist of large, 'lumpy' infrastructure projects which cannot be given to every region in the economy. A national regional planning agency would help assure that such choices are made neither according to purely national considerations nor as the mainly political outcome of regional pressures and bargaining.

The creation of a national system of regional plans requires considerable administrative changes. There is firstly the need to define the regions. This is a highly complicated problem to which there is no unique solution, but it has to be done. Existing regional divisions in most European countries are the result of an amalgam of pressures and events which in many cases are no longer the most important influences in the countries in question. New divisions have to be created which meet the main criterion of facilitating to the fullest possible extent economic development in the different parts of each country.

The administration of these new regions requires far-reaching reforms of existing administrative structures. The new regions are compatible neither with a large number of local authorities nor with a central administration organized on a vertical basis. The promotion of regional development requires co-operation between administrations dealing with a wide range of subjects and the creation of regional authorities able to organize and operate at a regional rather than a local level. There are, both in theory and administrative practice, many ways of meeting these requirements. There is, however, the additional and very important problem of ensuring that the emergence of a new level of organization, necessary for economic advance, midway between the elected authorities at the national and local level will remain subject to effective democratic control.

The next section of this chapter will examine how Italian and French experiments in regional planning have attacked these problems.

II

In the period since the Second World War there has been, in both France and Italy, a movement towards increasingly comprehensive and sophisticated regional planning. At the same time the two countries have displayed, naturally enough, interestingly different approaches to the problem. These differences are not simply the result of different circumstances but reflect differing views on how to promote and organize regional development.

Immediately after the war, both France and Italy were preoccupied with the task of reconstruction and the problems of particular regions were treated as part of the many pressing national difficulties involved in restoring the war economies of defeated and occupied countries. It was not until 1950 that the problem of regional imbalance began to attract official attention. In that year the Cassa per il Mezzogiorno was created in Italy; in France the Ministry of Construction produced a Plan National d'Aménagement du Territoire, and the National Fund for Regional Development (FNAT) was established to finance the building of industrial estates and other infrastructure works in regions where industrial development was required.

There is no doubt that the creation of the Cassa was the much more ambitious exercise. It was given a considerable allocation of funds and represented an active commitment at ministerial level to regional development. The French efforts were on a much more limited scale and amounted to little more than a diagnosis of the regional problem in France. The job of the Cassa was to act as a development agency for the whole of the South of Italy. It was to promote increased productivity in agriculture and organize the construction of special infrastructure works which were a necessary precondition of industrial development. The French plan d'aménagement, on the other hand, argued that the basic problem was the decentralization of industry from the Paris region. The French initiatives concentrated rather on encouraging firms to transfer or expand outside the Paris region. In a sense the Cassa had much more in common with the regional development schemes for a specific region such as Bas-Rhône-Languedoc which were beginning at this time than the rather academic *plan d'aménagement*

On paper the creation of the Cassa represented the beginnings of regional planning in Italy. It was to operate within a ten-year plan and co-operate with other Ministries who were to take the problems of the South into account in their decisions. The Committee of Ministers dealing with 'extraordinary' intervention in the South was to act as final co-ordinating agency. In fact, the results were disappointing. There was very little attention paid to the relationship between the Cassa's activities and national policies. The problem of the South was treated as a very large special case which had to be dealt with by special measures which it was hoped would increase agricultural incomes and employment and create conditions which would attract industry to the region. It was not, however, envisaged that development in the South and the North would become closely interrelated either as a result of emigration of labour to the North or large-scale expansion of industry in the South.

The co-ordination of public spending in the South between the Cassa and the other Ministries never really transpired. Individual Ministries pursued their own programmes with little regard to the ten-year plan for the South. Indeed, they tended to view the Cassa as the agency responsible for the South and to concentrate their efforts to some extent in other directions. A similar absence of co-ordination existed in France where the First National Plan (1946-52) contained virtually no references to the problems of regional development.

The absence of any effective regional planning in the two countries was reflected in the objectives and nature of the various government interventions. In the case of the Cassa, both its agricultural and infrastructure operations were in the nature of assistance to particular localities rather than the basis of planned long-term development and were consequently scattered throughout the South. In France the *plan d'aménagement* did insist on discussing regional development in a context of national economic development but its prime emphasis was on decentralizing industry from Paris rather than the nature of development process in the less-prosperous regions.

About the middle of the 1950s, regional development policies in Italy and France underwent important changes. In Italy it came to be recognized that reliance on increased agricultural output and the provision of infrastructure was insufficient to provide the required increases in incomes and employment in the South. Various other measures were accordingly introduced to attract manufacturing industry to the South, and in particular to those parts of the region where the conditions for industrial development were most favourable or most easily created. If they were to be officially recognized and to benefit from special aid these localities, designated as Areas and Nuclei, were each required to produce a *piano regolatore* to be prepared by a consortium of local authorities, Chambers of Commerce and other bodies, and submitted for approval to the Committee of Ministers for the South. The plans had to select a location for an *agglomerato* or industrial zone, and prepare a plan for its establishment. A system of regional plans was thus inaugurated in Italy based on regions chosen because of their economic potentiality.

In France, regional policy was following a rather different course. In June 1955 a number of measures were introduced, the most important of which provided financial aid to firms decentralizing from Paris and expanding in certain regions. The areas to which firms were encouraged to move were scheduled as 'critical areas' and consisted in the main of small localities where unemployment was particularly acute. The recession of 1952-54 had caused unemployment to rise sharply in certain areas which were already losing jobs because of their dependence on declining industries, and it was to these problem areas that the 1955 measures were especially directed. The French approach to regional development was, therefore, very different from the Italian tactics of selectivity and concentration and provide a clear example of a job creation policy which offered very little scope for regional planning.

This is, however, to exaggerate a little, for in the same batch of measures there was a decree authorizing the preparation of twenty-two regional action programmes covering the whole of France. These programmes or plans were designed to be integrated with the Third National Plan (1958-61), to provide an analysis of the problems and prospects of the regions and to serve as guidelines for the regional distribution of public investment programmes. The introduction of a formal scheme of regional planning, linked in concept at least to the national plan and based on regions very much larger than the small, scattered 'critical areas' and indeed larger even than the basic regional division of the *département*, was a very important step forward. It indicated a much wider approach to regional development than the policy of local job creation implicit in the other measures.

In both countries, however, the moves towards regional planning were very tentative. In Italy the constitution of the consortia and the preparation of the *piani regolatori* took a long time and at present only 6 Areas and 6 Nuclei have completed plans out of a total of 12 Areas and 30 Nuclei. The plans are, moreover, limited in scope and in particular are precluded from considering the urban structure of the Area or Nuclei although one feature both types of area must possess is a principal commune of a minimum size. The fact that only some of the Areas and Nuclei have so far produced plans indicates the absence of any effective national co-ordination of the different plans. Since the two types of area cover 44 per cent of the population of the South and include almost every locality where industrial development has occurred, the absence of some kind of national strategy must be considered fairly serious. If the Committee of Ministers for the South limits itself to considering each *piano regolatore* when it appears on its own individual merits, the possibility of factory space and infrastructure being built in the wrong places, at the wrong time and in the wrong amounts is very real.

The question arises, too, whether the Areas and Nuclei can reasonably form the basic units of a regional planning system. Forty-two regional plans for the South of Italy does seem to be a very large number if a policy of development based on selectivity, concentration and long-term infrastructure projects is the objective. Moreover, the 30 Nuclei with a population rarely in excess of 75,000 are by any standards, however imprecise, too small to form the basic geographical planning units in a country of Italy's size. While it is difficult and probably impossible to determine the ideal size of a planning region, the size of many of Italy's growth areas contrasts notably with that of the planning regions in France, the smallest of which has a population of just under one million. They are small too in comparison with the existing provinces in the South of Italy and it is interesting to note that in the regions where the policy of concentration and selectivity has been pursued furthest, those of Bari, Taranto and Brindisi, these three Areas have sought to co-operate with each other to create an *ensemble* of interrelated economic activity.

There is doubt, therefore, as to whether Italian areas of growth represent a sound basis for regional planning although they do indicate some shift of emphasis from simple employment creation to growth of output as an objective of regional policy. At the same time the Italian approach to regional planning may in one respect be superior to the French. In Italy certain growth areas, admittedly too many, were chosen as the places where the development effort must be concentrated. What was not done was to link them organizationally and functionally with each other in a way and on a scale which would permit them to form the basis of a regional plan for the whole of the South. In France things happened the other way round. The country was first of all divided into planning regions which were intended to give a 'regional dimension' to the national plan but their relationship to the growth areas of the national economy was not made clear. Indeed, the move towards planning was accompanied by a policy of widely diffused assistance to small localities. Certainly the planning regions were chosen with regard to their economic homogeneity defined very broadly, but there is a sense in which the Italian approach, beginning with the centres round which economic planning regions must form themselves, is a more fruitful approach.

The move towards regional planning in France shared many of the defects of the Italian experiments. The plans had no timetable despite their proposed insertion into the national plan and the consultations with the various regional authorities and personalities during their preparation were limited and sporadic. There was, naturally enough, a serious lack of statistics relating to the new planning regions for they cut across the traditional divisions of the *départements* and the numerous other regional divisions used by the various Ministries. A more serious deficiency was the lack of collaboration between the Planning Commission which was responsible for the regional economic plans and the Ministry of Housing which in 1957 began the preparation of a land-use plan for each of the planning regions. These latter exercises were 'to take account of' the economic plans but the two types of plan were essentially conceived as separate tasks. The regional plans were, however, in one sense an important innovation. They represented the first substantial modification of the system of administration based on the *département* and drew attention to the fact that economic development was going to impose new regional frontiers and consequently new forms of administration.

The tentative moves towards regional planning in France which have just been described marked the beginning of a new phase in French regional policy which is still continuing. The Fourth National Plan (1962-65) recognized regional development as one of the general objectives of the plan and set out in broad terms certain priorities. The publication of the plan was followed closely by a number of important new measures and procedures which established regional policy as a major, long-term national concern. Events moved less quickly in Italy, but in August 1965 an important piece of legislation, Law 717, was passed which renewed the Cassa's mandate and introduced important new measures to aid development in the South. In the following year a national plan for the Italian economy was published covering the period 1966-70; it contained a section which presented in quantitative form the broad objectives of southern policy. The Vanoni Plan in 1955 had similarly tried to integrate southern and national development. The relationship was, however, stated in less formal and quantitative terms and the plan never really became operational.

By the early 1960s, regional policy in France and Italy had become closely associated with national economic plans and policies aimed at producing faster growth. The primary objective of regional policy in both countries was now quite clearly to increase the rate of growth of income per head in certain less prosperous regions within the constraints set by the objectives of the national plans. The remainder of this chapter will seek to examine the way in which regional and national plans for growth have been developed in relation to each other in the two countries.

III

The most important question both countries have had to face is the extent to which regional policy can be pursued without lowering the rate of growth of output in the more prosperous regions below a level compatible with the maintenance of full employment in these regions and a competitive position in international markets (the latter position being determined largely by the levels and rates of growth of productivity of industries located in the more prosperous regions).

In France, regional policy has reflected an increasing awareness of the costs of aiding the less prosperous regions. In the Fourth and, even more noticeably, the Fifth Plan, doubts have been expressed about the wisdom of restricting too severely the expansion of output and employment in the Paris region. The point is made that regional development must not hinder the reforms in the structure of French industry and the various measures taken to increase the competitiveness of manufacturing industry. The effects of this constraint can be seen in the tension between the plans for a much expanded Paris region and the officially agreed target of the Fifth Plan to create 40 per cent of the total estimated new industrial jobs between 1966 and 1970 in the underdeveloped regions of the west—twice the proportion going there between 1954 and 1964—and to begin the build up of the *métropoles d'équilibre* as provincial counterweights to Paris.

It is possible, however, to discern a strategy beneath this apparent contradiction. The Fifth Plan admits that its regional policy may result in some reduction in the growth of national output per head but it is prepared to tolerate this in an attempt to create in the less prosperous regions centres where the growth of output and employment will become self-perpetuating after an initial transfer of resources. Such an eventuality would reduce the continuing costs which the underdeveloped regions, despite migration, must inevitably impose on the whole economy and remove some of the diseconomies of scale and external diseconomies arising in the Paris region as well as satisfying the social and political aspirations of the regions. This policy implies a certain boldness both in the scale of operations undertaken and in the selection of areas, within the poorer regions, as centres of growth. If the west is to have some industrial centres it is necessary at some point to make a serious effort to transfer industrial expansion to a limited number of suitable areas. And if some of the metropolitan features of Paris necessary to industrial and commercial expansion are to be provided in the provinces the build-up of the centres must be at such a rate and on such a scale as to give the necessary initial impetus. Similarly, the expansion of the Paris region must be carefully planned in both its physical and economic aspects. The controls on expansion in the region must therefore be applied selectively. Those activities which require to be in the Paris region should wherever possible be permitted to locate and expand there provided they meet the real costs created by their choice of location.

The conflict between regional and national interests has also occurred in Italy. The new measures introduced by Law 717 in 1965 strengthened and extended the various types of financial aid available to firms located in the South. At the same time it made them more selective both in terms of the geographical areas within which assistance could be obtained and the types of industries and firms eligible for assistance. It did not, however, include any measures to restrict the expansion of private industry in the North of Italy. The need to keep Italian industry competitive and avoid the risk of an outflow of firms and private capital to other Common Market countries has caused the Italian authorities to fight shy of even the limited restrictions applied in France to the Paris region. Much more extensive and powerful controls such as those used in Britain in the form of the Industrial Development Certificate are apparently still considered too damaging to the economy as a whole. The 1965 reforms, therefore, followed a strategy somewhat similar to the French, insisting both on the costs of regional policy and the need to be more deliberately bold and selective in implementing it.

The integration of plans and policies for the South with the national plan is in many respects a less significant event than the reforms announced in Law 717. The targets set for the South in the plan are extremely ambitious; 40 per cent of the new non-agricultural jobs are to go to the South compared with 25 per cent in the period 1959-63, and 18 per cent between 1960 and 1965. To attain these targets the national plan estimates that gross fixed industrial investment of 4,500 billion lire will be required. This is twice the figure for the period 1960-64, and even if the state-controlled firms fulfil their obligations in the South it still seems highly unlikely that the target will be attained.[1]

It requires a large assumption about the increased effectiveness of regional policy to justify such optimistic targets. There is, moreover, no indication in the plan that the national rate of growth will be substantially lower than past trends as a result of the sizeable transfer of resources to the South. This is surprising, for in spite of the new orientation (and efficacy) of regional policy it is difficult to believe that the resources invested in the South will yield as high a return in terms of real output as they would have done in the North. Nor is there anything in the plan to suggest that the creation of a higher proportion of jobs in the North (implying higher immigration from the South) would generate more demand than output over the period of the plan and thus create inflation. Indeed, the reluctance of the authorities to impose restrictions on development in the North indicates a belief that the northern economy is capable of further expansion without inflation. There is, therefore, some reasonable doubt whether the implications of the new policy for the South have been fully taken into account in the national plan.

This uncertainty is reinforced by the fact that the allocation of funds made to the Cassa for the period 1965-69 was decided before the national plan was published. As a result the amount which the Cassa will be able to spend on financial incentives to induce industries to locate in the South and to recompense them for their initial disadvantages, falls short of the sum that is required to fulfil the national plan's forecasts of industrial investment in the South. The Cassa's funds for industrial incentives were in fact exhausted in 1968. Contrary to the expectation of many observers, some extra funds were made available. The point still remains, however, that the allocation of funds to the Cassa was never at any time consistent with the contribution expected from it towards the achievement of the national plan's objectives.

Any discussion of the relationship between regional and national

[1] See pp. 100-108.

growth raises the question of the time-scale of regional planning. In France the regional breakdown of the national plan has to perform two functions. It represents the working out of the national plan in the different regions, indicating the regional distribution of manpower, jobs, and investment which is compatible with the national forecasts of the medium-term plan and particular regional needs at the time, e.g. in the Fifth Plan the creation of a larger number of industrial jobs in the west than original employment forecasts there suggested. At the same time, the regional divisions of the plan represent a phase of a long-term national regional development programme. For the Fifth Plan the main features of such a programme were sketched out in the first report of the National Committee for Regional Development (CNAT). These were the industrialization of the west of France; the introduction of new industries to the older industrialized regions of the north and east; the creation of provincial cities to act as counterweights to Paris by providing 'metropolitan services' for their regions; and the development of agriculture in the light of increasing mechanization. These problems were all studied in terms of a time horizon of 1985 using three different regional divisions. Initially three main regions— the Paris region, East and West—were distinguished; the studies then went on to use an 8-region breakdown which was finally translated into the 21 planning regions.

It is more difficult to detect a long-term strategy in Italian regional policy. In 1950 the Cassa was established and requested to organize its operations on the basis of a ten-year plan to 1960. It was, however, quite clearly regarded as a special agency for a special problem and although an interministerial committee was formed to co-ordinate its 'extraordinary' efforts with the ordinary efforts of other Ministries the arrangement worked badly. This is hardly surprising, for the Ministries were often operating in terms of the annual budgetary vote and there was no national plan to provide longer-term guidelines. Admittedly, in 1957 a law was passed requiring that the South should get a share of public works programmes at least equal to its share of population, but there was no plan indicating the type, location and timing of the projects and the target was not attained.

In 1966, in an effort to improve co-ordination, a *Piano di Coordinamento* was drawn up setting guidelines to which the Cassa and the other Ministries (in so far as expenditure in the South was concerned) had to adhere when allocating their expenditure. It is not, however, clear how this public investment plan relates to the national plan. It should also be noted that while Law 717 in 1965 prolonged the life of the Cassa until 1980, funds were allocated to it for only a five-year period, 1965-69, which became the effective planning period. Despite the emphasis on long-term growth, much of Italian regional planning, even in the area of public investment, still rests on very uncertain *ad hoc* co-operation between government departments.

One of the key elements in a system of regional plans based on a long-term view of the distribution of economic activity is public investment. In most Western economies, the state controls a sufficiently large proportion of capital expenditure to be able to exercise a considerable influence on the development of this or that region. The integration of regional and national plans must begin, therefore, with the introduction of regional development as one of the criteria determining the distribution of public investment. It is on this point that most of the emphasis has been laid in France and the basic framework of French regional planning is provided by the *tranches operatoires* of public investment projects, which set out for each region for the period of the national plan its share of publicly financed investment schemes.

To a large extent, of course, a region's share of public investment is determined by its share of national output and employment. What a positive regional policy seeks to do is to reverse this relationship and influence the location of output and employment, both new and existing, by laying down infrastructure in advance of possible demands upon it. This was the kind of policy begun in Italy in the early 1950s and is still the basis of policy in France. The location of private industrial output and investment and commercial activity has been largely left to the private individuals or groups concerned except, in the case of the Paris region, where a direct negative control has been exercised. In Italy, however, there exist two important state holding companies, IRI and ENI, and these agencies have been obliged to locate a specified proportion of their investments in the South. Since these two bodies control a large range of industries the state has through them been able to direct output and employment to the South.

The existence of such powers clearly widens the scope of regional planning beyond the provision of infrastructure and the limitation of development in certain regions. There are two respects in which state-controlled groups like IRI can make particularly important contributions to regional development. They can, firstly, decide the location of large new plants. The steel-mill at Taranto and the Alfa-Sud motor-car plant near Naples are examples of this kind of operation. The installation of large new units of expanding industries can sometimes be a necessary condition for 'take-off' in regional development. The second and perhaps even more valuable activity which organizations like IRI can organize is the direction of related ancillary industries to locations surrounding these large plants. In a market economy without an organization like IRI this is the stage of development of an industrial grouping in a region which is the most problematical and one upon which information about the critical factors affecting the location decisions of the industries concerned is most lacking. The existence of an IRI should make the gathering of such data easier and permit the required ancillary industries to be located around the parent plant at more or less the same time, thus ensuring that the efficiency and successful growth of the complex will not be hindered by excessively piecemeal development.

The power to shift industrial output between regions makes regional planning more powerful, but it also requires a fairly thorough knowledge of the consequences of such intervention. Regional policy based on the provision of infrastructure involves the risk that some of the infrastructure may remain under-utilized if it does not succeed in attracting firms to the regions concerned. But these risks are less serious than the dangers involved in imposing a particular location on more directly productive resources. To avoid this, operations such as those carried out by IRI have to be accompanied by fairly detailed calculations of the costs they impose on IRI, the economy of Italy and the benefits they will bring to the South. The more powerful regional planning becomes the more important it is that its relationship with national economic policy should be carefully assessed.

Finally there is the question of the institutions and administration of regional planning. On this question the French and Italian experiences are very different. In Italy, regional development has been treated as an 'extraordinary' task and entrusted to a special Committee of Ministers with the Cassa as its executive arm. At the regional level the Cassa was to deal with the consortia formed to organize industrial development in the Areas and Nuclei. With the very important exception of the Cassa this scarcely amounts to a significant reshaping of administrative structures to aid regional development and in practice the Cassa's operations have been very imperfectly linked with the 'ordinary' activities of government departments in the South.

In France, however, regional development has provoked much more far-reaching reforms of administrative practices. After a rather ad hoc and confused start, a new administrative hierarchy was created to prepare and carry out the planning of regional development. In February 1963, the Délégation a l'Aménagement du Territoire (DATAR) was created. This agency, like the Planning Commission with which it has close relations, is attached to the Prime Minister's Office and is essentially concerned with the co-ordination of regional planning at the centre and acts as liaison agency between the regional prefects and the central administration. The DATAR is more like the Planning Commission than an independent fully staffed Ministry. Its Director is of Ministerial rank and is represented on all bodies, both legislative and executive, dealing with questions of regional development. His staff is small and the DATAR works more as an agency of consultation and persuasion on the lines of the Planning Commission. Despite a certain disillusionment with indicative planning, the habit of non-imperative planning through discussion and consensus is sufficiently embedded in the post-war French administrative practices to allow the DATAR to fit more naturally into the administrative system than it could in Italy or indeed in Britain. Along with the regionalization of the budget and the longer-term researches of the CNAT it is an indication of the extent to which regional development has become a national policy issue in France.

The creation of the regional prefects is a further reflection of this approach. The prefects and the planning regions for which they are responsible have not yet supplanted the *département* and commune as the basic administrative divisions in France. But they mark the harnessing of an essentially centralized, vertical system of authority to deal with the problem of regional development in a manner which respects the need for national co-ordination (or to use the current and emotive French term, 'coherence') and for development to be organized on the scale dictated by modern economic and technological pressures. Despite the limitations put on the regional prefect's powers, there is now in place in France an administrative structure which matches the new physical divisions of the country. The creation of urban communities in the *métropoles d'équilibre* is the beginning of a further extension of this principle.

The creation of a regional prefect does not of course automatically ensure the 'horizontal' co-operation between government departments at the regional level. This was not always impressive at the level of the *département* and some of the particularist habits still remain. The regionalization of the budget and the preparation and execution of the *tranches opératoires* are, however, bound to lead to improved co-operation.

Perhaps the major lacuna in the French arrangements is the absence of effective participation by regional interests. The Regional Committees for Economic Expansion (CODER), it is true, are a formal attempt to meet this need but although they are well organized and have specifically indicated rights of consultation, the nature of French regional planning makes it difficult for them to exercise real control over decisions. The amount of information in the hands of the regional prefect and his staff and the established channels through which it moves allows the 'official' case to be put with powerful effect. There is, in addition, an increasing tendency for decisions about regional development to be made according to criteria other than that produced by the competitive bidding of different regional interest groups. The regional allocation of budget credits and the compilation of the *tranches opératoires* are two important instances where a national 'social welfare function' approach is as much in evidence as a concern to arbitrate between different regional demands and indeed between the demands of different areas and groups within each region. It is extremely difficult for the CODERs to present alternative proposals in the context of such a nationally-oriented and directed system. And if it is accepted that regional development is properly an issue for which a national policy is required and which can be successfully implemented only if there is co-ordination at the centre, it is equally difficult to see how more directly democratic regional bodies can be given sufficient powers to justify their existence.

CHAPTER 13

GROWTH AREA POLICY[1]

The general aim of this chapter is to examine the advantages and disadvantages of pursuing a growth area policy and the extent to which the policy has been implemented in the United Kingdom, France and Italy. The chapter is in three parts. Part one is a brief introductory section which outlines the strategy of growth area policy and prepares the way for the following two sections. Part two is a more detailed section which tries to evaluate growth area policy as a measure for regional development. Part three discusses the attitudes towards growth area policy and the extent to which it has been pursued in the United Kingdom, France and Italy.

I

Growth area policy is a strategy for regional development. It is a strategy which can be used in non-depressed as well as depressed regions. We want in this chapter, however, to limit ourselves to a discussion of its role in the depressed regions. The strategy involves the selection of a few areas within the broad problem region and the concentration of development effort in the form of infrastructure as well as industrial development upon these areas. The areas selected are physically quite small—usually the travel-to-work area around a centre—and considered capable of sustaining rapid growth of

[1] Growth area policy has its theoretical origins in the writings of Perroux and others working on the general theories of unbalanced growth. See F. Perroux, 'Note sur la notion de Pole de Croissance', *Economie Appliquée*, 1955. Also by the same author, *L'Economie du XXe Siècle*, Paris, 1961. See also G. Myrdal, *Economic Theory and Underdeveloped Regions*, London, 1963, and J. R. Boudeville, *Problems of Regional Economic Planning*, Edinburgh, 1966. For more practical evaluations of growth area policy see G. C. Cameron and G. L. Reid, *Scottish Economic Planning and the Attraction of Industry*, University of Glasgow Social and Economic Studies, Occasional Paper No. 6, Oliver & Boyd, 1966, Chapter 4. Gavin McCrone, *Regional Policy in Britain*, Allen & Unwin, 1969, chapter 9. A detailed evaluation of the policy has recently been completed by an EFTA working party and published as *Regional Policy in EFTA: An Examination of the Growth Centre Idea*, University of Glasgow Social and Economic Studies, Occasional Paper No. 10, Oliver & Boyd, 1968.

income and employment. They will normally be areas which are experiencing a rapid growth of employment, an inflow of new firms and immigration of labour. The prime characteristic of growth area policy is its selectivity. It accepts that development effort should not be spread evenly over a whole region nor should effort necessarily be directed into those areas where problems of depression show themselves most acutely. Rather, policy should be directed at building up and developing those areas which are capable, and have shown themselves to be capable, of rapid economic growth. The major consequence of a growth area policy, and one from which most of the benefits of the policy are derived, is that it will result in an increase in the average size of settlement and a larger proportion of a region's population living in large settlements.

The alternative to a growth area policy is a policy of spread. This involves the spreading of effort over the existing settlement structure or the direction of effort into areas and settlements which are problem areas—areas with high unemployment, low incomes, low activity rates and heavy out-migration. Implicit in a spread policy is an acceptance of the existing settlement structure and a belief that this is adequate for the long-term needs of people and industry. Growth area policy, on the other hand, is based on the belief that the existing settlement structure has no long-term validity. It argues that a policy of spread is a short-term policy—one which, even though it may shore up the settlement structure for a long period, but at high cost, will not provide a long-term solution to a region's problem. A long-term solution will have been attained when the region has rates of growth, unemployment, activity, emigration and income which are, over a reasonable period of time, approximately equal to the average for the nation and when there is no need for further assistance, i.e. when the characteristics of depression no longer exist. Growth area policy is an attempt to reorganize the settlement structure in order to lay the foundations for long-term growth. It accepts the corollary of this—that the populations of some settlements in the region will decline or at best remain unchanged.

To a large extent, a growth area policy represents an acceptance of a natural trend. There is a tendency in most developed countries for people and industry to move into the larger population centres where both seem to enjoy advantages not found in the smaller centres. The justification of growth area policy is based on the belief that this trend has good economic foundations and that policy should try to plan this movement in order to ensure that it takes place efficiently. Growth area policy is, to a large extent, a form of anticipatory planning.

Merely because there is a visible tendency towards greater levels of urbanization and a movement of people and industry into the larger centres does not, of course, necessarily mean that policy should attempt to further this trend. Market forces do not always bring about the most economic solution. The evaluation and justification of a growth area policy has to be made in terms of the advantages of having a larger proportion of a region's population and employment in large centres for this is the major outcome of the policy.

In order to evaluate growth area policy it is necessary to define clearly the objectives of development policies in the depressed regions. Obviously one objective must be to promote the rapid growth of employment, output and income. In one sense this is no great problem. The posting of £20 per week to all the inhabitants of Scotland would considerably increase the region's rate of growth. This, however, would be costly and it is extremely unlikely that it would be the best policy from the national viewpoint. In most countries an important objective of national economic policy is to secure rapid growth of output. Regional development policy must be compatible with this national objective and must attempt to develop individual regions in such a way that the cost to the nation is minimized or, to put it in another way, so that each region's contribution to national growth is maximized. More formally, the objective of regional policy must be to secure the fastest regional growth of income and/or employment at the lowest possible cost to the national economy.

It is in the light of this objective that we shall now examine growth area policy. Since one of the main consequences of a growth area policy is an increase in the average size of settlement and an increase in the proportion of people living in larger settlements, our analysis is basically concerned to assess the possible advantages of larger settlements. The section which follows discusses firstly the advantages for industry of being in a larger rather than a smaller centre (in terms of population) and thus whether a growth area policy will lead to faster industrial growth in the region. Secondly, there is a brief discussion of the advantages to the region in terms of infrastructure costs, of having a larger proportion of a region's population in bigger centres. The third part moves on from these two aspects to a discussion of other regional and national benefits arising out of a growth area policy as well as some of the problems.

II

Firms located in a big centre enjoy many advantages not available to their counterparts in smaller centres. There are, however, also disadvantages in the form of higher labour costs as earnings are forced up by competitive bidding, and productivity is affected by a high rate of labour turnover and costs arising out of congestion. These, however, do not seem to offset the advantages, and the trend in industrial location is increasingly towards the larger centres or close proximity to such centres.[1] The principal reason behind this trend is the importance of external economies to modern industry and, with the more intensive competition in today's economies, the increasing need to exploit such economies. There are three basic types of external economies or economic advantage for a firm arising out of location in a large centre. First, there is a greater likelihood of its being close to suppliers and markets; secondly, it can obtain the benefits of a larger and more diversified labour market; and, thirdly, there is greater availability of services for both people and industry.[2] These are discussed below in this order.

Specialization as opposed to vertical integration is one of the basic characteristics of modern industry. A firm is thus likely to be at an advantage if it can secure a location close to suppliers capable of satisfying its needs. The larger the centre the greater is the probability of a firm being able to find suppliers on the spot. This probability arises not only from the simple statistical probability but also from the fact that a greater range and number of suppliers is economically feasible the larger the centre because of the greater number of firms demanding their services.[3] The benefits of having more suppliers in close proximity are twofold. First, transport costs are likely to be lower and, secondly, there will be greater certainty that production is not halted by the late arrival of supplies. Although transport costs frequently account for only a small proportion of a firm's total production costs, they still remain an important factor affecting location decisions. No matter how small they are, they do represent an additional cost and, furthermore, being one of the more quantifiable location factors, they have a weight in the businessman's mind greater than their value alone would suggest. Certainty concerning the arrival of supplies is an important though often neglected location factor. Without this certainty, it is necessary to carry higher levels of stocks and this, though less costly than

---

[1] See R. L. Morrill, *Migration and the Spread and Growth of Urban Settlements*, Lund, 1966. See also the EFTA study, op. cit.

[2] All three points are treated in detail in the EFTA study, op. cit.

[3] A simple example may explain the point. Although a packaging firm may not be economic in a centre on the basis of the demand by one firm, a larger centre with more firms demanding packaging materials may, with their joint demands, have sufficient demand to make a packaging firm economic.

production stoppages, still represents a cost which could have been avoided.

The larger and more diversified labour markets provided by large centres are a further reason for industry choosing to locate in them. The larger centre will have available a greater variety of skills while the labour reserve, as measured by unemployment, is also likely to be larger. Even a centre with a population of 30,000, and a labour force of 12,000, would not usually have a large number unemployed. At 5 per cent, the unemployed would number 600. Unemployables and the frictionally unemployed often take up two-thirds of such a number, so the true reserve is likely to be only about 200.

The firms providing most of the new employment in the depressed regions have very heavy labour demands and need a correspondingly large labour reserve and market if they are to secure the labour which they require. The smaller centre is at a severe disadvantage. Figures in the Northern Ireland Development Plan are instructive on this point. Between 1945 and 1964, 70 per cent of new jobs created in co-operation with the Ministry of Commerce were in concerns of 300 employees or over, with about 50 per cent in the size range of 500 or more.[1]

The question of size is extremely important in relation to the provision of services. Many services require a large population before they can be provided in full on an economic basis. This applies both to services for industry and people and to both the publicly and privately provided services. Where the population is below the threshold number, the services will either not be provided, will be provided at a lower standard where possible, or will be provided at a higher cost—the latter being borne either by the individuals in the centre or by the State. Other things being equal, industry will be reluctant to locate in a centre which cannot provide for its demands or legal and financial services, export agencies, maintenance and repair services, training schools, etc., or where these are provided at a cost which is higher than elsewhere. Availability of industrial services on the spot is particularly important, probably more important than materials and semi-finished products, for many service inputs cannot be stored, e.g. maintenance and repair services, but at the same time it is costly to pay for the firm to provide such services for itself.

Industry not only needs to be able to secure services for its own use, but will prefer a location where its labour force can enjoy ready access to its own service requirements. Some personal public

---

[1] *Economic Development in Northern Ireland*, Cmnd. 479, HMSO, 1966, p. 37. Similar figures apply to Scotland. See EFTA study, op. cit., p. 77.

services like hospitals and schools require quite large dependent populations if they are to be provided in full. A reasonably sized hospital by today's standards (300 beds) would, for example, require a dependent population of about 45,000 if it was to be used to anything like capacity.[1] Personal services supplied by the private sector are more variable in their dependent population requirements. Many retail services are often available at very low population levels and there is evidence that a dependent population of 5,000 would be able to support most of them.[2] It is important to note, however, that higher population levels would be able to support a greater number of similar types of services, thus giving rise to competition, a greater range of choice, and probably increased efficiency. Higher populations would therefore tend to produce a higher quality of service. Lastly, the bigger form of low-price retail establishment, supermarkets and department stores, require quite high populations of 30,000 or more before they can be assured of the level and turnover required for their successful operation.

Private non-retail personal services usually require high populations before they can develop. Bowling alleys, theatres, cinemas, concert halls and zoos, for example, usually need dependent populations of well above 30,000,[3] though, of course, it must be remembered that factors other than population alone will determine whether or not these exist, e.g. income levels, socio-economic class structure, extent of local subsidy, etc. It should also be noted that discussions of threshold populations for particular services usually refer to a standard form of service. Modification of design or perhaps a lower standard of service can often lower the threshold population levels.

Nevertheless, the general point remains that larger centres can support more services and/or a higher quality of them than can a small centre. This will make the larger centre more attractive to industry in as far as there is a greater likelihood of its own service needs and those of its employees being met in such a centre.

On all three points discussed above, there is evidence that, the larger the population of a centre, then the more attractive it is to

[1] This and other service figures below are taken from the EFTA study, op. cit.
[2] See B. S. L. Berry, and W. L. Garrison, 'The Functional Bases of the Central Hierarchy', in *Readings in Urban Geography*, edited by Mayer and Kohn, where a threshold population size of 1,500 is never exceeded for a considerable range of retail services.
[3] For a discussion of threshold populations for these services and some quantification of their values, see Robert Matthew, Johnson-Marshall & Partners, *Central Lancashire*. For a critical discussion of threshold values, see *Central Borders: A Plan for Expansion*, Vol. II, HMSO, 1968.

industry. A growth area policy, being concerned with concentration of effort on selected areas in an attempt to build these up to a larger size and increase the average settlement size in a region, seems likely to give faster regional growth because it makes the region more attractive to new firms and provides a better economic environment for existing firms. A growth area policy recognizes that many smaller settlements are not suitable for the majority of industry in that they are unable to offer the kind of advantages mentioned above. They may be suitable for non-industrial activities like tourism where the importance of external economies arising out of large population sizes is not so great. They may even be suitable for some types of industrial development, though this will normally be small-scale industry. The majority of new industrial employment is likely to be in or near the larger centres. The concentration of industrial growth on large centres (or in an attempt to build up large centres) will, by increasing the prospects of industry securing external economies, make the centre and the region more attractive to industrial development and secure faster regional growth. This is the essence of the growth area argument.

The attainment of faster regional growth arising out of a growth area policy has two indirect advantages for the state. First, because the region is part of the nation, faster regional growth contributes to faster national growth. Second, faster regional growth will generally diminish the increasing pressures on the congested regions into which the development might otherwise have gone and this should reduce the inflationary forces in the congested regions and in the nation as a whole. But a more direct state advantage of growth area policy is that the cost or providing infrastructure is likely to be less costly if the settlement pattern is more concentrated. Up to a point it is less costly to provide infrastructure for a large than a small community. The indivisible character of much infrastructure means that it can only be provided for large population groups or else provided at a high cost per head—a cost which is met either by the resident population, or the State. A growth area policy, by securing larger population groupings, will enable a greater proportion of the region's population to enjoy infrastructure provisions and at a lower cost per head.[1]

[1] A recent study of infrastructure and public service costs in relation to centre size suggests that the average cost curve falls steeply to a minimum point at a population of about 30,000-35,000 after which it rises slowly. At a population of 100,000-250,000 the index number, taking 20,000-50,000 as 100, is however not more than 110. See *Ricerca sui Costi d'Insediamento*, Svimez, Rome, 1967. The Svimez estimates would appear to overstate the rise in costs after the population level of 30,000-35,000 in that qualitative aspects are not taken into

It is not appropriate here to go into any great detail on infrastructure costs. It is, however, worth while to add that we are still relatively ignorant of the relationship between infrastructure costs and population size. The information we do have indicates that although the infrastructure average cost curve, up to a point, is lower in a large than a small centre, this is only a very general rule.[1] Costs will vary enormously according to the shape of the centre, density of population, geological conditions and standard of infrastructure provision. For our purposes, however, and recognizing the qualifications, the conclusion that small population centres can either not be provided with much of the infrastructure considered basic today or else provided at a high cost and that large centres can be provided with such infrastructure and generally at least as cheaply (and generally more cheaply) as the small centres, is sufficient.

So far we have argued that a growth area policy, by concentrating development is likely, in general, to bring about a more suitable settlement structure from the viewpoint of industrial development and also from the viewpoint of infrastructure and public service provision. It is likely to create conditions which are more conducive to faster regional growth and a settlement structure which will result in lower infrastructure costs—relative to the alternative policy of spreading development.

Another advantage of growth area policy is that it provides the framework for a national regional planning strategy, isolating the foci of development and providing a basis for the planning of the region of which it is the centre. Implicit in a growth area policy is the recognition that the existing settlement structure is inappropriate. The desired structure, having been stated through growth area policy, can then be catered for in terms of infrastructure and service provision both within and outside the growth area itself.

Having decided to pursue a growth area strategy, there are basically two lines to follow in order to select the areas. The first is a 'passive' or 'reinforcing' approach and the second is 'positive' or 'initiating'.

account and some of the infrastructure, e.g. hospitals, were not treated as truly indivisible. For most practical purposes the average cost curve after an initial steep fall appears to be virtually flat between populations of about 35,000 and 250,000. The Svimez study is based on the 'standards' technique. For a very interesting study of infrastructure costs and their relation to population size based on observation, see *Infrastruktur*, Institut für Orts, Zurich, 1966. This study stresses in particular the wide variations of cost for towns of similar population sizes and thus warns against generalizing too much on the subject of infrastructure threshold populations. A discussion of both the Italian and Swiss study can be found in the EFTA study, op. cit.

[1] See footnote above.

The passive growth area policy involves the selection of those areas which are already large and growing fast in terms of population, income, employment or immigration. They will already be well endowed with social capital and it has been suggested that they should have a population in excess of 30,000.[1] The basic argument behind the passive approach is that industry will already be enjoying external economies and that further development would be relatively easy and add to the existing external economies, thus making the area yet more attractive. The passive approach is very much a case of anticipatory planning based on the expectation that past growth will be repeated in the future. Designation and planning as a growth area would allow development to take place more smoothly and efficiently and also more rapidly.

A passive growth area policy, by concentrating on existing fast-growing and well-populated centres, has the disadvantage, however, that it could leave a considerable part of a region outside the selected growth areas and their sphere of influence. This is particularly likely to be the case in the sparsely populated regions of Scandinavia and the Highlands of Scotland. The alternative, or supplementary, form of growth area policy is to create growth areas. This is the positive or initiating approach. It involves the concentration on, and building up of, areas which in the normal way of things would not have developed or developed only very slowly. The difficulties of this approach are fairly obvious. Industrial development is difficult in small centres because they lack external economies and this produces a vicious circle which it is difficult to break out of—industry is reluctant to set up because there are no external economies; external economies are not built up because industry does not develop.

The dangers of 'creation' are as important as the difficulties. Political factors may force the designation of too many growth areas, many of which will be of the positive type, with a consequential spreading of effort and the weakening of the industrial advantages arising out of more concentrated policy. Proliferation will inevitably slow down the speed with which growth areas can be developed.

---

[1] A population minimum of 30,000 is suggested in the EFTA study, op. cit., on the grounds that this population will probably be able to support the most indivisible piece of basic social capital—a general hospital. Although, as mentioned elsewhere, a hospital requires a population of around 45,000 before it is likely to be used close to capacity, the coverage area of a hospital is generally greater than the travel-to-work area around the centre itself—the usual basis for delineating a growth area. Using average population densities for the area around the growth area the report finally suggested the rough minimum population figure of 30,000 for the growth area itself.

This gives rise to disadvantages, for the quicker that growth areas can be built up the better. Discrimination in terms of industrial incentives can help in this speeding-up process and help therefore in building up external economies. Furthermore, a big and rapid expansion of an area can offer substantial economies of scale in infrastructure provision, but these benefits will be offset if the infrastructure capacity is left underutilized. Proliferation will thus deny some of the economies of scale in infrastructure provision or diminish the prospects of using such infrastructure quickly. It will also add to the problems of phasing development and could create a situation where infrastructure, far from lying idle, is not being supplied quickly enough to attract and stimulate industrial expansion in the area.

The temptation to proliferate growth areas is an understandable attempt to include as much of a region as possible inside a growth area and hopefully to reduce the amount of intra-regional migration required to operate the policy. It must be admitted that a growth area policy will involve intra-regional migration which in some instances may be so severe as to reduce populations in some outlying areas. This element of the policy, though unfortunate, must be viewed rationally. The problem of maintaining the existing settlement structure has already been mentioned. Migration and perhaps even some depopulation would be probable even if an attempt was made to spread development effort. The important point about a growth area policy is that by building up an economic environment more favourable to industrial development it will give a greater likelihood of migrants finding employment within their own region, i.e. within the growth area, rather than having to migrate to other regions. This seems preferable if the assumption is accepted that short-distance migrants suffer less welfare loss than long-distance migrants. A growth area policy does involve settlement structure changes with consequential intra-regional migration, but such changes are what the region needs if the foundations for long-term economic growth are to be laid. It should finally be recalled that the region's settlement structure is probably anyway already undergoing spontaneous change with a growth of the large centres and decline of the smaller ones. Growth area policy merely tries to plan the change, making it more efficient, speedier and more economic.

Our arguments so far have been couched largely in terms of a growth area policy stimulating faster regional growth because the growth area itself is likely to grow faster and, through this growth, to give to the region of which it is part a faster rate of growth than the alternative policy of spread. The population expansion of the growth area is fed by intra-regional migration. In the short term this is likely to be the pattern. In the longer term, however, it is probable that even the outlying smaller settlements will be able to secure industrial development with the growth area acting as a service centre. This is the centrifugal effect of growth area policy. It seems that industry finds no great disadvantages from locating in the smaller centres if these are in proximity to a larger one. Certainly, regions without a large centre capable of acting as a service centre seem to have very slight prospects for industrial development on a scale adequate to overcome their problems. In Denmark, for example, only those parts of the country without a reasonably large centre have remained problem regions while in the rest of the country industry seems to have moved on quite a considerable scale into the smaller centres where these are in proximity to a larger centre. The problems of those regions in Europe, which through the redrawing of political boundaries lost their natural centre, have proved difficult to resolve: again underlining the point that a region without a fairly large centre has fewer prospects for development than one with such a centre. A growth area policy, by building up a reasonably sized centre, will probably make the whole surrounding and dependent region more susceptible to industrial development.[1]

Growth area policy is a long-term policy aimed at altering the settlement pattern and providing a structure which is suitable for more rapid regional economic development. To operate such a policy today implies a belief that the factors which make the existing settlement patterns inappropriate will continue in the future. All the signs are that they will. Infrastructure, like hospitals, seems likely to become even more indivisible. The specialized character of industry with its heavy reliance on other firms will probably increase. Increasing economies of scale in many industries will bring about a yet greater need for large labour markets as firms grow in size. While transport and communications are likely to improve and perhaps become cheaper, it is doubtful, particularly in the light of increased industrial specialization, whether the value of the transport input as a proportion of total production costs will fall, and this is the relevant point. Improved communications anyway, though at first sight seeming to allow greater industrial dispersion, may in fact, by widening markets and increasing competition, force firms to exploit yet more the economies present in the large centres.

[1] This point, with more details on the Danish case, is argued in the EFTA study, op. cit.

III

The arguments used above for growth area policy are now becoming fairly standard. They have been used, in one form or another, in many European countries. Some have stressed one aspect of the argument in their case for growth areas while others have based their case on other aspects.

In Italy the stress has been largely on the need to build up external economies in the South in order to stimulate the conditions of the North.

'The primary and induced effects of public expenditure do not create *per se*, in the absence that is of an autonomous mechanism of development, a sufficient flow of private investment. Public infrastructure expenditure furnishes only part of the advantage that an entrepreneur gains by operating in a zone already economically developed: one can provide roads, bridges, rail junctions, water, but one cannot bring about those external economies that the firm derives by being near complementary industry, by the availability of specialized manpower, trained manpower, by the existence of a market for its products, etc.'[1]

In France the major agrument behind the creation of the *métropoles d'équilibres* has been based on the need to simulate the external economies and metropolitan functions of Paris. But it has also been recognized that they would allow infrastructure cost savings and would be the foci for the redrawing of the general framework of the French transport and communications network.

In the United Kingdom, as we shall see, growth area policy has never been adopted with anything like the French and Italian enthusiasm. The justification for pursuing such a policy has not been discussed at any great length though the need to develop external economies figures in some of the earlier writings on the subject.[2] When, in the early 1960s, the first tentative moves were made towards the policy in the north-east of England and Scotland there was no detailed public explanation as to why the policy was being pursued. In the north-east of England, the policy was merely

[1] Comitato dei Ministri per il Mezzogiorno, *Relazione al Parlamento*, 1960, p. 5.

[2] The earliest and tentative suggestion of growth area policy as a means in regional development in Britain was probably Scottish Council for Development and Industry, *Report of the Committee on Local Development in Scotland*, 1952—better known perhaps as the Cairncross Report. 'The community must have something more to offer than unemployed workers: it must have the facilities and the atmosphere that will let transplanted enterprise take firm root', p. 29.

defined, not explained: 'The additional effort will be mainly directed to the part of the region best fitted to support rapid economic growth'.[1] The Scottish counterpart to the north-east of England Plan was equally vague:

'. . . certain parts of the area have shown remarkable capacity for change and expansion. It is these districts . . . that point the way to what can be achieved in the future by integrated investment deliberately concentrated and designed to promote faster growth . . . this modernization exercise will be based on major focal points—defined in this White Paper as growth areas. Experience has shown that in the circumstances of Central Scotland this is the best way to co-ordinate effort and spending so that economic growth can take place on the right scale and with speed.'[2]

In Northern Ireland the rationale of the policy was much clearer: 'Many advantages accrue to a firm that is situated in or near an industrial centre of some size. The most important consideration may be the greater ease with which it will be possible to recruit experienced managerial and supervisory staff and workers with adequate industrial training. In such a centre there are likely to be supporting industrial services . . . A plan for regional development must recognize the need to build up industry in centres of growth of reasonable size and good location and must accept the corollary that some mobility of labour is an indispensable condition of economic advance.'[3]

The growth area debate has not of course been limited to the United Kingdom, France and Italy. The policy has also been argued in other countries. In the sparsely populated regions of Scandinavia, in Sweden for example, the main claim for the policy has been that 'there exists in Sweden, for economic reasons, a certain need to concentrate the population. There is great difficulty in providing different types of services in sparsely populated areas and effort must be directed at a controlled concentration of the population to fewer and larger centres and settlements.'[4] In Norway, similarly, 'It is the opinion of the government that if one is to avoid further concentration of the industry and service bodies in and around the centres that have already been strongly developed, efforts should be made,

[1] *The North East: A programme for regional development and growth*, Cmnd. 2206, HMSO, 1963, para. 38.
[2] *Central Scotland: A programme for development and growth*, Cmnd. 2188, HMSO, 1963, paras. 9, 10, 11.
[3] *Economic Development in Northern Ireland*, op. cit., paras. 12 and 13.
[4] See the EFTA study, op. cit., p. 131.

on a larger scale than hitherto, to help in the development of a limited number of centres in the Districts. . . . The development of larger centres in the Districts will also provide the population of these areas with a better possibility for taking part in the social and cultural amenities of a modern society . . . .'[1] In Denmark there are plans afoot for creating larger service centres in the west in the belief that these will then make the whole region more viable.[2]

Although at some stage there has, in many countries, been agreement that growth area policy has benefits to offer, the implementation of the policy has been difficult. The political problems in particular have been such as to force serious modifications of the policy and in some cases brought about its abandonment. The progress of policy in Italy and France has already been treated in some detail.[3] We therefore want now to survey the trends and experiences of the policy in the United Kingdom and then briefly review the position in France and Italy.[4]

In Britain, the Conservative administration, towards the end of its period of office, pursued a declared growth area policy for the north-east of England and for Scotland. The policy was initiated in 1963. This was a period when something positive and of a novel character, for political reasons at least, needed to be introduced in regional policy. Unemployment in the north-east was at an all time post-war high. More important, perhaps, the introduction of the policy occurred at a time when it was becoming increasingly recognized that regional policy was capable of contributing to overall national growth,[5] and that the mopping up of the pockets of unemployment in the small Development Districts was not the best policy from either the regional or national viewpoint. The Development District policy was too much in the nature of assistance and was too little oriented towards a long-term solution of the regional problems. It was a short-term policy aimed at alleviating the problem of unemployment in small areas. It was costly in terms of infrastructure and the dispersion of effort was not creating the required external economies.

[1] *Norwegian Parliamentary Report,* No. 29 (1963-64).
[2] Many of the problem areas in Europe are areas without a suitably sized service centre as is the case in western Denmark. Areas which through the redrawing of political boundaries have lost their service centre are all problem regions, e.g. the border area of western Germany, northern Finland, north-west Eire. [3] See Chapters 2 and 8 above.
[4] The difficulties which the policy has encountered in various EFTA countries, including the UK, can be found in the EFTA study, op. cit.
[5] National Economic Development Council, *Conditions favourable to Faster Growth,* HMSO, 1963.

It was decided, therefore, that development should be concentrated in those areas which were considered susceptible to fast growth. The corollary of the policy, the decline of some areas, was courageously accepted. 'In several parts of the region there are a number of communities where the economic activity which called them into being is in permanent local decline and it would be unrealistic to expect the emergence of alternative local employment on anything like a comparable scale. Many such places are also poorly equipped in housing, public services and amenities, and the government feel it is right that the local planning authorities concerned should concentrate their future improvement and development efforts, or encourage population movement, into those towns or villages which are of a size and condition to make any substantial further public investment in them socially and economically worth while.'[1]

The selection of growth areas was a result of detailed and careful, but unpublished, studies. The areas selected had usually, though there were some exceptions, experienced rapid growth in the past or shown their potential for growth, already had a wide range of services and infrastructure, had large populations and, finally, were physically capable of absorbing the planned expansion and without undue costs.[2]

Not only were growth areas designated but they were given preferential treatment through the industrial incentive schemes though the element of discrimination was not as open as in, say, Italy. Discrimination arose out of the fact that the growth areas were permanently eligible for assistance. This differed from the situation outside the growth areas where a Development District would become ineligible for assistance if its rate of unemployment fell

---

[1] *The North-east*, op. cit., para, 122.

[2] *The North-East*, op. cit., para. 38, describes its own major zone along the following lines which indicate its reason for selection: 'It covers only a small part of the area but takes in the main existing centres of population and economic activity and includes some of the country's most up-to-date steel, engineering and chemical units, nearly all the coal-mines likely to endure, a highly skilled labour force, a wide range of facilities for technical education and two universities. It includes the major ports, is well served by the main lines of road and rail communication, and has growing facilities for travel by air. It is relatively free from high ground and has adequate land and basic services for expansion.' The Scottish growth areas were selected with similar criteria in mind. See *Central Scotland* op. cit., paras 105-111. In Scotland, following designation, a number of detailed studies were made of the areas in order to form a framework for planning their expansion. See *The Lothians Regional Survey and Plan*, 2 Vols. HMSO, 1966, and *The Grangemouth/Falkirk Regional Survey and Plan*, 2 Vols., HMSO, 1968.

below a particular level. The level was never specified but, in practice, was around 4 per cent. This element of permanence represented an attraction to industrialists, and thus discrimination in favour of the growth areas. It gave an assurance to industrialists that after their decision to locate, any further expansion would also benefit from the incentives. Only if there was strong 'evidence of a general and sustained improvement in employment in the region as a whole',[1] would a growth area lose its eligibility. This can be interpreted as meaning that they would remain eligible for as long as the regional problem persisted.

As well as discrimination through incentives, the growth areas were to be favoured by being the centres of public investment: '. . . increased public investment will be undertaken to modernize the "infrastructure" services which a modern industrial economy requires . . . to have the best chance of success this modernization exercise will be based on major focal points—defined in this White Paper as growth areas'.[2]

In contrast with the open acceptance of growth area policy in the mid-1960s, the current view is difficult to interpret. On the surface, growth area policy does not seem to form a part of present regional policy. Under the Industrial Development Act, 1966, the Development District policy was abandoned and replaced by the Development Area policy.[3] The Development Areas are geographically very large—virtually the whole of Central Scotland is one. They cover 'over 40 per cent of the land area of Britain and 20 per cent of the population compared with 16·7 per cent for the Development Districts in 1966'.[4] The old growth areas have been merged into these Development Areas. There has been no admitted abandonment of them, however, though references to them in government documents is now cautious and more implicit than explicit. Because the whole of a Development Area is now eligible for virtually permanent assistance, the discrimination through incentives in favour of growth areas (mentioned above) has now disappeared. Recently (1967) there has been a policy change which in fact represents a move

---

[1] *The North-East*, op. cit., para. 41.

[2] *Central Scotland*, op. cit., paras. 10 and 11.

[3] The Act also changed the system of incentives. The major change was to replace the previous system of tax allowances on industrial investments by a system of investment grants. See *Industrial Development Act 1966: Investment Incentives*, Cmnd. 2874, 1966. For a comprehensive discussion of the evolution of regional policy and the current position, see Gavin McCrone, op. cit. For a very good official description of UK regional policy, see *Report of the EFTA Working Party on Industrial Estates*, EFTA, Geneva, 1970.

[4] Gavin McCrone, op. cit., p. 126.

back towards the Development District policy and to some extent away from the principles of growth area policy. Special Development Areas have been designated. These are small coalmining areas with heavy rates of unemployment or potentially high rates (though the absolute number of unemployed will generally be low) within which the Board of Trade intend to site advance factories; to be let in some instances for a five-year rent-free period. Firms within the special areas will be eligible for incentives which have a slightly higher value than those in the Development Areas as a whole.[1] The designation and treatment afforded to the Special Development Areas would appear to represent a weakening of the belief that development should be concentrated on growth areas and the need to recognize that certain areas have no long-term future.

The present government's attitude towards growth areas in England is very vague. Although the growth areas in the north-east have not explicitly been abandoned, there has at the same time been no confirmation that the principles behind them are still operative. If a growth area policy is being operated in England at present it is a hidden one. It may in fact be that government departments are still operating on the old designations and using them as a focal point of their development plans and actions. A hidden policy, however, as we argue below, lacks many of the advantages of a more open policy where growth areas are clearly and publicly designated.

In Scotland the situation is a little less confused though hardly more open. Although designated growth areas disappear from the maps in the current development policy document, the policy still seems to be courted:

'The studies carried out by the Scottish Economic Planning Board and the Council have shown that in Central Scotland the economically and socially directed strands of post-war planning are essentially complementary and that, properly integrated together, they could help to create in certain key areas of new development a powerful stimulus to economic growth. They have also demonstrated that the labour mobility, which the provision of new houses in new growth areas can provide, is an essential ingredient to faster industrial expansion. The government therefore propose to build on these past successes and to intensify the provision of housing and other essential services in suitable locations in Central Scotland where the necessary movements of population arising from the

[1] For a list of the Special Development Areas and the incentives available, see *Government Help for Your Business*, February 1968—a Board of Trade Booklet.

decongestion of towns and cities can be matched with new industry steered by the government's distribution of industry policy.'[1]

Mention is made elsewhere of the need for a 'strengthening of other promising places throughout the central belt where progress can be rapid',[2] and later, more explicitly: 'The first phase, to 1970, will see the continued and rapid expansion of those places in Central Scotland which have the benefit of complexes of new fast growing industries, and which are well placed in relation to communications and other services'.[3] It goes on to specify the old growth areas. In other areas outside the central belt there is an explicit recognition of the need for concentration. In the Western Borders there is a need to 'turn Galashiels into a more sizeable centre of population than at present existing in the Borders. This would afford the first stage of a more sustained expansion leading eventually to further spontaneous growth.'[4] In the Eastern Borders the concentration of effort will be on Berwick-on-Tweed, 'the natural focal point and the place best able to draw on the maximum labour potential. It is probable that in its early stages development will be concentrated there; but the aim of the programme will be to benefit the area as a whole and to ensure that expansion at any one point will have a revitalizing effect on the surrounding districts.'[5] Similar strategies are outlined for other non-central belt regions.[6] In the Highlands there is mention of the need to 'identify and develop viable communities to form holding points and, possible, centres of modest expansion'.[7]

In Scotland, then, growth area policy would still seem to be in operation though it is less open and a little weaker than before 1966. It is weakened furthermore in as far as in Scotland, as elsewhere in Britain, Special Development Areas have now been designated and this is at odds with the principles of a growth area policy.

In Northern Ireland, policy is much clearer and more open than elsewhere in the United Kingdom. A growth area policy was proposed, and areas suggested, in the Northern Ireland Development Plan.[8] Fourteen growth areas were selected covering 20 per cent of the region's population. In Northern Ireland, as elsewhere in the United Kingdom, there is no discrimination, through industrial inducements, in favour of the growth areas. The authorities doubt that discrimination is required: 'Experience suggests that firms need

---

[1] *The Scottish Economy* 1965 *to* 1970: *a Plan for Expansion*, Cmnd 2864, HMSO, 1966, para. 155.
[2] ibid., para. 164.   [3] ibid., para. 229.   [4] ibid., para. 231.
[5] ibid., para. 237.   [6] ibid., paras. 238-41.   [7] ibid., para. 242.
[8] *Economic Development in Northern Ireland*, op. cit.

no prodding (to go to selected growth centres); if they are prepared in any way to consider a difficult area of high unemployment their own preference would be for the centre, the expansion of which is being encouraged'.[1]

The current situation with respect to growth area policy in the United Kingdom is varied, but in general is more vague than it was a few years ago under the Conservative government, and certainly more nebulous than in France or Italy. Growth area policy today is not in general a firm and declared part of United Kingdom regional development. The recent designation of Special Development Areas represents a definite move away from the policy. There is, furthermore, less openness about the policy and considerable caution in making an open designation of growth areas or even an open declaration, one way or the other, towards the policy.

A more open pursuit of the policy has a number of advantages and there are dangers in allowing policy to become too hidden or implicit. First, it is difficult enough to secure interministerial co-ordination even with open and publicly declared objectives. Without such a declaration it is likely to be even more problematical. An open declaration of policy would provide a spatial framework for action within which each department could co-operate. Such a framework cannot be provided by a less open policy. Secondly, the clear designation of growth areas would give a firmer sense of direction to policy. It would imply a recognition of the need to alter the settlement pattern as well as providing a base for the necessary restructuring. It would also make it easier for other necessary changes to take place. It would, for example, allow and encourage detailed planning studies within the growth areas to be carried out.

In both France and Italy the situation with respect to growth areas is much clearer.[2] The policy has been generally accepted, growth areas declared and policy openly oriented towards them. In France the *métropoles d'équilibre* are to be given privileged treatment in terms of infrastructure provision. Such a clearly selective policy is at first sight quite remarkable when compared with the much more attenuated policies in other European countries. It involves the singling out of a very small number of cities for a role which is bound to confer considerable and lasting economic privileges upon them. There are, however, three important factors which help to explain this exercise in selection which might, at first sight, seem to be rather too exclusive.

[1] EFTA study, op. cit., p. 125.
[2] Growth area policy, its form and development, in Italy and France, is discussed in Chapters 2 and 8 above.

The first is the disparity in size between Paris and every other French urban centre. Apart possibly from Lyons, there is no other city in France capable of offering anything like the range of locational advantages possessed by the capital. If provincial counterweights to Paris were to be created their identity had then to be established definitely and openly, for in the case of several of the smaller *métropoles* it would have been difficult otherwise to justify the special, selective treatment they were to receive. A second factor is the emphasis which French regional policy has come to place on the service industries in regional development. This orientation of policy has naturally made the choice of an urban centre the key decision in the development of a particular region. In the absence in many regions of a 'natural' main centre, this meant the designation of one city (or two physically contiguous ones) to fulfil this function. This is naturally a sharper and more clear-cut choice than the denomination of large areas of a country (sometimes containing several *métropoles*) as regions deserving particular treatment.

Finally, there was the question of the cost of regional development. By the early 1960s it was becoming apparent to French policy makers that the France of Paris, average size towns and villages was no longer tenable as a physical or social framework. The mechanization of agriculture was bringing about a migration from the countryside which made it uneconomic to modernize each village so as to bring its amenities nearer to those enjoyed by town-dwellers, and which was by-passing the larger provincial towns in favour of Paris and, to a much lesser extent, the Lyons-St Etienne-Grenoble complex. Rapid selective development was thus required in order to build up, at one level, rural centres suited to the new patterns of rural life brought about by a less labour-intensive agriculture and, at another, provincial cities which would mitigate the attractive power of Paris. At the same time the cost of regional development in terms of increments of national output foregone were coming under close scrutiny, as the French economy became more and more open to competitive pressures from her partners in the EEC. In such circumstances it was becoming less easy to spread resources thinly, widely and, in political terms, more or less satisfactorily about the economy. What had been locationally unattractive peripheral areas in the French economy were doubly (and more) so in the economy of the EEC, and the cost of putting resources in them also greater. Under the constraint of having to do something, the logical solution was to select the most promising parts of these regions and build them up as centres of growth.

The principle of selectivity has also been followed in regard to financial incentives to industry. The importance of developing a wide range of services within the *métropoles* has been recognized by the financial benefits made available to firms establishing their 'service' activities within them. The incentives available to industry have also been made more selective by the establishment of a distinction between areas where aid must continue to be available for an indefinite period and those which may be declared ineligible if a reasonable improvement in their economies can be induced. Special industrial incentives have not, however, been created in the *métropoles*. Their primary function is to act as service centres, in the widest sense, to their regions within which industrial development may take place in several localities. The advantage which the *métropoles* enjoy in the allocation of the national quota of industrial estate space will, of course, be an important factor in attracting manufacturing industry to expand within their boundaries.

In Italy there is fairly strong discrimination in favour of the designated growth areas: first, through the industrial incentive schemes; secondly by the purposeful use of state-controlled firms as propulsive industries in the growth areas; and, thirdly, by the fact that the Cassa per il Mezzogiorno has been increasingly restricting its intervention to the growth areas—a process which has now resulted in the Cassa operating almost wholly within these areas. The Italians are pursuing a policy of concentration not only in the industrial sphere but also with agriculture and tourism. There can be little doubt, and indeed planning is based on the assumption, that the greater part of future industrial development will be in the growth areas. The Italian National Plan anticipates that 80 per cent of new industrial jobs will be in the designated industrial growth areas. This fact alone reflects the extent to which a growth area policy has been accepted in Italy. Italy is undoubtedly pursuing the most developed and purposive growth area policy in Europe. The corollary of growth area policy—the need for net emigration from those parts of the South outside the influence of the growth areas—has also been accepted, reflecting the recognition that many areas in the South are not suitable for industrial development on any scale. It is recognized that concentration of industrial development on more suitable locations will build up the external economies which are needed if the South is to simulate the North, and also that concentration will represent infrastructure savings.

The selection of areas as growth areas in both Italy and France has been based on fairly rigorous economic criteria. The criteria for selection have been openly announced. In the United Kingdom, even though the selection process was just as rigorous, the detailed reasons for selection were not made public. The growth areas selected in both Italy and France, and also the United Kingdom, have largely been of the 'passive' type,[1] i.e. they are, on the whole, areas which already have large populations and have grown rapidly in the past. The major exceptions have been in Britain when new towns and growth areas coincide. This is a more positive form of policy.

Political factors have, however, to some extent forced a move towards a more 'positive' growth area policy in both France and Italy, and particularly the latter, with the designation of areas which have not, in the past, shown rapid growth. This has also been the case in the United Kingdom to some extent. The desire for rapid regional growth has had to be moderated by political forces demanding a more even regional distribution of development. In Italy more than forty growth areas have been designated. Although the Areas of Industrial Development (*Aree di Sviluppo Industriale*) have been selected very largely on economic grounds and have excellent prospects for rapid development, many of the Industrial Nuclei have very slender prospects.[2] Many were undoubtedly selected for political motives. There is certainly no past or present economic growth which would justify the selection of some of the Nuclei. The designation of unpromising growth areas, though perhaps understandable in political terms, is wasteful from an economic viewpoint. Infrastructure laid down for development which does not take place, or which takes place too slowly, is very costly. Excessive proliferation, as in Italy, also runs the further risk that by dispersing development one dilutes the possibilities of rapidly building up industrial external economies. Similar points apply to France, for there, too, the policy of concentrating development on the large and economically promising *métropoles d'équilibre* has been tempered by the designation of rural development centres[3]; though admittedly no large-scale industrial development is planned for these smaller centres. Indeed, it can be argued that these centres are to act as the *métropoles* for the new, larger-scale agriculture which is transforming large areas of 'the France of small villages'.

In both France and Italy there has been a recognition that the local authority structure at present existing is not appropriate to the tasks at hand and an attempt has been made in the growth areas to create more appropriate bodies. In Italy this has been done with the creation of consortia made up of local authorities, chambers of

---

[1] See p. 302 above.
[2] For the distinction between Areas and Nuclei, see pp. 68-72 above.
[3] See p. 191 above.

commerce, etc., though the process has probably not gone far enough as their tasks are very much limited to matters relevant to the *agglomerati* (industrial zones) and there would be benefits in giving them wider powers. In particular, in view of the very deficient level of urban planning in Italy, and if the consortia were strengthened, there would be a good case for giving them greater powers in the field of urban planning and development. In France, the local authority structures in the *métropoles d'équilibre* have been reorganized in order to make them more suited to the tasks which they face. It is a great pity that local authority reform was not an integral part of the early growth area policy in Britain.[1]

The attempt to industrialize growth areas rapidly has been taken much further in Italy than in France or the United Kingdom. In French regional policy generally there is not much stress on industrial incentives. The approach to industrial development in the growth areas does not differ from this general attitude. There is a belief that the adequate provision of infrastructure is the main factor required to attract industry. In the United Kingdom, where incentives play an important role in regional development, the lack of any strong discrimination in favour of growth areas would seem to imply a belief that the location of the growth areas plus the plans to provide adequate infrastructure are sufficient to ensure their rapid development. It could indeed be argued that if growth areas have been chosen correctly, then industry would anyway have a preference for a location within them and that discriminatory incentives are therefore rather superfluous. In Italy, however, quite strong measures are used to ensure that the greater part of industrialization takes place in the growth areas and indeed in the *agglomerati*. The incentive schemes discriminate in favour of growth areas, state-controlled firms are encouraged to set themselves up in growth areas while at the same time they are to be well-endowed with infrastructure. Further to these points, however, the Italians have taken more interest than other countries and gone further in the planning of interrelated industry complexes in an attempt to secure rapid industrial development in the growth areas. To some extent France also has shown some interest with their schemes for the Gulf of Fos and the Lacq natural gas complex. It is in Italy, however, that the use of these complexes has gone furthest. Although at present a scheme of this nature has so far only been drawn up for an engineering

---

[1] The detailed plans for some of the growth areas in Scotland did contain strong recommendations on local authority reform. See *The Lothians Regional Survey and Plan*, op. cit., and *The Grangemouth/Falkirk Regional Survey and Plan*, op. cit.

complex in Bari-Taranto, it is possible that similar schemes may be developed for other areas. The scheme represents one of the most interesting post-war developments in regional policy.[1]

CONCLUSIONS

In Italy and France the benefits of pursuing a growth area policy have been recognized and acted upon. Their governments have recognized that a growth area policy will help build up external economies for industry and thus give faster growth; that the policy provides a framework for regional and national infrastructure planning and will make the provision of that infrastructure cheaper. The corollary of growth area policy—the fact that some settlements are not appropriate for industrial development and will probably decline—has also been accepted. It has been recognized that a growth area policy, though requiring some migration, will at least provide a greater opportunity for the migrants to find employment within their own broad region. Without a growth area policy, when effort is spread over the existing settlement structure, one merely prolongs the decline of the unviable settlements, with the migrants slowly moving out of the region altogether and usually into the already congested and pressured regions.

In the United Kingdom there is a considerable lack of clarity concerning growth area policy. The clear-cut acceptance of the principle in 1963 has been replaced by a more nebulous and uncertain policy. This, to our way of thinking, is a great mistake. Growth area policy is required in the depressed regions like Central Scotland and particularly if overspill policies are ever to be efficiently implemented. In the sparsely populated regions like the Highlands of Scotland, a growth area policy is required in order to build up a few settlements of reasonable size which will then be attractive to industrial development and also act as service centres for the larger region. Without these centres the future is not bright. With such centres the whole region becomes far more viable. In the United Kingdom there is a need for a reappraisal of growth area policy.

---

[1] A short appendix is provided at the end of this chapter which describes the scheme.

APPENDIX

A NOTE ON THE INTERRELATED INDUSTRY COMPLEX IN SOUTHERN ITALY[1]

Plans for the creation of an industrial development pole in Puglia, based on the simultaneous location of a series of interrelated industries, have aroused considerable interest among economists working in the field of regional development. The study of the pole was commissioned by the EEC and carried out by an Italian consultancy firm, ITALCONSULT, under the direction of Professor Tosco. The report took three years to complete, was presented to the Italian government in the latter part of 1965 and is at present at a stage where an attempt is being made to recruit the principal industrial units needed for the implementation of the study.

The basic aim of the study is simultaneously to locate in the pole a complex of industries which are interrelated in as far as they make demands on each other. The complex needs to be of such proportions and such a composition that the principal units of the complex can be assured of their input requirements from the immediate vicinity and that the intermediate units supplying the principal units will have a market of sufficient size to ensure profitable operations. In this way an industrial complex can be created which is sufficiently close knit to continue its development by the interplay of market forces once the initial nucleus has been established.

The need for such a planned complex in order to secure regional development is founded on the present-day factors involved in industrial location decisions.

In the twentieth century, the need for industry to be located close to raw materials has lost much of its significance, mainly through changing energy systems and improved communications. At the same time, however, new establishments continue to show a preference for the location in the already industrialized areas of the country. The reason for this preference is based on four main characteristics of these industrialized areas:

—An existing infrastructure network.
—A large product market for industries producing final products as well as those producing intermediate products.

---

[1] Most of the information in the appendix was taken from Istituto per L'Assistenza allo Sviluppo del Mezzogiorno, *Studio per la Promozione di un Polo Industriale di Sviluppo in Italia Meridionale.* (mimeographed). All quotations are from this source.

—An integrated and diversified labour market.

—A complete system of industrial interrelationships formed by reciprocal interdependence between principal industries producing for the final market as well as for subsidiary and auxiliary industries which furnish the former with a whole series of intermediate products and services.

All four characteristics are important factors in industrial location decisions. The Tosco study suggests, however, that the latter is the most important factor and the one which represents the greatest impediment to regional development.

The lack of the fourth factor is not one which easily resolves itself spontaneously. The lack of supporting industries in the backward region deters the movement of principal industries, while supporting industries who need the principal industries as markets are unable to move or, if they already exist, find great difficulties in the way of their development. The result is a vicious circle. Industry A cannot move into the depressed area because industry B does not exist, while industry B cannot move or develop without industry A. The problem is of course even more difficult than the simple use of the two characters A and B would suggest, for frequently it is not merely a case of B developing or moving because A has developed in the region. Industry B may need more markets than the single unit A can provide in order to give it a sufficient market for profitable operations. At the same time principal unit A may need far more supporting industry than the intermediate B. It is difficult to imagine a quick *laissez-faire* solution to this problem. The present haphazard regional policies of accepting any firms which offer themselves are not likely to get round the problem quickly. The use of a big plant as a propulsive industry is likewise likely to fail unless a careful evaluation is made in the first instance of the size required in order to ensure adequate numbers of intermediate units setting up around the main plant. This was the case, for example, in the relocation of the British motor-car industry where surrounding development has been extremely disappointing.

It is against this background that the Tosco study should be viewed.

The first step in the study was to select the sector which would form the basis of the complex. It is obvious that it would need to be a growth industry. It was decided also that there would be advantages if some semblance of the industry already existed in the region. Heavy and medium engineering fulfilled both these criteria and was chosen as the industry to be studied. The existence of the steel-mill at Taranto undoubtedly played some part in the selection of this industry.

The principle of the study is that the complex should be 'composed of a limited number of principal units chosen in such a way as to sustain by their demand . . . at least a type of all the intermediate and auxiliary units essential to the sector'. One would therefore create 'an auto-sufficient system' capable of inserting itself in the general development of the industrial area in which it was located, but one would also have created conditions for the spontaneous development of other initiatives according to a natural mechanism of expansion similar to that taking place in the industrial zones of Western Europe.

Having limited itself to the heavy and mechanical engineering sector, the report goes on to narrow down this broad group, first, to choose a limited number of principal units which satisfy various criteria and, secondly, to select intermediate units which are essential to the efficient operation of the principal units; but also, in this second phase it was necessary to decide whether these intermediate units would enjoy sufficient demand from the principal unit in order to ensure their profitable operation.

Principal units

The selection of the engineering industries which were to form the principal units was made by a process of elimination consisting of three stages.

The first elimination came with the removal of electrical and precision engineering from the list of potentialities. Electrical engineering was eliminated because it is present to a large extent in another southern Italian pole (Caserta-Naples-Salerno) and it was felt unwise to disturb the external economies for this industry which were gradually building up in that pole. Furthermore, the industry is almost totally absent in Puglia. The second group, precision engineering, was excluded because it needed more specialized manpower than could be gathered together in the short or medium run within the Puglia pole.

The second stage of elimination, like the first stage, involved broad cuts. Using the NICE[1] classification for engineering, three production groups were excluded from any further analysis at this stage:

(*a*) Those groups which are of a heterogenous production character. These were excluded because of the difficulties involved in measuring their input requirements.

[1] *Nomenclature des industries établies dans les communautés européennes,* published by SOEC, June 1965.

(*b*) Primary metal industries.

(*c*) Those sectors of the engineering industry which are of an intermediate or auxiliary nature. These are treated later.

Even with these exclusions there still remained, from the NICE engineering classification, eighty-nine groups or lines. These are now whittled down further in the third elimination stage. This third stage is based on seven criteria for exclusion. The criteria used and the types of industry lines which were eliminated were:

(*a*) Lines which for technical and economic reasons needed very high levels of concentration in order to compete internationally, e.g. the automobile industry.

(*b*) Lines which constitute a specialism in northern Italy, e.g. production of light arms and the construction of packaging material.

(*c*) Lines which constitute a specialism in other southern Italian poles, there being no desire to disturb the external economies which were slowly building up, e.g. metal furniture, office machinery, railway rolling stock, powered and non-powered cycles.

(*d*) Lines which need highly specialized manpower because of the difficulties likely to be encountered of recruiting specialized manpower in the area above a certain limit. A 'training time' criterion was used and lines were excluded where Italian experience suggested that more than 30 per cent of the manpower needed a training period of more than one year. This excluded, among others, the manufacture of safes, textile machinery, cookers, chemical machinery, tower cranes, dry-cleaning machinery. Machine tools were not excluded, however, because of the sector's importance in engineering and as a trainer of labour.

(*e*) Those lines in which the corresponding establishments in the North are not of great size and lines which therefore do not make very great input demands. A minimum size of 200 employees was used here. Among other lines, this excluded: agricultural tools, knives, non-electric industrial ovens, automatic vending machines, fire-fighting equipment, gas, water and other liquid containers.

(*f*) Lines for which units have recently been set up or are being set up within the Puglia pole. Needless to say, these are later taken into account in calculating the total needs in terms of intermediate units. This criterion excluded, among others, light metal lathes, large gas and liquid holders, industrial taps including valves, assembly of industrial vehicles with special equipment.

(*g*) Lines which do not present sufficient market prospects in the medium term. The market prospects considered were those for Italy, the EEC and the Mediterranean basin. This saw the exclusion, among

L
321

others, of cast iron radiators and baths, tower cranes and balance manufacturing.

Following from these exclusions there remained twenty-one production lines which escaped exclusion.[1] These could be grouped according to engineering criteria and homogeneity of production processes into eight production units.[2]

The eight principal units selected were considered to be the necessary minimum for the creation of an auto-propulsive complex. If some of the planned lines do not in fact present good prospects it is suggested that they can be replaced by others with greater market possibilities which have perhaps been eliminated by an over-vigorous selection process.

'Furthermore, there is nothing to stop the inclusion of other initiatives, in the field of heavy and medium engineering, which are susceptible to rapid development. The only problem to take into account is to make the subsidiary and auxiliary unit adequate to the additional demands of the principal units.'

These arguments would seem, however, to weaken the basic idea of the pole. One wonders what is the value of the analysis of intermediate units if the principal units are changed. Indeed, because the profitability of the principal units is linked to the presence of specific intermediate units, one wonders what is the value of the detailed study of the principal units.

However, having by the process of elimination described above made the selection of eight possible principal units, each of these units was then subjected to a feasibility study. These studies were in three parts. First, the commercial aspects with particular regard to Italian and EEC prospects were studied. Market forecasts were calculated up to the year 1975. Secondly, there was an examination of production processes with an eye to making the units competitive with their actual and potential competitors. Transport, machinery, labour, stocks and land requirements were carefully catalogued. Finally, the financial-economic aspects were studied: investments, financing, revenue, costs, as well as the regional development incentives for which the units would qualify.

Intermediate units
The study of intermediate units covered the examination of intermediate units which in one way or another are associated with the

---

[1] See Note A at the end of this appendix.
[2] See Note B at the end of this appendix.

principal unit types already chosen and finally the selection from the possible intermediate units of a number which would be sufficient to enable the principal units to operate profitably. At the same time it was necessary to confirm that the intermediate units themselves, with the markets available from the principal units, could operate profitably.

Potential intermediate units were divided into three types:

(*a*) Auxiliary units—those supplying machinery, equipment, plant and specific services needed by the principal units.

(*b*) Subsidiary units—those producing elements (raw materials and semi-finished products) 'which form an integral part of the products of the principal and other intermediate units and which it is not considered could be economically produced within their own plants', e.g. stampings, castings, extrusions.

(*c*) 'Other' intermediate units—'those which furnish products of a wide range of industrial uses', e.g. paint, pneumatic and hydraulic cylinders, electric motors, nuts and bolts, cables, compressors, internal combustion engines, wire, etc.

In order to determine the number and size of the intermediate units needed by the selected principal units, the first stage of the analysis was the identification of all the possible intermediate lines which could be used by the principal units, i.e. a list of all the types of input which the proposed principal units could use. Secondly, these intermediate lines were examined to see whether their presence within the pole was absolutely essential. Lastly, after a valuation of the input needs of the complex and other engineering concerns already in the pole or being set up, the analysis proceeded to a quantification of the essential inputs and possible units which could be created in order to profitably and efficiently produce these lines.

The identification of the inputs needed by the selected lines was based on two main hypotheses. First, that the production of the principal units corresponds to the biggest units of their type in Italy. Secondly, that the form of organization and production adopted by the principal units was that followed by the same industries in the most industrialized countries of Western Europe.

In point of fact, a first examination revealed that the principal units used virtually all the intermediate category lines listed in NICE. It was, however, considered inconceivable to realize all these lines which would in fact, if they were to operate efficiently, need an increase in the number of principal units. This would make for difficulties in the simultaneous promotion of the complex and in the recruitment of labour. It was therefore necessary to examine which of the intermediate lines needed to be close to the main unit if the latter were to avoid costs so high as to carry them outside the limits of competition.

On the basis of such an examination, it became clear that proximity was essential for all supplies from the auxiliary and subsidiary units. Transport costs and the penalties of any interruptions of production through shortages made their proximity vital. Only in the case of a few products which were not important in terms of value and weight, such as extrusions, could an increase in stocks be considered as a valid alternative to the presence *in situ* of the production units themselves.

It was considered, however, that the 'other' intermediate lines, mainly commercialized and standard products, need not necessarily be in close proximity to the principal product. 'The characteristics of these products, having a high level of standardization and high substitutability with other products available on the market, leads one to conclude that a wide agency network could fully satisfy the needs of the principal production lines. In any case, even on the hypothesis of supplies direct from the north, the incidence on the price of the finished product would not exceed 1 to 2 per cent.' The only exception here were bolts, which, because of their importance in engineering and because of their not indifferent transport costs, were considered to be needed within the pole.

For the quantification of the intermediate inputs of the principal units it was necessary to determine the likely demands of the principal units as well as plants already existing in the pole or in the course of being set up. At this point a difficulty is encountered. 'It is not possible *a priori* to determine what kind of product will be chosen for the new lines. This is a choice which is obviously up to the entrepreneur who sets up the plant.' The study, however, considers that it can avoid this difficulty by assuming for each principal unit a 'product type' and calculating input requirements for this type, 'leaving to the entrepreneur to decide the range or type of product to make'. Thus, there is hypothesized a 'product type' for each principal line of production. Input requirements for these lines are then calculated.

The use of 'product types' would seem to be a further weak point, and one wonders whether the work on the intermediates is not largely academic. If, for example, an entrepreneur of the eight principal units selects a line which is not of the selected 'product type', does this mean that a recalculation of the intermediate requirements is then needed? Obviously the answer depends on how far the width of choice available to the principal-unit entrepreneur would, if he chose a line other than the selected type, change the pattern and quantities of inputs. It need hardly be added that if there is doubt about the intermediates then there must also again be doubts about the feasibilities of the principal unit.

Nevertheless, from the input demands made by the principal units producing the suggested product lines as well as from the inputs of existing plant and plants being set up[1] and also the input demands of the intermediates themselves, a schedule of total input requirements is drawn up.

Having calculated total potential demands for inputs, the test then was to see whether the total demands would be sufficient to sustain, at an economic size ('referring that is to the minimum production levels which would permit competitive costs with similar units in the North'), one or more intermediate units of each line.

An estimate was made of what was considered to be the minimum economic size, in terms of output, for each of the potential intermediate units. It was found on calculating the demands that could be expected from the complex that twenty out of forty of the units (with one unit for each line) did not reach the minimum size. Quite a number of these units would have been operating at levels well below the minimum economic size even supposing a quintupling in size of the principal units.

In order to increase the number of products which could be economically produced, a re-grouping was made of intermediate units which would anyway have been producing similar products. Such re-grouping made many more lines a feasible proposition and indeed reduced by half the number of lines which had a level of demand which was insufficient to sustain them. The kind of re-grouping which took place in order to make up units of an economic size was for lines which were similar and/or where such groupings were common in the more progressive industrialized regions. An example of the re-grouping was in the manufacture of bolts and specialized bolts. These two lines would now, after the re-grouping, be produced by one single unit rather than two.

After this re-grouping it was found that twenty-three intermediate units could operate profitably within the complex, three of which already existed in the pole. The final outcome of the complex was therefore thirty-one units in total, of which twenty-three are intermediate and eight principal.

The complex as a whole is expected to require industrial investments of 79 milliard Italian lire (1965 prices) of which 63 per cent will

[1] The assumption made for existing industry is that intermediates will cover between 40 and 80 per cent of their essential intermediate inputs.

be in the principal units, 34 per cent in the subsidiaries and 3 per cent in the auxiliaries. The complex when fully working is expected to give a total employment of 8,210, of which 72 per cent will be in the principal units, 24 per cent in subsidiaries and 4 per cent in the auxiliaries. It is intended that construction should start 1968-69 and that production will commence in 1970-71. Normal production is expected in 1972.

The complex is at present being promoted largely under the control of IASM[1] which is attempting initially to recruit the principal units. This task is not proving easy and is well behind schedule in spite of the fact that the firms in the complex would receive the maximum regional development incentives available. It is of course essential that the complex should be a complete success. It is rather like a jigsaw puzzle and a few pieces missing could ruin the whole project.

The response to the recruitment campaign has not been very lively so far, with very little interest being shown by the northern Italian firms. IASM has been looking abroad for its recruits though so far without any great success. One should not perhaps be too depressed about the results so far. The project could gather momentum as it goes along. At the present time IASM is concentrating on the principal units, hoping, with some justification, that having been assured of the principal units, the intermediate units will not be so difficult to recruit.

Some conclusions
The planned interrelated industry complex described above has stimulated a great deal of interest already. Indeed, there was considerable enthusiasm in many circles well before anything but the vaguest hints of its form or content became generally known. This is hardly surprising. The need and benefits of finding some new approach to the regional problem are very great. The possible use of a similar complex in developing a growth centre or giving impetus to a small growth centre is fairly obvious.

It is perhaps rather easy to find faults in the scheme, faults which have become rather troublesome at the promotion stage. The imperfect data which were sometimes used, the bold assumptions concerning size of principal units, the time it is taking to implement (with consequential suffering in terms of data validity), the impossibility of being more specific about the production lines which the principal units will enter and which therefore throws great doubts on the relevance of the intermediate analysis. These are but a few of the points which can be made against the study. Yet at the same

[1] *Istituto per l'Assistenza allo Sviluppo del Mezzogiorno* see pp. 60-61 above.

time it would be shortsighted if these problems were to be used as excuses against acceptance of the basic principles lying behind the study, or as an excuse for not trying to modify the approach so that these difficulties could be overcome in another similar complex. Of all the recent advances made in the science of regional development, the interrelated industry complex is one of the most interesting. It warrants attention and further study.

Note A: Metal structures (bridges, viaducts, hangars, industrial building equipment, prefabricated components, metal frames, etc.); cookers and domestic heating appliances; oil burners for domestic heating and similar purposes; sheet-metal radiators; metal hollow-ware; bath tubs; combine harvesters; fodder presses; walking tractors, motor mowers and other farm machinery (other than combine harvester-threshers); metal-removing machine tools; earth-moving equipment (mechanical shovels, excavators, etc.) and crane lorries; pulley tackle and hoists; jacks; winches and capstans; mobile and fixed cranes (other than tower cranes for the building industry); travelling cranes and the like; elevators; continuous mechanical conveyors; lifting grabs, buckets and the like; lift and carrier trucks; centrifugal pumps.

Note B: Manufacture of metal structures, bridges and structural steel. Manufacture of cookers, bath tubs, sheet-metal radiators and metal hollow-ware. Manufacture of oil burners, centrifugal pumps, pulley tackle and hoists. Manufacture of farm machinery. Manufacture of metal-removing machine tools. Manufacture of earth-moving equipment and crane lorries. Manufacture of lifting gear and equipment. Manufacture of lift and carrier trucks.

CHAPTER 14

THE EEC AND REGIONAL POLICY

The aim of this chapter is, first, to outline the consideration given to regional problems in the Treaty of Rome and discuss the Community's policies for regional development and, second, to examine briefly the likely impact on British regional problems and policies if Britain joined the Common Market. First, however, there is a short introductory section on the extent of regional disparities in the EEC.

I. REGIONAL DISPARITIES IN THE EEC

In as far as disparities in regional well-being exist within member states of the EEC it is inevitable that disparities also exist within the EEC as a whole. The disparities are in fact greater than within any single country. Southern Italy, poor relative to the North, is even poorer relative to the more prosperous regions of Germany or France. The disparities between the poorer and richer regions within the EEC are quite startling. Income per head in the richest region is six and a half times as great as that in the poorest; the highest regional unemployment percentages are seventy times greater than the lowest; the highest regional percentage of active working population in agriculture is twenty-eight times the lowest.[1]

The problem regions are largely on the periphery of the EEC; the South of Italy, the south-west of France, the eastern border areas of Germany and the south-east of Belgium. The areas which represent very serious problems are in Italy and France.

Since the creation of the EEC regional disparities within it have not diminished. 'Whilst it is unquestionably true that all regions of the Community have overall benefited from the general tendency towards expansion, it should be noted that notable and excessive divergencies remain between the various regions. In certain cases

---

[1] N. Novacco, 'Considerazioni sui Problemi Territoriali dello Sviluppo e sui Livelli a cui Misurare gli Squilibri', in *Scritti di Economia e Statistica in Memoria di Alessandro Molinari*, Giuffrè, 1963.

territorial imbalances in fact became more pronounced.'[1] For a number of reasons the continuation, or even widening, of the regional disparities is not surprising.

First, the increase in competition arising out of the creation of the EEC has tended to encourage firms to move into, and develop faster within, the central area of the Community and has made them reluctant to locate in the peripheral areas. They are able to secure greater external economies in the former and are also closer to the main markets of the Community. The majority of new foreign industrial investment has taken place, not in the peripheral areas, but in the heart of the Community—an area roughly within the square of Hamburg, Paris, Genoa and Turin. The free movement of capital within the Market has facilitated the expansion of this area.

Second, the problems in the peripheral areas have been exacerbated by the reluctance of member governments to interfere too much with the location of industry and run the risk of diminishing their country's industrial competitiveness. In particular, policies aimed at curbing development in certain areas, unless organized at a Community level, can be very costly in the competitive environment of the EEC. It is interesting to note that the French policy of restraining industrial and commercial development in and around Paris has been relaxed in the last five years, in recognition of the fact that Paris is the natural centre of growth in the EEC economy which it is impracticable and undesirable to constrain to any great extent.[2] In Italy, after considerable debate, it was finally decided not to use disincentives in the North because of the possible weakening of Italy's competitive strength and the fear that firms which were refused permission to expand in the North might leave Italy altogether and move further into the heart of Europe rather than into the South.[3] A further example of the reluctance within the EEC to sacrifice efficiency for regional development is the growing acceptance by the Community members of a Growth Area policy—a policy which at least reduces some of the possible national disadvantages of regional development policy.[4]

Third, the rapid movement towards free trade in the Community and the greater Community approach to the problems of certain industries—coal, steel, agriculture—have both given rise to regional difficulties. The rapid removal of tariff barriers almost inevitably means that some previously protected industries will suffer and if

---

[1] Lionello Levi Sandri, 'The Contribution of Regional Action to the Construction of Europe', in the *Report of the Third International Congress of Regional Economies,* Rome, 1965.   [2] See Chapter 8 above.
[3] See Chapter 3 above.   [4] See Chapter 13.

these are concentrated in particular areas, then the areas also will suffer serious transitional problems if adequate measures are not taken. All three industries mentioned above gave rise to regional problems as free trade was attained. The rapid rationalization which took place further aggravated the difficulties. The regional problems arose in spite of measures taken by the Community, and described below, to alleviate the difficulties. Apart from these three industries, few others were sufficiently concentrated to give rise to serious regional problems except perhaps the Italian sulphur industry—centred in Sicily and long protected by the Italian authorities. Its vulnerability and importance to the Sicilian economy was, however, recognized at an early stage and provisions (delayed tariff reductions and a loan from the Investment Bank) were made by the Community to secure an easier transition.

The three factors discussed above have all tended to widen the regional disparities in the EEC or at least have kept them from being reduced. The first two factors will probably remain as permanent influences while the third is temporary—though it will be some time before its force is spent. There is, however, a fourth factor which has prevented a narrowing of the disparities. This is the inadequacy of the regional policies pursued at a Community level. These are discussed in some detail later. It is surprising that while common policies have, to varying degrees, been developed in the fields of trade, transport, energy and even taxation, regional development has been largely neglected. The measures taken so far have been generally *ad hoc*, unco-ordinated and with few supporting funds. Regional policy has been left almost entirely to the individual member countries in spite of the fact that the ironing out of regional disparities is an important objective of the Treaty of Rome.

The EEC, so far, has been a group of countries whose economic policies have been very much oriented towards rapid growth. In both the directing agencies of the EEC and in the member countries, the view that regional development can contribute to national economic growth has commanded less support than in the United Kingdom. Although it is recognized that the backward regions contain unutilized and under-utilized resources and that these, if brought into use, could aid growth, there is a very strong recognition that the cost of using these resources in their own regions is likely to be very high. It is probably the case, given the nature of the regions involved—isolated, poor in infrastructure, almost completely lacking in industrial development—that the costs of development are likely to be higher than in the United Kingdom.

II. THE TREATY OF ROME AND REGIONAL POLICY

Regional policy figures early in the Treaty of Rome, and indeed in the preamble the signatories express themselves as being 'anxious to strengthen the unity of their economies and to ensure their harmonious development by reducing the differences existing between the various regions and by mitigating the backwardness of the less favoured'. On the other hand, one of the prime objectives of the Treaty is the free movement of goods, capital and labour. Any measures which distort competition are deemed incompatible with the Treaty. Thus, 'any aid, granted by a member state or granted by means of state resources, in any manner whatsoever, which distorts or threatens to distort competition by favouring certain enterprises or certain productions shall, to the extent to which it adversely affects trade between member states, be deemed to be incompatible with the Common Market' (Article 92). The same article, however, lists exceptions to this general rule which *shall* or *may* be considered compatible. Under the first heading are: 'aids of a social character granted to individual consumers provided that such aids are granted without any discrimination based on the origins of the products concerned'; aids to 'remedy damage caused by natural calamities or other extraordinary events'; and finally aids to certain regions in West Germany 'affected by the division of Germany, to the extent that such aids are necessary in order to compensate for the economic disadvantages caused by such division'. The exceptions which *may* be deemed compatible include aids of a regional character: 'aids intended to promote the economic development of regions where the standard of living is abnormally low or where there exists serious under-employment' and 'aids intended to facilitate the development of certain activities or certain economic regions, provided that such aids do not change trading conditions to such a degree as would be contrary to the common interest'.

The decision as to what regional aids are acceptable is the responsibility of the Commission. It is to be informed of new measures intended to promote regional development and member countries cannot apply such measures without a favourable decision by the Commission. The Commission has the right to demand the abolition or modification of any regional aid which it considers unacceptable (Article 93). It is very difficult to be precise on the extent to which the Commission has in fact influenced the regional policies of member states through its powers as laid out in Article 93. Its deliberations are not made public. It has been suggested that the recent Italian transport subsidy for the South came under criticism.

331

The Commission also apparently expressed its dislike of Belgian regional policy which isolated a large number of small areas for assistance. In both cases, however, policy does not appear to have been modified. In 1968, when there was growing concern in the EEC over the apparent escalation of regional development measures in member countries, the Commission attempted to strengthen its powers of control by requiring that all subsidies for projects having a value of more than half a million dollars be submitted for approval. Italy and France have, however, openly refused to co-operate in this respect.

In addition to the Treaty of Rome itself, all countries had 'protocols' attached to the Treaty which covered aspects of policy which were important for the individual countries. The protocol for Italy in particular recognized the need for the Italian government to continue its efforts in the South and indeed an assurance that the Community would help them in this task.[1]

III. THE COMMUNITY AND REGIONAL POLICY

There are a number of Community agencies which have been created to promote regional development. These include the European Investment Bank, the Social Fund, the Agricultural Fund and the European Coal and Steel Community. (The latter, though existing and pursuing regional policies before the Treaty of Rome was signed, can and should be considered as an EEC body.) The EEC has also taken regional development into account in its formulation of general policies on trade, energy and transport. It has furthermore been responsible for financing a number of studies of problem areas. These EEC agencies and aspects of policy are discussed briefly below.

The European Investment Bank

The European Investment Bank represents one of the most positive efforts of the Community to encourage development in its more backward areas. It commenced operations in March 1959, with the aim of encouraging more balanced development in the Community by means of its loan and guarantee facilities.

The direction which its efforts were to take was set out in the Treaty of Rome (para. 130). It was to aid:

'*a.* Projects for developing less developed regions;
b. projects for modernizing or converting enterprises or for

---

[1] For a good description and discussion of the protocol for Italy, see Umberto Leanza, *Legislazione per il Mezzogiorno e Mercato Comune Europeo*, Giuffrè, 1963.

creating new activities which are called for by the progressive establishment of the Common Market where such projects by their size or nature cannot be entirely financed by the various means available in each of the member states; and

c. projects of common interest to several member states which by their size or nature cannot be entirely financed by the various means available in each of the member states.'

Since the early 1960s, the Bank has also made loans to the Associated Member Countries and Turkey. The value of these loans has expanded rapidly and by the end of 1967 represented over 20 per cent of the Bank's total loans.

The Bank has a capital stock of 1,000 million dollars of which 25 per cent is paid up with the remaining 75 per cent in the form of capital guaranteed by the member states.[1] The Bank was expected to expand its capital by resort to the financial markets of member states and other countries though it has the right to borrow from member governments if it needs funds for the financing of specific projects and is unable to obtain these in the capital markets on suitable terms. The Bank went to the capital market for the first time in 1961.

The Bank conducts its operations on fairly strict banking principles. It lends money at about the market rate and aims at covering its expenses. There is no element of subsidy in its operations except in as far as it is non-profit making.[2] Member states can, however, subsidize the interest on loans made to bodies in their own country. The Cassa per il Mezzogiorno, for example, has done this in the case of loans made by the Bank for projects in the South of Italy. Loans by the Bank must be guaranteed by member states or some other reliable body. The Bank does not make loans to cover the whole cost of a project. In the past it has, on average, covered about 22 per cent of project costs though the proportion varies considerably 'according to the nature and size of the projects'.[3] The loans are usually long term.[4] The Bank has financed a great variety of projects

---

[1] Countries contributed to the 1,000 million dollar capital stock in the following proportions: Germany and France, 300 million each; Italy, 240 million; Belgium, 86·5 million; Netherlands, 71·5 million; Luxemburg, 2 million.

[2] An exception to the principle of no subsidy is in the case of Greece, where an interest subsidy can be granted.

[3] European Investment Bank, *Annual Report* 1966, p. 51.

[4] For industrial loans, the repayment period is between 11 and 15 years and 16-20 years in the case of infrastructure and agricultural projects. There is usually a period of grace before the repayment of principal and interest commences.

as illustrated by the loans made in 1966. These varied from a Sicilian irrigation scheme to the construction of a hollow-glass factory at Neuburg in Bavaria, from the erection of the M'Bakaou barrage in the Cameroons to a gas production unit in West Berlin. Most of its projects, however, are large scale—the average loan being around 5 million dollars. Up to the end of 1967 industry took the largest proportion of the Bank's loans, about 40 per cent. Transport, energy and agriculture took 28, 15 and 13 per cent respectively.[1]

The most important direction of the Bank's efforts has been towards projects concerned with regional development. This orientation of its activities was encouraged from the start. In the general lines for its credit policy laid down in 1958, the Bank was directed to 'devote a large part of its resources to the financing of projects likely to contribute to the furtherance of less developed regions'.[2] The Bank has largely held to this directive. A large proportion of its loans has gone to southern Italy. Between 1959 and the end of 1967, about 53 per cent of the Bank's loans went to Italy and the majority were for southern development. About 58 per cent of the Bank's ordinary loans (i.e. excluding loans to Associated Countries and Turkey) has been for projects in southern Italy and 'shows the constant interest attached by the Bank to the fulfilment of its mission of aiding the less developed regions of the community'.[3] The loans to many of the other countries have also to a large extent been for the development of their problem regions.

It is important, however, to keep the value of the Bank's loans in perspective. In relation to total investments in the Community they are very small indeed. In the nine-year period 1959-67, the Bank made loans to the value of 978 million dollars—a very insignificant proportion of the Community's fixed capital investment which in 1966 alone had a value of 73 billion dollars. No official figures are available, but it seems likely that loans to the value of around 700 million dollars have been made by the Bank for projects in the backward regions of European member countries—an average of about 80 million dollars per annum. It could and, if the Communities

---

[1] European Investment Bank, *Annual Report* 1967, p. 22. These proportions have changed somewhat over the life of the Bank. Up to 1962 industry was receiving 55 per cent of the loans. The decline in this percentage after 1962 coincides with the expanded role of the Bank in associated underdeveloped countries where loans for infrastructure represented the greatest demand.

[2] European Investment Bank, *Annual Report* 1958, Appendix II, p. 38.

[3] European Investment Bank, *Annual Report* 1966, p. 47.

verbal commitment to regional development is to be put into action, should play a bigger role. Its adherence to commercial principles severely limits its scope. Its efforts and usefulness could be strengthened if it were to lend at cheaper rates and lengthen the duration of its loans for regional development projects. Perhaps equally important, it needs to assume more of the character of a development bank prepared to support risky, long-term prospects. Another field where it might intervene is in the setting up of a finance company to take shareholdings in industrial ventures in the depressed region. At present the Bank is playing an extremely cautious role.

2. European Social Fund

The activities of the European Social Fund have been disappointing both relative to the Investment Bank and other institutions having a similar role to the Social Fund, such as the Social Fund of the European Coal and Steel Community.[1]

The basic role of the Fund is to assist financially in the retraining and resettlement of workers who become unemployed and to assist workers whose incomes are reduced or temporarily suspended as a result of the conversion of their enterprises to other forms of production.[2] In all cases, assistance is limited to 50 per cent of the expenses incurred, and payment is made to the member state or other accepted agency and not to individual firms or workers. Workers qualifying for the retraining and resettlement allowance must have commenced their new jobs or taken up residence in their new homes before payment can be made. The same point applies to the conversion allowance. The Fund's grants are thus retrospective. Conversion plans must receive prior approval by the Commission before they qualify.

The Fund is financed by member states, its annual budget being prepared a year in advance based on the demands expected to be made upon it.[3] From 1960, when it commenced operations, to the end of 1966, the Fund spent 40 million dollars[4] to the benefit of half a million workers. The vast majority of its expenditure has been on

[1] See p. 339 below.

[2] *Treaty of Rome*, para. 125.

[3] Contributions by member states to the Fund's budget are out of line with those paid to the general EEC budget. Italy pays less than its usual EEC proportion and Germany and France pay more. Italy takes about 65 per cent of the Fund's expenditure. See Yves Delamotte and Erika Georges. 'The Role of the European Coal and Steel Community and the Common Market in Regional Policy', in *Area Redevelopment Policies in Britain and the Countries of the Common Market*, US Department of Commerce, 1965, pp. 469-72.

[4] By the end of 1968 it had spent over 70 million dollars.

retraining schemes (37 million dollars) though a greater number of persons has benefited under the resettlement schemes—291,000 as against 216,000. The third activity of the Fund—that of maintaining the income of employees who suffer temporarily as a result of conversion schemes—has never been undertaken. This is probably due to the long and difficult procedure involved, including the need to secure the Commission's permission in advance, plus the fact that, although all member states have resettlement and retraining schemes, and the Fund can therefore play its role through these schemes, few have conversion schemes.

The Fund has a strong regional character in as far as it aids regions which have run into structural difficulties or are likely to do so. It does, however, play a much more passive role than the European Investment Bank, limiting itself to picking up the expenses incurred by member states. It is up to the member states to make the positive intervention. The Fund's objective is more to encourage member states by helping out financially rather than to intervene positively. This is perhaps inevitable and probably advisable. A more interventionist Fund would be administratively unwieldy. There is anyway little point in duplicating, at a Community level, the already fairly satisfactory interventions by member states. Where criticism can be levied at the Fund is in respect of its restricted mandate. The Fund has no responsibilities for juvenile training, no responsibilities for retraining the underemployed and it makes no provisions for the Associated Territories. In these respects the Fund is a poor shadow of what it could be. It particularly needs to be reorganized in the light of the EEC's present attempts to expand and standardize training. Here it could play an important financial role, particularly in Italy where training, in quantitative and qualitative terms, is still much less developed than in the rest of the Community.

Proposals to increase the effectiveness of the Fund have long been awaiting Council approval. In January 1965 proposals were submitted aimed at channelling the Fund's action 'more in the direction of the immediate aims of Community policy. The special purpose of these proposals is to associate the fund more closely with member states' efforts to maintain a high level of employment, ensure more balanced development of regional economies, and improve the living conditions of migrant workers and their families.'[1] There were four major proposals put forward: first, that the Fund should help with the vocational training not only of unemployed and

[1] European Economic Community Commission, *Eighth General Report on the Activities of the Community*, 1964-65, p. 250.

underemployed workers but also employed workers whose jobs are threatened because they lack qualifications or because the qualifications they already have are no longer adequate; second, that it should help maintain the earnings of workers who have lost their jobs in regions suffering from, or threatened with, unemployment and who are waiting to be re-employed in the same region; third, that it should help in building training centres in depressed areas; and fourth, that it should help to finance low-cost housing schemes for migrant workers and their families and the social services provided for them.[1]

These proposals, if adopted, would considerably strengthen the Fund and give it a function more relevant to 'the Community's economic and social evolution'.[2] It would also allow it to play a larger role in a key area of regional development policy. The Fund was originally set up with very limited aims and quickly needed to be reorganized. It is a great pity that proposals to do this have still not received approval.

3. *The European Agricultural Guidance and Guarantee Fund*

Agriculture remains an extremely important industry in the Community, employing 17 per cent of the civilian labour force as against 4 per cent in the United Kingdom. In France and Italy it employs 19 per cent and 25 per cent respectively. The sector is not only quantitatively important but is also to a very large extent inefficient. A long history of protectionist policies has left it in great need of rationalization and modernization if it is to overcome the problems of underemployment, fragmentation, small units and undercapitalization.

The Agricultural Fund has two main roles and two sections to implement them. The first is to intervene in commodity markets and prices; this is the task of the Guarantee Section. The second is to improve the productivity of agriculture; this is the function of the Guidance Section.

Agricultural prices are fixed each year by the Council of Ministers according to 'the agricultural situation and the trends of production and consumption within the Community, the financial cost of market support, and the situation on international markets'.[3] The role of the Fund's Guarantee Section is to maintain these prices by

---

[1] ibid., p. 250.
[2] ibid., p. 251.
[3] European Economic Community Commission, *Tenth General Report on the Activities of the Community*, 1966-67, p. 46.

support buying when market prices fall below the intervention price. The Section has, however, a further role beyond the support of domestic prices. It gives refunds in respect of exports to non-member countries which are sold on international markets at prices below the EEC support prices. Outlays under this head take up about four-fifths of the Guarantee Section's expenditure. Of the 50·6 million dollars expended by the Fund on guarantees in respect of 1963-64, 45·4 million went to France—the majority being export refunds on French cereal production. Italy hardly benefited at all, receiving a mere three-quarters of a million dollars.

The Guidance Section of the Fund is concerned with the financing of projects through grants, normally of around 25 per cent, aimed at raising agricultural productivity. Its expenditure is divided fairly evenly between projects for the improvement of agricultural marketing schemes and projects directed at improving production structures, e.g. consolidation of holdings and provision of agricultural infrastructure. The Guidance Section of the Fund is much smaller, in terms of the expenditure, than the Guarantee Section. For 1965 its expenditure was 17 million dollars. Its efforts have been more evenly divided between the member countries than have those of the Guidance Section with about 35 per cent going to Italy, 28 per cent to Germany and 20 per cent to France.

Although the Treaty of Rome requires that agricultural policy be pursued with due regard to the 'structural and natural disparities between the various agricultural regions',[1] the Agricultural Fund as a whole has not so far made any great contributions to the Community's backward agricultural regions. The majority of its expenditure has involved the Guarantee Section and most of this has gone to French cereal producers. These are not in the depressed French regions and most of them already enjoy high living standards. The situation in the Community in this respect is not dissimilar to that of the United Kingdom, where the greater part of expenditure on agricultural subsidies is for agricultural output which is already quite profitable. The Community's backward agricultural regions profit mainly from the Fund's Guidance Section though the size of its budget obviously limits the assistance it can render. Six million dollars to Italy in 1965 can do very little to improve the unbalanced agricultural structure of southern Italy, and by no means all of this aid went to the South. The inadequacy of funds going to those areas of the Community where help to change the structure of agriculture is so much needed now seems to be recognized. 'Structural policy should also aid—and even give priority treatment to—backward

[1] *Treaty of Rome*, Article 39, para. 2.

areas whose mainstay is indisputably farming, so that with the Community's help they can overcome the handicaps which have so far condemned them to lag behind economically.'[1] In 1965, the General Report of the European Commission intimated that expenditure by the Guidance Section would be around 300 million dollars per annum after 1967.[2] It remains to be seen whether such hopes are fulfilled.

4. *The European Coal and Steel Community*[3]

The ECSC, a forerunner of the EEC, has been an important force in region development. Although its activities are limited to the coal and steel industries, the geographic distribution of these industries is such that any decline almost inevitably creates regional problems. Most of its activities are, therefore, in the nature of regional policy. The policies developed by ECSC to cope with the changing character of the industries for which it is responsible, and to offset the damage caused to particular areas by such changes, are very comprehensive. It plays the combined role of European Investment Bank, the Social Fund and, for its own sector, a role similar to that of the Guidance Section of the Agricultural Fund.

The regional or area activities of the ECSC take two main forms —adaptation and conversion. The first involves the payment of unemployment compensation, resettlement allowances and vocational training allowances. Conversion assistance takes the form of loans to help firms, not necessarily in the coal and steel sector, whose development is likely to employ redundant workers. The ECSC thus operates the two normal prongs of regional policy—the training of workers for new jobs and the encouragement of new industrial development.

Arrangements and conditions for adaptation and conversion payments were laid down in Article 56 of the Treaty setting up the Community—signed in April 1951 and operational from January 1952. The arrangements were never in fact applied in their original form (which lasted from 1952 to 1960) because the conditions for eligibility were never met by any applicant. Assistance could only be given if *all* of three conditions were met: first, that unemployment

---

[1] *Tenth General Report on the Activities of the Community*, 1966-67, op. cit., p. 46.

[2] *Eighth General Report on the Activities of the Community*, 1964-65, op. cit., p. 224.

[3] On July 1, 1967, the ECSC, Euratom and the EEC were merged into a single Council and a single Commission. A single treaty covering the fields of operation of the three communities is being drawn up. Until this is completed, the roles of the three groups remain virtually as independent as before July 1.

was the result of technological change; second, that the unemployment was on a large scale; third, that re-employment of the discharged workers, without assistance, would prove especially difficult. 'The few applications for assistance received under Article 56 had to be rejected by the High Authority as all three of the conditions were never fulfilled simultaneously.'[1] However, although Article 56 was inoperative up to 1960, the ECSC was able to assist areas and firms through Section 23 of the 1952 'Convention containing the Transitional Provisions'. This section of the Convention contained provisions for area assistance through adaptation and conversion policies during a five-year transitional period. The provisions were similar to those laid down in Article 56 of the Treaty itself though without its stringent conditions. The application of Section 23 was extended in 1957 to 1960 while the High Commission began to study possible amendments to Article 56 of the Treaty. The amendment finally accepted was one which incorporated Section 23 of the convention into the Treaty itself. This was in January 1960.

Up to 1960 there was no expenditure by the Community on conversion schemes, the whole of its funds going to adaptation. Between 1954 and 1960, it spent a total of 42 million dollars and assisted 115 thousand workers.

After 1960, the expenditure by the Community on both adaptation and conversion grew rapidly. Between 1960 and 1966 it spent 85 million dollars, 54 million dollars in 1966 alone. Its interest in conversion schemes grew rapidly during the period, and by 1966 it was spending three times as much on conversion as adaptation. However, its efforts in this direction were limited to loans which, before 1965, were negotiated individually. In 1965 standard rates were introduced. The loans could be up to 30 per cent of capital costs for a period of 10-13 years at a rate of interest of 4·5 per cent for the first 5 years and 6·5 per cent thereafter. Most of the conversion schemes have involved the iron and steel sector, though one of the most notable and interesting exceptions was in Belgium where the ECSC participated in a mixed industry programme prepared by the Société Provinciale d'Industrialisation for Liège.[2]

5. Other EEC Regional development actions

In addition to the efforts of the four bodies mentioned above, there are three other ways in which the EEC is trying to further regional

---

[1] *Area Redevelopment Policies in Britain and the Countries of the Common Market*, op. cit., p. 443.

[2] ibid., p. 454.

development. The first is through the exchanges of information between member countries on regional problems and policies. Second, the Community has carried out a number of studies of problem regions and regional policies in member states. Third, and most important, the Community in its formulation of general economic, social and industrial policies has taken into account the regional consequences of its actions.

The exchange of information between countries and the collection of data on regional problems and policies is of course an essential prelude to any 'community' regional policy. 'For the Commission hopes that through the establishment of closer relations between the national regional experts and policy makers, the kind of "atmosphere" can be created which is the necessary precondition for the development of regional thinking from a Community point of view.'[1] One outcome of this sentiment was the Conference on Regional Economies organized in Brussels in 1961. A second conference was held in Rome in 1966. Smaller groups of experts, encouraged by the EEC, are studying more specialized aspects of regional problems and policies. In many respects, the results of these meetings have been disappointing. In particular there is no evidence to show that the EEC has yet formulated a Community-accepted view on what are its problem regions and the forms of the problem. This is an extremely grave shortcoming, for such a view is required if the Community is to operate a meaningful Community regional development policy or if Community general policy is to have a serious regional dimension.

More positive results have been produced by a number of special regional studies initiated and financed by the Commission. These have been of two types. First, area studies, including detailed studies of the Franco-Belgian frontier area (dealing with the effects of the removal of tariff barriers, labour and capital restrictions, etc.) and in particular the less-developed parts of the area. The second type of regional study have been those concerned with industry and of which by far the most important has been the analysis of the possible interrelated industry complex in the Bari-Taranto area.[2] A study has also been made of the problems and prospects of the Sicilian sulphur industry.

Lastly, and most important, in this list of 'other' Community regional efforts, are the regional aspects of general Community policy. The Community has been conscious of the need to prevent its general policies aimed at free trade from severely damaging particular areas and also of the need in its energy and transport

[1] ibid., p. 465.
[2] Details of this study are given on pp. 318-327 above.

policies to ensure that the benefits are dispersed into the problem regions. Sulphur is one of the better examples of the first type of consideration, where it was recognized that too swift an opening up of the Italian sulphur market would hit Sicily particularly hard. Action was therefore taken, using the safeguard clauses of Article 226 in the Treaty of Rome,[1] in order to slow down the freeing of trade in this commodity. At the same time, a detailed study was made of the prospects for reorganizing and strengthening the industry. Other commodities have been put under the safeguard clause, e.g. lead, zinc and silk, but none has had such a strong regional character as sulphur.

The Community recognizes that in energy and transport there is a need to take regional considerations into account in the formulation of policy. On energy, the rationalization of the coal sector in particular and the regional consequences of this have long been considered important though largely left in the control of the ECSC. The attempts at improving and placing the transport networks on a Community rather than national basis have obvious regional consequences. The Commission realized that the peripheral regions must enjoy some of the benefits of this action. It has accepted that an important aspect of development policy for these regions is to improve their links with the more central regions of the Community.

'An important role will also be played by the common transport policy, chiefly by influencing the choice of the main arteries of communication. The development and modernization of the networks serving outlying areas can help to secure a more balanced distribution of economic activity throughout the Community.'[2]

But it needs to be added that no comprehensive tying of Community transport policy, or policies generally, with regional development can be achieved until, as mentioned above, the Community forms an accepted Community view on its regional problems.

IV. THE NEED FOR A STRONGER COMMUNITY REGIONAL POLICY

Considering the extent of the regional problems in the EEC countries and considering the commitment of the EEC through the

[1] 'In the course of the transitional period, where there are serious difficulties which are likely to persist in any sector of economic activity or difficulties which may seriously impair the economic situation in any region, a Member State may ask for authorization to take measures of safeguard in order to restore the situation and adapt the sector concerned to the Common Market economy . . . .'

[2] European Economic Community Commission, *Fifth General Report on the Activities of the Community*, 1961-62, p. 139.

Treaty of Rome to reduce regional economic disparities, the Community's regional policy has been very disappointing. The funds spent on regional development have been small while so far the EEC cannot be said to have much semblance of a co-ordinated policy for regional development. The lack of a co-ordinated policy is discussed below, but it is instructive first to have a look at the size of the funds which the EEC devotes to regional development.

The expenditure on regional development projects by the four bodies discussed above has so far been quite small. It is not possible to make a detailed calculation, but the total amount probably averaged less than 85 million dollars per annum[1] during the first half of the 1960s, though higher at the end of the period as the various bodies expanded their operations and others like the Agricultural Fund commenced operations. The annual average for the two years 1964 and 1965 was around 100 million dollars. About three-quarters of this expenditure involved loans by the Investment Bank. It will be remembered that these loans are made on strict banking principles and are not subsidized by the Community. Even when these loans are included, the Community's expenditure on regional development is well below what the United Kingdom government spends on regional development. Over the period 1960-65, Community expenditure on regional development amounted to less than half a dollar per EEC inhabitant. This expenditure is, of course, supplementary to the efforts by individual member countries to develop their own problem regions, but the amount is so small that the addition is relatively insignificant. If expenditure is any indication of priorities, the EEC gives a fairly low priority to regional development. It spent more than half as much on agricultural guarantees, and these are non-repayable grants, for 1963-64 as it spent annually on regional development between 1960 and 1965. Regional policy is still left very much to the individual member countries and, apart from what appears to be *ad hoc* vetting of policies and measures by the Commission, there is very little which could be called a common policy for the depressed regions.

The need for a Community regional programme or at least a

---

[1] This is a rough calculation only and if anything errs on the side of generosity. It is based on the assumptions that

—all of the ECSC expenditure on conversion and adaptation is in depressed regions,

—all the agricultural Guidance Section's expenditure (but none of the Guarantee expenditure) is in the depressed regions,

—all of the Social Fund's expenditure is in depressed regions,

—three-quarters of the Investment Bank's loans are for projects in the depressed areas of Europe.

firm Community view on regional problems and policy is no less important than the need for national regional programmes and views in individual countries. Without it a number of problems are bound to arise. First, there is the risk that countries will designate as depressed, regions which from the viewpoint of the Community as a whole would not be considered as requiring assistance. The danger arises that incentives given to such regions by an individual country will, by over-compensating industrial development in that region, distort competition in the Community. Second, and allied to the first point, there is a need for firm Community action if there is not to be an escalation of regional incentives as countries compete for third-country firms. Such competition, apart from distorting trade patterns within the Community, is also likely to be extremely wasteful of resources. There is evidence, as mentioned elsewhere, of such developments in the second half of the 1960s and the Commission became increasingly concerned. In 1968 it introduced a scheme whereby it would agree to the introduction of systems of regional aid only on condition that member countries gave it advanced notification of decisions to aid projects involving an expenditure of more than half a million dollars. Italy and France have, however, refused to co-operate on the grounds that the effectiveness of their incentives would be diminished if there was the chance that the Commission would disallow aid in particular instances. Both countries wished to retain autonomy in the field of regional development, thus posing a largely political problem which appears at present to be unsurmountable. Third, a Community approach is required if any negative policy weapons, such as controls on development in congested regions, are to be implemented. Any serious restriction on development in congested regions, whether in the form of administrative controls like the British Industrial Development Certificate or fiscal disincentives, would need to be introduced at a Community level. The use of disincentives by individual countries would otherwise result in some firms moving across the border into other countries and not into the depressed regions as they were intended to do. The point has been made elsewhere that the lack of a Community policy on controls and disincentives has been one of the factors which has led some member countries to weaken their control of the congested regions. Finally, a Community approach is required in order to coordinate and expand the efforts of the various EEC bodies which have regional development responsibilities: the Investment Bank, the Social Fund, the Guidance Section of the Agricultural Fund, etc. It is difficult at present even to know precisely what proportion of the expenditure of these bodies is in the depressed regions and, in consequence, difficult to evaluate their contribution to regional development.

In brief, Community effort to promote regional development has been far from adequate though this has sometimes been the result of actions by member countries, and in particular the reluctance to surrender autonomy, rather than a lack of inclination on the part of the Commission. There is not yet an accepted Community view on which regions are depressed; there is little co-ordination of member countries' policies and no significant Community policy for the depressed regions. The regional development efforts by the various Community development bodies have been small and largely unco-ordinated. The Treaty of Rome laid down that the Community had a responsibility to foster regional development. If this is to be fulfilled and if regional development is to proceed more rapidly and efficiently, then there is a need for greater Community effort and, more specifically, a Community development body having responsibility for regional development. It would have the role of designating depressed regions, of co-ordinating member countries' regional policies and of organizing greater Community intervention. It would also be required to keep an eye on the regional implications of general Community policy.

The shortcomings of the Community's regional development effort, the need for change and the need for greater funds, are increasingly being recognized in the Community. The need for more serious effort was recently expressed in the medium-term economic plan for the Community[1]: 'Efforts must be made to establish in the less-favoured regions conditions facilitating business initiative thus enabling unused resources to be brought into use. At the same time undue concentration of economic activities in certain areas must be prevented, as it leads to disproportionate economic and social costs and consequently limits the possibility of overall growth.'[2] The regional policy suggestions made in the plan were however very weak, being limited largely to the gathering of information on member states' problems and policies and estimates of the impact of past Community policies on the less-favoured regions. The only positive section was a recommendation that the Community financing agencies should contribute more to regional development. This latter has since had a favourable reaction from the European Parliament, and in mid-1966 they called on the Community authorities to consider the establishment of a special fund acting together with the

[1] European Economic Community, *Preliminary Draft of the First Medium-Term Economic Policy Programme 1966-70*, Brussels, 1966.
[2] ibid., chapter III, p. 16.

European Bank which would further the Community's regional development policy. So far, however, no positive action has been taken. Even so, the growing interest and concern with regional development will, undoubtedly, result eventually in greater effort being made in this direction by such bodies as the Bank and the Guidance Section of the Agricultural Fund. However, in those areas of activity where a greater Community role is dependent upon member countries accepting inroads into their autonomy, progress is likely to be slow and difficult.

To date, then, the Community's regional policy has been disappointing. Relative to Community's advances in other fields, the backward regions appear to have been largely neglected in spite of the recognition of the need for more efficient and large-scale intervention and the commitment to regional development set out in the Treaty of Rome. An organization as rich and strong as the EEC and with such great regional problems should be expending more money and effort on regional development. The action taken so far indicates that the Community considers regional development as having a low priority. There is some reason to believe that the future will see more attention paid to regional development. This is very much needed, for without more co-ordination of effort, the introduction of some control on development in the congested areas and more positive financial intervention, the EEC's regional problems are unlikely to diminish and may well increase.

V. BRITISH REGIONAL POLICY AND THE COMMON MARKET

The purpose of this section is to consider briefly the likely consequences for British regional problems and policies if we join the Common Market. Any such discussion will inevitably be largely speculative, for among other things the consequences will depend on such imponderables as the provisions made specifically for our problem regions in the application for entry, the transition period allowed for the British economy in general, whether the Commission will consider some of our regional problems as being sufficiently serious as to need regional aids and also how far the Commission will consider some of our policy measures unacceptable.

There are a number of reasons why Britain's problem regions will probably not benefit initially from Britain's entry into Europe. The disadvantage that these regions suffer because of their remoteness from major markets in Britain will be intensified when the major markets are in continental Europe. Firms will thus probably be more reluctant to move into the problem regions, the more so because of the greater pressures to be competitive which membership of the EEC will bring. At the same time, indigenous industries in the less prosperous regions will be exposed to greater competition from EEC firms. There are a number of industries which will find themselves under intensive pressures, e.g. textiles, coal, castings and shipbuilding, though the rationalization of recent years has made them more capable of competing successfully with Europe. They still have some way to go, however, and may face serious declines unless adequate safeguards are ensured. There are, of course, other industries in the problem regions which are capable of withstanding the new pressures and even benefiting from the easier access to wider markets. Electronics, chemicals and motor-cars are cases in point. It is likely, however, that the decline of uncompetitive, traditional industries will at least offset the increased employment arising out of the expansion of the more modern industries. The basic problem of our backward regions, the decline or slow growth of traditional industries and the lack of adequate development of new industries, could be exacerbated by entry into Europe.

If the regional problem appears likely to increase as a consequence of entry into the EEC, what of our regional policies? The basic question is of course whether the Commission would consider that our problems are of a sufficient scale as to justify the current level of incentives. It seems likely that, as with the other member countries, the Commission would allow Britain to pursue whatever regional policies it thought fit to introduce, though it might be reluctant to admit the Regional Employment Premium (REP) as a valid weapon since it is an unselective subsidy of current costs. The Italian transport subsidy for the South—a current cost subsidy—did not apparently find much favour with the Commission, and the REP is a much more powerful weapon applied to a less serious regional problem. The removal of the REP would represent a severe blow to the British system of regional aids for, no matter how critical one might be of its form, it does represent an important measure of aid to producers in the depressed regions. With a value equivalent to $1\frac{1}{2}$ per cent (after tax) of an average producer's total production costs it is a significant addition to the existing forms of financial aid.[1]

A more serious blow to Britain's regional policy could be the removal or weakening of the Industrial Development Certificate (IDC) system of control. This, however, would not be because it is

[1] T. Wilson, 'Finance for Regional Industrial Development', *Three Banks Review*, September, 1967. Professor Wilson estimated that the value of the whole range of British regional incentives was, after tax, about 5 per cent of an average firm's total production costs.

contrary to the Treaty of Rome or Community thinking but because the conditions after entry may discourage its use. We have already seen that French policy of controlling development in the Paris region has been noticeably relaxed lest it should weaken the competitiveness of the French economy. For similar reasons the Italians decided not to penalize or restrict expansion in northern Italy. In both countries the policy decision or reorientation was largely based on a recognition of the dangers of interfering with industrial development in a way which might place their industries at a disadvantage relative to competitors in member countries—with deleterious consequences for growth and the Balance of Payments. There was also a fear that industry restrained in Paris or northern Italy would move to other countries. These same fears must be present in the British context. Industry, refused permission to expand in the South, may well move yet further southwards. The free movement of capital would certainly not impede such a move. Most observers recognize the IDC control as being one of the strongest of British regional development policy. Its removal or weakening could have very serious repercussions for British regional development.

One final point concerns the effect that entry into Europe would have on the basic form and strategy of British regional policy. Most member countries of the EEC have now moved away from a regional policy of diffusing assistance over a large number of localities to one of growth areas in the belief that this gives better prospects for industrial development in the backward regions. It provides an environment which makes indigenous industry more competitive and one which is attractive to new industrial development. The high level of competition in the Community has been one of the factors which has forced such an approach. It seems likely that British policy would have to take a similar line, particularly if its incentives were weakened by the removal of the REP.

The British problem regions could, of course, qualify for assistance from Community bodies like the Investment Bank, the Agricultural Fund, etc., though we have already seen that their funds are small. The Investment Bank, to which Britain would be expected to contribute £100 million, seems likely, however, to be increasingly involved in the bigger problem regions like southern Italy and the Associated Territories. This is the pattern observable at present and it seems unlikely to change much in the future. One keeps returning to the point that Britain's problem regions, relative to the others in Europe, are not likely to be seen as being particularly important at a Community level. The Agricultural Fund, as we have already seen, is devoting the greater part of its effort to the French cereal producers located in areas which are anything but a problem. Although the Guidance Section is expected to play a bigger role in the future, the relative unimportance of agriculture in our peripheral areas means that very little of its limited funds would come our way.

This discussion has not sought to be alarmist. The picture, however, is one which is bound to cause considerable gloom. It seems likely that British regional disparities may increase, at least in the short run, and that regional policy may be weakened. A most disturbing point is that there is no public evidence that the regional implications of entry have been investigated in any depth by the authorities. It is essential that a serious attempt be made at an official level to assess the likely consequences of entry into the EEC for British regional problems and policies. Armed with this information it will at least be possible to gauge the seriousness of the problem, to give thought to the necessary redesigning of policy and also, perhaps, to draw up some realistic conditions for entry, as did the other member countries of the EEC.

INDEX

INDEX

For Product Safety Concerns and Information please contact our EU
representative GPSR@taylorandfrancis.com
Taylor & Francis Verlag GmbH, Kaufingerstraße 24, 80331 München, Germany